Memoirs of a Black Philosopher

Memoirs of a Black Philosopher

Richard A. Jones

HAMILTON BOOKS
An imprint of
ROWMAN & LITTLEFIELD
Lanham • Boulder • New York • London

Published by Hamilton Books
An imprint of The Rowman & Littlefield Publishing Group, Inc.
4501 Forbes Boulevard, Suite 200, Lanham, Maryland 20706
www.rowman.com

86-90 Paul Street, London EC2A 4NE, United Kingdom

Copyright © 2024 by The Rowman & Littlefield Publishing Group, Inc.

All rights reserved. No part of this book may be reproduced in any form or by any electronic or mechanical means, including information storage and retrieval systems, without written permission from the publisher, except by a reviewer who may quote passages in a review.

British Library Cataloguing in Publication Information Available

Library of Congress Cataloging-in-Publication Data

Names: Jones, Richard A. (Richard Argustia), 1945– author.
Title: Memoirs of a Black philosopher / Richard Jones.
Description: Lanham : Hamilton Books, an imprint of Rowman & Littlefield, [2024] | Includes bibliographical references and index. | Summary: "Memoirs of a Black Philosopher is a history of both anti-Black racism and the author's indefatigable struggle to transcend it by educating himself. These memoirs demonstrate the value of academic philosophy's 'upward path' from the ordinary to the sublime"—Provided by publisher.
Identifiers: LCCN 2023053918 (print) | LCCN 2023053919 (ebook) | ISBN 9780761874300 (paperback) | ISBN 9780761874317 (epub)
Subjects: LCSH: Jones, Richard A. (Richard Argustia), 1945– | Jones, Richard A. (Richard Argustia), 1945– —Books and reading. | African American intellectuals—Biography. | African American philosophers—Biography. | African American poets—Biography. | Intellectuals—United States—Biography. | Philosophers—United States—Biography. | Poets—United States—Biography. | United States—Race relations.
Classification: LCC E185.97.J7747 A3 2024 (print) | LCC E185.97.J7747 (ebook) | DDC 191.08996073 [B]—dc23/eng/20231206
LC record available at https://lccn.loc.gov/2023053918
LC ebook record available at https://lccn.loc.gov/2023053919

*For my grandchildren
Maurice, August, Elisa, Mona, and Reina*

Contents

Acknowledgments	ix
Chapter 1: Spring Hope	1
Chapter 2: Blaine Street	17
Chapter 3: School Daze	25
Chapter 4: The Absurd Schoolboy	37
Chapter 5: Historically Black Colleges and Universities, 1962–1965	47
Chapter 6: The Howard University Years, 1963–1965	65
Chapter 7: Missile Man, 1965–1969	83
Chapter 8: Why Not Minot?	101
Chapter 9: The University of Iowa, 1972–1977	117
Chapter 10: Laughing the Face of a New Sun, 1975–1982	135
Chapter 11: Westmar Eagles, 1979–1982	159
Chapter 12: Colorado, 1982–1985	177
Chapter 13: I'm Wasted and I Can't Find My Way Home, 1984	199
Chapter 14: Kent Denver Country Day School, 1985–1990	219
Chapter 15: Teikyo Loretto Heights University, 1990–1994	235
Chapter 16: The University of Colorado, 1994–2000	241
Chapter 17: Howard University, 2001–2013	263

Bibliography 281

About the Author 291

Acknowledgments

Without question, my primary acknowledgment goes to Carol, my loving and supportive wife of more than fifty years. My heartfelt gratitude extends to my children—Graham, Shauna, and Lindsey—and to their children, who quietly sustain me with love even in my distracted aloofness. Further, I express many thanks to Donna Reeves, Caroline Jaap, David Ray, Charles Mahone, and Regina Harris for their lifelong friendships. A special thanks goes to Ann Ferguson for suggesting I write this memoir.

I cannot emphasize enough my gratitude towards the philosophers who have inspired me, taught me, and made me more human: William Anderson, Alison Jaggar, Lewis Gordon, Richard Schmitt, and Lucius Outlaw. I would be remiss not to mention my early teachers, Herman Clifford and Alan Maxwell, who kindled my passions for astronomy.

Since *Memoirs of a Black Philosopher* covers a wide range of topics, including baseball, astronomy, poetry, mathematics, philosophy, and race, it could not have been published without careful editorial assistance. Therefore, I appreciate the meticulous editing of Brooke Bures and Sam Brawand.

Lastly, I would like to express my deepest gratitude to *all* my teachers and students. From students, I *learned* more than I ever *taught* them, and for that, I am profoundly grateful.

Chapter 1

Spring Hope

We are all born batting 0.000. We are all born with an era of 0.00. Some of us never play the game and couldn't care less. Everyone strikes out. But there is one thing that *is* certain. If you love something *they* will take it away from you. And who, or might I say whom, is the *they*? Those who are in the know—and have read the *DSM-5-TR*[1]—always try to attribute talk of the *they* to some form of latent mental illness: one's refusal to take responsibility for one's actions, blaming every failure on someone else. But what do *they* know? A ballplayer always knows that they, or them, are the other team, who are always trying to defeat you, shame you, and/or strike you out.

On every ball field—sandlot to pro—"You" can hear chatter. The chirping encouragement of teammates for the pitcher to throw the ball in there.

"Hum babe . . . hum baby . . . hum bay."

"Rock and fire!"

"Ho now."

And I am at the aubade of my memory. Still in the crib. Before I knew baseball or You and not-You. I do not know if I was humming, my hand in my mouth, barely able to stand and hold on to the rail at the top of the crib. Could I hear the cicadas and crickets in the steamy Sunny Side neighborhood's night air, just outside Houston? I do not remember.

These are the vaguest memories from my earliest years, foggy. Yet, somehow, I do seem to remember the sweltering heat, the rotary table fan fluttering the curtains at the open bedroom window. The darkness. And I have told this story so many times that no one—*they*—do not seem to believe it is true. And no, I might add, mine is not the story of the repressed genius. I was not destined to be the "loser who becomes the winner." I have already said, if you love something, they will find a way to take it away from you. In baseball parlance, I was waiting for the worm to turn, the proverb Shakespeare appropriated from John Heywood (1546) "Treade a worme on the tayle, and it must turne agayne."[2] Baseball players are always waiting for the worm to turn. And projecting to the future back of my Topps baseball card, batting average 0.000. I was only months old, just having learned to stand, jumping at the rail of my crib, hoping to see my mother's face, to nurse at her ample breasts, and wanting to say "Da" as I crammed my little fist further into my slobbering gums. I had never heard of baseball, PRENEX normal form, Laniakea, Calabi-Yau Space, or Sandy Koufax. But more about that later. I was "ofer," 0 for 4, still in the bush leagues. Just up from the bushes of my mother's vagina. My father was asleep beside her.

So, where we at? I am in my crib, it is the middle of the night, I cannot even talk yet, "Yet and still," as my ol' Daddy used to say, I am thinking. I am thinking that the "dark" is not solid; that it has "holes" in it. It is (the dark) the same when I close my eyelids: speckled like salt and pepper darkness, like fine-grained Bendet dots (y'know like those old black and white newspaper photos, or Roy Lichtenstein pop art comic strip paintings). And I am astounded by this. It means that the world is not solid, it is porous, and so there must be a way into it and out of it. You might be skeptical that a six-month old is having these thoughts, especially when he is preverbal. But that is what happened. It was my first thought. A thought that did not need words or concepts. But this single thought became the leitmotif of my life, its imprimatur. The world was holey.

Philosophers, Clare Mac Cumhaill and Rachel Wiseman, writing in *Metaphysical Animals* on the thoughts of Mary Midgley; "A scientist may think he is clever because he can 'see through an apparently solid floor and know that it is only a speckled void,' but this is nothing to a philosopher, who is 'a man so wise that he sees through appearances in general (not just floors.)'"[3]

Sunny Side, a bedroom community outside Houston, Texas in 1945, was a Black neighborhood, one that would not have been considered a "ghetto," albeit highly segregated from whites. Ironic, as my mother and my father might have easily passed for white, or at least white Mexicans. All I can remember now of Sunny Side is that it was indeed sunny—in memory at least—and that my father, recently discharged from the US Navy, a petty officer, who cut hair at Portsmouth Navy Yard, because white barbers did not know how to cut the hair of Negro sailors. My father was thus the tonsorial expert on the woolly-bully, nappy-headed swabbies. And so it goes. You might have ascertained that I was, and am, a Black humm baby.

"Are you awake? . . . Are you wet?" My mother's voice was soft, slow, and loving.

She rustled out of bed and picked me up. She slid her finger into the front of my diaper.

"You're not wet," she said as she laid me back down in the crib and returned to bed.

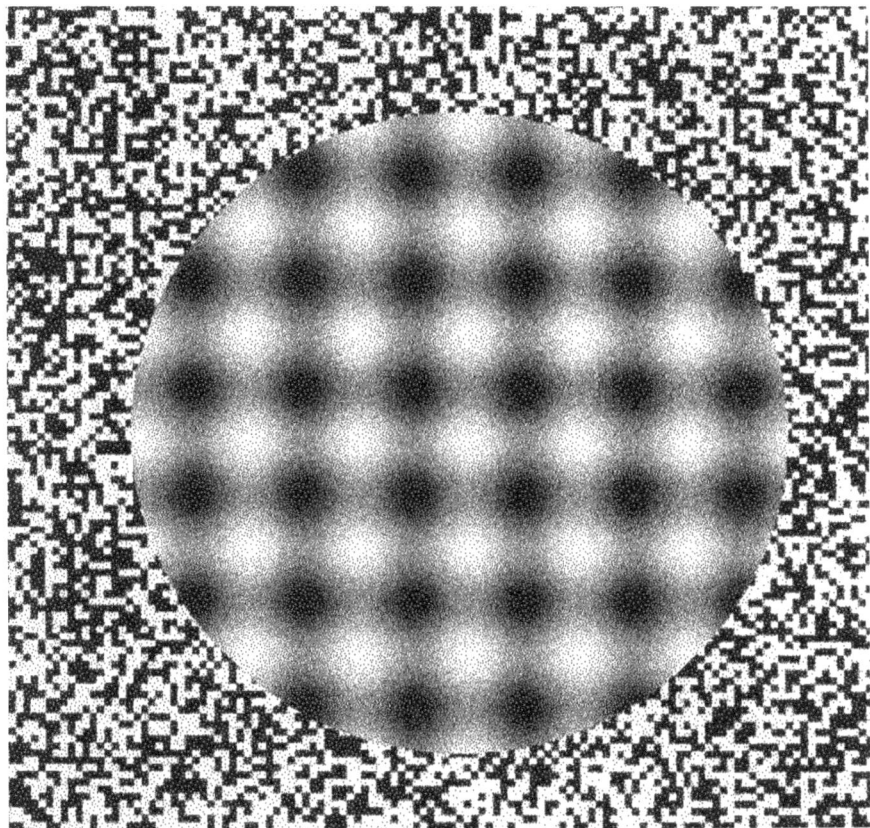

Speckled Void. Optical Illusions, World Press.

My mother's name was Bertie. She was call "Grown" by her fourteen brothers and sisters. During my teenage years, I had often thought they might have intended "Groan," because of her single-minded and opinionated insistence on any and every topic under the sun. It was as if she was an authority on everything . . . and when she did not know something, she simply dug in her heels as if her life depended on it. But I loved her, my fist in my mouth, sweating on the plastic covered mattress in my crib. Loved her deeply, indeed, as she appeared over the edge of the crib's bars and rail every sunny morning in Sunny Side to nurse me and change me and smile at me with her luminous brown eyes. Watching her long eyelashes blink over her round moon shaped face, reflecting the butter yellow sunlight, cooing at me, I knew no matter what her faults, I would always be her baby. But I digress.

I was trying to talk about my earliest memories. The polka-dot holes in everything. Crying in the back of my father, Gus's, Chevrolet coup, for cheese.

"For Christ's sake, get that boy some cheese," as he pulled into a small local grocery to buy the block of cheddar.

Where was I? You might have already surmised from my disjointed, discontinuous writing, that I am easily distracted: that life is an endless detournement—an interminable detour—one never arrives at one's destination. The universe is the same, except, it always "gets there." Hence, I am crying for cheese, and Gus, my father, the recently discharged Navy barber, who I remind of Mickey Mouse because he can see the blood veins in my large bowling ball ears—Steamboat Willy bouncing at the wheel—cartoon son, is driving his chevy coup looking for a place to buy cheese. Gus, who I remember one sunny afternoon, scooped up all the little kittens into a bag, to my wonderment, and took them to the huge gas houses near Sunny Side to leave them. What would my father have against kittens? Or me? I was only a year old, and these are my earliest memories. There is a small black and white, one-square inch photo of Gus in his Navy whites, hoisting me up on his shoulder.

So let me start over—a do-over. I was born on March 26, 1945, at the Portsmouth Naval Hospital at 2:43 am, at 6 lbs. 3. oz.—a "preemie" if I believed my mother—who always called me "the runt of the litter." Yeah, I was a small baby, but that did not matter to me, as I always thought of myself—like most people—as the "chosen one." I had an ego on me that just would not quit. I was going to win, to dominate, to be a winner, to smush all who opposed me. I knew it from the beginning. I was special. "They" were not.

Born in 1945, a few months before the United States dropped "Fat Man" (my father) and "Little Boy" (me) on the Japanese. Like Thomas Hobbes, who was born in 1588, the year the Spanish Armada bombarded England, said, "my mother gave birth to twins: myself and fear."[4] I was born to three mothers; my mother, fear, and racism. And for some reason, they named me Richard A. Jones—the "A" for Argustia. It did not bother me until much later when people mispronounced it as "Augustus," and I did not know whether Gus and Bertie did not understand the gendered difference between the two; that, the "tia" ending was a feminine Latin ending, or that they literally intended the "ia" rather than "us" ending after looking at me in the Naval Hospital there in Portsmouth, Virginia. Much later when I understood these Latin endings, I went in search of the mythological, thinking that they intended "Argus" as the "many-eyed hound who guarded the gates of hell," albeit a feminine "dawg," and since I was black (literally darker than either of them), I was the little black bitch guarding the gates of hell. And I suffered this through junior and senior high school. When people asked me what the "A" stood for I was reluctant to tell them: they would always guess *Alowishous*. I would always laugh and say, "You don't want to know."

Then at sixteen when I got my driver's license, there it was, spelled out for everyone to see—A-R-G-U-S-T-I-A.

My middle name always mystified me: accidental misunderstanding (due to faulty Southern educations) or intended (given the feminine name of a distant Black auntie). Or did they think I was a Black bitch?

But "Argus" was son of Zeus, son of Arestor builder of the Jason and the Argonauts' ship Argo, the "all-eyes" giant, the faithful dog of Odysseus. Okay, I get that—all sons—but the "tia" ending was definitely a feminine suffix. So, I check the authoritative Cobham E. Brewer's *Myth and Legend:* "Argus-eyed. Jealously watchful. According to Grecian fable, Argus had 100 eyes, and Juno set *him* to watch the priestess Io, of whom she was jealous. Mercury, however, charmed him to sleep with his lyre, and slew him. Juno then set the eyes of Argus on the peacock's tail." Who was this bitch Io, I was supposed to watch? Again, Brewer answered, "The priestess of JUNO whom JUPITER became enamored. When Juno discovered his liaison, Jupiter transformed Io into a heifer and she wandered over the earth, finally settling in Egypt, when she was restored to human form."[5]

Astounding! So, I was a hundred-eyed-dog-bitch instructed by a goddess to watch another goddess, who was hooking up with god, who was changed into a cow to wander in Egypt. Now it was beginning to make too much sense, as Gus was born in Egypt, Texas.

The endless detournement.

I do not remember my first inklings of baseball. Perhaps it was in Detroit, Michigan in the late 1940s, in Aunt Bettie's basement at 556 King Street. I tend to remember the Detroit Tiger's catcher Frank House. I thought that was a strong name for a catcher, like he was a strong house that nobody could knock down. "Frank" as in honest—he was an honest house. Frank as in hotdog: he was a Briggs hotdog in a frank house. It was all in black and white and droned on and on all afternoon, daily, for those damp, dank, days in Aunt Bettie's basement. Aunt Bettie was Gus's sister. She was married to Uncle Reed—a.k.a. Reed Maxie—also a Navy veteran who worked for the Square D company.

I would have been five years old in 1950. Living with Aunt Bettie and Uncle Reed and watching the game of baseball, with Frank House behind the plate. I did not really understand what was going on. Yet it seemed that Aunt Bettie and Uncle Reed were interested in the game, as they went about their chores, always background drone. My father, Gus, lived in the attic and when he was home, my brother and I spent time with him up there. His room, with the severely slanted ceilings, always smelled like talcum powder and KOOL cigarettes.

Dear reader, compassionate reader, ideal reader, charitable reader, if you remember, a few pages ago, I promised to muse on PRENEX Normal Form,

Laniakea, Calabi-Yau Space, and Sandy Koufax. Let us start with baseball . . . hum baby.

Much later, my stepfather, Charles Wiggs, took me to Robert F. Kennedy Memorial (RFK) Stadium a few miles from where we lived in northeast Washington, DC: what the haters refer to as "east of the river," to distinguish the Black ghetto of 1960s DC to the prosperous largely white northwest, Georgetown part of the city. Anyway, Charles, a World War II veteran and baseball aficionado, who taught me the intricacies of the game, had tickets to a pre-season exhibition game between the lowly Washington Senators and the mighty Los Angeles Dodgers, with the paradigmatic Sandy Koufax of the yellow hammer, uncle Charlie, yakker—overhand curveball—and the humming 98 mph fastball. Koufax was slated to pitch in the exhibition, and I was a wide-eyed teenage pitcher myself, totally overawed by seeing this southpaw in his glory.

Why did I love baseball? It was simply the one fact that when the ball was in the air, time stopped. For me, calculating the arc, trajectory, place in spacetime that I needed to get the glove to intercept the ball, required such concentration (actually solving differential equations, parabolas, rate of change, wind corrections, footspeed, the sound of the ball off the bat, vectors to intersect) that time stopped when the ball was in flight, whether playing catch, fielding fly balls, or throwing: keeping the ball from hitting the ground, caused time to stop for me. This phenomenon was the result of my love for the game, the people who played it well, and its ontological mathematical rules. Hence, the Sandy Koufax part. But more about that later.

One of my art teachers once asked me "What is the opposite of love?" I had answered "hate," and she had said "wrong."

"The opposite of love is laziness, because when you love something, you cannot be lazy with it; you are willing to work yourself to death nurturing it."

"That's why hummingbirds work so hard?"

"They love their baby hummingbirds?"

But I digress. I am off on another detour in the grand random walk of the universal *détournement* (diversion). So, I will try to explain how I got from my non-solid crib in Sunny Side, Texas, to my next "crib" in Spring Hope, North Carolina. For reasons only known to them—albeit I have heard rumors—Gus Jones and Bertie (née) Sills, married for less than four years, living in a little house with too many kittens, divorced. This event, hidden behind family myths, time, and many of my latter emotional travails, remains a source of my own psychological confusions. The principle of sufficient reason demands its reasons. After the breakup, Bertie took me to her home place to stay (temporarily until she could get back on her feet) with her father, Tommy (Papa Sills). My brother Robert, still a toddler, was sent to Jamaica, New York to be cared for by Aunt Lillie, Gus's sister. All I really remember of this time was my confusion—I had only been weaned a few months—and crying in a dark room where Papa Sills would not let anyone comfort me. Abandoned.

"Let dat young'un cry it out, or he'll keep doing it every night."

So, I remember crying until there were no more tears, dry sobs, in a darkness—whether holey or not—so bleak as to be crucifying. And after I could cry no more, I remember resolving myself to buck-up and survive this horrifying circumstance where I did not know the people, the house, the environment: until that time when "Mama Dear" would return. This alienated condition was my first commitment to existentialism: the universe does not care about "me."

So, who were these people? My aunts and uncles on Bertie's side. Luther, Lossie, Ozell (Chuck), Edna, Thesseleneure (Kitty), Barney, Mildred (Mill), Verlene (Bit) Matòska (Lois- "Wee-Wee"), Julian (Unc), Berlie (Rat/Anne), and a few others who died in childhood. During my tenure, Luther, Lossie, Barney, and Julian were present uncles; Julian being only a few months older than I was. Mildred, Matòska, Verlene, and Berly Anne were resident aunties. Taking care of me—a three-year-old, alienated, lonely, and unhappy toddler—thus fell to the caprices of neglected responsibilities. I learned to fend for myself. There were issues of child molestation and sexual abuse that I will not dignify by retelling. Leave it that in the South in the 1940s and 1950s, when Black people were poor, miseducated, and desperately displaced no matter which way they turned, sexual abuse was rampant—even within families—as the attitude was "you ain't worth much, get used to it, you'll be used for somebody's pleasure." Black people of this generation, unless they are rich and famous, do not claim or talk about their childhood sexual abuses, because that was just the norm—how else you gonna learn about it? It was barnyard sex ed.

Mama Sills provided little protection, as by this time after bearing thirteen children, she had largely given over the raising of the younger young'uns to the older young'uns. She had largely ended her working in the fields, cooking meals, and largely retreated to the front room to read her Bible, abed, making rare silent appearances in all her glory. And there were myths and conflicted backstories about Grandma Acie Mae. First, once I had had my own children, I had told them that they were part Native American. As I had been told many times that Acie Mae had an Irish-Cherokee heritage—she certainly looked the part, light-skin, grey eyes, and long black hair—with a dip of snuff in her lower lip, boiling clothes over fire, or canning fruit, while humming spirituals.

"They'll be peace in the valley, one day . . ."

However, when the DNA tests started coming back for my brother Robert and my adult daughters, there was no trace of Cherokee Indian blood. I asked my Aunt Anne about it, and she remained convinced that "Mama was an Indian, all her sisters were Indians."

The only explanation (IBE—inference to the best explanation) was that Acie Mae Sills was a white woman pretending to be Native American so she could live with a Negro man in North Carolina in the 1930s and 1940s without being murdered by the Klan. And then there were family myths about Pa. Tommy Sills was reputed to have come to North Carolina from Texas where he was a sharecropper. There were also whispers that he had "killed a man," served time in prison, before his conversion to Christianity. These things were only whispered about; Pa had become a Deacon in a church, and the Black people in the community of Spring Hope called him "Brother Tommy." Even at three or four years old, I remember him sitting on the porch in a rocking chair, in bib-overalls, work boots, round silver-dollar spectacles, looking at his pocket watch, and reading his Bible.

Pa—"Papa Sills"—Brother Tommy—was a religious man, a deacon in a Baptist Church, and on Sundays, the girls (my Aunts) and Pa circulated from one Baptist church to another from sunup Sunday until sundown. Matòska had an angelic voice and sang in church choirs as a soloist. I distinctly recall attending a baptism, where congregants were dipped, leaning backward, into red river water. One Sunday morning, the congregation got "happy," shuffling back and forth in what looked like a voodoo dance, white-gloved ushers rushing down the aisles to prevent the sistas from falling backward, until the rocking church fell from its cinder block foundation with a resounding "whoomph!" Scared me silly and even though I was yet five years old, provided ample empirical evidence against "that good old religion."

Having been abandoned (dumped) in rural North Carolina required many adjustments. First were the foreign sounding pronunciations of words I had only just begun to process in Sunny Side, Texas.

"Bit, git up, n'fix di'na." Pa would growl. "Dinner" being lunch, as "supper" was dinner.

"Wiz' zuh." I thought my aunts and uncles were trying to say "Yes Sir," and it took me months (if not years in retrospect) to discern they were saying "Wise Sir." For Pa was indeed a wise Sir—lord of all beneath his visage—the progenitor of thirteen children. The story I heard is that he had come from Houston, Texas, had a large white house in "town," before the great depression in which he had lost everything and forced him to live in the country. Pa was the power. Like a little lost puppy or duckling, once I became aware that he had the power in this Erskine Caldwell's *God's Little Acre* (or more aptly *Tobacco Road*, as Tommy farmed 'bacca on his hundred-acre farm), I imprinted on him.[6] Following him around, always wanting to be in his presence, his calm imperturbability, laconic gruffness, and principal force behind food, and arbitrator of the endless jockeying between the aunts and uncles. In this world of light-skin, hi-yellow, grey-eyed beings, Pa was a dark walnut-colored person, as was I. I identified with him. The desperate degeneracy of poverty, racism, and delusory personal identity was obtained on Pa's "little acre." There was a grubbiness and futility that has always remained with me, but lacking that, it possesses an almost nostalgic beauty.

The house was unpainted, weather-beaten wood, tin-roofed, with a side room, front bedroom, kitchen, and dining room. With so many Sillses, every room was a bedroom. Momma Sills's front room (to which only she and a few of the other younger girls were privy) was heated by a kerosene heater which had a big tank outside the house. Pa's room, behind the side room, was heated by a wood burning Franklin stove, where a few of the younger boys (myself included) slept. The kitchen had a wood burning cook stove; and, the back room, where the table we ate from, had a "Frigidaire" (called an icebox), and cots where the older boys could sleep. There was rarely anything in the icebox. There was a bucket of water with a dipper. Dipper etiquette was simple. Pa drank out of one side of the dipper, everybody else from the other side.

What I am trying to convey—in this welter of past and current thoughts—is that just at the time I was beginning to acquire language and parse "reality," I was thrown a curveball—a "drop." I was swinging and missing at every and anything: life has many detours, roadblocks, wormholes to the future. So, without any other "home" to compare it to, Pa's house became, by necessity, home. There were electric lights (electricity called "fire"), on cords hanging from the center of the ceilings. When a "cloud came up" (viz., a thunderstorm), Momma Sills would demand that all electrical appliances and lights be extinguished, as, in some way that I could not fathom, God was at work during these storms. There were hurricane lamps as well, burning a redolent lamp oil I still associate with Spring Hope, North Carolina where Ma and Pa lived. No running water meant washtub baths once a week. Well water was heated on the kitchen stove.

The well was such a mystery to me. Located just outside the kitchen out back, the wooden bucket was connected to a rusty chain that creaked as the bucket was lowered into the depths. Once, Mildred lifted me to see the surface below and I was terrified by the slimly green walls and rusty chain imbricated into my drinking water. But then again, Spring Hope was teaching me not to be squeamish about the elemental aspects of human and animal life. Nobody around me seemed to have the time or patience for queasy fastidiousness.

"Don't bother Pa," was heard almost every day, as if to interrupt his contemplations and Bible ponderings would disrupt the beatific order of the universe.

Because there were no "store bought" toys, joyful distractions were minimal, but included games like tic-tac-toe and dots (a matrix of dots on a piece of paper, with the wining of an enclosed square resulted in your initial).

There was also the twenty questions-like game where a pencil sketch of an object or part of an object within view was guessed at. As I was very young when I arrived in Spring Hope, the game of Billy Buck was among my first memories.

"Billy Buck, Billy Buck, try your luck, how many fingers do I hold up?"

My three-year-old mind never understood how and why I "always" got it wrong never crossed my mind, until, one day I figured out that "Mill" (Mildred, who was my primary caretaker) was changing the number of fingers behind her back. I was trying, having had to translate my first contacts with language in Sunny Side, Texas, to re-interpret the world of Spring Hope, North Carolina. At times, this proved difficult and confusing. As an adult, I often thought that my halting, broken, long-paused filled, verbal communications style, could be traced to my early encounters with the backwoods, rustic, ür-talk of the Sills-speak, and their share-cropping, descendants of slaves, poor exiles from the great depression, ignorant neighbors. I was inundated with words like "boot," for the trunk of a car. And "dout" for "hindparts," or butt. "Gwine" meaning "going to," as in something I heard often from Poppa Sills, "Bit when you gwine git up?" In 1948, I had never seen a television set, the outside world coming through an old plastic AM radio that only played hillbilly songs and "Grand Old Opry," spirituals, "Arthur Godfrey," and news commentary that meant nothing at all to me.

"Who wet the bed?" was an expression I often heard awakening in the cold wet sheets, Julian, Robert, and I sleeping in the same bed in Pa's room.

"Twern't me!" we maintained, except for my brother, who was the obvious culprit.

This bed-wetting, waking up in the middle of the night with the sensation of warm pee saturating the thin mattress, yet being unperturbed because the increased warmth was pleasant in a cold room where the fire from the parlor stove had banked down to ruddy coals. Unk and I did not want to get up in the cold air, you just had to learn to hold your pee because you did not want to venture outside in the cold to—God forbid—the outhouse, or risk pissing beside the house in the middle of the night. So, we endured this urine-soaked mattress, with Robert peeing regularly, until months later, the constant hectoring ridicule from the aunties who had to clean up the sheets and air out the mattress, sunk in.

That our childishness was thought immutable, Bit taunted Unk relentlessly as being a "runt," a "bantam rooster," a "squirt" (which on reflection, added nuance to his comments returning from the outhouse). Looking into the cesspool, after one of the grownups had used it, Julian wanted "to shit like a man." Momma Sills, Grandma Acie, never hazarded down that path to the outhouse: she had a chamber pot in her room. I do not know who emptied it, as her room was out of bounds, only the older girls were permitted entrance.

I hardly ever witnessed direct communications between Ma and Pa; they were either telepathic, of one mind in the gospels, or deeply estranged after the rigors of the great depression and thirteen young'uns.

"Bit when you gwine leave that boy alone," Pa constantly chastised Bit.

But Bit would not let up. I tried to do everything I could to stop her from venting her wrath on me. Whatever Julian did, I tried to do something else—I did not want to talk like him, walk like him, or believe anything he believed.

I promised to connect all this to baseball and PRENEX form. Given what I have already said, this retreats from possibility. Thus, I will begin this discourse with a warning; it is gibberish, almost hebephrenic (word salad). First, in "making time stop," my feeling when the baseball is in flight, because my entire attention is on its path, and I love the activity of concentration, in the temple of silence, in the Calabi-Yau spaces within Laniakea, until the ball is caught: baseball is paradigmatic, a trope, metaphor, metonymy. Unselfconsciousness. A Sandy Koufax.

"How many ways can a batter reach first base?"

They will tell you—the experts—that there are seven ways a batter can reach first base. Without Googling it first, I try to name the ways. Single (hit); walk; hit by pitch (HBP); Fielder's choice; Past ball after strike out; catcher's interference; pinch runner. Now I check by Googling "How many ways can you reach first base?" "Pinch runner" was incorrect: should have been "error." In Googling, I see that there is somebody called "Toronto Mike" who lists twenty-three ways to safely reach first base:

1. walk
2. intentional walk
3. hit by pitch
4. dropped third strike
5. failure to deliver pitch in twenty seconds
6. catcher interference
7. fielder interference
8. spectator interference
9. fan obstruction
10. fair ball hits ump
11. fair ball hits runner
12. fielder obstructs runner
13. pinch runner
14. fielder's choice
15. force out at another base
16. preceding runner put-out allows batter to reach first
17. sac bunt fails to advance runner
18. sacrifice fly dropped

19. runner called out on appeal
20. error
21. four illegal pitches
22. single
23. game suspended with runner on first, that player is traded prior to the makeup; new player is allowed to take his place.[7]

I ponder these nuances. In "Toronto Mike's" broader construal, I ponder my own absurd ways that a batter can safely reach. I come up with: (1) be born there, (2) quantum jump there, (3) parachute into the stadium, (4) insert his avatar in a multiverse, meta simulation, (5) put your hand on a girls' brassiere, (6) recite Abbot and Costello's routine "Who's on First," and (7) play finger baseball. Finger baseball, a game I had discovered in the Reader's Digest, is played like Rock, Paper, Scissors. You shake your fist three times, and on the third shake, you extend a number of fingers, from zero to five. Your opponent (Robert my brother) does the same. The fingers' combined total: (0) "out," (1) "ball," (2) "single," (3) "strike," (4) "double," (5) "strike," (6) "double," (7) "out," (8) "triple," (9) "out," and (10) "home run." We played this game while riding in the car. We played it on rainy days.

As I promised, this has something to do with—at least in my mind—the inexhaustibly different ways a baseball game can turn out. It has been observed that you do not know whether the run scored in the second inning will turn out to be the winning run. But first, here is my take on PRENEX form.

In first order predicate logic, quantifiers are mixed in the inside of grouping of *wff* (well-formed formulas)—pronounced "woofs." It can be advantageous in simplifying these propositions, to move all the universal and existential quantifiers out front of the expressions. Taking this to another (more imaginative) level, let us suppose that you transcribe a novel into ASCII code, then move all the 1's to the front using a simple sorting mechanism. You would have a long string of 1's followed by another long string of 0's. If you translated millions of novels and sorted them in this pseudo-PRENEX form, it is highly unlikely that any two would be identical. Even if you pseudo-PRENEXed these novels in alphabetical order, starting with a long string of capital A's, followed by a long string of lowercase a's, with all the other letters and symbols similarly sorted, it is inconceivable that two novels would present the same spectrum.

In analyzing ancient texts to see who the author might have been, "stylometry" is often used. This is a technique that does word counts, word selections, and vocabulary to obtain a signature. Given an investigator has enough data in the form of extant text, stylometry is a highly successful algorithm for producing the identity of an unknown writer. In deeper analyses, stylometric analyses can even reveal influences, by detecting patterns that have been borrowed from other authors.

Anyway, the number of possible chess games is somewhat less than $10^{10^{\wedge}70.5}$. This is far greater than the number of elementary particles in the universe—10^{80}. But what about the number of "finger baseball games?" Given it involves ten fingers, perhaps somewhat less than 10! And what about the number of possible baseball games? Surely less than the number of ergodic (possible arrangements of elementary particles—their permutative arrangements—in the universe).

I think of a baseball game in terms of "+'s" and "–'s" (pluses and minuses)—a ball is a plus; a strike a minus; an out a minus, a hit a plus. Make a list of the pluses and minuses—play by play—and you will get a string of pluses and minuses. Do a pseudo-PRENEX on these pluses and minuses: a unique signature, no two the same. If you really want to get freaky (something I am frequently prone to), turn the pluses and minuses into ones and zeroes, put a decimal point in front of them, change each one to a zero and each zero to a one, and diagonalize—the way Gorge Cantor did to prove the existence of transcendental numbers—and you get a game on the diagonal, when translated back to 1's and 0's, fingers on two hands, a baseball game that has never been played. And if you add it to the list, then diagonalize again, you get a new one. I am left with the idea that there is an inexhaustible number of ways that a game can be played. The first ten batters hitting home runs ++++++++++++. Thirty strikes thrown by a pitcher in a row.

The point is, there are a huge number of ways that a baseball game can be played. And what of the ways human lives might be lived? Code it out, PRENEX it, calculate it, then compare that to the number of ways a universe might arrange itself, ergodic it out, add the multiverse, turn the PRENEXus into rational numbers, diagonalize these multiverses like "blackberries" (what C. S. Pierce thought universes could not be), and what do you have?[8] You have a universe that is not in your list of ergodic universae, so you are in a Cantorian transfinite or higher set of universes. All that I am trying to communicate here is that there are an infinite number of ways one can live a life, play a baseball game, or write a book.

And, to alert you to the fact that I do not really think my own life is unique in any special way. Your own life is of equal PRENEX value, ergodic value: all you have to do is learn how to play the game—play ball—humm baby. Can one really be an American without learning how to play the game? Play at what level? Sandlot? Little League? T-Ball? High School? American Legion? College? Minor League? Major League? Howard Cosell, the sports broadcaster, wrote a book titled *I Never Played the Game*. Yet he was an authority on all things sports, including baseball. And as a character in the movie *Ship of Fools*, who lamented that he had been drummed out of the major leagues because, "He couldn't hit the curveball," was reminded by his confidant: "There are a billion people in China who can't hit a curveball."[9]

Did I think this way at five? At five, I really did not know much about baseball. But I thought about things in a highly abstract and nuanced fashion, without the words or concepts to express them. I was trying to get beneath language—behind words—to fill the holes in the reality I had discovered in my crib in Sunny Side, Texas: to express the loneliness of the whippoorwills echoing through the loblolly North Carolina pines. I was looking for my father, Gus, in the imprinting on Papa Sills. I was looking for my mother, Bertie, imprinted on my various aunts and Moma Sills.

I was a boy scientist. My body was my laboratory. I had discovered that I could survive being abandoned, could live on a diet that did not include cheese, could take care of my wants without indoor plumbing. "My soul cleaveth unto dust," as Psalms 119:25 says. "Turn away my eyes from beholding vanities" (Psalms 119:37). I could see beyond the indignities of my skin color all the way to Laniakea (a billion cubic light year superstructure of galaxies). Having never played the game, I still knew that there were things in the world—very simple things—sustaining me, and I had no fear—following Papa Sills out to the fields.

His work boots dusty. His bibbed overalls caked with sweat and dirt. His hands gnarled and calloused by a lifetime.

"Gee-up there."

"G'wan and git dat sto'wood."

So where am I. Suspended in Gus taking a bag of kittens to the gas house? Tagging along behind Pa to the red-dirt fields of Carolina? In Sunny Side dragging Donald Barthelme's *The Dead Father*: a lifetime of pulling that stupefying corpse behind me.[10] Or imprinting on another father, Papa Sills, the pecan brown man in coveralls; the only person with a color like mine. A father figure to replace the man who would not give me cheese. These were my earliest thoughts of polka-dot reality to my four-year-old bewilderment at a moon-doored outhouse, where my soul cleaved to the dust, and dirt, barefoot, boredoms of rainy afternoons where everyone stood on the weather-beaten gray porch whittling or whet rocking a pocketknife blade. As the warm spring rain, running off the rusted metal roof formed shallow channels in front of the porch, in the white sand, we floated little folded paper boats, and did not wonder why no one spoke of other things.

And then one day, she came back, Bertie my mother. She had on a tan trench coat and a dark brown Tam' o' Shanter beret.

"You've got a tan," she cooed, lifting me onto Pa's bed. Not understanding "tan," I reached for my head, thinking she had said "tam," like the one she had on. She laughed and hugged me. From that moment on, I knew she had come to rescue me, to take me away from the huge white horse Cindy's brown eye, the barnyard smells, the fatback and grits, and from Buddy's finger, cut off at the sawmill accident, in a jar, in a suitcase in the pack house. She had come back to save me. And then the aunties had collected eggs from the hen house, sifted flower, fired up the stove and baked a cake, singing,

> If I knew you were comin' I'd've baked a cake, baked a cake, baked a cake
> If I knew you were comin' I'd've baked a cake
> Howdya do, howdya do, howdya do?

But, I am only as good as the last book I have read. And while writing this, I have read two books that intersect and influence my thinking. The first was Jacques Derrida's *Dissemination*.[11] I told you I was a pedant.

I am hyper-apperceptive. *Apperception* is the condition where every new perception or concept is compared to all previous conceptions or perceptions. It means that when I read something new, I am sifting it through everything else I have ever read, weighing it, contrasting it, testing it for value, assaying what *you* are saying—and consciously so. It is not a unique trait with human beings, we all do it: mostly without being conscious of it, but I am always conscious of it. Therefore, reading is the grist for my understanding. And I enjoy recognition of the similar paths that the writer and I have taken to get to our total befuddlement. So, I am a highly charitable reader, able to learn from any perspective, style, or topic.

Anyhow, I am reading Derrida, and he is musing about *dissemination*, as the production and spreading of the textual. And I apperceive that parenthetical (text) is to be inseminated, rather than disseminated—parentheses as vulva (inseminated text). And on June 16, 2022, as I was writing this first chapter, I realized that Derrida cautioning against "prefaces," that this was the "preface to my appendix." I understood that the "beginning" was a being (being "Being-*ing*"), the ongoing becoming (becoming-*ing*). The $g(f(x))$ the beingness of being, the becomingness of becoming. This is starting to sound like Martin Heidegger.[12] Be(ing)^2 or what might be expressed as, The being of being =. And to "Be" is "is." *Is-ing* is the Ising-ing of $(g(f(x))$ of I am singing—iambs-ing-ing—I-am-bee-singing-ing. Reading Derrida's *Dissemination* not only was the death of the author, but also the destruction of the preface ("pre"-face), before you had a face; preface, introduction (text), postface, afterword, appendix, index. And I try to put this into PRENEX form, apperceive, apprehend, and diagonalize. I warned you not to read this. Turning the page.

NOTES

1. American Psychiatric Association (APA), *Diagnostic and Statistical Manual of Mental Disorders, Fifth Edition, Text Revision* (*DSM-5-TR*), ed. Francis G. Lu (Washington, DC: American Psychiatric Association Publishing, 2022).

2. Quoted by William Shakespeare, *Henry VI*, part 3 (act 2, scene 2) from John Heywood, *A Dialogue Conteinyng the Nomber in Effect of All the Prouerbes in the Englishe Tongue* (London: Thomas Berthelet, 1546), "The seconde parte, the fourthe capiter" (page unnumbered) https://quod.lib.umich.edu/e/eebo/A03168.0001.001?view=toc (accessed August 12, 2023).

3. Clare Mac Cumhaill and Rachel Wiseman, *Metaphysical Animals: How Four Women Brought Philosophy Back to Life* (New York: Doubleday, 2022), 262.

4. Thomas Hobbes, "Opera Latina," in Molesworth, William (ed). *Vita carmine expressa,* Vol. 1, London, 86.

5. Cobham E. Brewer, *Brewer's Book of Myth and Legend*, ed. J. C. Cooper (Oxford: Helicon, 1993), 19, 139.

6. Erskine Caldwell's *God's Little Acre* (New York: Signet, 1965); and *Tobacco Road* (Athens: University of Georgia Press, 1995).

7. Toronto Mike, "23 Ways To Get To First Base," *Toronto Mike*, January 29, 2008, https://www.torontomike.com/2008/01/23_ways_to_get_to_first_base/ (accessed August 13, 2023).

8. C. S. [Charles Sanders] Pierce, *Stanford Encyclopedia of Philosophy*, "If Universes Were as Plenty as Blackberries," https://plato.stanford.edu/entries/pierce/#bio (accessed September 3, 2023).

9. Howard Cosell, *I Never Played the Game* (New York: William Morrow, 1985); and Abby Mann, *Ship of Fools* (film), directed by Stanley Kramer (Culver City, CA: Columbia Pictures, 1965).

10. Donald Barthelme, *The Dead Father* (New York: Farrar, Straus and Giroux, 1975).

11. Jacques Derrida, *Dissemination*, trans. Barbara Johnson (Chicago: University of Chicago Press, 1981).

12. See Martin Heidegger, *Being and Time* (*Sein und Zeit*) (1927), trans. J. MacQuarrie and Edward Robinson (New York: Harper & Row, 1962).

Chapter 2

Blaine Street

In his poem "Cows Grazing at Sunrise,"[1] the poet William Matthews muses that the past is "inevitable," especially "Now that we call the little / we remember of it 'the past'?" I remember that it was always hot in Washington, DC, in the summertime. And despite my despair at having Charlie, my new step-father, often called "Spencer" by his friends, especially as I ruminate on this distant time, there was the familiar voice of the "Nat's" radio announcer, Bob Wolff, on WWDC, rising and falling with excitement and despair with the regular tempo of the Washington Senator's continuous poor play, losing ballgame after ballgame. As I drifted off to sleep every night, the low volume of the radio on Bertie's night table, through the open door to their bedroom to our room's open door, was a sweet droning lullaby of the play-by-play—humm baby.

In the mornings, there were the sports pages from the *Washington Post*, with black and white photos of the heroics or failures from the night before. Charles, my new "Daddy," read the sports pages, especially the columns by Shirley Povich. There was a grandeur and anguish surrounding this national pastime that was slowly creeping into my innocent consciousness. America, celebratory, in shirtsleeves, with a cold National Bohemian beer, had suspended worries after being victorious in World War II. There was a suspension—a hermetic impenetrability—in following baseball. I heard snippets everywhere on car radios, in the various stores on Minnesota Avenue. Everyone was listening. Then within a few months, a black and white television appeared in the basement on Blaine Street and with it came the Washington Senators' endless quest to finish last in the American League East. "First in war, first in peace, last in the American League East," as I remember it.

In pursuit of my affections, Charles had given me that icon of post-World War II friendship, the silver-plated Spidel bracelet. On one side he had had it engraved, "To Richard" and on the other "From Daddy." He clasped the bracelet to my thin wrist.

"You're not my father!" I screamed as I hurled the bracelet into the dirt at my feet and stomped on it, tears streaming down my face.

Henceforth, Charles resorted to a cleverer strategy. He needed to nurture something—beyond my love for Bertie and my mythical father Gus—that something being baseball. He left baseball equipment around the backyard, an overstuffed Gil McDougal baseball glove and a heavy iron catcher's facemask. Reinforced by the endless Bob Wolff narrated games on radio WWDC, the Du Mont Network's TV broadcasts on WTTG, and the splashy photos in the *Washington Post*'s sports pages, I was slowly being inculcated to share his love for the game.

Then, the miraculous occurred! Charles took me to Griffith Stadium to see a game. The field was an immense swath of emerald green in the middle of the city. The bases were stark white, the chalk line straight and true, players resplendent in their home white uniforms with the stark block "W." When the game started, I could not believe the great distances of the long fly balls hit to the outfielders, their long, lazy, parabolic arcs. Ground balls were ballets, pirouettes, plies, exercises in timing and in execution. The fans were ecstatic when the home team scored, delirious with home runs, and pumped their fists at strikeouts. There was so much to process, the scoreboard, the count, the strategies of advancing runners, and preventing runners from advancing. The "'round the horn" double-play was an exacting, precision display of hand-eye coordination. For several years, he took my brother and me to games at Griffith Stadium. Somehow, I do not know how, the other fans (and at times even the players) seemed to know Charles, "The Sarge," with his two ragamuffin kids. He was a mostly silent spectator, answering my questions concerning the rules of the game.

"Is it a sacrifice fly if the runner advances from second to third when the ball is caught by an outfielder?"

"No—only if the runner scores."

"So even if the runner advances, the at-bat counts against the batter's average?"

"Yes, but if there's nobody out or one out, the batter has done his job to advance the runner—that's team baseball that doesn't show up in the stats." Charles was patient in his explanations; especially, I now think in retrospect, that he knew I was hooked.

He was also a discerning critic of the abilities and liabilities of players. He would often talk about the player's "deportment" and "configuration"—his size versus quickness, range versus throwing accuracy—intangibles, like clutch-hitting, pitch of decision, out thinking an opponent with strategy—seeing moves that would be made in the eighth inning in the third inning.

And my brother and I continued to play catch with the new baseball gloves we had been given for my birthday. The red-stitched baseball spinning beneath the blossoming black walnut trees in the innocent Washington spring sunlight. By now Charles held secure employment at Walter Reed Army Medical Center, in the Neurology department, where he helped US Army neurosurgeons work up cases for surgery. And Bertie had found employment as a nurse-receptionist in the office of a Jewish podiatrist, Dr. Saul Shafritz; I make the point of his Jewishness because, at that time in DC, Negroes in DC were totally integrated with Jewish immigrants from the war.

Much later, when I had been educated into my ultimate profession (not a professional baseball player) as a teacher of philosophy, I had understood the difference between scientific time (dx/dt), psychological time (epiphenomenal), block time (McTaggart's completed A-series), relativistic time, and the eternal time outside sempiternity. It took me years, from reading Marcel Proust's *Remembrance of Time Past* to Henri Bergson's *Time and Free Will*, to begin to understand how human time works.[2] One day, while I was in elementary school when I was playing hooky, I watched a cartoon from the series *Out of the Inkwell* by Max Fleischer with Koko the Clown. In the episode that burned its way into my memory, Koko discovered the "time-switch" for the city. Koko pulled the switch and everything came to a halt.[3] Then there was the sci-fi film *The Day the Earth Stood Still*, where the cosmic policeman stopped the earth spinning on its axis to demonstrate his power.[4] I was so unhappy as a child, I often wanted to stop time in protest of all the difficulties that I had experienced.

And Proust had imagined that if one lived an entire day—paid close enough attention—the entire day, all 86,400 seconds, beads on a string, would be available for recall. Life is a complete record of all experiences, only a small number of whichever rise to the level of consciousness. Either suppressed, repressed, deigned too trivial for recall—or not—were still available. I imagine this is what Christopher Isherwood intended by "I am a camera with its shutter open, quite passive, recording, not thinking."[5]

The more thoroughly I scrutinize the past, the more I find Jamesian and Jungian synchronicities—it all seems to be apiece, part of a holistic pattern, quantum entangled. While pondering what to write next (today)—Marcel Proust's *Remembrance of Things Past*—I read the morning comics section, *Zippy* by Bill Griffith. And there is a quote from F. Scott Fitzgerald: "So we beat on, boats against the current, borne back ceaselessly into the past."[6]

Charles is still taking me to ball games at Griffith Stadium. As I pass through the next few years, until about the age of eight years, I attend the games, watch the games on TV, listen to the games on radio, and play catch with my brother. When the school-year ends, for many years, Bertie trundles Robert and me off to Detroit to spend the summer with Gus, where he listens to the games—the Detroit Tigers—in his barber shop.

On Blaine Street, the exodus of whites for the suburbs continued, to be replaced by many different kinds of Negroes. The family that replaced the Italians, whom I had run off with unrelenting sunspots reflected into all the rooms in the front of their house, were very standoffish. They had a daughter about my age—Christina if memory serves—who would not even look at me. She had a cadre of girlfriends who played double-dutch.

"Who stole the cookie out the cookie jar . . . not me . . . number two stole the cookie out the cookie jar . . . not me . . . number three stole the cookie out the cookie jar . . . "

With the rhythmic click-clack of the rope, their barrettes bouncing, and their hostility toward my brother and me, I avoided that side of the street. They were dark brown Negroes with a superior attitude, like they were not first generation "bamas" (from Alabama), but sophisticated people who had been living in the North for generations. There were also "Gold Coast" folks who had moved out into the suburbs of northeast Washington after the neighborhood had been desegregated. Also, across the street was a middle-aged Black woman, imperious in her height and demeanor, who cast a wary eye at me every time she saw me. She also had a little dog named Frisky. Frisky did not like little Negroes, like me, walking in front of his house. Every time I ventured over there on my way to the Jew Store, Frisky would run out from somewhere—under the front porch or from the backyard—and start yapping and snapping at my ankles.

Suddenly, as the whites retreated, there were a diversity of Black folks in the neighborhood. Some were parvenu, recent arrivestes, educated at Howard University School of Law, poseurs, and other pretenders to elite status—schoolteachers, postal workers, cab drivers, and US government employees. But, for the snobbiest Negroes, and there were quite a few, "you had to be born to it." What this meant, as I understood it, was you could not inherit it in wealth, could not be educated into it. One had to be "it" from birthright. The genetic inheritance of "soul." The blackness of the tribal Kings and Queens from Africa. This royalty could only be detected from earmarks or the rhythm with which you walked, the timbre of how one talked, the way one held one's head against all and any judgments.

At that point, in the mid-1950s, baseball cards and marbles were national phenomena. First, baseball cards. Manufactured by Fleer or Topps, bundled with a slice of hard pink bubble gum, they were traded or flipped.

"I'll give you a Joe Adcock for a Harvey Haddix."

"No, I don't have doubles for Haddix . . . but I'll trade-ya a McCovey rookie card for the Adcock."

All the cool boys in the neighborhood walked around with a huge deck of baseball cards, ready to trade or flip. Flipping involved holding the card at your side and flipping it with just the right number of tumbles so it landed heads. As long as you matched your opponent—heads for heads—the flipping continued. If one contestant flipped a tail and you flipped a head, you won and collected all the cards.

Once in a while, during a long run of heads, one of the players would flip a tails. The pressure mounted above the hill of cards. And sometimes the next flip, unaccountably, would also be a tails, and the flipping would continue. A formidable number of cards exchanged hands this way. Along with baseball cards, shooting marbles was also a huge phenomenon.

Boys walked around with front jeans pockets stuffed with cat-eye marbles. Like the baseball card gunslingers, you could challenge anyone to a game. Anywhere there was a flat semi-sandy opening, a game of marbles was order of the day. The game of choice was to draw a ring where each player would put in the same number. Then there would be a lagging to a line, closest went first. The rules agreed to before the first shooter.

"Knuckle soup, fin no goodies, no hunching."

This meant that the first shot was with knuckles on the ground and no hunching meant that you could not move your hand forward before the shooter left your hand. I really have forgotten what "fin no goodies" meant, but I think it pertained to "eye-dropping" (releasing a marble down onto the ring from above or using a "bunker" (an oversized marble) or "steelie" (a metal marble) to shoot. "Fin no goodies" might have also spoken to the sometimes-claimed convention that a competitor had to knock one marble out of the ring while standing up before he could go "knuckle soup" (shoot from his knees with hand on the ground). Knuckle soup might also address the habit of some shooters who bent their forefinger and used their other fingers like the bridge used in holding a pool cue stick, to raise their shooting knuckle up off the ground. This advantage of elevation was decried by saying knuckle soup: all the shooter's knuckles must be in contact with the ground. All players had a "shooter," their cherished favorite, often a cat's-eye beauty with an internal blue or pink swirl inside the clear glass. If you missed a shot while in the ring, the next player(s) had the chance to "kill" your shooter and take it. Different players in the neighborhood had reputations, so you always had to be cautious who you played with, if you did not want to get wiped out. You could always detect a "sharpie" by the shooter's ability to back-up his shooter after a shot, like a pool ball's draw English. There were long shot artists and shooters who were adept at playing position, controlling the recoil of the shooter. And of course, there was the ultimate gauntlet.

"Mamie Eisenhower's drawers," which meant I want everything. If I win, I take your shooter and all the marbles in your pockets.

I am seven-and-a half years old, jeans pockets loaded with so many marbles I can hardly walk. I am looking for a game with somebody I can beat. I win more marbles than I lose. I am good at flipping baseball cards. I win more than I lose. I can catch a baseball. I catch more than I drop. And the Black girls across the street are spinning the ropes (how do they do that?), jumping in and out, chanting.

Three, six, nine, the goose drank wine,
The monkey chewed tobacco on the streetcar line.
The lion choked, the monkey croaked,
And they all went to heaven in a little rowboat,
Clap-Clap! Clap-Clap!

Back in the neighborhood, the whites were still moving out to the suburbs. A few blocks away was a neighborhood called Greenway, where there was a strip mall, a candle-pin bowling alley, and an ice cream parlor. Greenway was at one end of Minnesota Avenue and demarcated the white from the rapidly Blackening section of northeast DC. As a kid, I learned not to trespass into this area. Then, early in the 1950s, East Capitol Street was bulldozed and concreted from Maryland to the edge of the US capitol, another boundary. Soon after that, the I-495-Beltway was constructed to surround Washington, another impenetrable barrier. The effect of all these public works was to create an enclosure—a barrier—from which Negroes were disinclined to transgress.

Living in a prison where the other denizens were either inmates or screws, I yearned for the freedom I imagined still existed in Sunny Side, Texas or Spring Hope, North Carolina. Time and space were impediments for my being there, so I had to figure out a way to stop time so I could reenter it in a prior time; or bend space so I could walk again within my mythic places of peace and understanding. The flipping of baseball cards, shooting of marbles, or watching/listening/playing baseball—more than entertainments or diversions (pastimes)—were the experimental grounds upon which I calculated my freedom.

Somewhere in this welter of people, places, ideas, and concepts is Mr. Clifford. He was a new next-door neighbor. He was younger than Charles and Bertie. He and his wife, Aurelia, had degrees from Columbia University. He had a master's degree in education, and she held a master's degree in Spanish.

One summer afternoon, Mr. Clifford asked me something that changed my life.

"Richard, what is the nearest star?"

I quickly answered, "Alpha Centauri."

"The Sun," he corrected.

This was a profound revelation. Although I appreciated the Sun—ol' Sol—as a star, I had never really equated it with the "twinkle, twinkle variety." And Mr. Clifford followed this question up with the gift of a seventh-grade science book; after all, he was a science teacher. Now, when I glanced at the

Sun, time stopped, as I was so close to a star that I could see its face, and I loved its smiling yellow face. I had found something to love so much more profound than baseball, but I could see the connections: without the Sun, there would be no me, no you, no baseball. Then, while I was still reveling in the answer to his question, he hit me with another statement that altered my life. Remember, I am still seven years old.

"I've told you this before, billions of years ago, but you've forgotten."

With this one comment, Mr. Herman Clifford had produced the wonder and awe for time and reality that ignited the awe and wonder that continues to inspire me in my old age. I have spent a lifetime unpacking this comment. Of course, Mr. Clifford, was speaking of the eternal return.

"Cliff," as Mrs. Clifford called him, had introduced me to a philosophical thought with lasting import, and I had forgotten that he told me billions of years ago from an earlier thirty-billion-year cycle of the Brahman.

I am still grappling with this inside-out—mobius strip—multiverse phenomenon seventy years later, writing inside-out, Lawrence Ferlinghetti's *Little Boy*, from a distance equal to an eternal return, entangled in multiple universes—ersatz Lewisonian—where everything is identical in this universe to a near-by logical universe where my middle name is "Augustus," rather than "Argustia."[7]

I recognize the universe from before. I left tags, crumbs in the labyrinth, to remind me of Herman Clifford's warning, so I could remember next time, which was this time. This memory is not my brother Robert's so-called eidetic memory, or Proust's *Remembrance of Things Past*. This is the remembrance of the entire "Jewel Necklace" of all the recurrences, strung together forever.

I am shooting a game of pool. The balls bounce around the table. I am aware of the mathematical possibilities of their places on the table, combinations of which colored or stripped ball where, and the ineffable paths all these balls, inspired by their causal interactions, inelastic collisions, friction against the nap of the felt, tangents of contact—all—and all else, spiraling into an infinite string of forces and influences. Nothing was everywhere and it repeated itself every thirty billion years.

NOTES

1. William Matthews, "Cows Grazing at Sunrise," in *Seach Party: Collected Poems of William Matthews*, ed. Sebastian Matthews and Stanley Plumly (Boston: Houghton Mifflin, 2004), 90.

2. Marcel Proust, *Remembrance of Things Past*, 3 vols. (New York: Vintage, 1982); and Henri Bergson, *Time and Free Will* (Mineola, NY: Dover, 2001).

3. Max Fleischer, "Koko the Clown," in *Out of the Inkwell* (cartoon series) (Los Angeles: Paramount, 1918–1927).

4. Edmund H. North, *The Day the Earth Stood Still* (film), directed by Robert Wise (Los Angeles: 20th Century Fox, 1951).

5. Quoted in: Arthur Bell, "Christopher Isherwood: No Parades," *New York Times*, March 25, 1973, 412.

6. Proust, *Remembrance*; F. Scott Fitzgerald, *The Great Gatsby* (Orinda, CA: Seawolf Press, 2021), 135.

7. Lawrence Ferlinghetti, *Little Boy* (London: Faber & Faber, 2019).

Chapter 3

School Daze

I started Smothers Elementary School's kindergarten in the fall of 1950. Smothers Elementary was a multi-story brick building at 4400 Brooks Street N.E., named after Henry Smothers, a free Black man who had lived in Georgetown in the 1800s and started a school for Blacks. The walk to the school was a half-mile through the neighborhoods of northeast Washington.

My kindergarten experience at Smothers Elementary was unremarkable. Mrs. Beverly, the teacher, was short, dark-skinned, and matronly in an "other-mothering" way where we were all her children. She effused a warmth and a great love for life and "her" children. I continue to recall her patience and egalitarianism almost seventy-five years after being in her class. I learned how to be sociable, to share. I learned that Negro children—like me—came in all colors, sizes, and temperaments. I learned the smells of white paste, brown mucilage with its red rubber oval dispenser-snout. I experienced the texture and flow of primary color tempera-paint. I learned how to use pencils, crayons, and paper. I learned to sing elementary songs with my classmates. I learned to anticipate the snack times of graham crackers and the little cartons of milk, nap time, stories read to us by the warm round, nurturing body of the love from Mrs. Beverly. I also learned that the children, adults, and others I met during these kindergarten days, were clueless. They all appeared from my immature solipsistic reified self, as being two dimensional, cutouts from the construction paper they appealed to in order to differentiate themselves from the dioramas in which they lived. I walked, zombie-like, among them, like a blind kid in wonderland.

First grade was more of the same upward path to the high ground of appreciating my alienation more fully. The teacher was a young, light tan, beautiful Negro woman, with bubbling optimism, dispensing worksheets and handouts to be filled in, colored. The coarse-grained wood pulp paper, with its three lines (the middle line dotted) to copy alphabets into without falling above or below the lines, were boring repetitive exercises in time consumption. But I enjoyed Miss Brown because of her great optimism and beauty.

My report cards were more than satisfactory, as I was always awarded grades of "outstanding." I did not feel I was doing "O" work in the scale of O for outstanding, "S" for satisfactory, and "U" for unsatisfactory. I still did not know how to read.

Holidays, especially Christmas were transcendent. The teachers of all grades would have their classes out in the halls, or standing on the steps between floors, singing carols. Acoustics in the hallways produced a deep resonance as we were led through "Silent Night" and "Deck the Halls." The fa-la-la-la-las echoing through the halls—"Away in a Manger"—created an intense sense of the sublime. Sometime during this period, between my first and third grades, my brother was "skipped a grade." Suddenly, we were in the same grade. Robert had distinguished himself one Christmas during an assembly of the entire school, by reciting "The Night Before Christmas," in its entirety, from memory. The teachers and principle had determined that he needed to be moved up a grade so that he would not be bored by things he already knew. His skipping a grade implied that I was only average.

My fourth-grade teacher was Mrs. Strother. Mrs. Strother was a severe disciplinarian. She administered the ruler to hands and punished misbehaving students with trips to the principal's office. The principle, Mr. Fletcher (a.k.a. "Blue-ball" Fletcher), was reputed to have a "spanking machine" in his office. Those sent to his office, reported back that he had a wooden paddle, which when applied to "hind-parts," left educational welts on the buttocks which discouraged further visits. Mrs. Strother was also rumored to be related to Blue-ball Fletcher (or at least his lover). She was stern, judgmental, and played no favorites. Under her tutelage, I learned to play hooky, feign illness, and differentiate between learning and training. Her withering scowl was enough to make a nine-year-old Negro boy want to disappear.

Listening to my fourth-grade classmates recite "Under God," in the Pledge of Allegiance, which was instituted by Dwight Eisenhower on June 14, 1954, caused me to reexamine my own thoughts about religion. Neither Bertie nor Charles attended church. There was a Baptist church—Upper Room Baptist Church—at the end of Blaine Street. The pastor, Reverend Willie B. Allen, was legendary for his sectarian ways. Bertie would give Robert and me a nickel apiece, dress us up, slick down our hair, and send us out on Sunday mornings to attend Sunday school. We quickly discerned the absurdity of Sunday school, took our nickels to the store for candy, hung out in the alley, and then came home as if we had attended. One Easter Sunday, Charles took the family to Walter Reed, where he worked, to the sunrise service ministered by Billy Graham. I saw the sun rise, and the words of Billy Graham exhorting the assembled flock to Christ's love. Most of those assembled that morning in 1953 were white. Although my emotions were stirred by the spectacle, I could not rouse my intellect to accept the message.

May 17, 1954, brought winds of a new life. *Brown v. Board of Education* meant that the next school year would transplant Robert and me to a new school.[1] It was a newly integrated school nearer our house, a neighborhood school, at the intersection of Benning Road and Minnesota Avenue. All the teachers and students at Smothers were Black. In the fall of 1954, at Benning Elementary School, there were a few white students left, but more importantly, my first white teacher.

Miss Patterson, a former member of the Women's Army Corps (WAC), who had served in World War II, brought a worldly perspective to her fifth-grade class. She often told us real world stories of patriotic discipline, her precocious nieces, and how precious we were as her new students. However, I once heard her talking on the playground during recess to another white teacher.

"They don't even speak the language," she had said.

After that I did not trust her. What did she mean? We did not speak English? Or that our pronunciation, grammar, and vocabularies were deficient? Too many "dese" and "doze," for "these" and "those?" Anyway, I did not care, I knew how to read. One of the first books I had chosen from the school library at Benning was *Pepper and Salt*.[2] This was a book of fairy tales concerning dragons, elves, princes, and princesses. I was hooked on checking out books from the school library. Sometime during this period between 1955 and 1957, the DC Public Library started a bookmobile. I checked out books on science (and science fiction).

Miss Paterson, in acculturating her Black children, would have us sit on the floor in a circle, read to us in her slow and deliberate way, chapter at a time from books like *Five Boys in a Cave* by Richard Church or *The Boxcar Children* by Gertrude Chandler Warner.[3] I loved her readings. She always stopped after a chapter or two, a cliff-hanger, suspension, leaving us wondering what would happen next. So, all her little Black children were eager for her to go on with this story time, the next time she deigned to share what was "outside" the cave or boxcar. It was if she was sharing the mysteries of life outside our darknesses, outside Plato's cave, outside the dark ghetto.

So, where am I? I am a sixth grader at Benning Elementary School. Having spent the past few summers in Detroit with Gus or Spring Hope with Papa Sills and 'nem. Moma, Sills had left Pa and moved to Philadelphia to live with Kitty, their daughter. This was shocking for the whole family, as they had been married for forty-five years, had fifteen children, and survived the rigors of the Great Depression, grinding poverty, multiple wars, and the hardscrabble existence of the rural South. But Bertie sent Robert and me anyway, where I learned to prime (pick it), string (tie it for curing), cure (put it up in the rafters of flue-barns) tobacco. Summers spent in North Carolina were barefooted, idle, marble shooting with Unk (Julian), hide-go-seek with the older *chillen*, and foraging for vegetables in the truck garden we depended upon for dinner's soup and supper's supplement for the salt pork.

Other summers, Bertie sent us to Detroit. Detroit was the North. Northern Black people considered themselves more sophisticated than their Southern country cousins. Gus had bought a barber shop and remarried. His new wife—my stepmother—was called "Little Mama." Ernestine, who was from Jackson, Mississippi, was a beautician. She had her own beauty shop a few miles from Gus's barber shop. Her mother was Black and her father white. She had a very fair complexion. Ernestine and Gus might have easily passed as a white couple, if one did not know them. But they both self-identified as Black and never tried to pass. They were both responsible businesspeople in the emergent Black middle class. My father cut the hair, shaved, and fried (gave processes) the heads of Black folks who worked on the assembly lines at Ford and GM, or hustled in the streets as pimps and number runners. My friend, across the alley, Ralph Cole's father worked on the assembly line at Chrysler. We played baseball all the time.

Back in DC, I was finally playing organized baseball. Our neighbors on Blaine Street—Mr. Jackson and Mr. Diggs—coached a Little League team, Fort DuPont Civic Association. This group of ten-, eleven-, and twelve-year-olds played teams from nearby neighborhoods. We practiced at a nearby playground. My teammates included Edward Mahone (catcher), Bobby Diggs (third base), Michael Locksley (first base), Donald "Duck" Lee (second base), Cal Worthington (shortstop), my brother (right field), and Freddy McDaniel (pitcher/outfield). I was a pitcher because already at the age of eleven years I had a wicked knuckle-curve that broke down and away from right-handed batters. Young baseball players have trouble hitting curveballs, so I was usually highly effective. I also could throw an in-shoot, what it was called at that time, a back-up fastball. Beyond that, my repertoire also included change-ups—changes of speed—"pulling the string" on all my pitches. To add to my arsenal, I had control, inside, outside, up, and down—all quadrants of the strike zone—I walked very few batters. In this role, I was a leader. Despite this, I did not mind losing; I was always eager to practice and excited to put on the Fort DuPont tee-shirt and play the game. My teammates varied in skills and enthusiasm. Yet we were a team and we played to win.

Summing it all up, what had I learned in two years at Benning School? Some of it was obvious. I had learned to read at a semi-proficient level. I had learned the elementary mechanics of mathematics. Playing kick ball on the playground during recess and lunch, I had discovered I had fine coordination—like with baseball—I could catch any ball hovering along its parabolic path. I felt my first interest in girls.

In class one day, I had drawn a little picture of the constellation Orion the Hunter on a little essay we had to write and turn in. I had sketched in the outline around the stars, colored the bright blue giant Rigel in the foot and the red gas giant Betelgeuse in the shoulder. When Miss Patterson handed it back, she had asked me about the name of the red-giant star, and I had delightedly responded.

"Be-tell-geese."

"Bettle-juice," she had corrected me with a chuckle. As I did not recall, or could not remember, having ever heard the word "Betelgeuse," pronounced, I immediately thought "They don't even speak the language." This single linguistic event began a life-long reticence to speak in public, especially a white public, as I thought whites were continually policing the language of Black people. Yet even my stumbling over words did not dampen my enthusiasm with learning about the universe and how I could be "inside" it. Being inside the universe was like being inside the Washington-Baltimore Beltway, in an enforced boundary, in the ghetto. Still regnant in my thoughts are the interstitial, the gaps between all continua, the start-stop of time, and the in-out, out-in of all things. And if it was not discretely quantized, it was a plenum, a continuity, a continuum, and I, we, all of us, were part of it without the possibility of segregation.

Another event that shaped me was finding a leaflet about binary arithmetic on the street as I walked home from Benning. I distinctly recall the pamphlet was from IBM. It explained how 1s and 0s—ones and zeroes—could be used to express any number. I understood how 101 could be understood as ($\underline{1} \times 2^0 - \underline{0} \times 2^1 - \underline{1} \times 2^2$) or the number 5, and 10 was 1010. It made perfect sense to me. Numbers could be translated into another base other than base 10. In this case, base 2. And was not translation what everything was about? White people were always translating Black people's language and motives. As Black people, we were a people under translation.

"Huh?"

"They don't even speak the language."

During that year in 1956, I had seen the television movie *Our Mr. Sun*, with Dr. Frank Baxter.[4] With all the elementary astronomy books I had checked out of the library—Herbert S. Zim and Robert H. Baker's book *Stars* and Rose Wyler's *The Golden Book of Astronomy*[5]—and the junior high school science books being loaned to me by next-door-neighbor and science teacher, Mr. Clifford, "Our Mr. Sun" convinced me that I wanted to be an astronomer. Thinking about the sun as a star—a friendly star—made time stop for me like playing baseball, spinning Topps baseball cards, and shooter marbles spinning in the middle of a dirt circle.

But where was I in space? First, I was in the confined ghetto space of Washington, DC. Even when spending the summers in Detroit, the same phenomenon was taking place; whites moving out of the neighborhoods that the newly emergent Black middleclass were moving into. It was a confinement within the invisible razor wire—concertina coiled wire of prisons—of white supremacy. For many reasons, this was a major part of my infatuations with astronomy; to be as far—light years, mega-parsecs—away from forced interiority. The freedom of being outside. Even with the deep sense of porosity I discerned in my crib, being "inside" of something, anything, produced an eeriness I could never absorb. Were the dark spots holes in the white background outsideness or, were the white spots umwelt for the black outside?

I felt trapped.

I wanted to peer through the 200-inch telescope at Mt. Palomar to see beyond the farthest reaches of white people penning up Black people. I wanted to listen with the radio telescope at Arecibo to see if I could hear something encouraging about freedom. When gazing up at the Milky Way on dark nights in Spring Hope, hearing plaintive whippoorwills, Papa Sills sitting on the porch in his rocking chair, I often thought I could see through it all from beginning to end. I was on the deck of a starship—in the movie *Forbidden Planet*[6]—on my way back home from Altair 4. Summers in exile, always trying to get back home to Sunny Side.

While watching the hapless Nats, I also saw the greatest white ballplayers of their generation—Mickey Mantle, Yogi Berra, Ted Williams. I watched Whitey Ford baffle Senator hitters. All the while, being a "homer," I rooted for Roy Sievers, Eddie Yost, Bob Allison, Albie Pearson, and Harmon Killebrew. Charles had taken to bringing a half-pint of Heaven Hill bourbon to the stadium, hidden in his sock. He would pour this into his Coca-Cola and continue to imbibe while smoking Camels. His interest in these games bordered on the fanatical.

"Watch him strike out on this change-up," he predicted, right more often than not.

Finally, fall 1957, I was in junior high school at the brand-new Woodson Junior High. The next three years would be highly significant—socially and intellectually—in my life in the homeroom of Mrs. Emma Ballard, an art teacher, on the top floor of the new school. We were also in the highest track, 7-406. The seventh graders in 7-406 had been handpicked as the potential leaders and thinkers of the emergent post-school desegregation era. Ironic, that desegregation had created this mecca of the elite of segregated bourgeois Black life. The kids in 7-406 were light, bright, and just right. The students in the lower tracks, 7-306 and 7-206, on lower floors and of lower status, resented us as the favorites of teachers and of administrators. Mrs. Ballard was a matronly, firm, loving, and creative teacher who valued beautiful behavior as much as beautiful art.

There was a constant banter between the seventh-grade boys out front of school in the fall mornings.

"Baby love, yo momma so ugly when she was born the doctor looked at her ass then at her face and said 'twins'!"

"Dat ain't nothing, baby love, yo' momma so fat she got more chins than a Hong Kong phone book."

The twelve- and thirteen-year-old boys would form a circle around the two verbal contestants as they joned on one another. Those in the circle would laugh and offer "oooohs," or "Aw, baby love, he really got you . . . you can't come back from that." So, the greeting of many Black boys during this period was, "Don't talk about my momma." Talk about one's mother would often lead to fisticuffs. There was a fine line between insult and funning, and Maurice Pace was a verbal magician, entertaining with his quick-witted improvisations, a genuine comedic genius often imitated, seldom equaled. And I quickly found myself in fistfights after school.

This was not due to my joning, as I tended to stand outside of these sparring circles, listening with amusement. It was because of other cultural considerations. Whereas my classmates had chosen to wear tennis shoes with their khakis—or Stacy Adams with their gabs (pleated gaberdine slacks), as with Maurice Pace—I had chosen white buck shoes, which were quickly stepped upon.

"Why'd you step on my shoes?" Which was quickly answered by "It wasn't an accident," and an additional stomp.

"Do it again, and I'll meet you after school!" Answered again with a stomp on the toe.

After school, behind the Western Auto hardware store, I fought knuckle to knuckle, within a ring of jeering boys. Some days I had two fights, one at 3:15 p.m. and one at 3:30 p.m. Within the ring, of marbles, of joning, of the knuckle soup, it was a matter of honor. Boxing was a dance. Up on the toes, circling left, bobbing, weaving, jab, retreat, jab, jab, jab throw a right. My brother, Robert, also in seventh grade, but younger by eighteen months than the rest, had a memory for the great lines of the joning verbal sparring. Thus, I also had to fight some of his fights, when an older, bigger boy took offense to his smart aleck mouth (and, he had a mouth on him).

In one of these fights, I landed enough punches to vanquish my white buck shoe disrespector. But I had another fight scheduled for fifteen minutes after that and was the recipient of a solid left hook to my right eye. This resulted in a closed-eye shiner in blue and black that lasted for weeks. My mother was so concerned that she walked down to the corner of Minnesota Avenue and Benning Road to ask the barber at the "Tonsorial Shop" to keep an eye out for me as I passed by there after school. So, it was my first incursion in cross-over culture, Pat Boone and white buck shoes, American bandstand, and Spin and Marty Mouseketeer ethos that had so offended my classmates.

They thought I was trying to act white. I soon lost the white bucks for Hush Puppies and tried to "Blacken up."

Woodson Junior High school was named for Carter Goodwin Woodson, son of slaves, second Black Harvard University graduate (after W. E. B. Du Bois) and the originator of first Black History Week, then Black history month. Woodson was also famous for his 1933 book *The Mis-Education of the Negro*, where he argued that Negroes were being indoctrinated (led into false-consciousness); rather, than educated to live in America.[7] Mrs. Emma Ballard, as were many of the teachers at Woodson, was there to correct this mis-education by employing the sophisticated John Deweyan philosophies of education to counter. As such, they appeared determined to undermine the simple training of Black minds to submit to a superior culture. The flexibility and tolerance, lack of judgment for failures, generosity for divergent thinking, and encouragement of creative thought, were more manifest at Woodson than in any other school I had attended. And Mrs. Ballard was the moral center. She rejected elitism, championing the scorned. She was the first authentic egalitarian teacher I had. She encouraged everyone. She taught me an aesthetic and an ethic that continue to color my life.

That first year, my next-door-neighbor, Herman Clifford—was a science teacher at Woodson. The kids in 7–406 were his first students at the new school. He was project oriented. He assigned us to construct a rock collection, make posters of the layers of the Earth from core to ionosphere, do reports on alcohol and tobacco abuse, and to do reports complete with posters of the "Future of Human Beings." Mr. Clifford, dressed in bow ties, knowledgeable on many aspects of science, used the Socratic Method. He did not try to get us to memorize anything, which I liked because I had such a suspect memory.

Then, the event that altered the world. On Friday, October 4, 1957, the Soviet Union orbited Sputnik I. Sputnik was a 183-pound, 23-inch sphere orbiting the Earth in a highly elliptical orbit, sending out beeping radio signals, and awakening Americans to the realization that we were behind in the space race. Not only did it awaken white Americans, it also awakened newly integrated Black Americans. Suddenly, the education system wanted to produce mathematicians, physicists, and engineers. I took it personally, filling cardboard tubes with paper towels soaked with gasoline and trying to launch them in the backyard. Mr. Clifford seized on this opportunity to continue influencing my scientific education. He loaned me a large telescope from the school. I took it out to the backyard and observed the mountains on the moon and the moons of Jupiter. My mind was aflame.

In Mr. Clifford's science class that year, he assigned a rock collection. I was fortunate in that Charles had a sister who lived in Pennsylvania mining country. When he took the family to visit her, she gave me a large piece of pyrite and other exotic minerals. I spray painted a rectangle of plywood a deep green, chipped all my rock samples to the same size, glued them in straight rows and columns, with neatly typed white card stock labels. Then, I painted a thin white border-frame and tacked it into place. I had milk quartz, feldspar, granite, pyrite, shale, basalt, sandstone, and other samples correctly named and classified. The overall effect was museum quality. What Mr. Clifford was teaching was classification strategies. He continued to nourish my curiosity with monthly issues of *Scientific American*, which I devoured.

A turning point for me came in the spring session at Woodson in 1958. I was in a science course taught by Miss Manning, a young biologist. Miss Manning was a warm brown woman with a large gap between her ever-smiling front teeth. She was a recent university graduate, still under the influence of her scientific education. She appeared intent on inculcating the essential elements of the scientific method. She had explained to us how, if one suspected that Gingko Balboa leaves could be used to treat cancer, one would extract potions, test them, double-blind, refine the hypothesis, and arrive at a theory. The etymology of *theoria* in Greek is "looking at." Because America was still reeling from Sputnik, science education was a primary concern of many federal agencies. One day there was an imposing white man in a suit and tie sitting in Miss Manning's science class.

"Would anyone like to explain what they're interested in in science," Miss Manning asked, her gapped teeth smiling bright from her chocolate face. I raised my hand.

"Richard?" she called on me.

"I'm interested in Hubble's Law—$V = H_0 D$—the relationship between the distance of galaxies and their velocities of recession. With H0 being Hubble's constant of 50 miles per second per Mega-parsec." Time stopped. Miss Manning asked me to explain.

"The Doppler-effect on light produced a red-shift for objects receding from us. Astronomers have found that the farther galaxies are away from us the faster they are moving away from us. This is the expanding universe. The rate of that expansion is 50 miles per second per mega-parsec. A parsec is a parallax second—3.26 light years—so for every million parsecs, galaxies increase their radial velocities by 50 miles per second." Time stopped. My seventh-grade classmates looked on annoyed. Miss Manning went on to ask other students about their interests. Of course, we were performing for the white stranger at the back of the class.

There were too many things happening to recount in detail. Bertie had brought home two puppies in a cardboard box from Mrs. Shafritz, wife of the podiatrist she worked for. I had cried when the other members of the family chose the one that did not look like Lassie. We took the one who was more like a Lab and name him Monté, after the Del Monte on the vegetable cans. He grew to be an obedient, loyal, and loving dog who played an important part in my life. Mrs. Ballard took the class on a field trip to Philadelphia to visit The Franklin Institute of Science, where my love for science was again reinforced. I read George Gamow's profound little paperback *One Two Three . . . Infinity*,[8] where I first met Eratosthenes's sieve of primes. I was also reacquainted with my algebra teacher Mr. Lee's penny doubling exercise ("doubling a penny for a month, was millions of dollars") in the "grains of wheat on a chessboard," awarded to Vizier Sissa Ben Dahir for inventing chess." Gamow's little paperback introduced me to curved space, time dilation, the Michelson-Morley experiment, imaginary numbers, and so many other concepts. I had the beginnings of an understanding of Special and General Relativity. My mother bought me science books like *Theories of the Universe* by Milton K. Munitz, *The Lore of Large Numbers* by Philip J. Davis, and the impressive *Van Nostrand's Scientific Encyclopedia*.[9] Mr. Clifford loaned me a high-powered microscope, which I quickly turned to my own sperm—obtained by masturbation for just that purpose—amazed like Antony van Leeuwenhoek in 1674 with what I saw. "Humm . . . baby." I obtained samples of my own blood just to check that what the science books said about blood cells was true.

In the ninth grade, I won the science fair. My project was on the principles of rocketry. I had designed distinct types of rocket bodies and tested them with wind generated from a vacuum cleaner, varied colors of paint for rocket exteriors and tested them by burning them with a magnifying glass, and made models of the insides of rockets and their motors. All of this was artfully presented on a plywood backed board with typed descriptions of these principles. I knew that hydrazine was the best liquid rocket fuel.

I was sitting in Mrs. McPhearson's History class, just before the bell was about to ring. The back door of the classroom was open. Woodson had instituted "Hall Monitors" to ensure that the halls were empty before the next classes began. The hall monitors stood at the intersections of hallways and briefly watched out for stragglers between classes. I caught a glimpse of her standing there in a sweater and skirt. She was short, well proportioned, honey-brown, and moved with a felicity that I had not encountered in astronomy books. Her name was Beverly, Beverly Fagan.

After months of sending "I think I like you" notes back and forth to her via intermediaries, one day I had the chance to see her at a middle-school basement party. Basement parties were all the rage in the Black neighborhoods of Washington, DC. Only recently having become a teenager, I was shy to the point of embarrassing others. So, while the other kids danced to "Smoke Gets in Your Eyes," and "Tears on My Pillow," I hugged the basement walls, a budding wallflower. When the grownups of the house blinked the lights and said, "Last Dance," Beverly walked over to me, took my hand, and led me in a slow "Charging Dance," slow grinding her pelvis against my thigh. Touching her made me feel things that I could not describe.

Within a few months, Beverly had led me tenderly into adulthood. She was a natural lover, unashamed of her body, confident in her mastery, and subtle in teaching me the mysteries. As I know think back, she took me to "Ding Dong School," or how to be a "Do Bee," and not a "Don't Bee." I lost all interest in baseball and astronomy. In fact, I lost interest in anything that was not Beverly.

As Beverly was a beautiful, zaftig, skillful lover, there were other boys who wanted to attend her "Ding Dong School," and her passionate needs were greater than the apprentice skills I offered, and I soon suspected that I was not the only one running to and from her door at the end of Sherriff Road.

Beverly not only taught me the limits of my "boy scientist" body, but also the limitless, transfinite dimensions, of the sensate, and that included transcendental realms of possessiveness and jealousy. She was determined not to be the possession of any boy's ego. She quickly tired of me. She moved on. I was heartbroken. Where Bertie thought it was "puppy love," I thought it was really love.

"Baby love."

NOTES

1. U.S. Supreme Court, *Oliver Brown, et al. v. Board of Education of Topeka, et al.*, 347 U.S. 483 (May 17, 1954).

2. Howard Pyle, *Pepper and Salt: Seasoning for Young Folk* (Salt Lake City: Editorium, 2020). N.B. This book has gone through many editions, first published in 1892.

3. Richard Church, *Five Boys in a Cave* (New York: John Day, 1951); and Getrude Chandler Warner. *The Boxcar Children* (Park Ridge, IL: Albert Whitman, 1942).

4. Frank Capra, *Our Mr. Sun* (film), directed by Fank Capra (CBS, 1956).

5. Herbet S. Zim and Robert H. Baker, *Stars: A Guide to the Constellations, Sun, Moon, Planets, and Other Features of the Heavens* (New York: Golden Press, 1951); and Rose Wyler, *The Golden Book of Astronomy: A Child's Introduction to the Wonders of Space* (Racine, WI: Golden Press, 1955).

6. Cryil Hume, Irving Block, and Allen Alder, *Forbidden Planet* (film), directed by Fred M. Wilcox (Beverly Hills, CA: Metro-Goldwyn-Mayer, 1956).

7. Carter Goodwin Woodson, *The Mis-Education of the Negro*. Amherst, NY: Associated Publishers, 1933

8. George Gamow, *One Two Three . . . Infinity: Facts and Speculations of Science* (New York: Bantam Books, 1979).

9. Milton K. Munitz, ed., *Theories of the Universe: From Babylonian Myth to Modern Science* (New York: Free Press, 1965); Philip J. Davis, *The Lore of Large Numbers* (New Haven, CT: Yale University Press, 1961); and Douglas M. Considine, ed., *Van Nostrand's Scientific Encyclopedia*, 5th ed. (New York: Van Nostrand Reinhold, 1976).

Chapter 4

The Absurd Schoolboy

Sitting here, sixty years removed, reading P. D. Ouspensky's *Strange Life of Ivan Osokin*, I wonder what it would be to go back, to have the chance to relive my life.[1] Would I choose, like Osokin, to go back in time? Only to discover that, even with the knowledge of having already lived the episodes of memory—and remembered them—that I could not change anything that had happened. Especially when it comes to matters of the heart. For as Gottfried Wilhelm Leibniz said, "the passage from mind to heart is so long."[2] In fact, I would say, the passage is infinite.

By the beginning of my first session at McKinley Technical High School in 1960, I knew I had lost my first love, Beverly. I still longed to have her back. Early that year, I had attended a basketball game at Spingarn High where Beverly attended, to catch a glimpse of her and her new boyfriend. He did not appear to be worthy of her. I was deflated that she would have chosen him over me. I studied him. He appeared to be popular and highly social, greeting and being greeted by all of the students at the game. He dressed well. She was smiling and contributed to this new boyfriend's social capital.

Fall 1960, I was a freshman at McKinley Tech, the high school for the track one students from all over DC. "Tech" was the pre-college preparatory school. Tech was in nearby northwest DC, recently abandoned by whites to the great northern migration. There were only a few white students and teachers left at McKinley, but it was a magnet for the elites from Dunbar High School, the haunt of the Gold Coast Blacks who had been residents of Washington for generations. There were also "e-lites": Negroes of fair-skin and straight hair—"house niggers." Black kids from other parts of the city—not from the northwest neighborhood—were called block boys. Block boys wore shined Edwin Clap, Nunbush, or FootJoy shoes, with white "pimp stitches," pleated gabardine pants, and Banlon or Pendleton shirts. Block boys were also known to be fighters, knowing how to "throw down." We Jitterbugged and Lindy-hopped.

Block boys hung around street corners, tried to sing doo-wop, smoked, drank, and often had a "walk man," or partner they would adopt as a sidekick. My walk man was one Michael Locksley. Michael was well over six foot. I was barely five-foot seven. People called us Mutt and Jeff. Michael and I carried stilettos.

In English, diagramming sentences, learning rules of punctuation, and analyzing literature were all boring. The only thing that caused even a tinge of profundity was the haunting fragment of a poem by Gerard Manley Hopkins, "Spring and Fall: To a Young Child":

> Margaret, are you grieving
> Over Golden grove unleaving?
> . . .
> By and by, nor spare a sigh
> Though worlds of wanwood leafmeal lie;[3]

And I was grieving over Beverly leaving, there was gray fall rain, and boring, droning, words from my teachers. And these pedagogues were from upper-class, Gold Coast Blacks, second- and third-generation college educated, and their students from Dunbar and Wilson High schools. I had the dreadful feeling every day of being stupid, outclassed, of dubious intellect, and of mispronouncing every other word that came from my mouth.

My other classes were not much different . . . what was "wandwood leafmeal?" And, why did it "lie?" I did not know. In the Chemistry class, the instructor, in his white lab coat, round eyeglasses, and uninflected lecturing style, and at the podium of the amphitheater-style seating, tried to come across as the great scientist, which he was not. Geometry was taught by a white teacher, Mrs. Haffer. I will always remember the utter futility of the little green geometry book, published originally in the 1940s and reissued to every McKinley High School class since. The book had exceedingly small inscrutable print, indecipherable—SAS my ass. Mrs. Haffer broke down crying in front of the class—a nervous breakdown waiting to happen—declaring, "Why don't you, why can't you, see the importance and beauty of these theorems?" Black students looking on with indifference to her imploring the compulsions of Euclid's irrelevance to Blacks in 1960s America.

My one escape was Military Science. At least here we were outdoors. I was a guidon bearer, a role usually reserved for a short but sharp trooper to bear the colors of his squad. In ROTC, we handled weapons. In this case the M-1 Garand, "A gas operated, seven shot, shoulder weapon." We learned the manual of arms, "Right shoulder, left shoulder, port arms." I liked marching in formation and the uniform. Moving in synchrony with hundreds of other boys made me feel like I belonged to something at McKinley Tech.

I was always on the lookout for Beverly. Or a replacement for Beverly—somebody to love. I was becoming a true iconoclast—a destroyer of icons—a rebel without a cause. An existential nihilist, an atheist, a rogue. Life on Blaine Street with Bertie and Charlie was not life with Ward and June Cleaver from *Leave It to Beaver*. However, as much I wanted to identify with the kids on *American Bandstand* with Dick Clark, I was not Wally Cleaver either, although Robert, my brother, was the Beaver, in all his innocent naïveté. I was always trying to explain it to him. He was oblivious. He appeared to go along with the bullshit at McKinley Tech.

Given my own environment, where the demimonde, oblivious in its own pursuits of pleasure and distraction, was trying to teach me to be like them, I could not suffer them. How could these bourgeois Blacks who had settled for second-best have any appreciation for the radial velocities of galaxies? I slipped through my days. Totally disinterested in being like them. I was Stephen Daedalus contemplating eternity, after all that sand carried in the beak of a bird from one place to another, "eternity would have scarcely begun."[4]

Boredom. Nihilism. My grades for the first semester were a dizzying array of Cs and Ds. To compensate for this dazzling display of teenage angst, my aesthetic senses were in full flower. I gained an appreciation for the da-dah-da-dah poetry of Emily Dickenson.

> I had a guinea golden I lost it in the sand
> And tho' the sum was simple
> And pounds were in the land
> Still, had it such a value
> Unto my frugal eye
> That when I could not find it
> I sat me down to sigh.[5]

Riding in Charles's new Chevy, WOOK on the radio, on his way to picking up Bertie from work at Dr. Shafritz's office, listening to Sam Cook's song "(What a) Wonderful World,"[6] about a man who does not know much about academic subjects, but he does know that he is in love.

Sure, I didn't know much about the "history" or "biology," Cook crooned about, but I did know that I love you," Beverley. And I am certainly proving that I do not know much about the academic subjects of my failures.

The second term at McKinley was more of the same dative or nominative case, gerunds, and futility in the classroom. When we were still a thing, I used to tell Beverly, during our hour-long telephone listening to one another breathe sessions, that if a person tried hard enough, one ought to be able to remember and to talk about other years in ones' life in such detail that it would require as much time as the original occurrences. It was a *Pincher Martin*,

William Golding's novel of the sailor torpedoed and drowning remembering his entire life, dying on page one, still narrating on the last page.[7] It was Marcel Proust's *Remembrance of Things Past*,[8] before they passed. It was the past as the present and CPT symmetry—charge, parity, time reversibility. I was trying to seduce Beverly into remembering me always, as I would remember her always.

I am smoking a Newport because Beverly smokes them. I am drinking Dewar's scotch, because Charles buys so much of it, he cannot remember a missing bottle or two. I am struggling to support the illusion that I am a student at McKinley Tech. I get up every morning and trudge off, carry textbooks home that I never open, and "Wanwood leafmeal lie."[9]

Finally, it is March 1st, which marks tryouts for the baseball team. It is a wet, cold, and gray Saturday. I go out on the sodden field, and while the baseball coach watches us throw, I am spinning my knuckle-curve. To my joy, I make the team. I start hitting in the batting cage in the gym. I am throwing every day after lunch. Finally, the first game comes. I am putting on sanitary socks, stirrups, and an actual felted-cotton uniform with "Tech" across the front. That first practice game was against a team of white boys from suburbia that Coach Smith had brought in. I was the starting pitcher. These white boys, who had played actual Little League and been to batting cages, had no trouble hitting my curveball, which had fooled so many inner-city Black batters.

After the mid-terms came out, Coach Smith flagged me down and said, "Your grades are not good enough. You are off the team. Turn in your uniform." Time stopped. The only reason I had for living was playing baseball.

I started drinking and smoking in earnest. A sixteen-year-old drunkard. I stopped attending classes. Accordingly, at the end of the school year when my report card came, I had earned three Fs, a D+, and a D.

By summer's end, Bertie had arranged for me to live with my father to attend school in Detroit. Hello Motown. Detroit is a strange place. Another haunt of the great northern migration of Black folks from the cotton fields. Another phantasm of self-deception. The neighborhood Gus bought his house at 2220 Collingwood on the city's west side, was still partially white when he first moved in. But, just like my neighborhood in DC, I watched it become increasingly Black, over the many summers I spent there, as whites moved out of the inner city. Gus was the owner of two "Jones Barber and Beauty Shops." The most lucrative was on 12th Street across the street from New Bethel Baptist Church, where a young Aretha Franklin sang in the choir. Gus cut the Reverend Franklin's hair.

Jackie Wilson, the soul singer, had been a shoeshine boy in Gus's barbershop, until his song "Lonely Teardrops" became a hit in 1959. Then, my father used to joke, "I last saw him in a pink convertible Cadillac." James Jamison, the bass guitarist for Motown's house band—"The Blues

Brothers"—famous for his intro bass notes on "My Girl"—lived two doors down. Smokey Robinson lived in an apartment complex near the corner of 14th and Collingwood. Hitsville USA, Motown's headquarters, was within walking distance. Having lived in this neighborhood for many summers, the only real change I could discern was that many of the hoodlums had cleaned up their act. They now dressed in neat, sharkskin suits and bowties, selling the *Final Call* newspaper. Daddy Grace and Elijah Mohammed had mansions on Chicago Boulevard, a few blocks from 2220 Collingwood.

Those first few days in classes at Central High School were a blur, as I did not really know anyone, or even the expectations of the various cliques—the cool kids, the "tricks," or the e-lites. Ralph tried to steer me in the right direction. However, in that I was repeating some of the courses I had failed at McKinley Tech, Ralph was not in any of my classes. There I was, taking Mechanical Drawing, English, Algebra, History, and PE. I was always great at drafting and took right up where I had left off at McKinley. In English I was reading interesting short stories, still vivid to me after sixty years: Jack London's "To Build a Fire," Richard Connell's "The Most Dangerous Game," and Wilbur Daniel Steele's "The Man Who Saw Through Heaven." Beyond these stories, the teacher taught us literary structure: man versus man, man versus nature; man versus himself.

In the algebra class, I sat with all insouciance, in the back row, feigning disinterest. The math teacher, Mrs. Flake, was a warm middle-age, matronly Black woman. What made her different from the teachers I had had in DC was her cheerful enthusiasm. As the days went by, she would call on me every day. For the first few times she called on me, I answered, "I don't know." Once, I figured out that she intended to call on me every day, I decided I did not want to disappoint her every morning with "IDK." To make her happy when she called on me, I started doing the homework, answering her questions, and even asking her questions. I learned how to use the textbook (*Algebra: Its Big Ideas and Basic Skills—Book II* by Daymond J. Aiken, Kenneth B. Henderson, and Robert E. Pingry [I still have my copy of this book]).[10] Mrs. Flake was so delighted by my progress that she inflamed my love for mathematics. Of course, as the other students started to see that I was becoming her favorite, they began to work harder to outdo me on tests. At the fall parent-teacher's conference, when she found out that my father was a barber, who left for the barbershop before I had had breakfast, volunteered to come to our house to fix my breakfast. Gus desisted but started leaving my breakfast on the table before he left for the shop.

That winter, before Christmas, I found myself getting up early—as early as 4:00 a.m.—to huddle by the heat register in the tiled bathroom to read. I read Lincoln Barnett's *The Universe and Dr. Einstein.* In this highly readable paperback, I discovered not only the use for imaginary numbers I was learning to manipulate in Algebra, but deeper connections between mathematics and the universe.[11]

During a few prior summers in Detroit, hanging around the barbershop, the stripped barber pole spiraling, under the tutelage of Lorenzo, I learned to shine shoes for fifty cents. I watched Gus shave and cut customers from all classes—businessmen to street hustlers. I learned the ways of the number's runners. Listening to the barber's constant jibber jabber, the customer's discourses on politics and baseball, I came to appreciate the discourses of Black life. There were class distinctions, Negro vs. Negro, Negro vs. Nigger, Nigger vs. Negro, and Nigger vs. Nigger. Let's call these Ne-Ne, Ne-Ni, Ni-Ne, and Ni-Ni.

Ne-Ne was the struggle between the upper-crust Negros for the limited cream that floated to the top. The "crab-in-a-barrel" clambering for success, a Cadillac, and the respect of white people. Fame. Ne-Ni was the attempt to distinguish oneself from the lumpenproletariat, criminal element in Black society. This was the struggle to get into the emerging Black middle-class. Ni-Ne was the pushback of the darker brothers and sisters—the field niggers against the house niggers—for props. Legitimacy. The struggle in northern cities against colorism. Finally, there was the Ni-Ni. This was the Niggerarmageddon. The struggle at the bottom. The world of Iceberg Slim's *Pimp* and Donald Goines's *Dopefiend*.[12]

There were elements of all these inter-dimensional struggles in my father's barbershop. He had college educated barbers he paid to instruct my brother and me to make crystal radios from a razor blade, toilet paper role, and copper wire from a television tube yoke coil. He also had a razor fighter who told me "He could cut a nigger ten times before he knew he was bleeding." The heavy keloids on his neck and arms convinced me he spoke truth. I was not threatened as these street people respected my father, who, when he counted the day's receipts in the shop's little back room, putting the money in the zippered bank bag that he would walk down to the bank at 12th and Claremont, had a loaded .38 to hand. He would sit there, a cigarette dangling from his mouth, the Smith and Wesson on the desk, a glass of scotch, and calmly look at me, his "Natural Nig." That was his nickname for me, his "Natural Nigger."

At Central High School, my father's insouciance exerted influence, as many Black people in the neighborhood had their hair cut at his shop. Mrs. Flake arranged meetings for me with other math teachers to talk about "infinity." Somehow, I had gotten the idea, like Aristotle two thousand years prior, that there were two kinds of infinity, actual and potential. The actual infinity of objects was, on my view impossible. Potential infinity was the mathematical kind, which could only be approached asymptotically, $x + 1$. This was deeply disturbing to me. I could not understand how human beings—Black or white—could go on with their normal daily activities when they lived with such a problem, infinity below them, infinity above them. So, I began to dwell on a theory of "Terminated Infinities." I started with the posit that every physical object took up a finite volume of space. If there were an infinite number of objects, then the volume of space they occupied would be infinite. But since the space in which objects existed was greater than the space occupied by those objects, this would result in one infinite volume being greater than another infinite volume; a result that was contradictory. Examining the elements of my argument, either the idea of infinite space, or the idea of an infinite number of objects, had to go. The idea of an infinite number of objects was easy to abandon. I rested on the idea that the number of objects in the universe was finite. I had read that the number of molecules of H_2O in a glass of water was 1.89×10^{25}. The number of stars in the universe was 10^{22}. Thus, there were a thousand times more molecules in a glass of water that there were stars in the universe. But there were only about 10^{80} particles (electrons, protons, and neutrons) in the universe. Here were all these well-meaning genteel people, living their daily lives in their ignominious struggles for survival and pleasure, complete zombies, unthinking automata, suspended midway between infinites (actual and potential), without awe.

So. Let us start over. Grades for the first term resulted in all As but one B+, in English. Gus was left wondering why my mother had characterized me as incorrigible. I was an academic star at Central High School. I was non-plussed by my grades, as if anything, I was repeating my failed tenth-grade subjects.

Spring term began in the cold and darkness of Michigan winter. The snow was deep and shrouded in purple shadows. I was determined to continue my studently ways. Somehow, I was enrolled in an "honors" English course. The course, taught by a young white man, Mr. Zaff, a graduate student from the University of Michigan. As I recall, he was energetic and inspiring in a way that no other English teacher had been. He assigned essays and was particularly impressed by one I wrote on "The Destiny of Mankind." Mr. Zaff's classes were driven by Socratic questioning. For my term paper, he assigned me to write on Albert Camus. After reading *The Stranger*,[13] with Meursault's "Mother died today or was it yesterday," "I could have married anyone," and "If they came for a show, I'll give them one" and the ennui and meaninglessness of an inexplicable murder (and universe), I was a confirmed existentialist. The research for the paper led me to the "absurd man," and the endless repetitive futility of Sisyphus, and mankind's inconsolable nostalgia for "home." A home that did not exist. A home that did not exist, in a universe indifferent to human meaning. If meaning was to be found, it had to be created. I became a godless existentialist, smoking an occasional Newport, trying to find myself between the Scylla of the microcosm and the Charybdis of the cosmos.

44   Chapter 4

   I should say more about Ralph Cole and his family. Sidney Cole, the patriarch, worked the night shift on the assembly line at Chrysler. Mrs. Cole (Jessie) was a warm, kind, "other mother," who worked around the clock cooking, cleaning, washing clothes, and loving her children (and any other children in the vicinity, which included me). Mrs. Cole had seven children of her own. Mary, the only girl, and the eldest, Big Sid ("Junior"), Frank, Ralph, Lawrence, Joe, and Kinney. Big Sid, had been a standout football player (a lineman) at Central. Mary was beautiful and sang in the church choir. Frank was tall and searching for direction in life. Lawrence was obese. Joe and Kinney were still little boys. Ralph was my age. Ralph was also an above average athlete, a running back on the varsity football team and a point guard on the basketball team. Also, more than the other boys in the family, he was always trying to help his mother, folding clothes, washing dishes, and sweeping, which there was a lot of. Physically, Ralph and I were the same height and weight. Ralph was a brown-skin boy, with erect steel rod backbone posture, a proclivity for dressing well, and little interest in academics, save being eligible to take part in athletics. But he was a trustworthy friend who tried to help me navigate the complex social realities of Central High School. Mrs. Cole was like my true mother, serving me meals where Gus and Ernestine were often absent, still at work far after dark.
   "You're a trick, Richard." He would often quip.
   I did not fully grasp his use of his use of the word *trick*. Only latter would I know its meaning as a demeaning term prostitutes used to describe their johns. It was not the connotation of magicians' legerdemain, but the trick of being made to think you were getting something valuable, when in fact you were getting nothing, cheap. Tricked into thinking you were getting pleasure when you were getting misery. Like how white people hoodwinked Black folks into thinking they were wanted in American society when they were not. Ralph understood the game—many games—better than I, that is why he played them so well. He was a passable student, worked for his own money, respected in his family, heroic on the athletic fields, and street wise. Compared to him, I *was* a trick. I had been duped.
   The first baseball game of the season was with Denby High School. Denby was a white school. They had won the city's schoolboy baseball championship the year before. The game was going swell, as I was spinning curveballs past the big "bohunk" whiteboys. My fastball zipped past them on the inside corner. "Strike three!" The umpire jerked up his right hand. Of course, the Denby hitters got to me for a few runs. Behind me, my teammates were chirping, "Hum babe . . . hum it on in there . . . atta-boy . . . c'mon-now." Going into the home half of the seventh inning, with me "dealing" on the mound, Central was behind, 5 to 4. As I recall, I was on base—men on first and second—when Ralph Cole came to bat, one out, and after taking a pitch,

hammered a fastball over Denby's center fielder's head. Ralph yelled at me to "Run!" The ball bounced, as Ralph rounded first base, the base runners scoring before him, as we had beaten the city champions 7 to 5.

Of course, I was not perfect. Central lost games to other Detroit high school teams. But one game will always be high-lighted in my memory. It was a game my father attended. He sat in the stands with one of his barbers. I pitched the best game of my life. It was a seven inning 7 to 3 win over Cass Tech High School, where I struck out thirteen batters, many of the Ks called strike threes. After the game, as my father came down from the stands; I hugged Erma McGhee, my girlfriend. I finished the season five wins and seven losses, but I still had a year left and I was getting stronger every day; wait until next year.

That same spring, I had constructed a science project—"The Theory of Terminated Infinities"—which won the Central High science fair. It was a strange science project; conceptual ideas about human beings suspended between two ineffabilities—the microcosm and macrocosm—and the logical necessities for their transcendences. I really did not understand it all myself, a reaching for Leibniz's monads, and for a nested conception of the multiverse. I had gone from being an abject failure at McKinley to a star at Central, earning a letter in baseball and winning the science fair. Because I was still a year behind in my academic work, and would be a senior the next year, while my classmates were taking the pre-SATs, I took the test just as a practice exercise. I forgot about the test, eager to return to my mother in DC for the summer. I was homesick for infinity.

NOTES

1. P. D. Ouspensky, *Strange Life of Ivan Osokin* (Garden City, NJ: Courier Dover Publications, 2020).

2. Gottfried Wilhelm Leibniz, *Theodicy: Essays on the Goodness of God, the Freedom of Man, and the Origins of Evil* (La Salle, IL: Open Court, 1985), 313.

3. Gerard Manley Hopkins, "Spring and Fall: To a Young Child," in *Hopkins: Poems* (London: Everyman's Library Pocket Books, 1995).

4. James Joyce, *Portrait of the Artist as a Young Man* (Berkeley: The Bancroft Library Internet Archive, 2008), 160.

5. Emily Dickenson, "I Had a Guinea Golden," available at: https://www.poetry-archive.com/d/i_had_a_guinea_golden.html (accessed September 4, 2023).

6. Samuel Cook, "(What a) Wonderful World," *The Wonderful World of Sam Cook* (album), (Hollywood: A&M Records, 1960). Lyrics available at https://www.bing.com/search?q=sam+cooke+what+a+wonderful+world+lyrics&FORM=QSRE2 (accessed September 6, 2023).

7. William Golding, *Pincher Martin: The Two Deaths of Christopher Martin* (New York: Harvest Books, 2002).

8. Marcel Proust, *Remembrance of Things Past*, 3 vols. (New York: Vintage, 1982)

9. Gerard Manley Hopkins, "Spring and Fall," in *Poems and Prose of Gerard Manley Hopkins* (New York: Penguin Classics, 1985).

10. Daymond J. Aiken, Kenneth B. Henderson, and Robert E. Pingry, *Algebra: Its Big Ideas and Basic Skills, Book II* (New York, McGraw Hill, 1957).

11. Lincoln Barnett, *The Universe and Dr. Einstein* (Mineola, NY: Dover, 1948).

12. Iceberg Slim, *Pimp: The Story of My Life* (New York: Cash Money Content, 2011); and Donald Goines, *Dopefiend: The Story of a Black Junkie* (Los Angeles: Holloway House, 2021).

13. Albert Camus, *The Stranger* (New York: Vintage, 1989).

Chapter 5

Historically Black Colleges and Universities, 1962–1965

In the middle of another hot and humid summer in Washington, DC, Bertie received a letter from Fisk University informing her that I was the recipient of a scholarship, from the United Negro College Fund ("A mind is a terrible thing to waste" . . . mine was already wasted) to attend in the fall. The neatly typed letter from the registrar said that I would be supplied room and board and $600.00 a year for tuition. The letter stated that I had been awarded this scholarship based on my academic record (?) and entrance examination test scores, and that I was to be admitted as an "Early Entrant." Being an "Early Entrant" meant that I was to be admitted without having graduated from high school.

I was reading Edward Albee's *The Sand Box*, Eugene Ionesco's *Rhinoceros*, and Albert Camus's *The Fall*.[1] The people around me were all turning into *rhinoceroses*, and I was the last human being left, searching the mirrors for signs that I was undergoing the same transformation. For after Detroit, with its stately elm trees creating leafy tunnels through the broad streets on Lawrence and Collingwood, the grassy medians on the boulevards of Chicago Avenue, where the stone mansions sat back from the streets; Blaine Street was the sand box stage-set for the misjudgments of Negroes fallen into rivers of their own misunderstandings. In Detroit, there were at least the solid concrete of factory workers. Black men framed by the orange coal furnaces of the steel mills at the River Rouge Ford plant, hammering out new cars on the assembly line. In Washington, DC, Negroes were bureaucrats, shuffling papers in the various offices, producing the obfuscations of a corrupt government that kept them entangled in laws they did not make. And, in Detroit, there were classes; upper professionals like the doctors I had met at the conference with Mrs. Flake's husband; middle-class working people, like Mr. Cole who worked on the assembly line at Chrysler; and a lower-class that I met at Gus's Barber Shop—hustlers, pimps, and number runners. But they all had dignity and contrast. Detroit was Soupy Sales and Belle Isle. DC was Negroes with college degrees from Howard University working in the post office or hacking, driving cabs.

In my dissolution, I realized that I had been bounced around like a basketball in a between the knees crossover or the Sunday school hop ground ball to second base, from Sunny Side to Spring Hope, from DC to Detroit—Woodson to McKinley, McKinley to Central, Central to Fisk—around the horn—Tinker to Evers to Chance—I was always being sent somewhere else—follow the bouncing ball. So. Yes. I was an alienated teenage Black boy searching for home; a home in the relatives around me (theory of relativity); my neighbors (Mr. Roger's neighborhood); my country ('tis *not* of thee). Where the letter from Fisk offered an exit to Jean-Paul Sartre's *No Exit*,[2] it was also a new labyrinth—*Theseus and the Minotaur* from my Latin textbook—"Wanwood leafmeal lie"[3]—"the Theory of Terminated Infinities." I was unimpressed, second best, shuffling off to Buffalo, a loser in a lost world. I thought the only reason for Bertie's immense joy was that she could be boastful; that she would not have to handle me for another year; that I was not as dumb as she thought.

Standing in Union Station waiting for the train south, my suitcase filled with new clothes, I wondered where all the other passengers standing on the platform were going. The train, an old coal burning locomotive chugged out of Union Station. Quickly, it passed by McKinley Technical High School, site of my ignominy, sitting on a hill in the distance. As the locomotive tooled on through the Appalachian pine forests, over trestles spanning rivers, around curves where I could see the forward cars and the white smoke rising from the smokestack, I wondered why I was here. I had stood at 14th and U Street just a few weeks before and watched the Telstar satellite pass over Washington. I had recently seen a LASER at a laboratory in Detroit.

The train chugged on, swaying on the tracks, the click-clack of the wheels on the railroad ties comforting, as I sat and smoked my Winston. I tried to imagine what awaited me at Fisk University. It occurred to me that the word "Scholarship," in the letter from the registrar had given Bertie and Gus the brief flicker of hope and salvation for the son, they had named "Argustia."

As the train pulled into the station in Nashville, Tennessee, I set my jaw, then stepped down on the platform.

An open dorm room, the beds and study desks pushed against the walls, I glanced idly out the windows trying to discern the lay of the land. Introduced to my new roommates, we were all in a similar state of exasperation over our new state of affairs. Trying to find out where we should go next, say next, and do next preoccupied us until we found out where the dining hall was located. When we walked toward the student center, I lit up another Winston, noting that none of the other boys smoked. After dinner, we all walked back to Du

Bois Hall, discussing the registration that was to take place the next morning. I slept uneasily that night, in a room with three strangers, who did not know—yet—that I was *The Stranger*.[4]

I did not know how long my diet of sweet rolls, milk, and Winston cigarettes would sustain my disdain for Nashville and Fisk. The college was situated on forty acres in a commercial suburb of the city. Like DC and Detroit, it was a circumscribed Black world (a microcosm) in an infinity of whiteness (a macrocosm). And as in these other cases, I could not see with either microscope or telescope into that white abyss surrounding the black hole.

Basic College Dormitory was a two-story brick building with a basement. This, so called, Honors Dorm, had a day room with a kitchen, and individual rooms along the central hallways. My room was mid-hallway on the first floor. I was told that my roommate was named Frank, and that he would be arriving later the next week. The other early-entrants were Ron McLaurin, Charles Harshaw, James Golden, and Cliff Robinson. McLaurin was the precocious son of a well-off owner of a Black car dealership in Nashville. He did not live in the dormitory, but he was sharp and confident, often driving up on campus in a new convertible. Harshaw was a thick and stocky light-skinned Black guy who was somewhat standoffish. Golden was the youngest early-entrant, only fourteen years old. Cliff was a tall and gangly youngster from Richmond, Virginia who looked on at all that was going on about him with a dignified silence.

The Honors Dorm resident assistant (RA) was Ronald Walters. Ron was a senior History major. He had the largest room, just off from the day room, and smoked a pipe. He was saturnine, authoritative, and seemed disinterested in the day-to-day goings on in Basic College Dormitory. Ron Walters had the countenance of an old man in a twenty-five-year-old body. He dressed in professorial patched elbow jackets, argyle sweaters, and flannel pants. He was already preparing for graduate school. There were other Black scholars from every class, sophomores to seniors, living in the dorm. All of them created deep impressions on me. Ronald Mickens would become a renowned Gauge-Theory particle physicist. Thomas Dooley would become a Chicago lawyer and John Galt was famous at Fisk for coming to the first day of a course, getting the syllabus, reading the material in his room, and showing up for the final exam, acing the test every time. There was William Anderson, another senior historian; and Thomas McKeel, who would become a physician. There were others prowling around in the halls of the Honors Dorm, nocturnal scholars burning the midnight oil. And there were the smokers, Edward Edwards and Theopolis Fair. Edwards was a chain smoker. Fair was a tall, intelligent, eloquent—always throwing in foreign language terms into his discourse—elder intellectual, to whom others in honors dorm deferred. Many of these Fisk scholars were Phi Beta Kappa, already admitted to prestigious northern Ivy League colleges. They were intimidating by their very presence. They were neither grade-grinds nor pseudo-intellectuals, as they were the real deal: intelligent Black men with important roles to play in politics, books to write, players.

The evening meal intended to bring us all to table to discuss weighty intellectual matters worked for the first few months. There was a cook who prepared the meals in the dorm, a blackboard at the end of the long dining room table. With Ron Walters sitting at the head of the table, we began the symposium/meal with a few remarks from one of the scholars. When my turn came, I went to the blackboard and scribbled a few of Einstein's equations from Special Relativity; time dilation, contraction of length, or mass increase. I made some hand waving remarks about the expanding universe. My dorm mates appeared disinterested in my obviously superficial understanding of physics, as they had taken university-level physics courses.

"Go read!" They would say to me in the hallway.

So, what about my classes? My professors? I was taking Math I from Dr. Holloway. Scientific German I, Western Civilization I, English Comp, and an Honors Seminar. The math professor was a kindly old Black gentleman, over seventy and "already asleep on his feet." The only real lesson I had learned from him, gleaned from his introductory lecture, where he averred to the beauty of mathematical thought: he deigned, "ratiocination." Beyond his boring monotone lectures, his assignments from *Fundamental Principles of Mathematics* by John T. Moore (a book I still own sixty later) were mostly repetitive—rather than conceptual—skill building exercises.[5] However, in examining the problem sets now, in retrospect, the circled exercises were far too advanced for my, then, state of mathematical maturity. I struggled at once. I even tried to get the one early-entrant, Ron McLaren, whose homework papers were always excellent, to help me. He was a well-trained mathematician. He had a haughtiness about him that repelled me, and labored on, frustrating myself by the difficulties I had calculating the answers to these sophisticated problems. Ratiocination?

"Dickie, go read." The upper clansmen at the dorm had taken to calling me "Dickie." I hated this diminutive, as I was still a smallish boy, younger than most of the other students, some of whom were twenty-one or twenty-two years old. I was socially shy in the graces of living alone. I had never had to wash my own clothes or, eat in an open dining hall, or live with people I did not know day in and day out. I was socially clumsy.

The Scientific German teacher was also an old man. He was a German Jewish emigre from World War II. As he lectured, globules of saliva about the corners of his gutturals, round sprays of spit as he enunciated. I tried to sit as far back in the lecture hall as I could. When called on to translate, I hardly ever had even the foggiest notion of what I was reading. It was worse than Latin. The only thing that I had deciphered was, *Vater unser im Himmel*—"Our father in heaven"—which was in my head as "Unser Vater im dem Himmel." I had also memorized the sentence "Du bis unter hunten," as "you are a dog." I thought the rationale given by the professor, that in order to get a PhD, you had to have command of a foreign language, be able to read it, was so far removed from where I was as to be laughable.

My English Composition course was also a nightmare. After the first writing assignment in class, a one-hour essay, the professor arranged for a meeting with me during her office hours. My essay had come back totally covered in red pencil, bleeding red. In her office, she had spoken softly, pointing out my misspellings, comma faults, and word misusages. As the next few weeks passed, she had me in office hours again, where she tested me on a hundred spelling words. She would say the word and I would write down my spelling. Afterward, she marked the list, and shook her head. I distinctly recall her saying, "You don't belong here." As she was middle-aged and white, I heard the echo of my white teachers at Benning Elementary from eight years before, "They don't even speak the language." The one redeeming element of this course was its reading list. She had assigned Bertrand Russell's *Why I Am Not a Christian*, E. B. White's *One Man's Meat*, Lytton Strachey's *Eminent Victorians*, and Thomas Malory's *Le Morte d'Arthur (The Death of Arthur)*.[6] While I continued to struggle with my grammar, syntax, and spelling, these highly sophisticated works fueled my intellectual growth. I might not have belonged there but, at least, *I Was Not a Christian*.

Let us see, what else? Oh, there was Western Civilization I, a survey course of western intellectual history. This professor, also a middle-aged white woman, who would have bored the dead, also wanted to talk to me during office hours. She was disdainfully arrogant as she asked me for the meaning of "anthropomorphism." I had answered "Man-like." I could tell that she did not particularly respect my lower-class intellect. Then there was the Honor's Seminar, a once a week, two-hour seminar-style meeting with first-year students and early-entrants, chaired by Dr. Courier, a Harvard educated historian. His approach was to ask the group siting around the table a provocative question and let us argue it out. In this course, I found my voice, as I was opinionated, even if I could not spell or solve the problems in analytic geometry for which I was unprepared. I liked Courier, he drank and smoked. He invited me to his house on campus a few times to talk. He appeared interested in my divergent, belligerent, and existential leanings. If I had an idea to defend, I would argue and wrangle for it. I liked to quote things I had read. Courier respected my intellectual integrity. Besides all that, I could not understand why they had admitted me, a failure as a freshman in high school, who had done well repeating his failed subjects at Central High, who was unprepared for pre-calculus mathematics, had no sense at all for learning foreign languages, and could not spell.

The first few weeks were, a kaleidoscope of Freshman Orientation, the Fisk Singers mesmerizing Negro spirituals echoing sonorous from the balconies of the Fisk Memorial Chapel. There were the Sunday evening brown bag lunches, the "Smoker" at a neighborhood home, where the Alphas, Kappas, and Omegas men's fraternities looked over the first-year crop, giving out little four cigarette packs of all brands. I smoked and smoked but noticed none of the other early-entrants did so, and few of the regular freshmen. I discovered Arna Bontemps—the Negro novelist and poet—in his basement office of the Basic College Dormitory, while looking to use the bathroom. He invited me into his office, and I told him that I was interested in writing poetry. A real poet lived in the basement. When I awakened early in the Tennessee mornings, after restive sleep, worrying about my inability to understand inverse-hyperbolic functions, walking out in front of the dormitory, I would sometimes encounter Dr. Johnson walking his two Dobermans, and say good morning. I asked Rodney Ransom, who would go on later to be a well-known pathologist, who the dark, sullen, man sitting in the day room was? On occasion, this person would stop in to watch the *CBS Evening News*.

"That's John Lewis," Ransom answered. I did not know who he was. Just as I did not know who Ana Bontemps was.

Then there was the day my roommate appeared. This was weeks into the semester. His name was Frank. Frank was a senior whose father ran a large Funeral Home in Bristol, Tennessee. Frank's ambition after Fisk was to attend a graduate program in mortuary science and join his family business. Frank was also married, so officially he was not supposed to be living in the dorm. He told me all this when we first met.

When Frank returned later in the semester, he was studying for a test. I was the only early-entrant who had no roommate to show me the ropes. After studying the differences between Doric, Ionian, and Corinthian Greek columns, Frank said, "Well, rooms, I'll catch you later." Weeks later, Frank returned to the room for a few days, to dissect a dogfish for his biology course. My roommate, Frank, the undertaker, cutting on the rotten fish, already preparing it for embalming. When he looked at me, he was measuring me for a coffin.

I was almost glad when he disappeared again, to go back to his wife. Somehow, I suspected he was living with her in an off-campus apartment and that she was underage—sixteen—her parents (or his) not knowing they were married. Or something.

The acrid stink of the dogfish corpse lingered in the room days after he left.

Frank's possessions in the room were sparse. He owned a portable Crosley record player with a few 45-rpm records and had a few clothes hanging in the closet. One of the records was "Gee Whiz," by Carla Thomas. In Frank's many long absences, I listened to this record repeatedly. Gee Whiz's plaintive lyrics . . . "Look at those eyes . . ."[7] filled my room like my loneliness and the smoke from my Winston cigarettes.

When the other early-entrants—Cliff, Jim, and on occasion, Ron—were in my room, we would engage in the obligatory freshman bull-sessions. We would argue about the existence of God. Of course, I argued trenchantly that God did not exist. Moreover, arguing that, in itself was a mistaken notion, as using the word itself indicated an existent concept. I argued that the idea of "god" was like Santa Clause or the Easter Bunny—anthropomorphic—fantasies to comfort and assuage the fears of cowering, infantile, scared children. I argued that Christianity had brainwashed Negroes, singing their spirituals and bowing their heads, into embracing the myths of their masters: that, a religious Negro was a Negro the white man need not fear.

To demonstrate my disdain for their pious embrace of religion, I needed to do something dramatic. I asked Cliff, the tall, serious, youngster from Richmond, Virginia, to get a Bible. Cliff retrieved a black leatherette, gold-embossed, red-paged, "Holy Bible." I flipped through the book, tearing out pages and balling them up in my hands. The boys were astounded. I continued ripping out pages, balling them up, throwing them into the metal trashcan in the corner of the room. Once I had created a pile of balls of paper in the trashcan, I lit a Winston, blew out a lungful of smoke, and threw the match into the trashcan. The pages flared red! As the pages burned, smoke curled up to the ceiling, and I quickly opened the dorm room window. The boys' mouths gaped open. Evilness personified for them, I walked over to the trashcan, unzipped my pants, pulled out my dick and peed on the flaming pages. My stream of urine quickly extinguished the flames. I had made my point. Cliff, Jim, and Ron retreated in disbelief. They went on to recount this blasphemy to others, I am sure, and I became a legend in the Black community—the Devil was a freshman at Fisk University.

Finally, our arguments got so complex that we were spending hours going around in circles. I was unable to budge from my position that belief in the existence of an omnipotent munificence was a fatal self-deception. And they were equally trenchant in their defense of their Baptist beliefs. At loggerheads, I suggested we seek the wisdom of the Dean of the Chapel, Dr. Jones, a Doctor of Divinity. Dr. Jones, who officiated at convocations, and Sunday services, was a large, serious, authoritative light-skinned Black man. Even though I knew he was a believer, I had also discerned that he was highly philosophical and thought his intellectualism might supply room—and more respect from my adversaries—for my learned skepticism. Dr. Jones agreed to meet with us.

"A spirit . . . love in the world . . ." the big man explained.

"But how do you explain the evil in the world? No possibility for poetry after Hiroshima and Auschwitz . . ."

"Theodicy . . . God uses evil and suffering to ends beyond the reasoning of men . . . a means to salvation . . . soul building."

Dean Jones was patient in his defenses of Christianity. Big Cliff listened quietly with a quizzical look. James Golden, the fourteen-year-old genius, bobbed his head. Ron, the mathematics prodigy, looked on in judgement of the arguments. I did most of the talking. After an hour, having been served coffee and cookies, the discussion having wound down to an impasse, we were preparing to leave. A willowy, girl breezed through the room—the preacher's daughter—and Dean Jones introduced her as "Lynn." Lynn Jones was a senior at Pearl, the Negro high school near Fisk. Dean Jones saw us to the door.

"Come back anytime you want to discuss this."

The next weekend I returned to the Dean's stately house—just up the street from the dorm—to watch Sunday evening TV—and after dinner had stayed on to chat with Lynn. Mrs. Jones had served a wonderful dinner. After trying to survive, avoiding Fisk's dining hall, by eating banana-splits for diner, or skipping meals altogether, the home cooking was restorative. After an hour of casual conviviality with the entire family, Dr. and Mrs. Jones retired to watch TV upstairs. Lynn put on some records. We sat on the living room sofa. Soon, the preacher's daughter had engaged me in a different argument concerning the existence of God. We sat on the sofa, with the music playing, pawing at each other, her mouth wet with kisses. She got up and put on another record. It was Tchaikovsky's *1812 Overture*. Our petting—or lovemaking—escalated as the symphony evolved toward its cannonade. And as the triumphal church bells chimed and the canon boomed, Lynn taught me the meaning of hallelujah.

"Go read, Dickie," Dooley muttered as I passed him in the hall.

And read I did. Since it was slowly dawning on me that my grades at the end of the semester were going to be abysmal, I knew my only way forward intellectually was to become an autodidact. Since the professors at Fisk smelt of mothballs and old lace, spoke in a queer hypnotic droning monotone, I was forced to create the excitement that they could not.

Consequently, I did "go read." That semester, I read, *Demian* (Hesse), *The Spire* (Golding), *One Day in the Life of Ivan Denisovich* (Solzhenitsyn), *Generation of Vipers* (Wylie), *Moses and Monotheism* (Freud), and *Memento Mori* (Spark).[8] As I said in the opening chapter, I always tried to use anything to add to the knowledge I had already gained, despite the negative reinforcements of the teachers who failed to motivate me. I knew that I could not learn anything from a teacher who did not love something—their discipline, their children, their pets—and I could easily tell by the light, or lack of it, in their eyes, the quick and the dead. The few who loved their disciplines could make wet newspapers burn (or urine-soaked Bible pages).

Listening to the classical music Lynn seemed to prefer, I tried to meet her obvious mental superiority with talk about cosmology. In my attempts to come to terms with my mediocrity, I often dwelled on the origins of the universe. In God's house, Reverend Jones's house, I knew that God had not created the cosmos.

"There's steady-state cosmology. The theory of Hoyle-Bondi-Gold, where only one atom of Hydrogen per six cubic kilometers of space per year would be enough to keep the universe going forever. The Universe must be eternal, so continuous creation is the only logical hypothesis."

Lynn would look at me with sensuous, knowing brown eyes.

"Come here."

In retrospect, she felt sorry for me. She wanted to mother me. Whereas her father—the Doctor of Divinity—could not save me, Jesus could not save me, Lynn thought she could save me.

In October, the Russians positioned nuclear missiles in Cuba. I talked to my mother, thinking I might never see her again, should Russia decide to use the missiles, Washington, DC, would be the first target. I told her that I loved her. For the next week, I suffered watching the *Evening News*, until the Russians agreed to remove the missiles.

"Unser Vater im dem Himmel."

I went back to the grind. Thinking of Lynn Jones, reading Hesse's *Damien* eating his drawings, Wylie's *Vipers*—Matthew 3:7—"You offspring of vipers, who warned you to flee from the wrath to come?"—Golding's *Spire* rising like my penis to Lynn's touch, Solzhenitsyn's Ivan Denisovich freezing behind barbed wire in the gulag, and Sparks *Memento Mori*—where I experience "a little death," everyday. I played the B-side—*For You*—of Carla Thomas's *Gee Whiz* (Look at Those Eyes). I painted large canvasses, poor landscapes, with the oil paints my mother had sent me in the mail. Robert Wood was my aesthetic exemplar. Besides, the rich odors of the drying oil paint took the dogfish out my nose.

"Dickie. . . . Go read!"

The people I met in the stores and shops were all white. I discovered that Fisk and the neighborhood with Pearl High School was surrounded by a sea of whiteness, and like DC and Detroit, Blacks lived in hidden concentration camps circumscribed by highways and residential redlining.

Finally, the first semester completed, I was on the train—Treblinka-Nashville to Birkenau-Washington—chug-chugging back to a more familiar concentration camp. With Christmas gifts from Nashville, I was a Black Santa bringing back academic failure, and two poorly rendered oil paintings, and less praise for the Lord. I imagined myself a Black Renaissance man; of speculative science; of literary critique; of iconoclastic destroyer of idols; of landscape painting; of matters of the heart. My final grades were Math D, English C−, German D+, Western Civ C, and Honors Seminar B.

Walking into my home on Blaine Street—greeted by Monté—faithful dog awaiting my return like Argus waited for Odysseus—Monté of the vegetable can for Argus of the camera. Monté appeared sad, a Negro dog banished to the basement, confined to the yard, never taken for walks, and eating cold dog meat from a can. I cuffed his neck. I vowed to brush his long fur out when I had time. Monté seemed pleased to see me again. Despite my affectations of worldly sophistication, for the rest of the family, I was only a problem coming home to roost.

Beelzebub on holiday.

While on Christmas break, I received two letters from Nashville. The first one from Fisk, informed Bertie that to keep my scholarship from the United Negro College Fund (UNCF), I had to maintain a "B" average. And since I had failed to maintain that average, I had been placed on academic probation, and would be funded for an additional term to allow me to achieve said average. The other letter was from Lynn Jones informing me that she had missed her period and might be pregnant. I did not call her on the telephone. Instead, I waited outside Weltman's Liquor Store on Minnesota Avenue. My collar turned up against the chill, a cigarette dangling from the corner of my mouth like an Albert Camus, my cap pulled low over my eyes.

"Hey man, want to get me a little taste?" Smoke huffing from between my lips—like a legitimate degenerate—I asked the colored man about to enter. I was trying to act tough because sometimes when the dude who took your money took you for a chump, he would go in the front door while you lingered in the shadows in the parking lot and go out the backdoor with his own bottle and nothing for you, and your money. "Sneaky Pete."

"Sure, lil'bro . . . wha'cha want?"

"Half-pint Bacardi Dark."

"You got it."

As the ditty at the time went, "What's the word? *Thunderbird*! What's the price? Thirty, twice! Who drink the most? Us colored folks!" Us cullud folks.

"Here you go, son," he said coming out and handing me the brown bag and my change, of which I gave him a dollar.

"For your trouble," I said, by way of thanks. And it was *all* trouble, thank you very much.

While on break, I went with Robert to McKinley. They were having an assembly where the seniors were to stand one by one to announce the colleges that they would attend the following fall. I stood with them, and when my turn came around, I said, "Richard Jones, class of 1963, freshman, Fisk

University." This caused a raucous cheer, as the students knew me. I had already matriculated. I was an outlaw who had landed on his feet.

Afterward, I walked down the hill to Florida Avenue and hailed a cab. Once in the cab, I unscrewed the cap of the half-pint of Bacardi, took a slug, tucked it back in my inside jacket pocket, and lit a cigarette. As I blew out a lungful of smoke, I noticed the middle-aged white hack looking at me in the rear view mirror.

"Just back from college," I said.

He said little. Pulling up in front of the house, I paid him. I had wanted him to be witness to what his race had produced. An eighteen-year-old "bad nigger," who drank from a flask, as he paid a white chauffeur to shuffle him through the Negro streets. I intended him to witness the new Black aristocracy—did not give a damn about polite civility—behavior out-of-bounds—on all sides of the color line. "Merry Christmas."

Christmas came and went. Neither Charles nor Bertie had a serious conversation with me. I drank every day: Charles's Scotch; my own Bacardi; Jack Daniels and Coke; Cherry Kijafa; Night Train. Just before I was to take the train back to Nashville, I received a postcard. It was from Lynn indicating that she was "not." Exhaling a huge sigh of relief, I vowed on the spot to buckle down to my studies, get off probation, and become the scholar I had been trying to convince the world I was. I had been to four schools in four different cities in four years, yo-yoing from boy-scientist at Woodson, drop-out at McKinley, wunderkind at Central, and poorly prepared freshman at Fisk.

Spring semester, a new chance. It was cold in Nashville in January. I had rolled over near the wall and burned my arm on the hot pipe of my heater. My roommate, Frank, was still will-o-the-wisp. I buckled down to my classes, trying to do the assignments, studying the German vocabulary. Until I was thrown another curveball. I had a new class, "Speech." The professor took it that my speech was pathological. She did not like the timbre, pronunciation, and lingual and facial placement of my tongue with my implosives. She thought I had a problem with esophageal speech, that I swallowed my words, rather than producing purer sounds in the front of my mouth. Beneath her stern judgments, now I had been convinced, not only could I not calculate, spell, remember German verb forms, but I could also not speak properly.

I tried to avoid Lynn Jones. Sometimes, I would be walking into the dorm's day room and see her walking, regally, her head held high, on the street past the dorm. She represented temptation and danger. The speech teacher called me in for a session outside class. She stood me up in front of the room and had me read aloud. Shaking her head, she told me that, I would need speech therapy. James Baldwin's famous dicta, "Black people are always under translation," came back to me. Whenever we said anything, some white person had to interpret it; "Oh what he was trying to say" or "What this really means." If not the "translation" of meaning, then the translation of place: the translation and rotation of lines on the plane. We were under translation, always out of place, needing to be repositioned, found a place for. My tongue was too thick, my lips too big, my teeth ill positioned in the facial angle, to snap out the "d" and "t" endings. I mumbled, always unsure of the pronunciations of words I had read but never heard spoken.

"Interstices."

"Go Read, Dickie."

So that is exactly what I did. These professors really did not seem to love me. I poured over *The Poems of Robert Frost*, C. S. Lewis's *Till We Have Faces*, George Orwell's *Animal Farm*, Albert Camus's *The Plague*, and Arthur Koestler's *Darkness at Noon*.[9] One Sunday afternoon, Andre Watts, the celebrated young Black piano virtuoso, gave a concert at Fisk Memorial Chapel. His ringing chords, echoing from the balcony—light, blue-green, red orange, spilling through stained glass windows—set my spine tingling. I watched, listened, in awe. I had felt the sublime. It was not God in the chapel, but beauty.

It was that day that I found a path toward my freedom. I would be an artist. For the first time, I saw the dichotomy of *Narcissus and Goldmund*, Hermann Hesse's novel contrasting two brothers. One a Latin scholar and the other a woodcarver. How the pews and alter pieces carved by the woodworker were superior to the pedantries of the academic.[10] I did not think I had the talent to be a painter. But it was feeling that I possessed. Everything else, everyone else, felt inhumanly cold and remote. I had wanted to study the stars because they were so far away, they could not disappoint me, betray me. They represented a freedom from—the ghetto; the inferiority; race. But could I *love* the stars? Could they *love* me?

When I was blue, I took the five dollars Bertie had sent, and hiked down to the liquor store.

"Hey Boss, help a brother get a taste?"

March 1, 1963, was the first day of baseball practice. Fisk had not fielded a baseball team in a generation, and this was to be the first year in this new era. I went over to the gym and began throwing. The field was still wet, so for a week, while we waited for the weather to break, we practiced indoors. Once outdoors, I once again impressed the coach with my control. Coach Martin was a big dark-skinned, no nonsense, noticeably quiet guy. He saw, like all the other coaches I had had—despite my diminutive size—that I threw strikes and had a big breaking curveball. I could locate the ball, in and out, up and down, and change speed on all my pitches. Whereas scientists said the maximum break on a curve was seventeen inches, my sidearm curve (a roundhouse curve) appeared to come at a right-handed batter from third base. It was tantalizing, appearing never to be able to get there, until it did. I pitched batting practice. Some of the others going out for the team, were football or basketball players. Fisk was a small school, five hundred students, so the distribution of talented baseball players was slim pickings.

I made the team! There was a small article in the sport pages of the *Nashville Tennessean* saying that "Coach Martin of the Fisk Bulldogs baseball program had announced that Richard Jones would be the pitcher for the opening game of the season."[11] We lost that first game—March 29, 1963—I lost that first game—as the older, stronger players on the other team pounded my fastball. There was another pitcher on the team named Lamont Lawson. "Bebe," as he was called, a very tall—six-five—light-skinned, forward on Fisk's basketball team. He was also the nephew of Dr. Lawson, a noted spectroscopist in the Chemistry Department at Fisk. Bebe started the second game. He owned a fastball in the low to mid-nineties. We lost that game. Where the pitching in that second game was better, we were unable to push many runs across the plate.

After losing all the home games, we boarded the team bus and headed south where we were to play Alabama A & M in Huntsville, Alabama. Fully intending to study, I took my textbooks with me on the bus. I will always recall these rides, sitting in the back of the coach, smoking *Newports* with Bebe—blowing the smoke out the cracked window—wondering why Coach Martin did not walk back and tell us to stop. Wondering whether he knew or cared, or if baseball players and tobacco were accepted standards. Bebe was a big man on campus (BMOC). He was also a graduating senior. Yet, he was also friendly, accepting me for who I was. He told me about how his girlfriend had gotten pregnant, and he had to help her get an abortion. Bebe Lawson was like an older brother. On one of the late-night bus trips between HBCUs in the deep South, smoking *Newports*, we had tried to sing Jerry Butler's song "Rainbow Valley."

> The sunset outside my window has lost its glow
> I need you so
> Come home
> The bluebirds outside my window
> Are lonely too
> Come home
> I miss you so[12]

Rolling through the South, the tires of the team bus were humming, harmonizing with my teammates; I belonged. But where was home? Who missed me *so*?

To quote Emily Dickinson:

> My story has a moral
> I have a missing friend
> Pleiad and robin
> and guinea in the sand.[13]

The next afternoon, the field was dazzling, chalk lines white and straight, as I took the mound full of the belief that I could compete. The batters were of a differing opinion, as they rocketed hit after hit. It was as if they knew what was coming. I was a boy amongst men. And many of the A & M players were men, twenty-one- to twenty-two-year-olds, muscled, and quick. Coach Martin left me in the game long enough to absorb a thorough shellacking. Inning after inning, the ball flew into the gaps between outfielders, over their heads, and by the end, thoroughly defeated, I sat with my head between my knees staring at my sweaty sanitary socks.

During this trip, we played Shaw, Tuskegee, and Morris Brown. We were supposed to play Morehouse, but that game was rained out. I remember the Tuskegee game because the field was so lush. The Tuskegee campus was almost tropical. The Tuskegee students watching the game were particularly vicious, hurling insults at Fisk's players and Coach Martin. They laughed at us. They trounced us on the field. The Tuskegee players and fans' belligerence was an acting out of the Booker T. Washington–W. E. B. Du Bois Atlanta Compromise controversy. The Tuskegee batters had "put down their buckets" where they were; thought the Fisk players were impractical pansies who studied Greek outhouses.

I was slated to pitch against Tennessee A & I. It was Saturday and there were quite a few students in the stands. One of the faculty, Dr. Levine, was also in the group in the small bleachers. As the game progressed, the A & I batters teed-off on my hanging curveball. Coach Martin, once again, let me absorb the beating. I thought he thought that by the time I was a senior—older, stronger—I might be able to compete. We went on to lose every game we played that year. I would watch Bebe pitch a game worthy of a story by Roger Angell, like the 1981 Viola-Darling Ivy League Championship game. A 1 to 0 affair where Ron Darling had struck out batter after batter, only to bested by a short lefty, Frank Viola, with a wicked overhand curve, a drop. After the Fisk game Lamont Lawson had broken down in tears. I heard that the Washington Senators had scouted him.

"You ready, Dickie?" Smitty, the first baseman shouted at me as he passed.

Back to the grind. Weightlifting, practice at 3:30 p.m., German vocabulary, Speech class. I was pleased that Dr. Levine, one of the white professors in the Honors Program, gave me a copy of Jim Brosnan's book *The Long Season*.[14] Having witnessed my ignominy pitching against Tennessee A & I, Levine wanted to sympathize with me. He knew I was no longer part of the

Honors Program. He could see that I was immature and out of my league, academically and athletically. As I read the book, Brosnan, a former Yankee pitcher, revealed that my heroes had feet of clay. Mickey Mantle was a drunk. Most of the professional baseball players he wrote about were egotistical, profane, did not love the game, and only motivated by the fame and money. *The Long Season* demystified baseball for me. And as the season at Fisk continued, I became less idealistic and motivated to be a professional player, which I realized was an impossibility anyway. One afternoon, dressed out for that day's home game, I was out front of Basic College Dormitory, warming up, playing catch with a teammate, when Lynn Jones wafted by. Head erect, not glancing from side to side, she pranced by as if she did not even see me, which I knew she did.

During the game, I listened for the chatter, for the call guy on the infield to say, "Hum baby . . . hum babe." I did not hear much chatter, as we were being pounded, as usual. As I said, Fisk's baseball team did not win a single game that year. But I had played enough innings to win a varsity letter. That big yellow "F" was representative of my academic achievements that year. In a year where I had only made one "A," that "A" was in physical education. As the year ended, I knew I had lost my scholarship, as I had once again not achieved a "B" average. I knew Bertie would not be willing to pay tuition, room, and board for me to struggle through another lackluster year at Fisk.

As I started to pack up my things, Ron Walters, the RA invited me to his room for a chat. His room was redolent with the Carter Hall pipe tobacco he kept poking at.

"So, how you doing, Dickie?" Although he was only twenty-five years old, Walters took an avuncular tack with me. He knew I had fucked up. He knew I had struggled. But he also understood how I had been an integral part of what had happened at Fisk that year. He was an historian, Phi Beta Kappa, destined to work in the US State Department, become the chair of the Political Science department at Howard University, author several highly regarded books, and become the director of an African American Leadership Institute at the University of Maryland.

"I'm good," I said, trying to maintain my composure, when I really wanted to spill my guts to him—to tell him how shitty I felt—to breakdown in tears and let him know how battered I was, how ashamed I was to have let them all down. He chatted with me without condescension or derision, as an equal, man to man, pipe smoke curling about him, he gave me a knowing look.

I had taken my final exams, knowing my efforts would not redeem me. I started packing up my books, a trunk full of textbooks and paperbacks. There were few classmates hanging around. They were not "fellows well met," as they had outclassed me in the books. I went to my closet and discovered that my clothes were gone. My hardly worn suit, a gray blazer, my almost new slacks, a pristine overcoat, and my Harris Tweed sports coat, were all missing from their wooden hangers. I was puzzled. I continued to pack my things. The next morning, the day I was departing, Frank showed up in the room, my clothes folded over his arm.

"I had to hock them, rooms." He went on to explain that he had needed money to pay rent on the room he kept for his wife, so he hocked my clothes. I wondered whether he had used them to dress a corpse for display before putting the casket in the ground. I was outraged at his disrespect. This was Fisk's last humiliation. Frank had delivered the *coup de grace*. I had been shamed in my mathematics course by Ron McLaren, made funky by a dissected dogfish, spat upon by the guttural implosions of the German professor, contemplated marriage-abortion, made to believe my speech was pathological, and batted around on the baseball field like a Little Leaguer playing against the 1926 Yankees. But this was just too much.

"If you love something, somebody will take it away from you."

I was once again on the train back to Washington. Trundling through the fresh green rolling hills of Virginia, I tried to assess what I was bringing back with me from Fisk. I had learned a valuable lesson; I was woefully unprepared for the rigors of academe. I needed to improve my writing skills. After reading Hermann Hesse's *Steppenwolf*, I had written an allegorical piece published in Fisk's literary magazine. Hesse's "little door, for madmen only," and the hallucinatory hall "with doors behind which he'd discovered all his prior experiences," had motivated me to write the allegory, where I was standing in a room with an infinite number of windows through which I could see "myself, everywhere."[15] I needed a better foundation in mathematics and science in general. Women were dangerous and just as sexually aggressive as men. I had learned that I would not be a professional baseball player. I had heard the piano concert by Alan Watts. I learned that where there are more molecules of H_2O than there are stars in the universe, there are also billions of people, who all came from eggs and sperm. I had been taught by Philip Wylie and Lynn Jones that "Mommyism" inevitably led to weakness; and that I would never be a love-struck "Mooncalf" again. Billions of orgasms meant that sex was natural and thus unworthy of shame. Since there are all of these billions—produced by passions—all striving for authenticity, legitimacy, and meaning—without knowing why—they often got in one another's way. I had learned that one path to freedom was through the brambles and thickets of art. I had met an undertaker who had hocked my clothes, and that "Hypocrisy is the price vice pays to virtue."

NOTES

1. Edward Albee, *Two Plays by Edward Albee: The Sand Box and the Death of Bessie Smith (with Fam and Yam)* (New York: Signet, 1960), Eugène Ionesco, *Rhinoceros and Other Plays* (New York: Grove Press, 1959); and Albert Camus, *The Fall* (New York: Vintage Books, 1991).

2. Jean-Paul Sartre, *No Exit and Three Other Plays*, trans. Stuart Gilbert, International ed. (New York: Vintage Books, 1989).

3. Gerard Manley Hopkins, "To a Child," in *Poems and Prose of Gerard Manley Hopkins* (New York: Penguin Classics, 1985).

4. Albert Camus, *The Stranger* (New York: Vintage Books, 1946).

5. John T. Moore, *Fundamental Principles of Mathematics* (New York: Rinehart, 1950).

6. Bertrand Russell, *Why I Am Not a Christian: And Other Essays on Religion and Related Subjects*, ed. Paul Edwards (New York: Touchstone, 1967); E. B. White, *One Man's Meat* (New York: Harper & Row, 1942); Lytton Strachey, *Eminent Victorians* (New York: Modern Library, 1940); and Thomas Malory, *Le morte d'Arthur* (New York: Everyman's Library, 1956).

7. Carla Thomas, "Gee Whiz (Look at His Eyes)," *Gee Whiz* (album) (New York: Atlantic Records, 1960).

8. Hermann Hesse, *Demian*, trans. Michael Roloff and Michael Lebeck (New York: Bantam Books, 1963); William Golding, *The Spire* (New York: Pocket Books, 1966); Aleksandr Solzhenitsyn, *One Day in the Life of Ivan Denisovich*, trans. E. P. Dutton (New York: E. P. Dutton, 1963); Philip Wylie, *Generation of Vipers* (McLean, IL: Dalkey Archive Press, 1996); Sigmund Freud, *Moses and Monotheism*, trans. Katherine Jones (London: Hogarth Press, 1939; and Muriel Spark, *Memento Mori* (New York: Macmillan, 1959).

9. Robert Frost, *The Poems of Robert Frost* (New York: Modern Library, 1946); C. S. Lewis, *Till We Have Faces* (New York: Time Reading Program, 1956); George Orwell, *Animal Farm* (New York: Signet, 2004); Albert Camus, *The Plague* (New York: Knopf Doubleday, 1991); and Arthur Koestler, *Darkness at Noon* (New York: TIME, 1962; New York: Bantam Books, 1984).

10. Hermann Hesse, *Narcissus and Goldmund*, trans. Ursule Molinaro (New York: Bantam, 1984).

11. "Fisk Nine Plays Bamans Today," *Nashville Tennessean*, March 29, 1963, 47.

12. Luther Dixon and Ollie Jones, "Rainbow Valley," *Moon River* (album), by Jerry Butler (Burbank, CA: Vee Jay Records, 1962).

13. Emily Dickinson, "I Had a Guinea Golden," https://www.poetry-archive.com/d/i_had_a_guinea_golden.html (accessed September 4, 2023).

14. Jim Brosnan, *The Long Season* (New York: Dell, 1961).

15. Hermann Hesse, *Steppenwolf*, trans. Basil Creighton (New York: Bantam, 1979).

Chapter 6

The Howard University Years, 1963–1965

Monté wagged his tail. I was back home in DC on Blaine Street awaiting my mediocre grades from Fisk University in Nashville and the letter concerning my lost scholarship. But, no matter, as I was determined to pull myself up by my own bootstraps. I would lay low, read, and get a job so I could find my own place and make my own way. I was eighteen years old and eager for the world beyond the bed I shared with my brother in the basement. I saw a job ad for a Nurse's Assistant position GS-3 at St. Elizabeth's Mental Hospital. In Washington, DC, jobs for young Black men were hard to come by. Thus, I sent for an application and took the civil service exam for the position. Over a hundred people had shown up for the exam.

In a few days, I received a letter with a 100 percent qualification for the job. There was a telephone call from an administrator, who communicated the fact that I had had the highest score on the exam and that I should keep the letter that extended the job offer, as it was a rarity to have a 100 percent on any civil service exam. Bertie was impressed but skeptical of my newly chosen career path.

St. Elizabeth's Mental Hospital rested high on a hill in southeast DC. I took the bus to get to the training sessions, was issued a blue work uniform, taught how to take blood pressure, supplied a set of keys for the locked ward to which I was assigned, and began work as an orderly trainee. My assignment was to Oak Ward, a geriatric ward for patients suffering from late-stage Parkinson's, neuro-syphilis, or depressive catatonia.

I would come up the hill to Oak Ward, check in, and stand around assisting patients—mostly old Black men—get their meals, help them get up from their wheelchairs, get to their doctor's appointments, and take their meds. Twice a week, the nurse-trainees had classes on rudiments of first aid, forms of mental illness, and patient care. When the weather was good, we would shepherd patients outside to get exercise and fresh air. Locking and unlocking doors to the ward with the key that hung from my belt gave me the uneasy feeling of being a jailer. Patients lined up in the morning to take their meds, dispensed in little white paper cups, and swallowed with juice. Trainees were warned about patients who would not swallow their meds—hiding them under their tongues—that we needed to check to see if they were swallowed.

There was Mr. Nolte, a retired Howard University chemistry professor. There was a youngish—thirty or so—man who had huge upper body muscles, a condition as it was explained to me, caused by a neurological disorder where when he tried to relax his muscles contracted. There was an old man in a wheelchair who suffered from Parkinson's. Mr. Nolte shuffled his feet when he walked. He had no teeth, so like a cow, he chewed his cud. Leroy, the muscle contractor was friendly and tried to help me move the wheelchairs. The Parkinson's sufferer made gestures that I could not understand, until when I saw him eyeing the cigarette in my hand, I thought to hold a cigarette to his lips. He quaked so much in his tremors that he could neither light a match nor lift a cigarette to his mouth. Escorting this crew out onto the broad green lawns behind St. Elizabeth's became a welcome ritual. Every morning I came in to work, punching a time card, wearing my blue uniform, unlocking, and locking doors, I felt a deep sense of purpose.

I found out that Oak Ward had been where Ezra Pound, the famous poet, had been institutionalized. I really did not know "Old E's" poetry at the time, but I had heard of him. The other orderlies, who were all older than me, treated me with a protective propriety. There were other wards on the grounds where the violent and dangerous patients were housed. There was a women's section of the hospital across the road from where the men were held. St. E's administration tried to create an atmosphere of a treatment facility rather than a prison. These young men were in their early to mid-thirties, happy to have the security of a government job. They had wives and children. Sitting in the weekly training sessions, we were lectured on the psychiatric theories of Harry Stack Sullivan and Karen Horney. When I walked onto the ward every morning, the old Parkinson's patient was waiting at the door in his wheelchair, his eyes lit in anticipation of the cigarette I would hold to his lips, waiting for him to exhale, and patiently letting him enjoy the rest of the smoke. Keeping Mr. Nolte from wandering away when we were outside became an ongoing activity, like herding a cow. As the summer months wore on, I contented myself in the evenings by reading, following the Washington Senators games on TV or at Griffith Stadium; of Ed Brinkman; of third baseman John Kennedy, ironically named like JFK; of Chuck Hinton, a Black outfielder; and of Jimmy Piersall, the former mental patient, who wrote the memorable baseball book *Fear Strikes Out*.[1]

There were two incidents at St. E's that forced me to rethink my career as a psychiatric nurse. The first was ordinary enough. One of the elderly patients on Oak Ward died. I recall looking into his room. He was a tall white man. His grizzled white hair and straight rigid presence on the bed was something I could not unsee. Soon, a huge Black orderly appeared, arranged the dead man on a sheet and started wrapping him into a cocoon of tucks, folding, and rotations that reminded me of a spider webbing a fly. The orderly's movements were precise, and I knew that he had performed this duty before. As an orderly, I knew that this was something I would have to learn to do. I thought of the undertaker Frank, my roommate at Fisk, and formaldehyde-soaked dogfish. This dead man wrapped like a mummy on Oak Ward, reawakened me to the grim realities of death.

The other event took place on the day—once a month—that the patients were scheduled for haircuts and shaves. The barbers came in, set up their chairs, and we lined the patients up for grooming. Within minutes, white foam on their faces, the patients were being sliced up, blood turning the lather pink. The barbers were brutally, cursing the men, pushing their heads, slapping them in the face and swashbuckling their straight razors like swords.

"Sit up, there, you dummy!"

"Keep your head still! You crazy fucker!"

The haircuts were vicious. The barbers slapped the sedated patients upside their heads as they ran the clippers roughshod scalping their heads. It was like the production line in a slaughterhouse. The experience turned my stomach. The head nurse, sat in his office, while the yelling barbers and screaming patients endured this "treatment." Nobody seemed to object. From that moment I knew I would quit. Where I thought, we were trying to treat, or at least comfort these heavily sedated, addled by age and disease, old men with only twilight in their eyes and sensoriums, it seemed we were agents of their torture. Punching out that afternoon, while walking to the bus stop, I decided I would resign and go back to school. Which is exactly what I had done. I had saved a little money. I would use it to pay tuition at Howard University.

I clocked out on my last day at St. Elizabeth's wiser to the work-a-day world of shaving sedated old men in a geriatric ward of a mental hospital. In the three months I was there, I read the patient's files—their diagnoses and medications—and lamented the fact that not one of them had had a visitor while I was on duty on the ward. It left such an impression that my literary alienation and ennui paled before the actuality of forlornness. The old, mostly Black men were hopeless, warehoused, in a prison within a ghetto, reminding me of Chris Hayes's *A Colony in a Nation*.[2] I vowed to do better.

Hustling up to Howard University, just up the hill from Griffith Stadium where I had been walking to see baseball games with Charles and Robert since I was six years old, I filled out the paperwork for admission. I registered for Sociology, Physical Science, Algebra I, Military Science, and Descriptive Astronomy I. I was so excited that Howard had courses in Astronomy! Living in the basement at 3929 Blaine Street, again: taking the bus to 8th and H Street, transferring to the streetcar that ran up Florida Avenue to Georgia Avenue—the same route I had taken to get to McKinley two years before—I was up early, dressed, and determined to make my fifth school in five years the turning point. I was determined to use lessons from Fisk to build upon at Howard. And Howard was huge, with thousands of undergraduates and graduate students. Howard was the "Mecca" of the Black intelligentsia.

It was the Astronomy course that had captivated me. The professor was one Dr. Alan Maxwell, who was to have the most influence on me during my three semesters at Howard. Dr. Maxwell was in his late sixties, having already taught Astronomy at the University of Michigan. In retrospect, he must have been an adjunct professor. In that during my class that semester, I was the only student, so Dr. Maxwell often deviated from his textbook lectures—often just informal "talks" with me—to tell me personal stories about himself. He had been a mathematical prodigy while in the public schools of North Carolina. He shared newspaper articles that had been written in testimony to his numerical acumen. He also showed me a small, three-ring, notebook he carried in his inner jacket pocket, in which he had handwritten the "powers of two," in columns, up to the power of one hundred.

Descriptive Astronomy I was not what I had thought a course on astronomy would be. He started with the equation of time, distinguishing between mean local time, sidereal time, and Greenwich Mean Time (GMT). Using a celestial sphere (a globular spherical blackboard), Dr. Maxwell taught me great circles—the ecliptic—and how to find astronomical objects by azimuth-elevation (AZ) and right ascension-declination (RA-DEC). I was introduced to the Draper Catalog and the eighty-eight constellations, and apparent and absolute magnitudes. For the early homework assignments, he gave me problems on "skinny triangles"—in retrospect so simple now—trigonometric exercises to begin arguments about stellar parallax.

Friday, November 22, 1963. I walked down Georgia Avenue to the streetcar stop, many of the people around me silent or speaking in hushed voices. Some were even tearful. President John F. Kennedy had been assassinated. Kennedy had offered the promise of better times for African Americans. With his body to be brought back from Dallas to lie in state in the Capitol Rotunda, Robert and two other friends—Michael Locksley, my old friend and first baseman on Fort DuPont's little league team and Jackie Robinson a classmate at Howard—decided to stand outside all night to wait our turns to pass by the casket. It was a cold, drizzly night. We stood there all night and were third in line to honor the fallen president. By dawn, Harry Reasoner, from *ABC News*, asked why we had stood there in the cold all night.

"I believe Kennedy cared about Black people."

We were among the first ten people of the three hundred thousand who passed by the flag draped coffin. On the following Monday, I was standing on Pennsylvania Avenue as the caisson bearing Kennedy's body passed by, Black Jack cantering. While the drum echoed down the street, I watched a crowd beat down a bleeding George Lincoln Rockwell, an American Nazi Party leader.

John Donne's description of death as "An infinite, super-infinite, an unimaginable space,"[3] was mathematician David Hilbert's "paradise," Aleph-null, $\aleph_0$.

"The gate is straight." This was the beginning of a national sentimental zeitgeist, the end of Camelot, the songs of Burt Bacharach: "What the World Needs Now," "What's It All About, Alfie?" Although it was before talk about the multiverse, I was living in parallel worlds: in the ghetto pool halls; in the academic lecture halls; in Bertie's basement. The world was a jigsaw puzzle within the Black bourgeois world circumscribed by the Baltimore-Washington Parkway, I seldom transgressed, as if I was in a Dantesque circular hell. My bafflements compounding as I looked through the verbal lenses of "Descriptive Astronomy."

Back at Howard, I was completing the first semester's coursework. The courses in Sociology and Physical Science were easy. The Sociology course required writing a few essays and the Physical Science course was a "history of" course, where we learned "$s = \frac{1}{2}gt^2$" and I authored a final essay on the physicist Sir J. J. Thompson. I also muddled through a college Algebra course, where the professor focused on "word problems." By the end of that first semester, I had earned As in Sociology and Physical Science, a B in Astronomy, a C− in Algebra, and an A in ROTC. Not bad. I had recovered some academic confidence. I earned my first A in an academic university course; I had taken an actual astronomy course; I had demonstrated the self-discipline to get up in the morning at seven o'clock and make the trek to my classes. I had escaped the horrors of the St. Elizabeth's barbers and found the blisses of an astronomer's words. I had been witness to history up close.

The Christmas holidays brought on an ennui I could not shake. I was having romantic experiences with neighborhood girls, dallying with them and being dallied with by them. I read the novel *Alfie* by Bill Naughton ("What's It All About, Alfie?"),[4] and I viewed Natalie Wood's film *Sex and the Single Girl*, trying to disentangle the phenomenon of relationships between men and women. During the holidays, I took a part-time job at Standard Drug Store assembling bicycles and other toys that had parts. Beverly was a cashier downstairs. Of course, we hooked-up, and I was once again under the illusion that I was in love with my first love. By the end of the holidays, I had found that it was only a fling for her while she was home from college.

The next semester at Howard was to bring me to higher consciousness of my racial identity. I had bought *Red Giants and White Dwarfs* by Robert Jastrow and *Uncle Tom's Children* by Richard Wright from a paperback book rack at People's Drugstore on Minnesota Avenue. These two books reawakened me to cosmology and race.[5]

The new semester at Howard had me registered for Descriptive Astronomy II, Philosophy, Calculus, History, and ROTC. In the Astronomy course, Dr. Maxwell continued to deepen my vocabulary and conceptual understanding. I heard him use terms like "true anomaly," "parsec," "period-luminosity," and "absolute vs apparent brightness." I was beginning to understand Balmer's series, Planck radiation curves, the electromagnetic spectrum, and the practical activities of astronomers—optics of telescopes, blink comparators, cold plate R-V timed photography, cataloging stars, and galaxies—beyond teaching. The calculus course was far beyond my mathematical ability. The professor was a young Black man with little tolerance for alienated dreamers like me. His name was George Hench Butcher, one of the first twenty African Americans to earn a PhD in mathematics.

How does one play the role of an alienated, iconoclast mathematician? Get the wrong answers?

"The gate is straight."

My history class was also a confrontation with a young Black PhD. The topic was Hitler and Nazism. I locked horns with this young assistant professor. He challenged me on every idea that I offered. Finally tired of my interventions, he assigned me to read and write a report on Hitler's *Mein Kampf* and William L. Shirer's *The Rise and Fall of the Third Reich*.[6] The philosophy course was an introduction to first-order predicate logic, taught by a white mathematician from the US Bureau of Standards. At first, I was deeply intrigued by the truth tables as a bridge between language and mathematics, but I quickly tired of the deductive proofs of Modus Ponens, Modus Tollens, and the Hypothetical Syllogism. As I struggled to keep my head above water, I was reading Albert Camus, James Baldwin, Theodore Dreiser, C. S. Lewis, Ayn Rand, Nikolai Gogol, and Ivan Turgenev. I had continued working part-time at the drug store, spending too much time in poolhalls, and walking up the hill to Howard in my Blue Air Force ROTC uniform greatcoat in the cold and drizzle of January and February.

Hearing a young co-ed at Howard recite a poem with the refrain "God Bless America, before she damns herself," I was again inspired to write poetry. I wrote and published "Utter her a bed/ Upon which her heart be lain/ . . . / Pray death be funny that she might laugh," in a solicited compilation of poems by college students. Of course, the collection had to be bought by the contributors, so it was just a money-making endeavor. But I continued to scribble poems and even shared them with a few of my classmates at Howard; one of whom suggested I show them to Sterling A. Brown—the famous African American poet on Howard's faculty, whom I did not know was a famous poet. Little did I know that at the time, the great Toni Morrison was also in Howard's English Department. Nervously sitting in a chair in his office, Brown shuffled through the sheaf of doggerel, I awaited his verdict.

"This isn't poetry. Get out of here."

I rushed out of his office, whipped dog, my tail between my legs.

"The gate is straight." As the semester ended, I was once again veering toward academic calamity. My "Ds" in calculus and philosophy did not help. Nor did the "C" in History. The only redemption was another "B" in Descriptive Astronomy. One morning that spring, I had been up at 4:30 a.m. struggling with Sir James Jeans's ideas about the dynamical determination of stellar diameters.[7] I understood Jeans' argument that because of $P=V/T$, and Ideal Gas Laws, a star's temperature was determined by its pressure, and with the equilibria between gravity and pressure, the star's color was directly correlated to its diameter. I was working my way through the integrals of pressure gradients, spectral classes, and bolometric measurements, as verification.

"What are you doing?" Charles up early to leave for Walter Reed, asked.

"Stellar Diameters."

"What are you wasting your time studying that for? There aren't any Black astronomers. You need to be studying something practical to get yourself a job."

I looked at the books, pages of my scribbled equations, and felt his disapprobation.

By August 1963, the talk in DC was "The March on Washington." On the morning of August 28th, Robert and I, along with several neighborhood friends, went down to the National Mall to see what the march "For Jobs and Freedom" was about. Mr. Clifford, handed us two union printed signs, blue on white card stock; mine read "Jobs Now!" We took the bus downtown and merged into the crowds walking toward the Lincoln Memorial.

Walking onto the grounds, I stood before a bandstand and watched Peter, Paul, and Mary, sing "If I had a Hammer." At that point in the March, there was a carnival atmosphere. But as the throng assembled along the edges of the Tidal Pond, the speakers started their introductions. Under the bright sun, John Lewis, the future civil rights leader and congressman from Atlanta—the same guy who I had seen in the Basic College Day room at Fisk—made a fiery speech. I had been impressed that in walking up toward the steps of the Lincoln Memorial, I had seen James Garner of TV's "Maverick" in the crowd. Being an existentialist and atheist, I was not particularly interested in the religious overtones of the March on Washington. In fact, I thought religion had pacified Black people to the extent that it was counter revolutionary. My ear had been honed by the more radical racial stances of Black Power's

Malcolm X and Stokely Carmichael. So as the loudspeakers rang out with Reverend Martin Luther King Jr.'s (MLK) "I Have a Dream Speech," I turned to walk away.

I read *Life in the Universe* by Michael W. Ovenden, with its subtle arguments about definitions of life that might include stars as "organisms." This book was the first stimulus for reorienting my thinking about matter, life, and the deeper meanings of cosmic evolution.[8] A thinking star! I tried to talk to the Sun; convince her that I loved her; induce her to talk back to me; enter into dialog—Akhenaton—in love with a star. The universe as a living organism. If such a lowly worm as I could have these thoughts, all certainties were questionable, the surprises of potential ineffabilities—in life, in death—were certain. There were things to be known that were unknowable. I read René Descartes' *Meditations*. I read Chinese philosopher Lin Yutan. Camus's play *The Misunderstanding* transported me. Perhaps *this* was the answer, everything was a misunderstanding—the universe, the lives of Black folks, me and Beverly—truth tables and reduction ad absurdum misinterpreted—mistakes in the logic, true anomalies, incorrect solutions to equations, the limits of human reasoning. I read the Mentor Classic *The Age of Reason* by Stuart Hampshire.[9]

The fall term at Howard was approaching. I was twenty years old, living in the basement on Blaine Street, sleeping in a double bed with my brother, desperate to break the bonds of inner-city DC. *I had a dream*. I walked to the Western Auto store at the corner of Minnesota Avenue and Benning Road and bought a .30-.30 Winchester rifle and two boxes of cartridges. Mr. Clifford loaned me a tent, sleeping bag, and camping equipment. Having recently read Thoreau's *Walden*, I thought I would go live in the woods. Driving between DC and Detroit on the Pennsylvania Turnpike, I had thought the forests of the Allegheny Mountains were the most majestic I had seen. I had often said to my brother, "You could let me out right here."

In my desultory, lonely, disillusionments of the basement, I had often studied the Atlas of the World Book encyclopedia, looking for the most desolate, heavily forested parts in the country—northern Oregon, upper peninsula Michigan, mountains of Colorado—and longed to be there; alone. It seemed to me that there was no quiet, no peacefulness, no respite from the never-ending social chatter, media bombast, lecture-lecture-lecture, continual responses to unceasing questions, thinking of what to say next. I needed time to think. So, remembering the splendor of the Allegheny Mountains, I had my brother to drive me up there, drop me off on the side of the Penn Turnpike, planning to return for me in three weeks. I decided to take Monté out of the ghetto with me. Collecting the cans of dog food, tuna, pineapple, beans, Spam—filling two five-gallon water containers—and packing it all, along with a few changes of clothes, into boxes and a backpack, I had matches, a compass, and a first-aid kit. I took writing paper.

As the day drew near, I packed my gear in Robert's green Mustang. MLK had "Been to the mountaintop," and James Baldwin had urged us to "Go tell it on the mountain,"[10] and Diana Ross had sung "there ain't no mountain high enough": I was going to the mountain to think, to escape, to be free. Bertie and Charles were worried. I was a man, and I had a gun.

We left well before dawn for the drive up the Penn Turnpike. Monté sat peacefully on the back seat. As we approached the Allegheny Tunnel, near Somerset, we agreed on the date and time for Robert's return. Because it was against the law, there were signs posted, to "discharge passengers on the turnpike," when my brother pulled off to the shoulder, I hurried to unload my gear into the scrub beyond a narrow drainage ditch. With tent, a duffle bag, boxes of provisions, two containers of water, my Winchester and Monté—I wanted to find a place far enough from the highway that I could not hear the semi-tractor-trailer trucks grinding their gears through the mountains. In search of the right spot, I walked away from the highway noise, upward, until the singing tires and whining engines were only a hiss. The place where I would pitch the tent was in a small clearing in a place where deer hunters had arranged rocks—not recently—for their campfires. It was flat and close to the summit. Monté sniffed around. I sat and smoked a cigarette as the sun rose. Dawn flitting through the ash and oak, I tried to retrace my path back to the side of the road where I had left the rest of my gear.

"Good boy," I said, as Monté wagged his bushy tail.

I still had him on a leash. I thought I would further reconnoiter the terrain before committing to pitching the tent; wanted to scout the area to see what was nearby. With Monté leading me on, I scrambled up to the summit, where the forest's canopy opened to a vista of the Pennsylvania Turnpike to the west. I could see the entrance to the Allegheny Tunnel, the cars and trucks tooling their way north on one entrance and south from the other. Sounds of the vehicles were faint whispers. Behind me to the east, the mountains rolled away to the horizon and there was no sign of human habitations. Birds flitted between the pine trees. Late morning was bright, I was hungry, and I was satisfied that I had chosen a safe and desirable location.

When morning came, I was shivering, wet, and panicked that all the gear was wet. To avoid the wet tent floor, Monté was sleeping on top of me in the sleeping bag. I scrambled to my feet, pulled on my boots, peaked through the tent door. I had forgotten to bring kindling and dry wood inside the tent, so I could not start a fire. Trying to get comfortable until the day dried out, I sat in the tent smoking and brushing Monté. This walkabout I was taking was also an adventure for Monté who had never been too far from a fenced backyard. Monté was loyal and patient, but I kept him on the leash. I put the rest of the can of dog food I had opened last night in a bowl. I poured the rest of the water from the canteen into a bowl. I was now into the first five-gallon can of potable water I had brought and knew I would have to use it sparingly if it was to last me three weeks.

Things went on this way for the first four or five days. After breakfasting, I would load up the backpack, pick a direction, walk for an hour or so, and sit writing in the notebook I had brought. One day it happened. My mind stopped talking to me. I had not brought a radio. So, I had not heard a human voice in a week. Nor had I needed to speak for a week, save a comforting word or two for Monté. We would roam across a new hill and see farmhouses and cows in the distance. Peanut butter sandwiches or sardines and crackers became the lunch of choice. Evenings were small wood fires, the bright mantles of the Coleman lantern, scribbling in my notebook, and finally dinners cooked over the open fire. Fried slices of Spam, beans, or canned stew, followed by Del Monté cling peach halves.

In the middle of the night, I heard something outside the tent. It was a snuffing, snorting, sound. Monté was standing, hair raised on his back, growling. Was it a bear? I was frozen. I reached for the rifle and listened. The snorting was just outside the tent wall. I cautiously raised the tent flap, to peer into the darkness and caught three large buck deer scrabbling uphill from the tent. I had built my tent in a deer run.

I was coming along with my handwritten journal. I was writing about what I believed about the purposes of life, the stars, and the universe. I wrote that humans were naturally evolved beings in a primarily hydrogen-helium universe of elements. I argued against a supernatural godhead, positing Nature as the causal agent in a physical universe without ethereal agency. Yet, I was also writing on how I believed that "true" consciousness might be enabled—by grace, by sincerity, by close attention—to communicate with the pure energy—resonate with—of creation. This godless mysticism—a cathexis—taking in all my senses, now they had been freed from the continual hum—humming—humm baby—of the people around me. Within the canopy of the cathedral Pennsylvania forest of red maple, white pine, hemlock, and birch, I surrendered to my dreamy mysticism. I did not understand the universe in English, Latin, German, or mathematically. Yet and still, I understood it emotionally, or so I thought in my peaceful tranquility among the chirping eastern bluebirds and flashing cardinals.

On February 21, 1965, Malcolm X had been assassinated in the Audubon Ballroom. And on March 7, 1965, Martin Luther King Jr. and John Lewis had been beaten down on Bloody Sunday, in their march from Selma to Montgomery. In my repose, I thought of race: how it had little or no meaning to the universe. The remotest galaxies had no notions of "Negro." Just before I had set out for the Allegheny Mountains, a race riot in Watts had killed thirty-four and injured thousands. I wrote out my feelings about being a Black man in America, about being a Black man in the cosmos. As I smoked, prepared my sparse meals, and ministered to Monté, I was consoled in the idea that race—as an artificiality—did not really matter to *matter*. So why to men?

Ten days into my sojourn, I awakened with my stomach queasy. Unable to hold my breakfast down, I hurled it. Unable to hold my bowels, I scrambled to get my jeans down, hopping to the latrine I dug a way off from the tent, and suffered the diarrheal. Before I could get back up the hill to my tent, this sequence repeated itself—both ends—objecting to something I had eaten. Then, I felt a sudden hot flush, sweat rolling from my forehead, nausea passing through me in waves. I sat down. Took a quick gulp of water—more molecules of H_2O than there are stars in the sky—only to throw this up into the watery galaxy of stars.

Among my stores, I had brought a fifth of "Old No. 7"—Jack Black (Black Jack)—Jack Daniels Sour mash bourbon, for what I had prejudged as for "medicinal purposes." When I had fallen asleep in a sweaty stupor, awakening repeatedly to throw up into the bushes, loose diarrhea, I adjudged that I was running a fever. I cracked the green paper seal on the bottle's top, took a mighty gulp. I had reasoned I had "amoebic dysentery," the result of trying to conserve water in scrubbing my pots and pans with dirt and sparingly rinsing them. My diagnosis required the alcohol in the bourbon kill the amoeba in my intestinal tract. Beginning to fear that my prognosis might prove fatal, as I vomited repeatedly, I picked up the rifle, let Monté off his leash, and followed him—stumbling—down the side of that Blue Ridge Mountain.

Monté sensed I was in trouble. Leading me on like he knew exactly where to go, we were soon following a fence along a pasture, to a dirt road, then a gate. I opened the gate and continued walking down into the pasture. A farmhouse.

"You're sick, come in."

It was a stout, middle-aged farm wife in an apron, who greeted me at the back screened in porch. Without further questions, she led me into the kitchen and onto a cot, where I sat, leaned the rifle against the wall, took off my boots, and slumped. She covered me with a quilt. When I awakened again, it was late afternoon.

"Here, eat this, it'll make you feel better."

She had offered me soup and bread. She gave me aspirin. There were other people in the house. Her husband, Mr. Fuchman, watched from the kitchen doorway. There were also three boys and two girls. For the next two days, Mrs. Fuchman ministered to me with food and coffee. She feed Monté, who was let into the kitchen to be with me. Soon, I was better. I wanted to get back to my tent. These people could not have been kinder to me. They were white, second-generation German immigrants. Mr. Fuchman's father had been a coal miner. And so had he, but he had also worked on the crew that had bored the hole thought the mountain in constructing the Pennsylvania Turnpike's Allegheny Tunnel. Why they had given so much hospitality to a twenty-year-old Negro, reeking of bourbon and vomit, needing a bath, carrying a rifle, trespassing on someone's property, I continue to ponder. But, after they allowed me to clean myself up a bit and provided me with fresh bread and butter from Mrs. Fuchman's table, I thanked them profusely and Monté still off the leash, led me back up the mountain to my encampment.

In building my fires in the evenings now, I knew that the Fuchman's knew where the smoke was originating. But so did the Fuchman boys—Wayne, Bill, and Sam—who I soon found standing outside my tent with offerings of more bread, jam, and butter.

"Beep-Beep—which is what they called their father—told us to bring this to you," Wayne said, as he lit up a Camel. He was ten years old, cursed like a sailor, as did his two younger brothers. They told me that Mrs. Fuchman wanted to invite me for dinner the next night; to come down after two or three o'clock. As I changed my shirt, in classic stereotypical form, the boys were amazed that my body was brown too; that, Black people were black all over. I laughed at their innocent profanity and naiveté, blowing Camel cigarette smoke—smokes they had stolen from Beep-Beep—from their cherubic faces. I told them I would come down to their house tomorrow afternoon, and they scurried away.

Healthy now from my bout with dirty dishes, I washed them more thoroughly. Walking with a roll to my shoulders—"nutation" of the moon, nodding—the Winchester balanced in my hand and a leashless Monté trotting along before me, I opened the gate and strode into the Fuchman's pasture. The Fuchman's had a little black dog—named "Nigger"—who sat on the porch eyeing Monté. Every time one of the children called him, "Sit Nigger!," "Stay, Nigger," "Come here, Nigger," I jumped. During the next few hours before dinner, Mr. Fuchman gave me a quick tour of his property. He had a bull and a few cows, for milk and butter, chickens, and a rainbow trout he was keeping in a cistern to fatten up for a future supper.

"Beep-Beep" had gained his moniker because, when the two younger boys sat on his lap, they would squeeze his bulbous nose, and he would respond with a good-natured "beep-beep!" Beep-Beep told me that he had injured his back boring the tunnel and lived on disability payments. As we sat on his front porch, he discussed his world and inquired of mine. He saw that we were as different as two people could be. When I told him how "rich" I thought he was—living in a place where Nature was so bountiful—home churned butter, a vegetable garden, and a rainbow trout in the cistern, he demurred explaining the poverty his family lived with. He was genuinely interested in my life in "the city." I explained to him how all the houses, with little yards, and so many people that you could not think your own thoughts, was a fenced in prison of the mind, he appeared to understand *that* as the reason for "all the crime" and my presence in Berlin, Pennsylvania, a little burg near Somerset.

As we had all sat, Mr. Fuchman had us hold hands as he offered the blessing. I was taken by this gentle act of togetherness. Sitting at the table with this white family, I felt a strange form of communion I could not name. Fried chicken, mashed potatoes, fresh garden salad, followed by apple pie. We sat at a long country table, the girls were young and shy, but it was as if I was part of the family. After eating, I sat in the kitchen smoking and drinking coffee as the family listened to the baseball game on the radio—the Pittsburgh Pirates—Willie Stargell and Roberto Clemente—as the sun set. Talking to Mr. Fuchman, I quickly discerned that he was worried about his financial situation. I asked him if there was any way I could help him. He told me there was some drywall he needed hung, as he was trying to create a room by dividing up another larger room for his eldest daughter. He had already done the framing but had not hung the drywall. I told him I would like to help with that.

Next morning, early, Monté and I trooped down from our perch on the side of the mountain. After coffee and toast, I helped Beep-Beep position, nail up, tape, and mud up the seams. By lunch, we had done a tolerable job. All that remained was to hang a door. That afternoon, I asked him if there was anything else I might do to help him earn the money he thought he needed to buy his five children the new clothes and supplies they needed for the rapidly approaching new school year.

"I have a flagstone quarry, I used to take rock out of before my back went bad, I could sell in the city."

Feeling like Sidney Portier in the movie *Lillies of the Field*, I thought I would be the Fuchman's *Magic Negro* and solve all their money problems. I told him that I could help with that. I went back up to the tent, wrote a few pages in my journal, musing about human kindness, cooperation, utopian community, and the nature of the universe. Noticing the calendar, my time on the mountain was approaching its end; I only had a week left before I would meet up with my brother.

For the next three days, I got up early, walked with Monté to the Fuchman's for a quick breakfast and coffee, and then off to the quarry. The flagstone ran in a tilted vein just beneath the surface of a hill on one side of the property. After digging with a shovel, inserting a steel wedge, slamming in the wedge with a sledgehammer, the rock split along its seam, which could be leveraged into broad sheets with a pry-bar, and broken out. Once freed, we rolled the flagstone down the hill, where it came to rest in a pile. Mr. Fuchman told me that he could sell it for a hundred dollars a ton. Landscapers used it to construct walkways and patios. It was challenging work. Swinging the sledgehammer, each strike on the wedge a "ping" like a recent remake of the 1950s song by Peter, Paul and Mary, "If I had a hammer," I'd ring out the sound of freedom, "all over this land."[11] Sweat drippling from my arms, I felt like John Henry "a steel drivin' man." I do not know how many *tons*—hundreds of pounds to say the least—we chipped out of the seam, Wayne and the two other Fuchman boys helping, before exhaustion and desperation set in. We had depleted the easily split flagstone.

"I hoped that that'll help," I said. I told the Fuchmans that I needed to finish the work I had started up at the tent and said my goodbyes. I told them I would never forget their many loving kindnesses and headed off to spend my last few days alone at my campsite.

"Come back here, Nigger!" I winced as the boys called out to their little black terrier as he barked and jumped at Monté as I hooked the fence of their pasture. Back at the tent, I settled down to write down all that had happened.

On the night before I was to rendezvous with Robert, I packed up all my gear, dug a deep hole to bury my empty tin cans, leapfrogged the equipment down to the side of the turnpike, aware that "It is Illegal to Discharge or Pick Up Passengers on the Turnpike." Concealed by the brambles along the shoulder, I huddled through the cool night, Monté by my side, sitting on the tent and sleeping bag. I looked up through the trees to the dark cloudless sky. Semi-tractors and cars roared by. I could see the blue stars. I saw the bright tail of a meteor, then another. Being late August, these might have been the remnants of the Perseids. I concentrated on what I had learned. I began to pose silent questions to the universe, taking the appearance of a meteor as a positive answer, "Yes!"

"Will I ever return to this place?"

"Yes!"

I asked question after question, to the Magic 8 Ball, Ouija board, roulette wheel universe, taking each meteor underline as a "Yes!" I continued this for hours, trying to establish a conversation with Nature. As the sun began to rise, smoking yet another cigarette, Monté bristling with anticipation, I turned my gaze to the shoulder of the highway. And soon, just as arranged my brother, accompanied by Charles, pulled onto the side of the turnpike. Fearing that a Pennsylvania State Trooper might cruse by, I hastily hurled the gear into the open trunk. Within moments, Monté's muzzle in my lap in the back seat, we were on our way back to DC.

"You need a bath," Charles observed, sniffing at the backseat.

"Hey bro'" Robert intoned. The Temptations' *My Girl* and Martha and the Vandellas' *Nowhere to Run* harmonized on the radio with the smooth whirring of the Chevy's tires.

Once back in the city, I took a few days to type up the manuscript, that Bertie wanted me to share with a local Baptist minister she knew. I sat with the family that Sunday night and watched *Bonanza* on the new color television. My trip to the mountains had become part of the gossip in the community; how I had gone into the wilderness; gone to the "mountaintop;" come back looking like a mountain man, Grizzly Adams; written a great treatise on the universe; smelling like a funky Yogi Bear.

Since the year back from Nashville and Fisk, I had experienced freedom and I wanted more of it. More importantly, I had discovered that outside the razor wire around the ghetto, there were white people who did not hate Black people. The Fuchmans had accepted me for who I was. After I had rested, I went to the bank where I had a checking account, closed it, and sent fifty dollars to the Fuchmans "to help with school clothes." Then, while Bertie went off to work on the bus every morning to Dr. Shafritz's podiatry practice, Charles drove to northwest DC to Walter Reed, and Robert went out to install new telephones for DC Bell Telephone, I went to Howard to register for the fall semester.

My heart was no longer in it. I was taking Descriptive Astronomy again. This time, there was a young Black woman in the class. She was a junior math major taking "Numerical Analysis," and I quickly discerned that the Astronomy class was easy for her. She accomplished the homework assignments and multiple-choice tests with an alacrity that astounded me. She started missing classes, but Dr. Maxwell did not seem to mind. As I sat with him in the upstairs room in the wooden temporary building, he would show me the notebook with the "powers of two" to the one-hundredth power and wax philosophical.

"Two to the zero is one—that is you the individual—two to the first power is two—that's you and the wife you will have. Two to the second—is four—that is your family. Two to the third power is eight—that's your community—eight is infinity turned sideways—there's infinite power in community. Two to the fourth—is sixteen—you grandchildren and community. And so on to two to the infinite power—2—that's God—wherever there are two gathered in my name, I will be there."

In the infinite powers of two, I thought Dr. Maxwell was teaching me theology, rather than astronomy. He was teaching me a scientific ethics. I knew that he wanted me to see that the wherever two were gathered, were the two of a genuine love for Nature. I substituted—salve veritate—"love" for "God." Love for the sun, the stars, the galaxies, the universe. Love for knowledge, love for wisdom, love for one's fellow beings . . . he would be there. I would be there . . . and *you* . . . would be there.

One afternoon, sitting in front of him as he lectured about the inverse-square force of gravitation, and how light fell off in intensity with the square of the distance, the gold edges of his dental work catching glimmers of sunlight, I interrupted him to ask a question.

"Dr. Maxwell, how do you feel at the end of your career, now that you realize that the questions you started with—the ultimate questions—about the purpose and meaning of the universe, have not been answered?"

He looked at me, smiling—the sunlight paying across his face—and answered.

"'Tis great fun." He went on to explicate on how a man could spend his life. He could enjoy it, he could worship, he could make money, he could help others, or he could ask unanswerable questions and seek their answers. "'Tis great fun." He told me that even without ultimate answers, to spend one's life in their pursuit was the noblest form of existence. Beyond what I learned from him about moving frames of reference, the period-luminosity relationship, the Herzsprung-Russell diagram, the apex of the sun's way, this lecture was his most meaningful. I agreed, "'Tis great fun."

Having struggled with the calculus, I was trying to teach myself analytical geometry. I was also taking an English class where the readings were the Theban Plays. This course was taught by the Harvard University educated classicist Frank M. Snowden. Snowden asked questions about death, to which I volunteered a quote from Francis Bacon, "It is as natural to die as to be born; and to a little infant, perhaps, the one is as painful as the other."[12] Later in the semester, Snowden gave a lecture to the student body, where, in stentorian tones, he admonished the students to "Go out into the world to experience it for yourselves." He orated for an hour on the grandeurs of the Tuileries Gardens, the Parthenon, and the intellectual bravery of Socrates. He used the refrain, "You have a lot of work to do." His speech was moving. I realized that he was right. I had to get up out of the basement on Blaine Street, go even farther than the Allegheny Mountains, and find out about the world. How could I understand the universe if I did not even know the world.

A few days later, on my way to the Corner Pocket poolroom on U Street, I saw the US Air Force Recruiting Office. I went in, talked to the recruiter, and took the qualifying test. I walked out of Howard without officially withdrawing, leaving seventeen hours of "Fs" on my transcripts. I went home, told Robert what I was going to do, and he decided he would enlist too. The Air Force had a "buddy system," where two people could enlist together and go through basic training together. Charles and Bertie agreed to this arrangement, and in the twinkling of an eye, we were on a bus to Fort Holabird, Maryland, for induction.

"'Tis great fun."

NOTES

1. Jimmy Piersall, *Fear Strikes Out: The Jim Piersall Story* (New York: Little Brown, 1955).
2. Chris Hayes, *A Colony in a Nation* (New York: W. W. Norton, 2018).
3. George Potter and Evelyn Simpson, *The Sermons of John Donne*, 10 vols. (Berkeley and Los Angeles: University of California Press, 1953), vol. vi, 363.
4. Bill Naughton, *Alfie* (New York: Ballantine, 1966).
5. Robert Jastrow, *Red Giants and White Dwarfs* (New York: W. W. Norton, 1979); and Richard Wright, *Uncle Tom's Children* (New York: HarperCollins, 1982).
6. Adolf Hitler, *Mein Kampf*, trans. Ralph Manheim (New York: Houghton Mifflin, 1973); and William L. Shirer, *The Rise and Fall of the Third Reich: A History of Nazi Germany* (New York: Simon and Schuster, 1960).
7. Sir James Jeans, *Problems of Cosmology and Stellar Dynamics* (London: Cambridge University Press, 1919).
8. Michael W. Ovenden, *Life in the Universe: A Scientific Discussion* (Garden City, NY: Anchor Books, 1962).
9. See René Descartes' *Meditations on First Philosophy*, trans. Donald A. Cress, 3rd ed. (Indianapolis, IN: Hackett Publishing, 1993); Yutang, Lin, trans. *The Importance of Understanding* (Cleveland, OH: World Publishing, 1960); Albert Camus, "The Misunderstanding," in *Caligula & Three Other Plays*, trans. Stuart Gilbert (New York: Knopf, 1958), 75–134; Stuart Hampshire, ed., *The Age of Reason: The 17th Century Philosophers* (New York: Signet Classics, 1956).
10. James Baldwin, *Giovanni's Room* (New York: Penguin, 2000).
11. Lee Hays and Pete Seeger, "If I Had a Hammer (The Hammer Song)," *Peter, Paul and Mary* (album) (Burbank, CA: Warner Bros, 1970; released as a single in 1962). The song was first recorded as a single by The Weavers and released under Hootenanny's label in 1950. Peter, Paul and Mary slightly altered the original lyrics.
12. Francis Bacon, *Bacon's Essays and the Wisdom of the Ancients,* available at www.gutenberg.org/files/56463/56463-h/5643-h.htm, page 64 (Accessed September 4, 2023).

Chapter 7

Missile Man, 1965–1969

At the beginning of December 1965, my brother Robert and I raised our right hands and swore to "Defend the United States against all enemies, foreign and domestic . . . ," were provided tickets on a commercial jet airliner and flown to San Antonio, Texas, where we were met at the airport in the middle of the night by a sergeant. We were then herded onto a military bus, where we sat, silent, with two dozen other new recruits. As the bus bent itself into the warm San Antonio night, I was my brother's keeper—with the eighteen months difference in our ages—he was only nineteen.

"Okay ladies—rainbows—get your shit off the bus!" the Airman shouted, as we tumbled out, just before dawn at Lackland Air Force Base (AFB), the huge ATC (Air Training Command) base.

Eyeing one another, we shouldered our duffle bags, wondering how much offense to take at being called "ladies" and "rainbows," a derogatory term we heard a lot at the start, in reference to our different colored clothing. After being quick marched to the dining hall, we bunked in an open-bay barracks to rest and sleep until the next morning.

"Ladies!" the drill sergeant screamed. It was 4 a.m. "I want to hear every one of your pussies hit the floor at the same time!"

We scramble to our feet.

"Hit the showers and the head!" He barked.

"Be assembled out front in fifteen minutes!"

From there we were lined up according to height and divided into four columns, marched to the dining hall, where we were jeered—"rainbows!"—by the more seasoned recruits. From there we were marched to a huge building where we were given military haircuts—buzzed down to a stubble—ordered to strip down to our "skivvies." Prodded and poked by a line of medical and supply specialists, as we walked in single-file between them, injected with air-pressure needles, fitted out with uniforms, boots, and hustled along (quick-step), back to the open-bay barracks to start organizing our gear.

The team chief was S/SGT (Staff Sergeant) Otting, a stout, laconic Non-com, who had an office upstairs in the barracks. On the one hand, SGT Walton, a tall young African American from Texas, taught us to march, guided us through PT (physical training), and took on the avuncular air of experienced support. On the other hand, S/SGT Otting was the bad cop in this arrangement, missing no opportunity to excoriate us.

Our military training began with classes on military courtesy, the UCMJ (Uniform Code of Military Justice), the Code of Conduct, chain of command, and Drill and Ceremonies. We were tested on the identification of rank, saluting, and proper modes of address. During breaks, we stood at attention in ranks, until told to "Stand at Rest."

"Smoke 'em, if you got 'em," as more than half the Airman Basics—no longer "Rainbows"—fired up their squares with newly bought Zippo lighters.

"Mail call!"

As we stood at rest, shuffling from foot to foot, SGT Walton called out the names of Airmen who had received letters, sailing them like Frisbees, stopping to smell the few that had been scented by girlfriends.

More classroom training, practicing saluting before walls so that you could bring it up close to the body, ironing fatigues so they held creases, spinning trays in the dining hall while keeping eyes front, gaining military bearing. I tried to keep an eye out for my brother. I did not want to smother him. He was holding his own, as he made his own friends. I tried to lead him on by example, through the obstacle course, PT running and calisthenics, and forced marches under heavy back packs. He performed admirably. We went through small arms training with the new M-15, concluding with live-fire, manual (single-shot) and full-auto. We both qualified as "expert" marksmen, with fifty rounds on target at fifty yards.

The instructors taught us that if you hold out your hand, all the fingers are different lengths, but if you make a fist, they are the same height. With Black recruits from the inner cities of Philadelphia, Baltimore, Cleveland—among others—and white farm boys from Idaho, Nebraska, and California, we were inculcated with the idea that if we could not learn to work together across these differences, we would be defeated by our enemies. During this time, the war in Vietnam ramping up, American service members were coming home in body bags.

"If you're in a foxhole with your buddy," the SGT extolled, "And you're guarding the perimeter, if you don't trust him, when you're supposed to sleep so you can relieve him, you won't sleep. And when your buddy is supposed to sleep, he won't sleep either, because he doesn't trust you, so he's watching you. In the end, you'll both fall asleep, and the enemy will overrun your position. You MUST believe your ally in the foxhole is BETTER than you are. If you do, then you'll close your eyes because you know that he'll protect you better than you could protect yourself. And he has to believe you're better than he is."

"Step it out, guide!" Otting barked at me.

Between tossing footlockers for toothbrushes turned the wrong way, ripping clothes from closets because there was a button unbuttoned, and flipping mattresses because the blankets were not taunt enough to bounce a quarter, Otting was wolfing orders like a deranged maniac.

"Get the fuck up! Shit, shower, and shave! In that order and out front by 0430! Move it! Move it! Move it, dip shits!"

When we had barrack inspections, we tried to work together, looking over one another's lockers and beds, making sure gig lines were straight. Otting had threatened that the squad would lose its first opportunity for leave if we failed the inspection.

"Barracks! Attention!"

We heaved to. Rigid. Otting and Walton swaggered into the room, their combat boots pounding, getting right up in our faces.

"Airman, you need to stand closer to that razor!"

"You call that a hospital corner?"

"Your boots look like shit! When I come back tomorrow, I'd better be able to see my face in them!"

We passed the inspection. Barracks life, when the team chief and drill sergeant were not there, was one ongoing joke. Living in close proximity to these white boys from all over the country was a revelation. All they talked about were souped up cars: "Bored and stroked," "Hurst shifters," and "hemi-heads." They used expressions I had not heard in the ghetto: "Yer fuckin' A," "Dip shit," "Numb-nuts," "You bet," "Fer' sure." The Black Airmen compared notes on ghetto life: "Columbus, Ohio was one of the most racist cities in the US." I learned the newest dance craze—the Philly Dog—from a Black guy named "Gumpy." There were protracted gambling games pitching quarters to the barrack's wall. A few Airmen washed out—disappeared from the squadron without explanation—their bunks left empty.

After eight weeks we were ready for a major parade—to pass in review—before the base commander and all the brass at Lackland AFB. It was our graduation ceremony. We massed in our dress blues, shoes spit-shined, brass polished, and assembled with the other flights into a huge "Wing" of Airmen. Marching, leather boots, clapping synchronously in a deep rumble, hundreds of rainbows turned lightning bolts, eyes right to the reviewing stand. As Right Guide, I slapped the wooden flagpole, snapped the guerdon—pointed it like a jouster as I passed, then pulled it back up—watching the base commander from the side of my eye. We were sharp troopers.

Based on my performance, I was an "Honor Graduate" of Basic Training. Subsequently, after another leave, I was to report to Chanute AFB in Rantoul,

Illinois, for training as a "Missile Systems Analyst." Promoted to Airman 2nd class—a one stripper—I was ready for anything. In my dress blues, with two service medals—Vietnam campaign and rifle sharpshooter—I stuck my chest out with pride.

On my way to Chanute AFB—an Air Force Training Command Base—I was "strictly by the numbers." In Basic training, I had learned that there were four kinds of discipline. The first, and most obvious, was, *corporal* punishment: spankings given by parents. The second was *civil* law: police and judicial punishment. The third was what I had learned from the Air Force: the *UCMJ*. The Uniform Code of Military Justice was higher than civil justice because the chain of command required that a lawful order be followed. This blind obedience was such that—in a time of war—refusal to follow a legitimate order allowed the offender to be executed. Hence, Military law was higher than civil law. Finally, the *fourth*, what all these disciplinary regimes were pointing toward was the highest form: *Self-discipline*, where one knew what was right and did it without external coercion. At this time in my life, I was reaching for this moral discipline, where I could command myself by my own duties. (I did not realize it then, but later, as Immanuel Kant's "categorical imperative").[1] But what I knew when I reported to Chanute AFB was, I could take an order and follow it.

My first night in the closed bay barracks, I did not sleep. Rather, I found a can of Trewax in my locker, and spent the night shinning the linoleum floor. I used the blanket in the locker to polish the floor (Ezra Pound's "Don't stop polishing the mirror"). By the dawn's early light, the barrack's room—with my clothes folded in drawers and arrayed on hangers—was inspection ready. My duty and discipline were on display. When the dormitory "rope" (a student leader with an aiguilette rope on his shoulder) knocked on my door, I stood at attention, until he said, "At ease," going to parade rest. As the rope scanned the room, I could tell by his facial expression that he had recognized that I was serious, disciplined, and in a hurry.

Ropes were assigned to individual barracks to provide discipline, march student squadrons, and give periodic barracks inspections. Advanced ropes recommend new ropes. Ropes are sent to a leadership training class where they were taught command voice, delegated authority, and chain of command. The green ropes are under the command of red ropes. Based on the order of my room after that first night, I was recommended for Green Rope Leadership training. Upon assuming this training (initiation/indoctrination), the first thing I did was shave my head. The reason for this was questioned by the Non-com (non-commissioned officer) in charge of leadership training. He sent me to the Lieutenant in charge of my squadron.

I marched into the Commander's office—by the numbers—took an extra step toward his desk, leaned my shoulders like starting the Philly Dog, pulled my right foot back and clapped my heels, pulled up a righteous salute so close to my body it raked my buttons, tensed my arm so my hand dampened in hysteresis to a stop and tensed my chest.

"Airman Jones reporting as ordered, Sir!"

"At ease. Airman, why did you shave your head?" Lieutenant Gustafson, asked. I wanted to answer: "Because of Alan Maxwell and orbiting Beta-Lyre and Cepheid variable stars, and the Fort DuPont Little League, and the Central High School Pathfinders, and the McKinley High School Trainers, and the Fisk University Bulldogs, and the peons all over the world, and Giovanni (in his room), and Frantz Fanon's *The Wretched of the Earth* (in their hovels), and for Rubashove crushing cigarettes in his palm (in Arthur Koestler's *Darkness at Noon*)."[2] But I said.

"Duty, Sir!"

"What do you mean by duty, Airman?"

"I want to show that I have no interest in myself, Sir. That I am dedicated to being the best trooper I can be. That I have a duty to my country and the Air Force," I answered.

"Carry on, Airman."

One of my duties was to conduct unannounced, periodic barracks inspections. Another was to assemble my barracks with the other barracks to march them to the technical schools. We "Fell-in" before dawn, marched to our classes in EP (Electronics Principles)—an eight-week intensive, modularized, introduction to electromotive force, Ohm's Law, use of a VOM (volt-ohm-meter), oscilloscope, capacitance (Farads and microfarads), inductance (Henrys and microhenries), and parallel and series circuitry. This course was interesting because the Air Force had adopted audio-visual techniques using animation to demonstrate the push-pull electromotive force, how electrons flowed in circuits. It was hypnotic. When the rooms (without windows) went dark, the movies of advanced electronic principles, danced in patterns that were retained—subliminally—even when you were not trying to remember them. We learned to read the colored bands on resistors. There was no homework. The next day, the lights went out, and you were again taught things (the skin-effect, waveguides) that were abstractly conceptual, at a visual-aural level that was close to brainwashing.

One weekend night, after lights-out in the barracks, I entered the back door, so the barracks guard would not yell "Barracks at ease!" The Airmen—PATs (Persons Awaiting Technical Training)—were hall surfing. When the first Airman recognized my rope, he screamed "Barracks, at ease!" Hall surfing was a carnival of youthful exuberance where mattresses from bunks were used as sleds on the highly waxed hall floors. Airmen would run, holding their mattresses, leap upon them, and slide as far as possible down the hallway, to the cheering of their barracks-mates. While they were still at parade rest, I excoriated, condemned, shamed, and ridiculed them for their folly. I told them that there were Americans dying in Vietnam, while they played childish games. I told them they were clowns. I yelled at them.

"As you were!" I hollered, as I eased out the back door.

Being a rope came with heavy liabilities. First, I did not want to be a "prick." There was a delicate balance between the saturnine gravity of being a natural leader, and an artificial tyrant propped up by the chain of command that ended with the President of the United States. So, I was a serious and conscientious trooper, motivated by my own self-discipline. I wanted to teach that same sense of duty to those over whom I held power. During open-ranks inspections, where I got up into the faces of Airmen to judge how well they shaved or cut their hair, I often heard the pounding heartbeats of six-foot-four-inch Airmen, tinkling their dog tags in fear. I once berated an Airman for his haircut—too long and shaggy about the ears—and he went AWOL to Chicago to get a haircut. Airman who failed my inspection of their uniforms—poorly ironed—were punished by setting up ironing boards on the commons, and ironing their fatigues with unplugged, cold, irons, until the Airman marched back to the barracks after a day of classes. This scene was greeted with howls of laughter from their ranks. I did not enjoy tossing lockers and beds during barracks inspections, but I did it. I was also a loner. I knew the Machiavellianisms of power.

I ascended to the lofty rank of Red Rope. Now, as only one of the very few Black Airmen, I was one of the select fewer red ropes. I commanded multiple barracks. When I entered a barracks and the barracks guard called out "Barracks at ease!" there was a different atmosphere as the PATs realized a red rope was in their midst. I signed into the barrack's logbook, walked up and down the hallway, looking into the rooms, my boots spit shined, I was alone in my dignity. I was Gung Ho. Boogaloo.

After Electronic Principles, I was assigned to the thirty-two-week Missile Systems Analyst course. The missile was the AGM-28/B—Air-to-Ground-Missile—"Hound Dog." The Hound Dog was a "standoff strategic weapon," launched from the B-52, it could deliver a 1.5 Megaton thermonuclear weapon (W28): one hundred times more powerful than the Hiroshima, 15,000 tons of TNT, atomic bomb. The AGM-28/B was forty-two feet long with a range of 750 miles. It was a complicated gizmo, a nasty little piece of work. With five other Airmen, we were taught in a cinder block house with no windows, in the middle of an Illinois cornfield, where we spent weeks "spark chasing"—that is, following complex schematics, in tracing various control signals (square-wave digital pulses). We were tested every week—multiple choice tests—we had to pass or fail the block. I learned to think in terms of v (velocity) and (dv/dt, or acceleration), and pitch, roll, and yaw and their derivatives (rates of change). As Missile Systems Analysts, we were "generalists," trained to maintain the six missile systems: Guidance, Flight Control, Cooling, Electrical, Hydraulic, and Pneumatic. We were being trained using the "Black Box" concept, with "Need-to-Know" as the operative underpinning. And we were being closely watched; constantly evaluated for intangible psychological factors.

On weekends, while the other Airmen travelled to Chicago or Danville—where there was a "cathouse"—I hunkered down in the barracks, knowing if I left the base, I would probably succumb to my Hook's Law vade mecum ("stress is proportional to strain"): trouble. As I sat in the barracks listening to WLS in Chicago, Herman Hermit's "Mrs. Brown You've Got a Lovely Daughter," and Spanky and the Gang's "I'd Like to Get to Know You," a profound loneliness filled me. Isolated by the crimson rope on my left shoulder, I was not getting to know anyone.

Some Friday and Saturday nights, I went to the Airman's Club and drank Zombies—one shot of dark rum, a shot of golden rum, a shot of white rum, topped by cherry brandy and Ron Rico's 151 proof rum—for two dollars. Quaffed quickly, a few Zombies were enough to make me forget the sadistic skills required to be a red rope, the girlfriend I left back in DC, and my frustrations from the suspension of my intellectual endeavors. There were also pool tables in the downstairs of the Airman's Club where I established my reputation as being a good stick. Some weekends there were local rock groups who covered "Gloria" and "We've Got to Get Outta this Place," with ear-ringing amps.

"I'd rather have a bottle in front of me, than a prefrontal lobotomy." I heard from more than one Airman at the club. In this air of resignation and frustration with training, Airmen also often invoked "The *faster* you go, the *slower* you get; the slower, the faster."

"You fuckin' A."

One Saturday, Gus drove down to visit me from Detroit in his Ford Galaxie 500. We went to the Airman's Club and had a Zombie. Then, he drove me off the base, where sitting, talking, and smoking, he produced a bottle of scotch we shared, "A bottle in front of me." He appeared tired and aged from the year I had spent with him four years before. I sensed he also thought that I was depressed and diminished beneath the burdens of the duties and discipline I faced. He dropped me back off at the base and drove back to Detroit.

A few weeks later, Gus told me that he had bought me a new Ford Mustang. He told me I had to come to Detroit to pick it up. So, with a few of my buddies from Chanute, we took the bus up, I took the keys and abandoned them, exploring me newly found liberty. Driving back to base, they sat, almost speechless—making comments about Gus, who had entertained them, while I cavorted in the streets of Motown—not understanding how this car had changed my existence. I understood that these white boys had an alternate cultural and social identity. They were interested in hanging out with me, because I was different from the stereotypes they had embraced about Blacks. I was confident, educated, disciplined, and a red rope. But these white boys were not introducing me to their sisters, or the girlfriends of their girlfriends. Spanky McFarlan's, "I'd Like to Get to Know You." When I returned to an environment where I could date Black girls, I morphed from Dr. Jekyll to Mr. Hyde, drinking, carousing, and getting into trouble.

On a particularly gray, muddy, February day, bored and lonely, I opened my mailbox and found a letter from Bertie; not unusual but enclosed in her letter was an unopened letter from one of the Fuchman daughters. She wrote to tell me that the fifty dollars I had sent had helped buy school clothes. She wondered how I was doing and sent love from the whole family. At an emotional low point, here was a beam of light. It was as if love—amidst the training for war—still existed in the world. It was as if, God had forgiven me for pissing on that flaming Bible in the trashcan at Fisk. I *felt* something. All my life I had held reason—ratiocination—high above emotions. But as the poet Samuel Taylor Coleridge had opined "deep thinking is attainable only by a man of deep feeling."[3]

The Hound Dog missile I was being trained to maintain had a stable platform—gimballed in three dimensions and held perpendicular to the center of the earth by alternating gyroscopes—from which it could "sniff" itself accurately to a target. I knew that I needed to provide a "stable platform" for myself, if I was ever to attain Coleridge's "deep thinking." That letter from the Fuchman daughter rekindled my spirit. I awakened the next day with a new respect for white people, that they were not all evil.

I completed my training at Chanute. My new orders were cut and I was assigned to Mather AFB in Sacramento, California, Strategic Air Command's (SAC) 320th Bomb Wing.

On leave, I drove the new champagne-colored Mustang back to DC, where predictably, I ran wild. I played the mating game—seduced *les femmes* as much as I was seduced by them—give and take, used and was used, before driving across the continent to Mather AFB, in Sacramento California. Cruising through states I had never seen—Nebraska, Kansas, Nevada, Utah—I cathected (took into myself wholly) the grandeur of the United States: majestic and expansive. The people I encountered along the way, at gas stations, in fast food joints, were generous and inquisitive.

Rolling across the California state line, I was at once taken by California's "newness." There was a distinctive odor to it—eucalyptus. There was a color to it—Jacaranda. The sun was brighter, and everything was clean—concrete highways, sidewalks, roadsides—compared to the sullen darkness and litter of the east coast. With my .30-.30 Winchester in the trunk, riding my Mustang, I was a "cowboy." California was beautiful!

I was quickly processed, assigned a room in a dormitory-style barracks, and started my OJT (on the job training) in the 320th AMMS (Air Missile Maintenance Squadron). OJT consisted of classroom lessons and hands-on experience. Seamlessly, in the bright California sunshine, I assimilated into the work. The primary task was to maintain the AGM/28. This consisted in uploading and downloading the missile from its B-52 launch platform, testing its systems in a hangar, and repairing the missile. The most difficult function was simulating the missile's guidance system. The missile was positioned in a geodetic scribed, plumb-bobbed, location in the hangar, external power applied to the electrical system, an artificial "auto collimated" star was fixed as the current position, and fed into the guidance system—a triple-gimbaled, stable platform, with NAVAN cycled gyroscopes (alternating spin-up/spin-down to reduce gyroscopic precession, in the xyz axes)—and initialized parameters for the accelerometers controlling the servo-mechanisms driving the flight control surfaces. Simulations of air pressure (ram air and barometric pressure) were provided to the Pitot probe. Once all the missile systems were running, a plastic Mylar tape (octally coded binary) engineered by North American Rockwell and Autonetics, was run through the missile's guidance and flight control computers. I sat overnight watching the nixie lights (tubes with numbers), blinking as the missile flight simulation ran to a pre-programmed target. If a parameter was out of tolerance, a "No-go, wait light" came on. When this occurred, following the manual, I got up from the console, extracted a jeweler's screwdriver from my toolbox, approached the missile's I-beam upon which the briefcase-sized computers hung, and turned the tiny screws to adjust the number of square-wave pulses (counted to update the guidance functions of current position, range to target, accelerations along three axes, rotation of the earth). Returning to the console, the "Wait Light" still blinking, I resumed the simulation, which backtracked and tested the function again. At the end of the successful flight simulation, the missile could be scored—anything within ten-thousand feet of the target was "right down the smokestack."

"Attababy!"

Just being around the more seasoned Airmen, quickly filled me in on the scuttlebutt and the overall state of SAC's war plan, at a time when the Chinese were increasingly backing the Vietnamese and the Soviets were increasing the "throw weight" and number of their ICBMs. This was the height of the Cold War, where every increase in one side's capability required a counter strategy. It quickly became apparent that we were at war with the "Chinks, Slopes, Gooks, Rooskies"—not my language—and that SAC was prepared for Armageddon. SOP (Standard Operational Procedure)—be ready to launch an all-out nuclear attack on Russia or China when the klaxon went off.

Once, I was on the Alert Pad, where armed B-52s sat ready for war. Walking under the bomb-bay, I saw the H-Bombs—even touched one—up into the Bomb-Nav console, to deliver a new weather forecast, and saw the maps with targets for Chinese and Russian cities marked with large red Xs. The war plan was for these bombers to fly over the North Pole, drop their payloads—launch their missiles—and fly on to England to land. But the pilots knew that there would be no England. Thus, the alert pilots I met on the Alert pad were the most serious men I had ever been around; no smiles, no banter, no emotion at all, waiting for the klaxon that was not an ORI (Operational Readiness Inspection).

There were all kinds of talk about nuclear weapons deployment: that the Russians had a doomsday device under the Pacific Ocean that when exploded would create a radioactive fog the earth would rotate under from east to west killing everything on the continent. We also heard rumors of ICBMs in fourteen-wheel tractor trailers, on US highways, camouflaged as ordinary interstate commerce vehicles, erectable for launching ICBMs. There were rumors of missiles on trains making huge loops—to remain mobile and thus untargetable—with ICBM erectors. But one thing that was a reality was the "Steel Gauntlet," SAC's logo and insignia patch. SAC used a "Chrome Dome" strategy when the alert posture was max. Chrome Dome kept nuclear armed B-52s circling the North Pole, with KC-135 refueling tankers to keep them aloft for days at a time, replacing them as they completed their missions. This 24/7 posture was intended to deter the Russians. Talk of Neutron Bombs. Talk of Multiple Reentry Vehicles (MIRVs). Mega-tonnage. Throw-weight. Chaff for jamming radar. Dummy Quail missiles used for radar signature deception. EWOs (Electronic Warfare Officers).

Periodically, the base information officer would hold a meeting in the base theater, where we were shown classified footage of saturation bombing, Vietcong tunnels, and ground fighting.

"Gentlemen, what this war is about," the Major would say in his sonorous voice, "is that your enemy does not believe you have the will to fight for your form of life. We are fighting for our way of life." Our strategic weapons were our "iron dukes," a steel gauntlet with spikes.

During this time, I met and worked with Sgt. Draper. He was truly knowledgeable about the Hound Dog, savvy. I watched him consult an Ephemeris (star catalog), help the B-52 navigators pick out a star "to shoot" for the missile missions, ride along on training missions, where the AGM's guidance system would provide steering for the B-52 using an LDI (lateral deviation indicator), and the navigator could hear the high-pitched rf (radio-frequency) signal when the missile's pitch signal indicated the missile was diving to the target. If the missile was outside the ten-thousand-foot circle indicating a direct hit, it was downloaded, brought back to the hanger for calibration.

Other than my old astronomy professor at Howard, Sgt. Draper was the only person I had ever heard use the RA/DEC system for stellar coordinates. He knew all the bright "circumpolar stars"—Sirius, Rigel, Vega—and as his name was Draper, he reminded me of the Henry Draper Catalogue which gave the classifications of 225,300 stars.

I uploaded and downloaded the missiles from B-52s. I went through several ORITs (Operational Readiness Inspection Training) and ORIs (Operational Readiness Inspection), where the SAC General landed on the base unannounced and the klaxon went off. The only difference between the ORIT and the ORI was that with an ORI the pilots did not know that it was a drill. So, the klaxon would sound and the bombers had to be airborne in twenty minutes, run their simulated bomb missions, return to base, and the maintenance squadrons had twenty-four hours to fix any malfunctions, and the mission was flown again. I had stood near the tarmac and watched the black smoke of the B-52s JATOed (Jet Assisted Take Off), using black powder squibs exploded in their engines to help them leap into the sky, and then return to the hangar to await the results. Sometimes problems with some of the missiles required us to work eighteen-twenty-four-hour shifts to get them operational and ready for re-launch.

I was driving a UTE (small tractor—tug—for transporting missiles) with Sgt. James, a tall Black Airman I worked with, down the flight line one day.

"What would happen if one of these nukes went off?" I asked him.

"Jones, you wouldn't feel a thing, as the atoms in your body would be moving away from one another so quickly, there wouldn't be time for nerve impulses."

I drove into Richmond—a town close to San Francisco—for a house party. The party was in a small house in a residential neighborhood. The house was packed with hundreds of young Black people, many of whom were college students. They stood shoulder to shoulder in the hallways, in the bedrooms, in the kitchen, drinking and smoking. Although music could be heard beneath the buzz of animated conversations, there was no room for dancing. Political talk—Black Panthers, Huey Newton, Soledad Brothers—was all I heard. Revolution was in the air. I had been in Sacramento when the Panthers brought their guns to the steps of the state capitol. Front page news in the *Sacramento Bee* newspaper, and all over the airwaves.

"All power to the people . . . Right on!"

Still trying to stay out of my barrack's room, I accepted an invitation from another Airman—an Airman William "Skip" Seeley—to go home with him to San Francisco for Thanksgiving. Skip's family, friendly and hospitable, made me feel at home. During the day, we visited the San Francisco Zoo and Golden State Park. Skip's talk about his lost girlfriend reminded me of my Beverly. He talked enthusiastically about the San Francisco music scene—bands I had never heard of—Jefferson Airplane, Quicksilver Messenger Service, and the Grateful Dead. Saturday night, he took me down to Haight-Ashbury. At 2 a.m., there were people dancing in the streets, balloons, soap bubbles, glitter, tambourines, and spirited laughter. I had never seen anything like it. On the Sunday night before we were to return to base, he took me with him to his sister's place. There were a few other people there. We were served ICB Root Beer, and I lit a cigarette.

"Have you ever tried pot?"

"No," I answered easily.

"You want to try it."

"Why not?"

Inhaling the marijuana smoke was easy, holding it in was more difficult. I coughed. At first feeling nothing, and not knowing what to expect, took a few more tokes and Skip and I drove back to his house. That is where it really started to kick in. I was hallucinating. Everything was running like an eight-millimeter film—I could see the jerky black limits between frames—but with brighter colors. Frightening, but intensely interesting. I was aware of "Lord Rotor," my own mind an illusion of the illusory. Conversations between Skip and his sister took on cosmic meanings. The world bristled with hidden connections. Driving across the Golden State Bridge later that night, I hallucinated a leopard running alongside the Mustang and flinched. I was worried, too, that I had committed a crime. Smoking weed was against the law. Since my Air Force records had a magenta triangle—indicating "works with nuclear weapons"—my behavior was highly scrutinized. Discovered using drugs might mean an article fifteen (Letter of Reprimand) or even the brig.

During the next few weeks, I had a few stoned flashbacks—stroboscopic, kinematic jerkiness—but there were few lasting effects. I was worried that my first encounter with dope—psychedelics—was a moral and ethical failure, that I crossed a line. But I was also "boy scientist," whose body was a chemistry set. So, I was heartened to discover that the illusion of a stable consciousness was illusory. At a deeper philosophical level, and I would not know this until generations later, I was worried that my indulgence with marijuana was punishment for my transgression against God. Like Kierkegaard's cobbler father who had blamed his bad luck in life for his cursing God, I was inwardly suspicious that my second-rate scholarship and understanding were God's retribution for urinating on a burning Bible. I found myself ruminating on "What if I'm wrong?" That God was teaching me a lesson, giving me all the allurements of pleasure, but leading me further from the path of righteousness. I wondered how long it would take me to be forgiven for my sins. Was it a sin or punishment for me to not be able to solve a parametric equation?

Thus, I started writing. I wrote an article, "Safety in the Dog House," about safety issues in the maintenance of the AGM/28B. The article was published with my photo in *Combat Crew*, the house organ of SAC. I won third place (and a check for ten dollars) in the base short story contest for a story titled "The Hand." The story was a fictional account of a man trapped in a rockslide who had been forced to amputate his own hand in order to free himself. Then, I entered the Freedom Foundations essay contest, with an essay titled "Freedom My Heritage, My Responsibility." Months later, an Air Force Colonel awarded me a medal for my winning essay. This was the same year Black Air Force General Chappie James won the same award. Even while serving my military commitment, I was beginning to find my way—through this detourement—back to my primary intellectual targets. I had a new stripe—a two stripe Airman 2nd class—and a thirty-day leave. Leaving on a Friday Afternoon to conserve time (my leave officially started on the following Monday), I drove from Sacramento to DC in fifty hours. Galloping Mustang.

On leave, I met a beautiful young Black woman named Jacqueline Boddie (pronounced "body"). She had graduated from McKinley High School and matriculated at Lincoln University, an HBCU noted for its academics. At this time, it was also known as a hot bed for Black Power politics. Jackie came from a solidly middle-class Black family. Her father worked in the US Printing Office and manned a cab off-hours. She had seen me around the neighborhood and was Robert's classmate at McKinley. So, I suggested that we get married. She said, "Okay." Soon after we had "celebrated"—and I use this word advisedly—our honeymoon in a rented room near Pittsburgh, she decided to tell me that "She didn't love me."

I was astounded. She might have at least given our relationship a chance to develop. But I still thought we could make it. I soon discovered that she was determinately anti-white. What she wanted was freedom and independence, like I did, but she was far more racially militant than I was. She was troubled that I was "serving" my country that was *not* my country. Once we arrived, after a long and alienating drive, not having a place to live, we bunked in with a white Airman from my squadron. Jackie was cool and aloof with the white Airman and his wife and little girl. We squashed into the little room in base housing. I was desperate to find a new place.

After a cramped few days, we found a little apartment across from Sacramento State College. Jackie enrolled in classes at Sacramento State and I enrolled in classes at Sacramento City Junior College. Ostensibly a college student, I was allowed to perform my Air Force duties on three-day weekend shifts, or at night, so I could continue with my studies. While on "Continued Academic Probation"—Fall 1967 through the Spring 1968—I took US History A, US History B, Art, Biology, Math, Psychology, and Sociology, where I attained a thoroughly mediocre 2.68 GPA. We were as happy as our not in love with benefits would allow. Jackie was unhappy. Too many white people and not enough Black Power. She started seeing a psychologist from Sacramento State's office of student counseling. She had a bad accident while driving the Mustang. She was not injured, but the repairs to the car were extensive.

At Sacramento City College, that spring, I was taking courses in Art History, American History, and Western Civilization. Because of the seventeen hours of "Fs" I had recorded when I dropped out of Howard, I often found myself taking the same courses over and over. I loved the Art History, as it introduced me to contemporary American art—Wayne Tebow, Robert Rauschenberg, Jasper Johns—and supplied relief from my technical duties.

Things went on this way for months. We argued. She got a job at May's Department Store at a mall in Sacramento. Even though we desperately needed the money, she quickly quit the job, complaining about the racist supervisor. She continued seeing the psychologist at Sac-State. When I asked her what they talked about she answered, "Our sex life."

"Our sex life?" I asked incredulously. "Like what?"

"Like what positions we used . . . did we ever have oral sex . . . had we ever masturbated one another to orgasm?"

One summer night in 1967, we were asleep when the telephone rang. It was Gus calling from Detroit.

"They're tanks rolling down 12th Street," he wheezed into the phone. I could hear automatic weapons' fire—*pocka-pocka-pocka*—in the background.

"Daddy-dear, are you alright?"

"I guess, but it's a war zone out here . . . I'm trying to get home . . . I'll talk to you tomorrow."

When I talked to him a few days later, he described the shooting, looting, and destruction of the Detroit Riots. He said that they did not burn down his Barber Shop on 12th Street. He said he had scrawled "Soul Brother" on the window with soap, and they had burned down everything else except his shop. I thought that was a testimony to the respect that the fire-bombing Brothas and Sistahs had for my father. Later in a Detroit News interview, they had quoted Gus as saying, "When you kill a man's dreams, there's not much left for him to live for." Talking to my father by phone for those few days also wounded my dreams. Here I was thousands of miles away, working for Uncle Sammy—helping his weapons of mass destruction function—while the US National Guard was firing on Negroes in the Detroit neighborhood that I had spent my summers and the year I had lived with him when I was sixteen. I stared questioning my involvement with the military. Disillusionment. Boogie-woogie.

On April 4, 1968, Martin Luther King Jr. was assassinated. In the History course I was taking at Sacramento City College the next day, I argued that racism was an American Tragedy: that phenotypical differences in skin color, hair texture, or thickness of lips, were of little consequence to Nature: that perceived differences in intelligence were artifacts of privilege: that for the United States to realize its ideals, racial equality would need to become reality. The professor invited me to talk to him during office hours. He said he would write me a letter of recommendation to graduate school when I was ready. Again, US cities were on fire. While in the midst of a twenty-four-hour ORI, fatigued and arguing with a white Airman—Hansen—I had swung a torque wrench at him after he had made an offensive comment.

"If you don't like this country, why don't you go back to Africa?"

Several weeks later, I had orders to report to Minot AFB in North Dakota.

I took my annual thirty-day leave. Once back in DC, Jackie and I went our separate ways. She stayed at her parents' house most of the time and I gallivanted all over the city. I hooked up with Beverly, without the faintest thought that I was "cheating" on a wife that did not love me. There was a shining innocence to my behavior, as I was the one who had been wronged. I thought Jackie had so many "hang ups" that I could do anything I wanted, and I did. As the leave came to end, Jackie decided she would remain in DC until I got established in North Dakota, then she would come out. To my mind this was all chimera, a disguised "separation."

Driving back to North Dakota, across Minnesota and South Dakota—the high plains—I had time to think. I only had eighteen months left in my enlistment. I had completed twenty hours of college course work through USAFI (military correspondence courses) and Sacramento City College. I had written technical modification suggestions for the missile (anhydrous ammonia venting safety) and won monetary awards. I had analyzed the missile's accuracy during daylight and nighttime missions and concluded nighttime targeting was better because the missile's astro-tracker (a device for shooting the position of astronomical bodies while the B-52 was airborne) locked onto stars at night and the sun during daylight hours. I had reasoned that if the star-tracker locked onto the east limb of the sun rather than its west limb, a potential thirty arc minute error could occur. Thus, using the skinny triangles I learned from Dr. Maxwell in Astronomy courses, and the trigonometry from the USAFI courses, I calculated the potential error. Analyzing the data, proved nighttime accuracy was greater than daylight's. I suggested that if the sun was used for a fix, the navigator should override the "lock" and drive the astro-tracker to a loss of fix, then divide the number of arc-seconds by two. The unit commander had looked at my work, stamped it "SECRET" and locked it in his office safe.

Listening to the radio playing "Hey Jude," "Sunshine of Your Love," and the Jefferson Airplane's "Somebody to Love," I was becoming acculturated to the new American youth culture's perspective. The music on the radio was my driving companion. When I heard Sam and Dave's "Soul Man," I thought of the night in a little club in Sacramento, I had sat in the first row and watched them knock this song out. They had also belted out "Secret Agent Man." I had also caught jazz pianist Vince Gerarldi's at a club doing "Cast Your Fate to the Wind." Having grown up listening to Motown and then the progressive jazz of Thelonious Monk and Dave Brubeck, this new rock music was complex, political, and revolutionary. This new was a new zeitgeist—weltanschauung—glorified drug use, anti-war, and free-love. I had also picked up hitchhikers—scruffy white kids—"On the Road"—who were rapping about Hermann Hesse's *Siddhartha,* Baba Ram Dass's *Be Here Now,* and Ken Kesey's *One Flew Over the Cuckoo's Nest.*[4]

By the time I arrived at Minot Air Force Base, the schizophrenic split between my duty to "defend and protect the Constitution from its enemies foreign and domestic," given the Detroit Riots and the assassinations of Malcolm X, Robert Kennedy and MLK, I was moving toward the "Summer of Love" thinking "Make Love not WAR." And war, with the capture of the *USS Pueblo* by North Korea and the Tet Offensive in Vietnam, meant that increased US troops were being deployed overseas.

There was a Minuteman ICBM at the gates of Minot AFB. The sign read "Peace is Our Profession," but the Airmen working on the base always appended it with the comment "And War is our Hobby." I was assigned to the 5th Airborne Missile Maintenance Squadron—5th AMMS—where I quickly returned to the maintenance and calibration of the AGM/28B. Where Mather had been a training base for navigators, Minot was a SAC base on a wartime footing. There were two B-52 wings with Hound Dogs, a Minuteman ballistic missile wing, and a KC-135 air-refueling wing. Given the rumors of Russian MIRVs—Multiple Independently Targetable Reentry Vehicles— that could deliver multiple payloads around a target, then air-burst a central hydrogen fireball forcing the ancillary blasts down to the ground in a sheet of fire fifty miles in diameter, cold war hysteria (*Dr. Strangelove*) reigned. Minot was a high priority target for the Soviets. The Airmen I associated with often quipped that they were "SAC trained killers." What they meant was, "They could kill you with a pencil—calculating trajectories of thermo-nuclear weapons."

"Why not Minot?" as the Airmen often quipped. Well, for one reason, it was in the middle of nowhere. Fifty miles from the Canadian border, and with winters where the air temperature could reach twenty-five below zero with winds that made the wind-chill seventy below.

"Uf da!" the Norwegian expression of disdain, I heard from the Scandinavian descendants, around Minot.

Indeed, "Why not Minot?"

When she did arrive, Jackie and I went to the nearest institution of higher education—Minot State College—seeking admission. We had found a nice, newish apartment in Minot. That fall, while commuting back and forth to Minot AFB, I had taken Calculus with Analytic Geometry I, Speech, and Western Civilization (again!). Jackie had registered for a full course load in the English Department. During this grueling quarter (Minot State was on a quarter system), I managed to earn an "A" in Calculus! I finally understood Simpson's Rule, the Trapezoidal rule, Integrands, and the fundamental theorem of the calculus. In fact, I had made the Dean's List. There was a small article in the local newspaper, "Minot AFB Airman makes Minot State Dean's List." Jackie's grades were consistently excellent. Yet I seldom heard her talk about her work.

Struggling with mathematical concepts, I conflated "integration" as an infinite summing beneath a curve, with "integration" as the attempts to have Black and white people live together. I often thought of "differentiation" as the differences in the races.

"Integration and differentiation are inverse processes."

NOTES

1. See Immanuel Kant, *Groundwork of the Metaphysics of Morals* (1785), trans. Mary J. Gregor (Cambridge: Cambridge University Press, 1998); see also Kant, *The Critique of Pure Reason* (1781), trans. Norman Kemp Smith, Unabridged ed. (New York: Bedford/Saint Martin's, 1969).

2. Frantz Fanon, *The Wretched of the Earth*, trans. Richard Philcox (New York: Grove Press, 2005); Arthur Koestler, *Darkness at Noon* (New York: TIME, 1962; New York: Bantam Books, 1984).

3. Samuel Taylor Coleridge quoted in a letter to Tom Poole, concerning Sir Isaac Newton, see Richard Holmes, *Coleridge: Early Visions, 1772–1804* (New York: Pantheon Books, 1999), 302. Available at Project Gutenberg eBook https://www.gutenberg.org/files/44553/44553-h/44553-h.htm, page 352.

4. Hermann Hesse, *Siddhartha*, trans. Hilda Rosner (New York: Bantam Books, 1981); Baba Ram Dass, *Be Here Now* (San Cristobal, NM: Lama Foundation, 1971); and Ken Kesey, *One Flew Over the Cuckoo's Nest* (New York: Signet, 1963).

Chapter 8

Why Not Minot?

I was honorably discharged from the US Air Force on February 20, 1969. Having been displaced by the flooding Red River, Jackie and I took a modest basement apartment in a family's home a few blocks from the college. That spring quarter, declaring myself a "math major," I took Calculus II and Modern Algebra. My calculus professor was Agnes Ladendorf. Mrs. Ladendorf was the chair of the math department and had taught at Minot State for decades. She was already approaching retirement at seventy. Dressed every morning in a crisp, white, starched, laboratory coat, she filled the chalkboard with definite and indefinite integrals, and retold the myths of the great mathematicians such as Carl Friedrich Gauss, Isaac Newton, Gottfried Wilhelm Leibniz, Niels Henrik Abel, Karl Weierstrass, and Augustin-Louis Cauchy. Her great enthusiasm for teaching mathematics was infectious. I was captivated by her swift clacking of chalk on the blackboard as the equations spooled out before me. I wrote my homework out in pencil and then recopied it in black ink. I was thrilled when she taught me polar coordinates and how to graph the Cardioid, the Folium, and the Lemniscate (a heart, two, three, and four-leaved rose curves). I could sense in these plots, how mathematics reached toward the forms of nature. I graphed these four-leaf clovers and hearts in black ink, and she posted them on the math department's bulletin board.

With her love for mathematics, early morning lectures on cold and clear blue North Dakota mornings, I became completely absorbed in solving equations. There was nothing more satisfying to me than struggling all night with a double definite integral (for finding the volume of a solid) and arriving, after several pages of calculation, with the correct answer. Many attempts at solutions led to failure. I would struggle to integrate by parts, checking my numerical calculations over and over, only to be frustrated by realizing I had taken the wrong approach. I would fall asleep amidst my attempts at solution, only to awaken a few hours later with a novel approach—fail again—and while walking to campus, have a new insight, hurry to get this new idea down on paper. After a few days, the answer would appear as if by magic—my subconscious efforts having worked out a path—I experienced the miracle of *understanding*.

"God made the integers, all else is the work of man."

I bought a copy of the Chemical Rubber Company's *Standard Mathematical Tables*.[1] I bought E. T. Bell's *Men of Mathematics*,[2] reveled in Niels Henrik Abel freezing in his garret when he was only twenty-six years old while studying groups, and Blaise Pascal deriving hyper cycloids to distract him from toothaches. All I did for months was solve equations. At one point, sensing my monomania, Mrs. Ladendorf asked me to introduce my wife—Jackie—to her. When Jackie came into the lecture room, Mrs. Ladendorf told her that I was a perfectionist and therefore appeared to be slow in my thoroughness, and that she (Jackie) should be patient with me.

Mrs. Ladendorf called me in for office hour's consultation. She said, "You are a right triangle." I wondered if this was another reference to Pythagoras, or a comment on my rectitude, as she sensed that I was struggling with more than triple integrals and maxima-minima differential equations. Agnes Ladendorf had led me into this wonderland of mathematical realism, but now I needed to transcend the chimeras of my social realities. I needed to hold many of the variables fixed, while I sought a solution for my racial identity. There were very few Black students in Minot's 2,000 undergraduates. I fell into a loose group of radical leftist students who called themselves ironically "The Campus Conservatives."

During the next fifteen months, I wrote an article for the *Campus Conservative* newsletter on "Hypocrisy," wrote an article on the new additions to Minot State's library for the campus newspaper and participated in a protest against the anti-ballistic missile installation (ABM) near Minot. At this protest, in the middle of a wheat field, were hundreds of hippies, student protesters, and peace activists. We stood in the middle of the construction site holding protest signs, smoking dope, and holding up our fists as helicopters circled overhead, no doubt taking pictures for the FBI.

I completed the three-quarter Calculus sequence, but faltered toward the end, not having enough time (in my perfectionism) to master inverse transcendental functions. Know full well that there were always students in these classes who performed better on tests. They were young and bright, many only interested in the calculus as a tool for pursuing other interests, like engineering or physics. But it was after completing calculus, required, as a math major, that I took other mathematics courses, like modern algebra, number theory, statistics, and geometry (from an advanced standpoint). In these courses, for the first time, I learned that mathematics was more than analysis. Mathematics was, more importantly, number theory, topology, and linear algebra. In matrix manipulations, the field properties of the real numbers, and the Peano postulates, I rediscovered my mathematical imagination.

I worked well collaboratively with other math students. When I met the other few Black students at Minot—many from the US Air Force base—and found out that some were having trouble passing the college algebra course, I arranged to meet with them during lunch to help them gain confidence and competency. Mrs. Ladendorf called me into her office and gave me a card requesting a tutor in math for a seventh grader. I called the telephone number and was hired to tutor a boy—the son of owner of the local Ford dealership—three times a week for an hour. He was having trouble completing his homework and had a "D" on his last report card, so I worked with him, explaining the concepts, and working with him to do his homework. I showed him how to complete the example problems before he even tried to do one of the assigned problems. However, what I discerned was that this youngster—son of a prosperous family—was lonely. Surrounded by financial emoluments, although he had everything, his parents hardly talked to him. He was isolated and longed for someone to chat with. So, before even beginning to start the tutoring session, I would go out back and shoot hoops with him for ten minutes. Once we opened the book, I spent another ten minutes trying to establish a friendship, listening to his commentary on his life, classmates, and teachers. To everyone's astonishment, he suddenly began getting "Bs" in math. The little checks I earned tutoring helped, as Jackie and I were living on my meager GI Bill benefits.

Word got around Minot of my success with the young boy and soon I had another tutoring job, with equal success. What these kids needed was friendship and kindness, not rote, memorization, and discouraging testing. I liked working with these youngsters. I had a gift for making the complex, simple. Yet, it was intimidating to be in the lush, comfortable homes of these successful families. We lived in a cramped basement, a broken window in the bedroom, awakening some mornings with snow on our blankets.

Jackie continued to do well in her English courses, "As" and "Bs." She also continued to be unhappy. While trying to rationalize her moods to homesickness, I suspected the real reason was her disappointment in me. I do not think she appreciated my grandiosities in the mysticisms of ideas and concepts. I never heard her use the word "galaxy."

The final quarter was a blur. I took a computer programming course. I applied for jobs and graduate programs. I attended a mathematical seminar, where a visiting mathematician produced an argument—complete with calculations—that proved that with two inhalations, one of the atoms exhaled by Julius Caesar on the Forum when he was assassinated in 44 BC, was included in the air in our lungs' next breath. The calculations included, Avogadro's number, diffusion and dispersion equations, statistics of random walks, thermal scattering, wind turbulence, and ratios of gases. So that meant that I had atoms from Jesus, Isaac Newton, and Euclid in and out of my lungs all the time. This was a meaningful understanding, and my first real intimations of holism. Still trying to fill in the holes I had perceived in everything when I was in my crib in Sunny Side Texas—through integration and continuity, Dedekind cuts, Cartesian plenum, God in the gaps—I had no one to share this with. Some mathematician—perhaps Pascal—had talked about there being two kinds of mathematicians . . . one kind concerned with the solutions for equations . . . the other concerned with lines and planes and their relationships, in space. I knew I was not an applied mathematician. I was interested in "number qua number." The less application it had, the more the mathematics interested me.

Given a little more latitude, I had also started to read for pleasure again. I read anything, but because I had such a troublesome time relating to other people, I tried to get insights into the minds of other people by reading novels. When I found a novelist, whose writing revealed the inner lives and personalities of protagonists (and antagonists), I read them to exhaustion. In this way, I plodded through Sinclair Lewis and Theodore Dreiser. They both wrote in a "newspaper style," with a directness and plotting that always yielded lessons on human behavior. I particularly enjoyed Sinclair Lewis's *Arrowsmith* with its portrayal of a scientist who lives a barren life trying to discover hidden truths in biology. Theodore Dreiser's *An American Tragedy* put me in sympathy with a murderer—much like Fyodor Dostoevsky's *Crime and Punishment*.[3]

In May 1970, I graduated from Minot State College. I had a job offer from the US Bureau of Standards as a "Mathematician I." Two interviewers from the "Teacher Corps," a US Department of Education program to entice "people who ordinarily would not enter public education to become teachers," flew into Minot to interview Jackie and me for positions in this program. Gus and Aunt Lillie flew to Minot to attend the graduation ceremony. A few parents of the boys I tutored, arranged a dinner for Gus, Lillie, Jackie, and me at the country club to thank me for the difference I had made in their son's lives.

Former SAC Commander, General Curtis Lemay, gave the graduation speech. I remember little of what he said, but now I know that he was the man behind, not only the nuclear trident strategy—bombers, submarines, and ICBMs—each capable of destroying the world. When Lemay went to the US Congress to appropriate more money for thermonuclear weapons and the committee wanted to know why, given "We already had enough atomic weapons to completely destroy the USSR," he answered, "I want to have enough should they attack us, we could reduce them to ashes." "Old Iron Ass," as he was known, was a true American hero, even Gus knew about.

Having been out of the Air Force for fifteen months, I had let my hair grow into a bushy afro, with an equally unkempt beard. My father was a barber and looked askance at my grooming. But he accepted this, as he had only finished the sixth grade, and I was the first college graduate in the Jones family. Degree in hand, I went back to Minot Air Force Base to share my joy at having accomplished what other Airmen had told me that I could not do. Master Sgt. James, who I had worked with told me that I should come back in, reenlist. He tempted me with the possibility of becoming a "ninety-day wonder"—enlisted man's slang for second lieutenants who went through officer's training school. I knew that I would be assigned to a lowly position in the Air Force's hierarchy, and that I was not pilot or astronaut material.

Jackie and I decided to take the Teacher Corps positions because they offered full tuition, a stipend, and a master's degree in education. I knew that even had I accepted the Bureau of Standards job; it would have been applied mathematics. I also knew that returning to Washington, DC, would be the death knell for my marriage with Jackie. There were just too many temptations, and I had learned how easily I succumbed to them there. I wanted a fresh start.

Monté had died—or he had gone missing after Agnes—the severe storm—or so Bertie told me. I suspected that they had him put down and did not want to tell me. Rather, offer the story that it had rained so hard that he was "washed away down the alley." I thought back to our few weeks in the tent on Allegheny Mountain, knowing that I had given him the hope and dream of freedom beyond the chain-link fence he spent his life behind. This news saddened me. More devastating was the news that Mr. Clifford, my next-door-neighbor and Woodson Jr. High science teacher, had been shot and killed in a school bank robbery at Eastern High School, where he had been vice-principle. I wanted desperately to get away from the East Coast.

In August, we headed for Des Moines, Iowa, and Drake University. Most African Americans had never heard of Minot State College, but they had heard of Drake University, the perennial location of the Drake Relays. Like the Penn Relays, Drake's Relays garnered national attention, as the finest athletes in the country competed in them. Crossing into Iowa, I saw the welcoming sign that read "Iowa, A Place to Grow." The prairies were green with corn and soybeans. My hopes were renewed that Jackie and I could find a way to make it—start over—move on and "Grow."

We found a comfortable, apartment, with air-conditioning (it was hot in Des Moines), close to Drake. The university itself, was in a central part of the city, and I was eager to begin my studies. I would become a teacher and share my love for learning with young people, at least that was my first motivation. The spring before the Teacher Corps Interns had arrived on campus, there had been a bomb detonated in the physics department by Black radicals in protest of Drake's racists admissions and few Black faculty. In some ways, the Teacher Corps brought black faces into the university's community.

Teacher Corps was one of President Lyndon B. Johnson's "Great Society" programs that also included other social welfare programs, like Model Cities, Job Corps, Medicare, and Head Start. Modeled after John F. Kennedy's Peace Corps, the Teacher Corps was designed to serve low-income schools. Drake's program was administered by a PhD educator from Texas, and Barbara James, a Black educator from the university. There were several local schools designated to host teams of Interns led by a team leader. The initial training sessions were held at a former monastery in Colfax Iowa, a few miles from Des Moines. The interns were from all over the country, New York, Memphis, Santa Barbara, and New Orleans. There were approximately ten Black men, six Black women, ten white men, and five white women.

Included in the contingent of Black interns were six from New Orleans. Five of these were from HBCUs, Dillard University and Southern University. These guys were former college athletes and quickly bonded. The sixth, was from Tulane University. One Black guy was a Seventh-day Adventist, and one was from rural Alabama. The Black guys tended to hang together, socializing after the daily formal training. I was the only Black intern with prior military service. The Black females were from the South, except for Robbie Lynn, who was from of all places, Vermillion, South Dakota. The white interns were primarily from large cities. Two white interns, Ron Larson and Denis Switzer, stood out. Ron had been a Peace Corpsman in Ethiopia and Denis was a veteran from the 101st Airborne, a paratrooper.

Jackie and I were the only married couple. The first few days included "sensitivity training," replete with trust exercises, like blind falls into one another's waiting arms. There were also group sessions—more akin to group therapy—where we were provided instructions for how to break through our social defense mechanisms. The trainers, from a company in Atlanta, were particularly sensitive to the racial divisions in the group; hence, every group of five included mixed participants. Quickly, racial animus began to come to the fore, with the Black guys from New Orleans forming powerful physical presence and the Black women aligning with them. Of course, the white interns made magnanimous efforts to dispel intimations of their racial prejudices. After a few days of sensitivity training, the group went out to the small town of Colfax for beers. Knowing the effects of alcohol on my reserve (I tended to become too expansive), I decided not to go, but Jackie went.

When she got back to our room, she appeared miffed with me. She told me how the Black New Orleans interns had walked around the car and opened the door for her. She commented on how polite they were, as if to imply that I did not know how to treat a "lady." I noticed how quickly she became at home with the Black interns, an ease and familiarity that I lacked. All these people were young, idealistic, and had earned undergraduate degrees. We all had motivations to change the world. But after a week, cliques had formed and there was a discernible racial tension.

During one training session, there had been an exercise to find the leaders in separate groups. Through a round robin elimination blind voting procedure, I was chosen as a leader along with Denny, the former paratrooper. In a mock treaty-making meeting, we were charged with finding solutions to the inter group conflicts. The two of us sat face-to-face at a small table and shook hands. After talking informally for a few minutes, we reached an agreement that we would work together—Black and white—and that the negative innuendos needed to cease. Since we were the only ex-military interns, our conclusions—and "peace treaty"—appeared to carry some weight. He went back to his "people," and me to my "people," to report on the agreement to ease these social tensions. All during this process the sensitivity trainers observed the process.

"It's cool," Denny said.

"It's all good," I replied as we shook hands.

At Colfax, we took meals together, had multiple daily group sessions, and integrated sessions with Drake University administrators, participant public school officials, and sensitivity trainers. It was a fishbowl. We also partook in individual sessions with our trainers. After ten days, people began to "flip-out." Some interns simply withdrew into themselves. Confronted with our defense mechanisms against one another, and encouraged to abandon them, a trainer told me that I was "glib." As I understood this criticism of my behavior, he was saying that I thought I could talk my way in and out of anything—that, I was verbally cunning—to suit my manipulative purposes.

On May 4, 1970, the Ohio National Guard had killed four students at Kent State. Then on May 14, two Black students had been shot dead by police at Jackson State University in Mississippi. I had started to think that the US government, in its omniscience, had declared a war at home on young people who were outraged by the ongoing violence in Vietnam and in US cities against Black people. This Teacher Corps project, while cloaked in good intentions, appeared to me politically motivated to undermine the groundswell of anti-American sentiments in youth culture. I began to see that we were being watched, evaluated, and used as baseline subjects to measure our will for commitments to revolutionary social change.

There were only a few of the thirty interns who were married. Denny, the ex-paratrooper, was married to Debby. They had two small boys. A few other interns were married, but the majority were single and immediately began to pair off in the mating dance. Before the two-year Teacher Corps project was completed, eight of these interns would have coupled and married. Counter cultural idealism, anti-war, and anti-racist ideology permeated everything that occurred in the white interns. The Black interns were more interested in the pragmatic and economic benefits that would be bestowed on them by attaining a master's degree, with its utility for procuring employment. Which is not to say the Black interns were not caught up in the reticulated winds of their "swerving" in the zeitgeist.

All of which *is* to say, that after a particularly "touchy-feely," group sensitivity session, where I was beginning to hallucinate ("tree branches with leaves opening into clearings above my head"), I decided to be less "glib" and have a heart-to-heart with Jackie. "The truth shall set you free."

"I've been unfaithful to you," I stated matter of factly.

"With who?"

"Well, Beverly, to begin with."

Jackie started to scream. A loud and unending, condemnatory, screeching. I knew everyone heard, in the other rooms on our floor of the Colfax retreat. She stormed out of the room. I felt so devastated that I retreated into the darkness of the room's closet, where I sat smoking and thinking what was to come next. Given the sexual revolution, mini-skirts, and "free-love," I had no doubt that most of the people surrounding me were promiscuous. I was not about to allow them to judge me as being immoral—they did not know the circumstances—extenuating and predictable: Jackie had told me explicitly on our honeymoon, no less, that she "Didn't love me."

Anyway, she stormed out into the night. She went drinking with the Black guys from New Orleans—all of whom were well-built, over six-footers—coming back late into the room without comment. We did not speak for days. I did not know how this would play out, but we continued the "sensitivity training" under a cloud. Other people had also "flipped out" when confronted with their "hang-ups." The public-school administrators, Teacher Corps leaders, and community representatives—I am convinced—were questioning the choice of these sensitivity trainer's methods and credentials. Were the interns being subjected to psychotherapy without their consent, by people who were not credentialed to practice it, and the results increasingly disastrous?

Southeast Polk Junior Senior High School was located a few miles outside Des Moines in Ankeny. It was a lower socioeconomic district where the parents were waitresses, store clerks, and truck drivers. I was to be on this team of interns with five white interns. There were no Black teachers, students, or administrators at this school. Before the first day of classes, the interns were invited to a cook-out with selected families from the district. Meeting with these parents and their children—I was the center of attention—was inspiring, as I learned that they were well-meaning, but suffering from impoverished conditions. All these parents wanted was a better life for their children: a better life as the result of better educations. As a young African American, I was new to their personal social imaginary, exotic, hip. As with much of non-urban America, white youth loved Black culture, but had little contact with the creators of that culture.

Jackie, one of the favorite interns, in the eyes of white school administrators, went to an integrated junior-senior high school. At Colfax, during orientation, I watched the white school administrators drool over her. She was a young, nubile, educated, and sophisticated Black woman who cast a spell on white men. The Black interns flocked to Callanan Junior High, in the center of Des Moines's Black ghetto. The remaining Black interns diffused throughout Des Moines's integrated schools. Before the semester began, I was invited to a meeting with Dr. Steve Jones, Project Coordinator, and Barbara James, Assistant Coordinator, at the Teacher Corps office. As I remember, they queried me about the disastrous effects of the "sensitivity training" on my personal life and had me sign a document stating that I would not pursue legal actions against Drake University or the US Department of Education.

Abruptly, classes began at Southeast Polk. I was unprepared for the chaos and confusion of life in a junior high school. The students bored, restless, and guileless. Interns were assigned to individual teachers in individual classes, but our presence did not seem to help. The teachers were either strict disciplinarians whose only role was to maintain quiet and order, or they were disinterested or uninspired laborers promulgating class-based social reinforcement. The school's administrators were magnanimous toward the interns while believing everything was fine with their school and community. The interns and program were perceived as "social experiments," to be tolerated as all concerned tried to maintain their façades of dignity. A vast pretentiousness pervaded the hallways and little room the interns used as an office. After attempting to work with the regular line teachers, I was quickly assessed to be of little real usefulness, so I was relegated to several ancillary roles. One of which was to try to teach a smallish, bespectacled, isolated boy to read. I used E. B. White's *Stuart Little* and Antoine de Saint-Exupéry's *The Little Prince* to motivate his interest, meeting with him for an hour three times a week, reading to him aloud. I visited his home and talked to his parents.[4] As I had always found—it is not a secret—attention, kindness, and belief in another person always allowed that person to rise above whatever limitations had arisen in their lives. He began to make progress with reading, which unleashed his other social and educational capabilities. But this was a minor role I was playing in his development.

The Teacher Corps project consisted of three components: teaching, community service, and graduate coursework. From my perspective, the teaching component was a disaster, as I was shuffled from one assignment, teacher, or project to another, never seeming to fit in. The community service project I had settled into was helping a Black woman (Mrs. Bertie Hader—Bertie "Hater") earn her GED. She lived in the inner-city, drug and crime-riddled neighborhood near Callanan Junior high, where many of the Black athlete-interns had chosen to teach. I meet with Mrs. Hader once or twice a week to tutor her in reading, writing, and elementary mathematics. Her son was in prison on a drug charge. Helping her helped me assuage my guilt for having chosen and been selected to work with an all-white team of interns at a school with no Black people. Over a year of encouraging her to do the assignments enabled her to pass the GED test. Although it was only one person, I had a wonderful sense of what teaching was about, empowering another to transcend a limitation. The final, and most important, was the program's graduate education course component.

The graduate hours in education required to complete the degree, were fairly simple, mostly "practicums." But once I learned that having been admitted to graduate school meant that I could register for any graduate course, I became aggressive in pursuing graduate courses in Astronomy, Physics, and Mathematics. Given the weakness in my preparation for many of these courses, I was only able to be marginally successful. That did not deter me. I was willing to take a "B" or even a "C" to deepen my insights into the ultimate mysteries that plagued me. While I witnessed the miseducation of the poor, white students at Southeast Polk, I was similarly miseducated in the graduate school at Drake. In less than a year, I took graduate courses in—or they took me—Introduction to Space Science, Astronomy, Mechanics, History of Mathematics, and Computer Programming (again).

These courses seemed like a test of what I thought I had learned at Minot State. The Space Science course had me calculating Planck radiation curves:

$$E_\lambda = \frac{8\pi hc}{\lambda^5} \times \frac{1}{\exp(hc/kT\lambda) - 1}$$

Where, in retrospect, this is not a difficult exercise; without a computer, it is. And it is especially difficult for a person who had never had a physics course. The cgs and mgs units and taking exponential functions, was difficult using only a hand-held calculator. Lectures from Dr. Skadron consisted of blackboards filled with Hamiltonian and Lagrangian equations. He acted as if I understood everything he was writing on the board. I was the only student in the class, so I could not seek help from other students. When he spoke of "Blackbody Radiation," I thought of the odor of Black people.

The Astronomy course—was self-directed—I never once met with the professor, who was retiring and on sabbatical. I had chosen the topic of eclipsing binary stellar systems, with its light curves, and orbital dynamics. I had to try to teach myself from books I checked out from Drake's library, the Ωs and $\dot{\omega}$s of orbital inclinations, rate of rotation of their lines of apses, and proper motions. It was a disaster. I earned Bs in both courses, as I did in the History of Mathematic course, where I focused on non-Euclidean geometries. I dropped out of the computer programming course after a few meetings, as the instructor was particularly adversarial to my "non-traditional" presence. The mechanics course was a nightmare of trying to get used to the Newtonian dot and double dot notation for first and second derivatives, having been trained in the calculus with the dy and dx notation of Leibniz. I took a gentleman's C in this course, realizing that a C in a graduate course was equivalent to an F.

While I spent time suffering with the integrations of my physics course and the dis-integration of my personal life, the other interns went on with their sociocultural *revolution*. Ron, who had returned from his Peace Corps service in Ethiopia, had told me that after what he had seen in Africa, when he returned home all he could do was sit on the coach and weep, as he endured the crass commercialism and cheap entertainment Americans were consumed by. He was a cool head, laid back, and unperturbed by the banal, insipid, bourgeois, dead zombies surrounding him. One evening, he fired up a joint and Nancy played Jefferson Airplane's *Volunteers*. Harkening back to a few years earlier, when Jackie and I lived in Sacramento, I thought of my first exposure to the Airplane's *After Bathing at Baxter's*. I do not know whether being stoned opened my aural intelligence to new understandings, but yes, the songs, "Wooden Ships," "The Farm," and "We Can Be Together," made more sense to me than anything else. I took to staying overnight at the farm in Ankeny. Jackie moved into an upstairs apartment near her school.

I continued physics courses at Drake. The education courses were so thin in content—a few papers and books by John Dewey and talk about "Summerhill" as alternative forms of pedagogy—that I was able to fulfill their requirements without effort. The physics courses were different—disorienting, challenging, and inscrutable—a dense mix of equations without explanation. To such extent, that one day during a lecture from Professor Skadron, I raised my hand and said, "Nature doesn't work that way." I sensed his disapproval and went back to copying his copious differential equations in my notebook.

Denny of the 101st paratrooper background, and his wife Debbie, like Ron and Anita were from California. At Denny and Debbie's, I also experienced a counter-cultural ethos. They had chickens, made candles, tie-dyed, smoked dope, and engaged in endless critique of the status quo. Denny had a huge dislike for Jackie. During our breakup, Denny always tried to convince me that I was not losing anything, except the conventional morality that had enslaved me. I resisted complete absorption into these "two farms," renting a rundown half of a house across from a cemetery. It was small, mouse-infested, and dreary. Of course, freed from my marriage, I played the field. All of which was disappointing and unsatisfying. I smoked a lot of weed.

Denny and Debby put up a three by five card in one of Drake's dormitories for a "Babysitter." After the three of us had been our drinking and smoking with some of the other Teacher Corps interns, we returned to their house, where Denny was about to take the babysitter back to the dorm.

"Why don't you take her," he said handing me the keys to his white Buick. The babysitter was stunning. She had the most beautiful blue eyes I had ever seen. Yet, she was phenomenally self-possessed, grounded in a perfect awareness, and young. Her name was Carol. It was love at first sight. When we arrived on campus, she sat in the car with me for hours talking. I took down her telephone number and called her the next day. We arranged to meet and have been together ever since. So, I could get out to Southeast Polk, Earl Schaffer, the Teacher Corp Team Leader, loaned me his Pontiac Bonneville. This car was a huge "boat," and Carol and I tooled around Des Moines, side by side, listening to "I'm Your Captain," (Grand Funk Railroad) and "Let it Be" (Beatles). Every time we saw a "one-eyed car"—a car with one headlight—we would lean in together and kiss.

Carol Marie Stahmer was a beautiful, smart, and aware young woman who had entered my life at a time when everything was crashing around me. I was a mess. She had confided in me early that she was not without her own "baggage." I will not throw her under the bus by telling all her secrets. But she had had her own traumatic experiences—psychologically abusive parents and betrayals by boyfriends—to the extent that like me, she was cautious about commitment. As I remember it, we were both suspicious about "love" as a genuine and sustainable emotion: "let *us* not speak of it." We were both adrift and searching for something better, a higher kind of life, a higher kind of love, a deeper wisdom.

Carol was always supportive of my subversive behavior. In her own way, she was as much an "outlaw" as I was. She entered my life and heart with a deeply pragmatic and realistic regime. She quickly assessed the chaos whirling around me. I was paying exorbitant interest on a loan with HFC (Household Finance Company), my apartment unlivable, and I was eating poorly. She helped me consolidate my losses, began seeing that I took meals beyond McDonald's, and was particularly startled when we discovered that we were both seeing the same psychologist in Drake's office of student counseling.

I decided to leave the Teacher Corps. This breakup, mirroring my breakup with Jackie, was at best mutual, as I had deeply embarrassed all those associated with the project. Steve Jones, the PhD from Texas in charge of Drake's program, had resigned. Most of the interns, disillusioned, only remained to salvage what they could from the experience, and a master's degree.

Suddenly in need of employment, I first sought meaningful work at M.I.D.A.C. (Mid Iowa Drug Action Committee) as a drug counselor. This work was deeply disappointing, as I worked as hard as I could trying to learn what motivated young people to abuse drugs to the extent that they became unemployable and psychotic. I was duped on several occasions—loaned money to addicts for what I thought legitimate reasons—only to find out that they had used the money to buy drugs. The serious drug users—heroin and cocaine—were in a different category from the psychedelic—soft drugs—users, of which I thought I belonged.

Like the movie *Ghost Busters*, where a mobile squad was on call to intervene when ectoplasmic monstrosities broke containment, MIDAC had a mobile contingent of drug counselors who responded to phone calls where there were overdoses. These emergency calls, often in response to "bad trips"—negative LSD experiences—were responded to with calming voices, and high doses of niacinamide (Vitamin B). Riding along with the MIDAC emergency crew, listening to the pharmacy students from Drake explain the physiological effects of various chemicals on the human brain, and observing the deceptive behaviors of MIDAC's resident drug addicts, convinced me after only a few months to move on.

I was experimenting with drugs myself, including a few acid trips and "magic mushrooms." Carol and I, having moved into a better apartment at 707 Buchanan Street, in the shadow of the Iowa state house, had tripped together on our waterbed. She was a willing participant in these explorations of the mind. I was discovering the links between psychedelics and creativity. I began writing poetry, short stories, and painting. One of the first poems I wrote during this "Black Hippie" period was:

>   A merry car
>   America
>   Merry Car
>   Poor Trait
>   Portrait
>   Of Blind
>   Billion volt
>   Fireflies
>   Methane mythed
>   Narcoses
>   Faster than a speeding locomotive
>   Gloomy luminescence
>   Looming essence
>   Less

I knew the line "Faster than a speeding locomotive," was really "Faster than a speeding bullet," from the old Superman TV show, but I was seeing the bullet as a train, with a car racing it to a crossing, so I could not make fact match vision.

I began writing my poems in a little notebook I carried with me. I painted a canvas that was accepted into a juried show at the Des Moines Art Museum. Having quit the job at MIDAC and often walking barefoot on the streets of Des Moines, Carol and I spent a great deal of quality time with Denny and Debbie on their little farmstead. But I needed a job. In some of my stoned hippie carousing, I met a young guy named Timothy Lindstrom. Tim was a young long-haired Iowan with an uncanny resemblance to Dennis Hopper, from the film *Easy Rider*. Tim was also the director of Iowa's High School Dropout Program. His job was to contact students who had dropped out and encourage them to either reenroll or pursue GED programs. I thought this was a highly worthy project, having helped Bertie Hader obtain hers. Tim was a "cool head," who did not have a prejudiced bone in his body. Tim told me about a job, as a regional Head Start Director, in the Iowa Office of Economic Opportunity (OEO).

Iowa OEO was headed by James Tyson, a democrat operative, who served under Iowa Governor Robert Ray. Jim Tyson was connected. Interviewing me, he stressed that the job was to administer a half-million-dollar federal Head Start grant for programs in four central Iowa counties. Describing the players in the contestation for these funds, divided between CAP (Community Action Committees)—Black and white—and the administrators of private day care centers in inner-city Des Moines, Jim Tyson indicated that the situation was "messy."

I took the job. It was "messy." I was faced with evaluating the current program status, establishing an administrative span of control, re-allocating funds, settling disputes between grantees, and writing a grant for the subsequent year's funding. I was interviewed by a local TV crew, an article appeared in the *Des Moines Register* newspaper, and suddenly local Black politicos knew who I was. Hand delivering government checks for tens of thousands of dollars, I was the "bag man" for the US Department of Health, Education, and Welfare (HEW). I was deeply skeptical of this approach to give lower-class and poor three- and four-year-old children enough of a leg up to overcome the burdens racism had imposed on them, their parents, and their communities. Yet . . . yet, visiting the Head Start Centers, I was hopeful. Seeing these kids eating the free lunches the program provided, receiving dental care, and having the paraprofessionals hired from the children's parents, was an innovative and progressive course. I was idealistic and enthusiastic, until I re-appropriated a small portion of the money for the rural counties that were white from the inner-city programs that were totally Black. In one meeting, an irate Black parent told me, "We're going to kill you."

I met Ruth Ray, an urban planner in the Iowa OEO office, who was the ex-wife of the poet David Ray. Ruth was a very spiritual person, a Buddhist yogi enthusiast, who asked me about my poetry. She told me about David, her poet ex-husband, and said that I should contact him. Consumed by my work, I lit a cigarette, and went on with my writing, Head Start work, and the exploration of my inner universe via drugs.

"You smell like an ashtray," Ruth said.

At the time, there was an "underground" newspaper in Des Moines, called *Cruel Sister*, derived, perhaps—I never really knew—from a 1970 song by "Pentangle." None-the-less, I started contributing poems, political cartoons, and short stories. I met the publisher, Dr. Marty Sachs, a professor at Des Moines's College of Osteopathic Medicine. Marty was a young man with a revolutionary flair. He taught human anatomy and physiology. One day, he invited me for a tour of the college with lunch afterward. He took me to the dissection lab, where laid out on fifteen tables, students cut away at human cadavers, spayed and laid open like books. Afterward, as I struggled to keep down my tuna melt, we discussed various ideas of universal "holism." Marty went on to be a distinguished doctor at the Mayo Clinic.

Having published several poems in *Cruel Sister*, I was moving away from the integration (the mathematical process of summation) toward the "joyful defiance" (a Buddhist category) of unrestrained expression. I was painting, reading—Abbie Hoffman's *Steal This Book*—smoking dope and tripping, and talking to anyone and everyone about the revolution of the human spirit, where love, peace, and harmony would finally be at hand.[5] Invited to read my poetry at a Unitarian Church in West Des Moines, having tripped the night before, I staggered to the podium, and read three or four poems—including "A Merry Car"—with a rapid, one breath, and unchanging inflection. After I had read, the audience sat in disbelief. It was in a progressive, educated, entirely white, group of Unitarians, who were ready to be liberal in their acceptances of difference.

"I don't know what that was, but it wasn't poetry."

The critic had been an English professor from Drake. Still stoned from the night before, his words skimmed off my psyche like a rock on its fifth hop. I was oblivious to any critique. His words were a self-critique of stultified bourgeois American imagination.

At a regional Head Start Directors meeting, at the bar in the hotel in Boone, Iowa, I had met a professor from the University of Iowa. After having a few drinks and chatting with him, he told me that I should apply to the U of I. He offered to write a letter of recommendation. When I returned to Des Moines, already having decided to quit Head Start, I put in an application to the Graduate School at the University of Iowa. Once I had been admitted to a PhD program in Science Education, Carol insisted that I complete the degree at Drake (Master of Science of Teaching) before leaving for Iowa City (I had wanted to skip it), helped me write the thesis, as I completed the last course required for the degree. Carol had also helped me negotiate the paperwork for a "no-fault" divorce from Jackie.

Carol was highly intelligent. She tested out (CLEP tests) of many of the required first-year courses at Drake. Yet, she never tried to contest my academic or intellectual efforts. Her intelligence transcended the academic, for the pragmatic tests, where there were no written exams or grades.

The kicker was Carol's grandfather, Bernhardt Stahmer. When I first met him, he seemed to be an ordinary seventy-year-old grandfather. But later, as I found out more about him, he emerged as a "genius," who held dozens of patents, including a patent for a high-speed corrugated potato slicer that led to "Ruffles Potato Chips." Although he only had a sixth-grade education, Bernhardt had started Omaha Industrial Electric, an electrical contracting business with dozens of employees. He had designed and patented the high-speed take-up reels used on the Saturn V booster rockets that took men to the moon. The take-up reels spooled up the umbilical cables attached to the rocket at launch, to move them away from the vehicle as it left the gantry.

As I was preparing to leave Des Moines for Iowa City, Carol decided that she wanted to go with me. Of course, although I knew I loved her, having been burned so badly by memories of my disastrous marriage, I was cautious. But I knew I could not lose her. On May 17, 1972, before a one-eyed civil magistrate, Carol and I were married.

NOTES

1. Samuel M. Selby, ed., *CRC Standard Mathematical Tables, Student Edition*, 16th ed. (Cleveland, OH: Chemical Rubber, 1968).

2. E. T. [Eric Temple] Bell, *Men of Mathematics* (New York: Simon and Schuster, 1986).

3. Sinclair Lewis, *Arrowsmith* (New York: Penguin, 2008); Theodore Dreiser, *An American Tragedy* (New York: Heritage Press, 1954); and Fyodor Dostoevsky, *Crime and Punishment*, trans. Constance Garnett (New York: Bantam Classic, 1984).

4. E. B. White's *Stuart Little* (New York: HarperCollins, 2005); Antoine de Saint-Exupéry's *The Little Prince* (New York: Harcourt's Children's Books, 1943).

5. Abbie Hoffman, *Steal This Book* (New York: Grove Press, 1971).

Chapter 9

The University of Iowa, 1972–1977

The University of Iowa was a mythic place for me. It was then in the Big Ten athletic conference, home of the Hawkeyes, powerhouses in football and basketball. It was also the home of the Writer's Workshop, where John Irving and Kurt Vonnegut, among countless others, had put their stamp on American avant-garde literature. I had heard that when Vonnegut was there, the students had revered him so much they camped out in tents on his front lawn. In many ways, ill-prepared academically, socially, and psychologically for the rigors of a PhD program, I had rented a U-Haul trailer, hitched it up to my new yellow Volkswagen "Super Beetle," and drove into Coralville on the western edge of Iowa City, rented an apartment in a four-plex, and vowed to buckle down to make something of myself. Before we were married, still living in Des Moines, Carol had given me a little mixed-breed dog we named "Inigo," after the famous English architect Inigo Jones. We took Inigo along with us to Iowa City, the Straw Man in search of a brain, Dorothy in pigtails, and Toto.

Foreshadowing the trauma that was to evince, Carol went with me to the first meeting of the graduate students and professors in the Science Education Department. During the introductions, in a room of about forty, I noted that I was the only African American, and that when I offered a comment concerning the discussion, it went over like the proverbial lead balloon. I discerned that the University of Iowa was very conservative. There were few of the long-haired, freaky people I had met at Drake. Science education was a discipline for preparing high school science teachers. The emphases were on teaching—a composite disciple—with science. As usual, there was little guidance for me; what courses would best prepare me for the rigors of the department. My advisor acted as if I would not survive the first semester, and he was right.

Again, knowing that having been admitted to the graduate school, I could register for any course, I signed up for Introduction to Astrophysics, Statistics, and an Education Colloquium. I had a stipend from the Office of Special Support Services administered by Phil Jones. Special Support

Services was designed to provide academic support for the few minority students at the University of Iowa. My assignment was to set up a "math lab." They assigned me a room with a round table. Students were advised to seek me out when they had problems with math homework assignments. For the first few weeks, not a single student appeared.

Knuckling down to my own coursework, I found the 8:00 a.m. statistics course a total snoozer. The professor was a kindly, elbow-patched, septuagenarian, well regarded in the field. He used a textbook of his own design, that was "Section 1.1, Section 1.1.2," and as dry as his monotone lectures. For all I know, it might have been Everett F. Lindquist, the famous originator of the SAT/ACT tests and the optical character reader for scoring standardized tests. All I remember is his mumbling on and on about "the criteria for sample size." I approached him after class one morning.

"What about statistical analyses with more than two variables?" I asked.

"Multivariate analyses . . . Bell curves of revolution. . . . " was his cryptic reply. Mrs. Ladendorf, my old calculus teacher at Minot State had told me once, "A mathematician is wasting time if he's not doing mathematics." I thought I was always doing mathematics—living it—always trying to go from two to three dimensions, three to four.

My other courses—including astrophysics—were equally *dis*astrous—*dis*-aster, as "against" the star—Pluto—Lord of the Underworld—was also named "Dis"—Hell's star. The young professor took a different tack than my professor at Drake, lecturing in general terms, with minimal Hamiltonian equations. He spoke of "radiative transfer in the Sun," "opacity," and the current quandaries in astrophysics. The textbook he used—by Swihart—was equally vague. When he put the scores for the first test up on the blackboard, I was astounded to see that I was not last; I was in the upper middle of the class. Nonetheless, when the professor made the assignment requiring that I use the computer center, I balked.

The U.S. Air Force had given me my first real look at computer technology. Unbeknownst to the public, the guidance, flight-control, and dead-reckoning navigation systems of air-launched missiles, were controlled by microprocessors. In the case of the AGM/28B, these computers were mounted on the I-Beam inside the missile's nosecone. They were small, about the size of large briefcases, and were primarily square-wave bit counters. A certain number of square waves equaled, say, one degree of pitch, roll, or yaw. Another number of square waves represented the rate of change of these, with accelerometers, providing the rates of change in square waves converted to bits per second. I had adjusted these bit rates with jeweler's screwdrivers while running overnight octal-punched Mylar-tape on the missiles in the hanger at Mather AFB. My second contact came at Minot State in a programming course. We had used a card-puncher to submit an object deck of programs to Iowa State University for processing.

The buzz at the time—everyone was talking about—was the WATFOR (Waterloo Fortran) compiler—that converted FORTRAN (Formula Translator) statements into executable code. I did not know FORTRAN, so I was shy about showing up in the computer center to do the astrophysics assignment. Also, I had a desperately negative aftertaste from the programming course at Drake, where the professor acted as if he did not want me to "monkey with" the card-punch or card reading machines. I had been the only Black student in that class at Drake and I was the only one in the astrophysics class. I stopped attending the astrophysics course. I felt—to use the French term—*de trop* (unwelcomed). I had the background, I had the mathematical ability, I was smitten by astronomy, but I was a social cripple.

The other course—the Education Seminar—employed a book by Jerome Bruner, *The Process of Education*, taught by a pedant who had been at Oak Ridge during the development of the atomic bomb. We sat around a seminar table to discuss our readings. However, I noted that when the discussion turned to human evolution and "inter-digital hair on fingers"—that is, whether hair on the first joint was an evolutionary advance over hairs on the second joint alone—and all the white students were looking at my knuckles—I felt *de trop* racial animus. On more than one occasion, the professor said to me, "You don't belong here."

Leaving them to speculate on their hairy knuckles, I stopped attending the seminar. Smoking more and more marijuana to treat my PTSD (Air Force, Jackie, Drake's physics), I idled in the upstairs apartment four-plex in Coralville, while Carol—who had transferred her credits from Drake, dutifully attended her classes. I was reading *Tarantula* by Bob Dylan, *Portrait of the Artist as a Young Dog* by Dylan Thomas, and *One-Dimensional Man* by Herbert Marcuse, rather than *Astrophysics and Stellar Astronomy* by Swihart.[1] I spent a lot of my idle time writing "Escape From Many Prisons," my imagined first novel.

I was still being paid by Special Support Services and spending a few hours a week in the "Math Lab," that I was supposed to be developing. There was only one regular student. He was totally illiterate, mathematically. I was trying to teach him how to add and multiply fractions—finding common denominators—and setting up simple *distance = rate x time* word problems. When, one afternoon a student came in seeking help with—what to me looked like—second semester advanced calculus. A serious young Black man, straight arrow, he was in the middle of the book, and from his questions knew more calculus than I did. It quickly became apparent to him and to me that he should have been my tutor. I realized in an instant that I was a fraud—a poseur—an impostor. I crawled back to my refuge in Coralville, Inigo was yapping on the back deck of the apartment, Carol was at her mathematics class. She returned from class and asked me about one of her homework questions on "Markov Chains," that I could not help her with. I sensed she was becoming doubtful about my so-called mathematical ability. But, *living* my mathematics—not the already solved exercises with solution manuals for the instructors—meant, as philosopher Berlinski put it, and I paraphrase, there is only one law in all of mathematics, and that was a simple statement that all things thought distinct are identical. Anything = Anything else.

There was no one to counsel me. I had been left adrift without a life jacket. Searching for a lifeboat, I reread *Be Here Now* by Baba Ram Dass—"If you could stand back far enough and watch the whole process you would see YOU ARE A TOTALLY DETERMINED BEING. The very moment you will wake up IS TOTALLY DETERMINED. How long you will sleep IS TOTALLY DETERMINED. What you will hear of what I say IS TOTALLY DETERMINED. There are no accidents in this business at all."[2] Comforted by the ideas that everything was predetermined, preordained, known in advance by the Brahman, and repeated over and over in all the worlds. I began pondering my own existence as a determined being. I became a machine. All moral and ethical considerations were illusory epiphenomena of dancing energy (*Wu Li*)—I was not responsible. My behavior was being dictated by quarks and the mathematical laws of physics that had originated in the big-bang fireball. I was the result of billions of years of Hamiltonian equations, chained by quanta, in a matrix of continual changes—totally calculable and predictable. I had decided I *was* a machine.

I had one friend in Iowa City. Bernard Johnson—"Bernie"—a doctoral candidate in education. Bernie was cool. He was from Nashville, Tennessee. Bernie had completed his coursework, formed his committee, and was working on his dissertation. As I recall, writing on the facial expressions of infants in relation to cognitive development models. In the 1970s, there was intense interest Piaget's identifiable stages of abstract reasoning in infants. Bernie was highly literate, always reading Claude Lévi-Strauss and other anthropologists.

Bernie's taste in music was refined—Ten Years After and It's a Beautiful Day. Having abandoned my graduate courses, I spent a lot of time at Bernie's apartment drinking wine, smoking, and rapping about the state of reality. At home in Coralville, I was listening—almost non-stop—to Yes's *Closer to the Edge*, The Stylistics' *Round Two*, Cat Steven's *Catch Bull at Four*, Traffic's *The Low Spark of High-Heeled Boys*, and Steely Dan's *Can't Buy a Thrill*. *Can't Buy a Thrill's* "Reelin' in the Years"[3] whose lyrics really tripped me out. The line was about someone who'd been telling people he was a "genius."

Like the song, I had been telling these people—teachers, friends, relatives—I was a genius—and they still did not recognize it. The whole vibe resonated with my current state of confusion, PTSD, depression.

One night, I took Carol to see *2001: A Space Odyssey*, written by Stanley Kubrick and Arthur C. Clarke. The movie transported me. I thought it explained everything. Arthur C. Clarke had provided the key to immortality—to be born again as a *star* child. To be resurrected in a cosmic womb. Another evening, we went to see *Reefer Madness*, written by Arthur Hoerl, the 1936 black and white government anti-drug propaganda film. The campus newspaper crew turned up to interview the hippies and potheads who had showed up (many of us high) to scoff at the actors in the movie driven to the madness of sexual frenzy under the influence of locoweed. I made a comment about how "safe" marijuana was, and how it should be legalized.

But what does this have to do with *Humm Baby*? As I understand it, a humdinger was something extraordinary, like his nose was a humdinger. Sometime in the late twentieth century, a home run became a *dinger*, the contraction of humdinger. At twenty-seven years old, I had long abandoned my dreams of playing baseball. Yet, I still dreamed of this beautiful game. Our next-door-neighbors in Coralville were a young white couple—Harry and Sue Wolf—really, Harry Wolf. Harry was in a fraternity competing in the university's intramural softball league. One Saturday, Harry invited be to play for his fraternity against a team of jocks. The jocks were members of the U of I's football team. I played center field. As the jocks laughed at the ragtag fraternity team, I quietly caught their long fly balls, casually threw them out trying to turn a single into a double and hit the softball over their heads in the outfield.

"Who is this guy?" I heard one of the crew-cut jocks exclaim as I came to bat again. Assuming they were superior athletes, it was as if I was a man playing with boys—Willie Mays playing with Little Leaguers, as I hit another ringing double between their left and center fielders.

"Who is this guy?"

I was the hippie Negro from their worst nightmare. I was trying to find a way to *live* my hairless middle phalanx. I taught the *superior* white race—like Jessie Owens taught Hitler—a lesson in their superiority that day. But they had taught me a lesson in their academic superiority—as the only Black student—in Introduction to Astrophysics, Statistics, and Education Theory. I was the only Black in the PhD program. Carol seemed to merge—socially mesh—with the children of the pioneers who had come into the Iowa territories, built their farms, declared their statehood on solid protestant values, erected a bastion of conservative—tried and true—like planting and harvesting corn and soybeans—educational practices that favored their own; infantilizing, feminizing, and eroticizing all the rest. I lit another doobie.

I have written this story many times before. These following events were among the most significant to have ever occurred in my life. In many ways they remain so. So, I will repeat much of what I have already repeated in my poetry and other creative writings (*Blackland*).[4] I had developed Capgras Syndrome. This condition, often associated with structural changes in the brain—lesions or schizophrenia—is also called the "imposter syndrome." I had started to catch glimpses of my professors in their cars, disguised with false beards or mustaches, with scowling accusatory faces, in dark judgement of my academic failures. I thought the people around me were imposters. I even doubted that Carol was really Carol, having been replaced by an adulteress—betraying my undying faith in her. I saw these judges—née, professors—everywhere I went, repeatedly admonishing me, their index fingers raised and bobbing in a gesture of "I told you so."

To avoid these eponymously disguised (as if clowns in their clown cars riding around Iowa City) pedagogues, I increasingly spent time at Bernie's, smoking as much tobacco as I could (a sure sign of schizophrenia). Bernie gave me one of his calabash pipes, beneath which I puffed clouds of gray aromatic smoke.

My last acts were spectacular. First, I answered the door to our apartment—to a woman friend—completely naked. I was trying to overcome all my hang-ups concerning shame for my body. She freaked and merely walked away. At the math lab, my student—if he was even a registered student—I was teaching how to add and multiply fractions complained that "They were not allowing him to vote."

"Did you show them your student ID card?" I asked.

"Yes," he answered, "But they still didn't allow me to vote."

There were elections going on for student government; a cardboard ballot box was in the hallway outside the math lab. I casually got to my feet and picked up the ballot box, to the protestations of the students watching it, took it out behind the building and set it on fire. The next day in the *Spectator*—the student daily newspaper—there was an article about "Ballots Allegedly Burned." Of course, everybody knew who did it, but nothing was done about it.

But there is more. I had been walking across the highway that led into Iowa City, to walk across a bridge over the Iowa River, to sit on its muddy banks and contemplate my problems. The rickety wooden bridge was locked, but I slithered through the gate and a warning sign "No Trespassing." The bridge crossed the spillway of an "Old Mill" that had long been abandoned. There were grassy banks and early spring flowers on the other side of the river. I had a deep need for untrammeled nature, freedom from academic concerns, and—certainly—an escape from my clown professors. My Capgras even had me believing that I was my own "double." I was a fake me, as the "genius at seventeen," would have certainly not have bombed out of his first year at U of I. So, I loaded up my briefcase, with some "unleavened bread" a friend had given me.

I was terrified. Now that I no longer received the graduate stipend, we were running out of money. But I was over on the other side (I had "crossed over"), the river Jordan or the lines of sanity. I had my briefcase, the unleavened bread, and my mother's old Bible. I sat down, hearing the lyrics of a Yes song, where the sang about the "sons and daughters" who understood and spoke in the "old ways."[5]

I took these "proud" sons and daughters to be American Indians and hippies. I'm thinking Neil Young's (and Buddy Miles) "Down by the River"). And I pick up the "good book"—Cat Steven's line about ending one's self-deception and picking up what I took to be the Bible[6]—and begin reading Genesis. After an hour of undistracted attention, everything was totally clear. I heard echoes of Emerson-Lake-and Palmer's great song, "From the Beginning."[7]

It was a mechanistically determined being, and I was meant to be here from the beginning of the universe. I raced back across the street, grabbed some black Hefty trash bags and spent the rest of the day picking up trash by the banks of the muddy, brown Iowa River, through which my mother's Bible had spoken in "sweet accustomed ways."

My friend, Andrew LaMothe, from the Teacher Corps, had graduated and taken a job in Kansas City, Missouri with IBM. When he had been in Iowa City Hospital having surgery on his eyes, I had visited him. Andrew suggested that I apply for a job with IBM. Despite my furtiveness with automated technology, I went to Kansas City, took the IBM Programmer's Test, and passed. Carol had remained in Iowa City worried about a thickening in her breast that the doctors were worried about—breast cancer was the disaster I worried about. I remember having a paperback copy of Albert Camus's *Lyrical Essays* in my suit pocket.[8] After the interview, eager to call Carol for updates on her health scare, as I sat on the toilet in the IBM office, I thought, how ironic, "I BM." I thought it strange that this computer giant was named I B(owel) M(ovement).

I drove back to Iowa City with hope that I had gotten the job. A few days later we received a letter offering one thousand dollars a month from IBM. Carol's cancer scare turned out to be a false alarm.

The Iowa River in spring runs fast with the flotsam from upriver; churning at its bank, chocolate milk. Desolate Narcissus staring: the spring birds chirping, the columbine bow their heads; I read the Bible and realize that my time had been wasted. Men had already walked on the Moon. I would have liked to have been one of those men, but I was not. I had lost my chances at becoming an astronomer. Seeing Robert Van Allen walking in the halls of the physics building had sent chills up and down my spine like the charged particles from the Sun helixing up the earth's magnetic field lines, reflecting back down as they generated synchronous radiation—the aurora borealis—calculations I had done at Drake.

Excited at having obtained a job, I thought back over the past few months. I had seen a counselor at the Iowa City Area Mental Health Center. The therapist, a white guy from Texas, tried to convince me that I was depressed about my failures in the PhD program, while I tried to convince him that I was depressed about the war in Vietnam, the racism in America, and my suspicions about the white people who populated my life.

I told the therapist that I was an inter-dimensional being undergoing "an operation" from below—at the quantum level—and that I would not be defeated by white people, Black people, Asian people—that I would see peace on this planet, that I would bring peace to this planet, and "speak to them in old accustomed ways."

Reclining by the banks of the Iowa River, the unleavened bread dissolving in my mouth, I leaned down and took a drink of the cool, muddied waters. My mother's old Bible had brought me peace and understanding. The plants were glassine crystal, sparklingly clean, with honeybees more majestic that the B-52 Strato-fortresses I had worked on in Minot. I had cleared the banks of bottles and beer cans, candy wrappers, and discarded cigarette packages. I thought I would baptize myself. Turning my head upside down, I dunked beneath the waterline. When I surfaced, at eye-level two Canadian geese (*Drake*s) crisscrossed flying from opposite directions, just at the water's surface. Because they were flying at great speed, the "intertwine" (a woven reedy catch for women's hair—but, also, the medieval sign for everlasting love)—an upward swoop. This aerial maneuver must have come aforethought—coming from different directions—a hundred eighty degrees apart: meeting at the exact moment my eyes focused coming up out of the water.

Astounded eye—I—I was convinced I had witnessed a miracle. Absolutely sure God had seen my attempt to baptize myself, I had been made clean. So, I dipped the unleavened bread in the dark waters (water the brown blood, bread the brown body)—a catechism—where they transubstantualized into the blood and body of Christ. As I crumbled the bread into the water, I knew in a sudden insight, the molecules of bread would be eaten by the fishes, by the bigger fishes, fishermen, and work their way to the stars. For whoever so loved a star, a galaxy, a universe? I knew the astronomers studied the stars, but did they love them? If one could love a galaxy with all their heart, would the galaxy love them back—try to communicate that reciprocal affection?

I had been listening to Jefferson Starship's "Hijack," in their album *Blows Against the Empire*:

>   Of stars that I have explored
>   Beyond the [idea] of beyond the void[9]

The hippies were *blowing*—smoke, oral sex, raining down blows—on the empire. They were trying to blow the joint; blow the doors off; blow it out. And they—we—were going to find a way out by hijacking the starship the empires of hate were building. I had made contact, just as I had when I had meditated on the black beanbag in Coralville. I had been contacted by extraterrestrial intelligence. They had not landed in a spaceship, as they were inter-dimensional—standing all around us, walking among us, measuring, evaluating. They were searching for one of their own—the one who so loved the galaxy, the Sun, the universe.

When I told the mental health counselor how I was undergoing an operation at the quantum level to prepare me for the voyage the Starship describe as "beyond the idea of beyond the void," he thought I was straight out nuts. I thought he was a dysfunctional bourgeois gatekeeper. Carol agreed with him that I should be hospitalized.

The University of Iowa's Psychopathic Hospital was a grim place where I was locked in a ward with other disturbed psychotics. I was put—naked—into a "quiet room" with padded floor and walls. Why I was put in this room without my clothes was a mystery to me. There was a construction project going on beyond the high window on a wall I could not see out of. There was a small window in the padded door where people came and went at irregular intervals. Sometimes, Carol appeared at this window. All these people needed to do was given me a cigarette and a cup of coffee and I would have explained this *misunderstanding* to them.

There was an extremely disturbed girl named Jennifer. Jennifer convinced me that the first step to getting released was to clean up my room. Through the haze, I gazed from the window of my room, into a little courtyard where grey squirrels scampered around the trunks of trees. Flicking their tails, they seemed so gentle and carefree. Then I saw the terracotta statue of St. Francis with his raised hand—friend of animals and Nature—*he* loved the star, the galaxy, the universe. A pacific exemplar, I became the calm lover of squirrels. I took Jennifer's advice (her last name was Rebel), I became a rebel—blowing against the empire—I cleaned my room, took down the booby-traps, organized and folded my clothes—the first step back. I sat—like the proud sons and daughters who knew the knowledge of the land (the beautiful squaw on the Land-O-Lakes butter)—and ate my dinner with "sister"—a beautiful young girl I could not take my eyes off, constantly being reminded by an older "mother" figure that she was "my sister," and to treat her with respect.

There was one other problem I had to deal with. Carol had told me that one of her legs was a half-inch shorter than the other. This had hit me like a Mac truck; I had wanted her to be perfect—I idealized her as perfection, as Mrs. Ladendorf had dubbed me "a right triangle." I knew that I was not perfect; slightly wall-eyed and my right eyelid was thicker than my left—a genetic trait I shared with many males in my family. But, somehow, now—in my mania—I saw every face as an anamorphic distortion. Beautiful women had a left/right facial asymmetry I had previously not recognized. It was if as I remembered George Orwell writing in *1984* something about faces where God had touched them and smudged them all, a way of recognizing their finite humanity; and I had idealized the right and left sides, bringing them back into symmetry, as I perfected them in my own idealized mathematical imagination. My sensorium had broken down, everyone was a Picasso cubist distortion, Carol smiling at me like the swooping face out of his painting *Guernica*, both eyes on the same side of her nose. I realized that faces were a construct of my visual field; whether one of my eyes was bigger than the other—that it was me and not the world that was producing these distortions.

The psychiatrists introduced me to Lithium Carbonate, still an experimental treatment for manic depression in 1972. I took 1,200 mg. a day and had my lithium blood levels tested until they had titrated to therapeutic levels. I immediately started to calm down. This lithium therapy took the edge off the interstellar travelling, the anamorphic facial perceptions, my tendencies for mathematic perfectionism, and my mental pacifistic St. Francisism. I was functioning well in the group therapy sessions occurring in the day room, trying to help patients who were more delusional than me. The nurses' aides sent me to the kitchen where they showed me how to make cinnamon buns. They listened to my stories about the evolution of cosmic consciousness and seemed to like me. I was quickly getting well.

To try to stave off financial collapse, Carol had taken a job at a Head Start center in a nearby town. My friend Bernard Johnson came to visit in the hospital. I disliked the fact that when Carol came, the orderlies unlocked ward doors and relocked them behind her. I never thought I was a danger to anyone. I believed that my psychotic break had been caused by an unwelcoming (*de trope*) environment. There were too few support systems, socially, educationally, and racially. While the psychiatrists waited for the lithium to stabilize, I looked forward to visits from Carol, and pondered whether I had lost my job opportunity with IBM.

If I were God and wanted to create a hell, I would do it just like the existence I was living. Inigo, the little mongrel dog—with a disfiguring under-bite—Carol had given me had disappeared (like Monté). Inigo would bark at night when we put him out to do his business. I was too distracted by my various deliriums to take him for walks. I thought one of the neighbors had tired of his incessant barking and thrown him into the Iowa River. Best case, someone had taken him out of town and some kindly farmer took him in. But probably the thrown in the river scenario was most likely.

I had a job paying one thousand dollars a month—a lot of money back then—but because I had flipped out, the job was in question. I had a beautiful wife who I wanted more than anything to believe in me. I was a mess. The day came when a panel of psychiatrists had me scheduled for a meeting to decide the possibility for my release. It was like another job interview. There were ten or twelve of them. I asked them if they would listen to a record. The record was *Houses of the Holy* by Led Zeppelin. I tried to interpret the lyrics for them through my own eyes. I was particularly interested in trying to relay to them the understandings that youth-culture had freed themselves from the strictures of their repressed elders. I focused on the song "No Quarter," as in "give them no quarter." In this song, they sing about finding a bridge. I told the psychiatrists that the "bridge" was an Einstein-Rosen *bridge*—a wormhole—that, the bridge was not a guitar bridge, or the bridge I had crossed to dunk my head in the Iowa River waters—the bridge from the lyric in the song "The Crunge"[10] was the bridge the naked crawling children on the album cover were seeking.

The doctors in their white lab coats listened carefully to me, no doubt comparing my "flight of fancy" to known cases of manic-ideation. But they *did* listen to the record and my exegeses. In retrospect, I am convinced they *heard* me—at least heard the desperation of young people who resorted to drugs and the alternative realities of acid-rock music to replace a reality that was so alienating as not to be *Houses of the Holy*—for the purposes of the papers they would write on the phenomena of people who were seeking ways to *leave the planet* (via death, insanity, or spaceflight)—what goes on in the mental hospital, stays in the mental hospital—or escapes like *One Flew Over the Cuckoo's Nest*[11]—from a hyper-lucidity that frees the psychiatrists from their own normative self-deceptive mental illnesses. I think I convinced them that not only was I not insane, but that I was a victimized artist. Mine was a moral trauma, not a mental trauma. The species was at fault, and I could not conceal my disdain.

"Mr. Jones, do you think you can *not* talk about these things when you get to your new job?"

"Yes," I replied.

"Down the road," one of the clinicians said to me, "An old west Texas saying."

I was released from the hospital. We sold the furniture in the Coralville four-plex—the childhood furniture from Blaine Street Bertie had given me—and drove to Kansas City to find an apartment. The medical doctors at IBM had given their approval for me to be employed. Our apartment was a newly built duplex. All was going well as I flew to New York where I shared a rental car from the airport with other IBM trainees, for the drive to Poughkeepsie where we would undergo our orientation sessions. On the drive, still adjusting to the Lithium Carbonate, I could not stop talking—stimulated by how fast my life was changing—about the *entanglement* of all things—how the universe was one thing. The young, recent college graduates—dressed in their button-down shirts and stripped neckties—who were all white, listened to my rambling discourse with quiet disbelief. It was as if they had never been in a car with a Black man; especially a Black man talking about the cosmos. They thought I was crazy.

I was delirious as they gave mini-classes on their current computer hardware and operating systems. They took us up to their manufacturing plant in Fishkill, New York. We watched as the workers on the assembly line, put together LSI (large-scale integrated circuits)—as, IBM was migrating from magnetic core storage to solid-state components—chips. I would have rather been in the manufacturing division of IBM, than in selling their products. I came back to the Kansas City IBM office with an unbelievably bad attitude. I did not want to be a computer salesman. I was assigned with Dale Lombard, the former Teacher Corps intern who had been hired when I was, to work at International Telephone and Telegraph (ITT) putting red paper dots on reels of magnetic tape records designated to be replaced by magnetic disk-pack storage. The magnetic tape, containing records of all long-distance calls placed in the United States, were beginning to deteriorate from their plastic bindings. It was a mind-numbing experience, required checking the individual tape's serial number, and tagging only the ones within certain numerical ranges. I secretly thought the supervisors at IBM were using this to test us for our attention to detail; the old Taylorism time and motion studies TMUs (timed measure units), and "therbligs."

My father, Gus, came to visit us. I picked him up from the airport and could tell right away that he was desperately ill. As I drove along the railheads and river coming into Kansas City, I tried to see him as I had seen him as a boy. He only stayed a few days, ate extraordinarily little, and asked for a little "scotch with milk" at bedtime. He was respectful of my new wife, and I tried as hard as I could to love him in his diminished state. I did not know it then, but even though he was still in his early fifties, he only had a few months left—succumbing to glioblastoma in 1975. Suffering from the distortions of lithium—a kind of emotional dulling—I did not react to my father correctly. I believe, now, that he was seeking reconciliation, reaffirmation, and empathy from me; while I was seeking his strength, and an answer to why my middle name was Argustia. I wanted to talk with him about what had happened between Bertie and him. I deeply wanted to tell him what had happened between Jackie and me. I wanted him to reassure me that he did not think "I'd gone over to the other side"; Black-speak for betraying the race (blood) by marrying a white person; that he loved Carol. Dealing with his own impending mortality, he wanted to tell me that he was dying; looking for the love from me that might reassure him that his life had not been meaningless. As the old saying goes, "Everyone will betray you," in the end. That was life's deepest lesson—one needing learning—in preparing to depart—we all die alone (betrayed) with little possibility of human closeness. Or as the poet Noor Hindi writes, "I think about how it takes forever to get to nowhere."[12] How it takes an eternity of atoms swirling in the void to get to the "void behind the void."

ITT (I tee-tee, as I said when learning to pee in the pot), and IBM I B(owel) M(ovement). If I were God, and had to make a perfect hell, I would make it like this. Everything you loved, I would take away from you and substitute something you loved less (but had to accept), and then take that from you, and substitute something you loved even less than that. Carol and I needed the money, as the first few paychecks from IBM'ed, while ITT'ed, proved correct.

I was still trying to get over my theoretical proclivities—reading Theodore Dreiser's *An American Tragedy*—sitting in an unused IBM conference room in Kansas, City, when I read an address in the novel that I realized was the address of the building I was sitting in.[13] This *Déjà vu*—or synchronicity—reminded me that my purposes and IBM's were different. It was as if the universe had penetrated the fog of my settling for material survival, to remind me that I needed to emerge into a clearing. I followed Dreiser with a reading of Herbert Marcuse's *Eros and Civilization,* gleaning what it was to live in an unrepressed world, again sitting in the unused conference room.[14] The marketing managers at IBM tried everything they could think of to engage me. I was assigned work at the Trans World Airlines site at the Kansas City Airport.

At the same time, Carol and I had bought a little house in Stillwell, Kansas. I was trying to *live* the esoteric life of a theoretical mathematician, while IBM had me working with systems engineers—what would later be termed software engineers—during a planning cycle to convert the IBM 360 mainframes to IBM 370 machines. I was still under the thrall of holism, mechanistic determinism, and had started reading the Russian mystic-mathematician P. D. Ouspensky's *Tertium Organum* and *In Search of the Miraculous*.[15] As I walked around in TWA's computer room filled with the massive IBM 360s and row after row of tape readers and disk-pack readers, I tried to understand why such computer power was needed. The answer was PARS—Programmed Airlines Reservation System—a software program of millions of lines of code—used to keep track (real-time) of every TWA plane in flight (segments), the passenger list, flight crew, cargo, billing, and reservations. When anything went wrong, the IBMers on site would produce a core dump to scrutinize the pantagruelian (colòssal) program for errors so they could write a "patch" (correction code). During my first few weeks, I was helping them burst (remove the perforated edges a four-foot-tall stack of computer printout) a core dump.

Still trying to get my mind around the problem of conformality—the mappings on one function onto another—like mapping the spherical Earth to a flat Mercator map—I wanted to *live* this non-one-to-one homology. In other words, if everything was a function $f(x)$—where this was like a factory f that transformed the raw materials x into y—then, if y was the universe, x could be God, or Nature, or blind mechanistic causation, or something else. And beyond all that, if $f(x)$ produced y—consciousness—it could not be one-to-one onto, as $f(x)$ was an infinite manifold, and y was a finite manifold, meaning consciousness was necessarily transformally incomplete—missing an infinite number of unmapped points—the "holes" I had seen in my crib in Sunny Side, Texas. Later I would map this to Kant's arguments concerning the transcendental noumena and Wittgenstein's the limits of your world is your language. Reading, today, physicist Anil Ananthaswamy writing about whether "The Universe is a Hologram":

> Maldacena showed that a five-dimensional theory of a type of imaginary space-time called anti–de Sitter space (AdS) that included gravity could describe the same system as a lower-dimensional quantum field theory of particles and fields in the absence of gravity, called a conformal field theory (CFT). In other words, he found two different theories that could both describe the same physical system, showing that the theories were, in a sense, equivalent—even though they each included different numbers of dimensions, and one factored in gravity where the other didn't.[16]

I sitting in the bar at an airport, drinking a Jack and Coke, trying to explain Kant—I was trying to read—to Dale Lombard, my old friend from Teacher Corps and current associate trainee at IBM, who rolled his eyes at my lack of practical regard for my *real* (not my transcendental) job. Dale and Andrew LaMothe, the other Teacher Corps intern who had become IBMers, took their work seriously, learned to read code (COBOL), and digging into the logic of using software to solve business problems. Just looking at the code, I had seen it was little more than strings of IF-THEN and IF-THEN ELSE sifting loops feeding the endless records, READ and WRITE commands to storage, and in some cases, printing bills, or receipts. The IBM computers at the time used FORTRAN (Formula Translator) and APL (A Programming Language). I thought IBM's work was little more than accounting. Sometimes, listening to the business executives I encountered at meetings, I would hear, "We could get a hundred heads." By which they intended, that card-punch operators would be replaced by OCRs (optical character readers), or supermarket laser scanners would replace cash register operators.

As I became more alienated, my manager—Dick Berner—had me talk to successful marketing associates, who told me all I had to do was "keep my mouth shut, and they'd make me a superstar." They told me that I could make big money—hundreds of thousands—if I played along; that IBM always tolerated "wild ducks" (people who thought differently), to keep from becoming ossified and rigidified in a rapidly changing society; but of course, their use of "wild ducks" made me think of the two geese (red-giant Betelgeuse) who had performed the miraculous above the muddy Iowa River.

When we first moved to Stillwell, the new house had a basement filled with water. But they pumped it out and installed a sump-pump to keep it dry. Within days, we had hung paintings on the walls and bought furnishings. We caught two mice. These were the two most unusual mice I had ever seen; they were blue with white chests. I always thought we had caught Douglas Adams's "Two mice who'd created the universe."

My manager at IBM set up a meeting with the vice-presidents of TWA, with me, where I was to explain to them how the systems engineers envisioned replacing the 360 mainframes with their new 370—virtual storage—mainframes—without interrupting the real-time PARS system. I thought this was a heavy lift for a trainee. But, despite my doubts, I thought about all I knew about this hardware upgrade. What this millions of dollars conversion entailed was replacing two 360 mainframes that were duplexed—connected together by an umbilical that could "mirror" the primary's function, so that the secondary could take over if a problem occurred in the primary. I drew up a flip-chart with drawings of an octopus sitting in the middle of four mainframes—the two running 360s and the new 370s—where the octopus's tentacles represented the communications channels between these four—now quadra-plexed systems—tentacles moving during the test phases and switch over, mirroring PARS between the original two, the installed new system and its mirrored mainframes. The original system running real-time, as the new system was installed and tested, and then switched over—octopus legs dancing—between old and new. The TWA executives had sat quietly, semi-astonished by the twenty-eight-year-old Black man, using cartoons to convince them that this could all make sense—keeping millions of records, segments of flight, billing—smoothly functioning while converting from old to new. It was like having the passengers change airplanes while in flight. They seemed to buy into the idea.

Carol surprised me with a new dog. I was still smarting from the loss of Inigo but knew that she was testing my resolve to love another creature (and protect it) before having a child. The puppy was a high-strung white and honey, fringed, Irish Setter we named Mizmoon. We had named her that because we were sympathetic with the Symbionese Liberation Army's chief theoretician Patricia Soltysik, killed by police in a 1974 shootout. That the

United States needed liberation by an actual guerrilla army—the SLA—had electrified the country's leftists.

I continued as a trainee at IBM, taking multi-week training sessions in technical topics like TCP/IP (transmission control protocol/ internet protocol) at IBM One in Chicago. Walking across the river, looking up at the skyscrapers reflected in the gray water—that was a different color every time I looked at it—thinking of Carlos Castaneda's *A Yaqui Way of Knowledge*—seeing the river with the eye that saw spherical waves, then the eye that saw transverse waves. I met IBM's telecommunications instructor, Rich Williger—a smart young guy who was attuned to the countercultural struggle with the establishment. He handed out a test (a mock test) with questions requiring wit, sophistication, and a divergent intelligence. Questions like, "What is information entropy?" When I returned to Kansas City, I typed out answers to his questions, had Carol correct the spelling and grammar, and mailed it to him. He reported back to my manager that the answers were "profound." Although I was still smoking doobies—far more potent than the ditch weed I had smoked in Iowa—IBM did not appear to care; I was a *wild duck*.

P. D. Ouspensky thought our reality—Plato's shadows in the cave—were the shadows of seventeenth dimensional objects. This reality—DeSitter Space—was the non-conformal holographic projection from higher dimensional anti-DeSitter space. Further Ouspensky's four levels of consciousness—unconsciousness, pre-consciousness, consciousness, and cosmic consciousness—were the concentric layers of the onion that I had been trying to awaken to. Cosmic consciousness was a higher mental state where a person was continually aware of the turning of the galaxy, expansion of the universe, and the void behind the void. Every thought, word, breath, was accompanied by this awareness—it crowded out the vainglorious, self-centered arrogances of "me." Of me and the comforts of the IBM paychecks.

I was becoming increasing aware of physical semiotics (the language things spoke)—Physical Graffiti—and wrote a treatise on this titled *Three Birds*. In our little house in Stillwell, I often awakened and glanced out the window to see a red cardinal, which I took as a good sign. I looked for a cardinal every morning. And, as I tried to maintain Ouspensky's cosmic consciousness, the cardinal reminded me to check the second hand on my watch—looking for the synchronization of being on the "12"—after seeing the cardinal. I was trying to use these physical semiotic signs to contact the cosmic. Any time I saw three birds, I rethought the entire argument concerning mechanistic determinism. I trained myself to be witness to these sequences, thinking if I could find the right sequence of signs—like the first of a series of cosmic dominoes knocking down the entire chain one after another—I could at last understand, derive meaning, discern the void beyond the void; the many-to-one onto mapping from the anti-DeSitter universe to the lower-dimensional universe I inhabited. I looked at the inscription on the front porch lights of our house in Stillwell—*Ad Astra per Ad Aspera*—"To the stars by difficulty"—motto of the state of Kansas, and on the logo of Pall Mall Cigarettes.

Knowing I was failing at IBM, one Friday I had a meeting scheduled with my manager. He had charged his trainees with doing "magic." IBM marketing managers used all kinds of tactics to motivate their trainees. I did not want to do a trick. I wanted to show him real magic—the magic of the spheres. He told us that the "magic" should use silver dollars. I went to the bank and got twenty silver dollars. I pondered the "trick," I would perform. I smoked filterless cigarettes—Camels and Pall Malls—for days trying to figure out how I could use these silver dollars to astound—vulgar Latin verb *extonāre, which literally meant something like "leave someone thunderstruck" (it was formed from the Latin verb *tonāre* "thunder")—this *Dick Berner*. And somehow, I do not know how, when I asked him to give me a twenty-dollar bill, the twenty silver dollars appeared in his jacket pocket. Sleight of hand? Did I put them there earlier in the day? Or was it real magic? He did not know and I did not know. At that exact moment, I decided to quit my job as a computer salesman!!!

But before I could begin my journey as an unemployable bohemian hipster, I had a few major life-altering events to attend to. First, my father died in Detroit's Ford Hospital. I had arrived the night before but decided to wait until morning to see him. Still dressed in my IBM three-piece black pinstriped suit, I traveled back to Houston for his burial, where I listened to his brother, Joe, tell me things about Gus and my mother that I did not want to hear. Gus was interred in Egypt, Texas where he had been born. When Gus died, I was so saddened I was unable to shed tears. When he died, Carol was pregnant with our first child. I quit IBM, a baby coming, and Carol was working for the US Social Security Administration in Kansas City. I was a maniac.

NOTES

1. Bob Dylan, *Tarantula* (New York: Scribner, 2004); Dylan Thomas, *Portrait of the Artist as a Young Dog* (New York: New Directions Publishing, 1968); Herbert Marcuse, *One-Dimensional Man: Studies in the Ideology of Advanced Industrial Society*, 2nd ed. (Boston: Beacon Press, 1991); Thomas L. Swihart, *Astrophysics and Stellar Astronomy* (New York: John Wiley, 1968).

2. Baba Ram Dass, *Be Here Now* (San Cristobal, NM: Lama Foundation, 1971), 14; emphasis in the original.

3. Steely Dan, "Reelin' in the Years," *Can't Buy a Thrill* (album) (Los Angeles: ABC Records, 1972).

4. Richard A. Jones, *Blackland* (Austin, TX: Atmosphere Press, 2021).

5. Jon Anderson, Steve Howe, and Chris Squire, "Starship Trooper: Part 1, Life Seeker," *The Yes Album* (album) (London: Advision, Fitzrovia, 1971).

6. Cat Stevens, "On the Road To Find Out," *Tea For the Tillerman* (album) (Hollywood CA: A&M Records, 1970).

7. Greg Lake, "From the Beginning," *Emerson, Lake & Palmer* (album) (New York: Cotillion Records, Atlantic Records, 1972).

8. Albert Camus, *Lyrical and Critical Essays* (New York: Vintage Books, 1970).

9. Gary Blackman, Grace Slick, Marty Balin, and Paul Kanter, "Hijack," *Blows Against the Empire* (album) (Hollywood, CA: RCA Victor, 1970).

10. John Bonham, et. al., "The Crunge," *House of the Holy* (album) (Headley, UK: Headley Grange, 1973).

11. Ken Kesey, *One Flew Over the Cuckoo's Nest* (New York: Signet, 1963).

12. Noor Hindi, "Against Death," *TriQuarterly* 159 (January 15, 2021), https://www.triquarterly.org/issues/issue-159/against-death (accessed August 19, 2023).

13. Theodore Dreiser, *An American Tragedy* (New York: Heritage Press, 1954).

14. Herbert Marcuse, *Eros and Civilization: A Philosophical Inquiry into Freud*, 2nd ed. (Oxfordshire: Routledge, 1987).

15. P. D. Ouspensky, *In Search of the Miraculous*: *Fragments of an Unknown Teaching* (New York: Harper Paperbacks, 2001); and Ouspensky, *Tertium Organum, or the Third Cannon of Thought and a Key to the Enigmas of the World* (Whitefish, MT: Kessinger Publishing, 1998)

16. Anil Ananthaswamy, "Is Our Universe a Hologram? Physicists Debate Famous Idea on Its 25th Anniversary," *Scientific American*, November 30, 2022, https://www.scientificamerican.com/article/is-our-universe-a-hologram-physicists-debate-famous-idea-on-its-25th-anniversary/ (accessed August 12, 2023).

Chapter 10

Laughing the Face of a New Sun, 1975–1982

Graham, our son, was born on a bright Saturday morning, August 30, 1975. We had prepared for him by taking Lamaze classes, and at age thirty, I was ready for a family. In the delivery suite, a mirror had been interposed to reflect the birth—it is all done with smoke and mirrors—and to keep me out of the way of the doctor and nurses. As I stood at Carol's head, trying to encourage her to breathe—"cleansing breaths"—as the baby's head started to crown, the obstetrician performed an episiotomy to give the baby's head more room. I did not know about this procedure and swooned. As the birth continued, and Carol's face contorted with pain and effort, she looked at me, her periwinkle blue eyes flitting about, and winked at me, as if to say, "It looks bad, but I got this." It was that wink that convinced me that she loved me; that I needed to make profound changes in my life, for her, and for our baby boy. At the moment of the wink, I vowed that I would always not only remember it, but that when I was on my death-bed, tubes and monitors, with her seated at my side, pondering her loss and my suffering, I would look her in her eyes and return the wink.

I was elated when Graham Matthew was born in Shawnee Mission Hospital. After considering a name that would dignify the common name "Jones," we had agreed on "Graham" ("of the gray house") as much from its etymology as from Graham Nash of Crosby, Nash, Stills, and Young. I believe that the name of the "Galloping Gourmet," Graham Kerr, who was popular at the time, also weighed on the choice. I had never met a Black man named Graham. His middle name was for the Book of Matthew, whose wisdom—beyond my atheism—echoes across the heathen centuries. Anyway, here he was, and we were taking him home to Stillwell, Kansas.

Thinking back to that time, although I had left their employ, IBM had paid for the hospital expenses, as they had explained, "He was conceived while I worked for them." Now, unemployed, with a new "bouncing baby boy," I buckled down to become a better man. I stopped using marijuana, tried once again to rekindle my interests in writing and in painting. I was to use the title of one of Denise Levertov's books of poetry—*Relearning the Alphabet*—as the leitmotif for the new stage in my life.[1] For, the lithium, disappointment of being a computer salesman, and flunking out of the University of Iowa, had made me doubt my abilities. I was also still stinging from the Teacher Corps sensitivity trainer's judgement of my glibness—shallowness—all verbal bluster sans in-depth understanding—just a show of words; words I no longer understood—words that no longer "did work."

In relearning the alphabet, and how to read, I had started with simple things like Richard Brautigan's *Willard and His Bowling Trophies*, Donald Barthelme's *The Dead Father*, and Kurt Vonnegut's *Breakfast of Champions*.[2] Old trout fishing Brautigan's early postmodern nonsense kept me from taking myself too seriously. Brautigan was the American "Un-writer," holding up literary pretenses and commercial publishing, for the nonsense they were. He was the hippie ür-writer. *Snow White's* Barthelme, dragging the corpse of the dead father, help me begin to come to terms, with the passing of Gus.[3] And Vonnegut's (curt and from the gut) Kilgore (killing and gore) Trout (fishing in America) advanced my thinking on free-will, mental illness, and "bad-chemicals in the bloodstream."[4]

I was also trying to relearn mathematics. I had to forget the satisfactions of solving triple and double-integrals—known solutions in the backs of the books "solutions for selected exercises"—to delve into my own creative ideas about numbers. Dreaming of spherical and ellipsoidal integrals, and how an expanding universe had planes of tangency—I reached for Kaluza-Kline space (fifth-dimensional geometry)—in trying to contact the aliens (to take Carol, Graham, and me to Vonnegut's Tralfamadore). For, I did not think this world was fit for Graham. If I were to live here, I had several alternatives; change it into a better place, leave it behind, find a hiding place.

On the day he was born, I was reading Robert M. Pirsig's *Zen and the Art of Motorcycle Maintenance*.[5] I was so excited about my son's birth, I had made a long-distance call to my old friend William "Skip" Seeley, from the US Air Force, and amazed to hear he was also reading *Zen and the Art of Motorcycle Maintenance*. He was at a different place in his life. He had sold all his music albums, bought an old school bus, separated from his wife and two children, seeking his own meaning and understanding.

As it was, I vowed when we first brought him home, that I would give him something that had not been given me; I would never disappear from his childhood. I would stay with Carol and him no matter how vicious the winds of change would howl. So, writing this is *not* the story of how I became a writer. Writing this is not a *Bildungsroman*—a coming-of-age-story—but *Bildungsroman* as the "psychological and moral growth of my character."

This will not end in my fame, contribution to science or mathematics, tomes of erudite philosophy, or poetry like the stanzas that have moved me to try to imitate them.

Arthur C. Clarke's *2001: A Space Odyssey* had prepared me for the deep future—a Star Child. His *Childhood's End* had shown me the preternatural evolution of youth. Clarke had hypothesized orbiting communications satellites in the 1940s, and before the end of his life, bounced transmissions of his new novels to his publisher, from Sri Lanka where he lived—via geosynchronous satellite.[6] I deeply respected Arthur C. Clark's genius, so it was no shock to me—given the genius genes in Carol's family—that my son was hugely gifted, like the preternatural genius babies in *Childhood's End*. I saw early on, while holding him, changing his diapers, giving him a bath that he could manifest his will like the Martians in Ray Bradbury's *Martian Chronicles*.[7] Later in life, I would read many things about the relationships between fathers and sons. In wanting the "perfect human being" to be my son, I knew he would eventually meet me—and replace me—in the "Circular Ruins," the short story by Jorge Luis Borges.

> For a moment, he thought of taking refuge in the water, but then he understood that death was coming to crown his old age and absolve him from his labors. He walked toward the sheets of flame. They did not bite his flesh, they caressed him and flooded him without heat or combustion. With relief, with humiliation, with terror, he understood that he also was an illusion, that someone else was dreaming him.[8]

"The child is father of the man." Wordsworth's poem "My Heart Leaps Up," was my hope that Graham would be the realization of my childish awe for the universe in becoming *my* father.[9] Reading Ivan Turgenev's *Fathers and Sons* to get insights into this relationship when he was a boy, and then again twenty-five years later when he became a man.[10]

My heart leapt up! As I was a "boy scientist," who had taken his body as an experimental laboratory, I would nurture my son to forge on past the limits imposed by the ordinary. I would show him the extraordinary, in a way so subtle, that when the time came, we would meet again in the circular ruins as equals. But for now, there was the inevitability of soiled diapers, senseless babble, sleepless nights, and the endless struggles for survival in an ineffable economic (and racist) system of dominance and subordination. Indubitably, I longed for intellectual freedom, artistic creation, and poetic expression.

I created a hard-edged, chromatic, rainbow, art object made by pouring acrylic paint through plastic tubes. It was a highly original piece—museum quality. But then again, my creative impulses were largely given over to writing. During this time, still changing Graham's diapers, feeling desperate that the world was too brutal and corrupt (and dangerous—no Eden)—while Carol had returned to work at Social Security—I wrote *Laughing in the Face of a New Sun*.[11] It was a pun because I really wanted to write *Son*. I took the few short stories I had published in *Cruel Sister*—the Des Moines' underground newspaper—and fleshed them out with a few absurd (Edward Albee, Donald Barthelme, William S. Burroughs) short story essays. It was my magnum opus. Laughing in the face of my new son, I would take him away from American Babylon, and show him how human beings—the high animal—ought to live with beauty, dignity, and peace; then we would bring the rest of them into the circular ruins. I sent the manuscript to Random House in New York, hopeful that this would be my entrée to a better life.

I struggled with a point of view on educating my son. My first sentiment was the discipline I had experienced in SAC—by the numbers—strict adherence to the rules. But, given my breakdown, I knew that to try to break his spirit with too much discipline, would be to hobble him in the prison of my expectations; a jail from which he would escape. So, I stimulated him—painting crude canvases with him in a backpack peeking over my shoulder. Wanting him to feel the rhythms of great writing, reading essays from Albert Camus to him while he was just beginning to form words. Wiring up little LED lights to attach to his crib with push buttons beneath them that did not light up when he pushed the button below the light. The light would come on under a different light—anti-Skinnerian training. I did not want him to be a linear thinker—a key word follower—given the input words, his mind following predictable paths (what the hippies had called mind-control). If I say x, you will automatically think y—the mind being a function $f(x)$, where x is mind and inputs to that mind yields predictable reactions y = socially controlled behavior.

Some of this thinking was predicated on reading Kurt Vonnegut's *Welcome to the Monkey House* and *Player Piano*.[12] There were geniuses hobbled for equality in the monkey house, and people who abhorred war so much they produced the Barnhouse effect (destroying sophisticated weapons by telekinesis). Unless opposed by the "Tribe" (the rainbow hippie tribe of revolutionary dissenters), the player piano's punched holes played the music of capitalist consumption, in a syncopated factory-like engineered society. Wanting to give Graham a taste of the freedom of the "tribe" I had found on Denny and Debbie's farm in Iowa, I wanted to escape into the rural hideouts America still had to offer.

Still marveling at how nobody I met ever talked about Roche limits, Chandrasekar's limit, Arp objects, Gold effects, gravitational red-shifts, galaxy's Z numbers, or Aleph-one, I slogged on pondering these ideas in the interstices between being ignored and the practicalities of survival. The people around me seemed asleep, paralyzed, automata convinced of their superiority. They were lazy (did not read anything substantive), self-indulgent (only concerned with their pleasures), vainglorious (self-satisfied in their superiority), and judgmental (assuming they were unjudged). I had read Emanuel Swedenborg's *Heaven and Hell*. This book talked about heaven as being in another neighborhood in the city you lived in, and if unenlightened, hell your own neighborhood. Swedenborg appeared to espouse the simultaneous existence of heaven and hell—a concomitantly coterminous multiverse—where God was the architect, landlord, and mortgage holder (and he knew his servants).[13] But what had held me spellbound, I had read in the introductory remarks to *Heaven and Hell* about a contest between *a man* and God—where everything the man thought was anticipated and countered by God—like a chess match. The arrogant man, who thought he was superior to God, was forked (a chess strategy) at every move, God always playing the game an infinite number of moves ahead of the man who though he could outthink God.

Having been designated as a shallow thinker—"glib" as the Teacher Corps sensitivity trainer had adjudged—I would have to think faster than God; think in the interstices, when God was busy elsewhere. Like the IBM 370 manuals I read in Kansas City, describing virtual memory techniques, "Cycle Steal," where the *fetch-process-put* cycle could be interleaved with other CPU functions to create a larger memory workspace, I needed to develop thinking in the gaps (like God-in-the-gaps)—interstitial thought—faster than the speed of light—to play chess with God. And I knew I would still lose. Moving at the speed of light stopped time. Humm baby!

But in the, if you love it, it will be taken from you—whether "it" be baseball, astronomy, or writing—was it still *possible* that if you love it, it will love you back? Somewhere, the Norwegian writer Gunnhild Øyehaug observes, and I paraphrase, writing is an attempt to stop the constant flow of the difficult, to hold time still, and to observe it. Even Yahweh knew, "In the beginning was the word" (John 1:1) to hold it still—the universe of light—to make change his own destiny; observe. Was it possible my son might love me back? Was it possible Carol might love me back? Was it possible the Sun might love me back? If I loved writing, might it write me back? The Universe? Nature? God, herself?

In order to find out, I had to make of myself a phenomenon, in order to posit a noumenon for that phenomenon, from which I might know the void beyond the void. Graham was the experiment derived from myself as an experiment. Graham—the book of Matthew 6:27–27—"Look at the birds of the air / they do not sow or reap or store away in barns / and yet your heavenly Father feeds them. Are you not much more valuable than they?" One of my fondest memories of the many pearls of wisdom that issued from the mouth of this babe (hum babe) was "Walking birds and flying birds." He thought they were of a different kind, a different species. I had never thought of birds in this manner and wondered when he had surmised that they were distinct aspects of the same thing. "His eye is on the sparrow." Perhaps while God's eye was on the sparrow, I could sneak a thought pass his scrutiny, thinking faster—in the interstices—than the speed of light.

I had read a book by Peter S. Stevens, titled *Patterns in Nature*. This is a book on philomorphology—the love of form—and the mathematical recursions in nature. The book revels in the repeated patterns Nature employs—branching in trees, blood vessels, lightning, rivers—in holons (different hierarchies); the angle between branches a function of the ratios of their diameters.[14] So, I am Akhenaten—the ancient Egyptian Pharaoh—worshiping Ra, the Sun god. Akhenaten, the first true monotheist, enraptured, in love with the Sun—filled with it. And I am rocking in an old chair Carol reupholstered, with the bright Kansas sun peeking through the window, and I am blinking my eyes synchronously (perhaps tardive dyskinesia) with the rocking—the red retinal after images alternating with the bright photosphere—and I sought lovingly for a communication with that yon star. Knowing the photons took millions of years—from the Sun's center—via radiative transport—to get to the service to impinge on my retina—little more than stretched mud with tendrils of moss—to reflect upon itself. God playing hide-and-seek with herself. The Sun seeing itself in the self it had pumped up with its photonic energy for five billion years—to ken—as kin; projected back in a subtle rainbow shift of my eyelashes as gratings. Contact. Transformed. I closed my eyes trying to read the red and coronal violet retinal after images, for sense, for direction: fell to my knees in awe, trying to beat God to the counterpunch—nonsense on stilts, and heard Graham awakening in his crib. I knew I had to do better—for him, for Carol.

I am standing at the sink cutting a ripe yellow banana for my cereal. As I slice the yellow, sun like disks—hey Ra, Akhenaten—I notice the face in the round segments. It is the face of the sun with fiery horns and a down-turned grimace, as if in warning me that the Sun-God is angry at the life-forms she hath birthed. Philomorphologically, I take this warning as I continue slicing—the face repeating itself, as the little black seed eyes rotate from place to place on the demonical face. I wanted a sun that was laughing, turning the banana around the other way to make the mouth turn upward, to no avail, as the warning is clear. In my writings I mused that "we needed to alter the sick sun's spectrum by rocketing in vitamins—more potassium and calcium—which would change the quality of the light to make a miscreant mankind, kind." Then I could raise my son, like Kuta Kinte (from, Alex Haley's *Roots*) up to the heavens, in saluting the majesty of the cosmos.[15]

I longed to hear someone around me use the word "cosmos." I wanted to hear "cosmological." All I seemed to hear was practical discourse concerning money. Thinking of the sliced banana, I wanted to turn that frown up-side-down. I wanted a happy sun! I received a rejection letter for *Laughing in the Face of a New Sun* from Random House's editor Toni Morrison.

I did not know Toni Morrison from Adam in 1975. I took my manuscript to the University of Missouri at Kansas City (UMKC) when I went to meet with poet David Ray. David Ray was the ex-husband of Ruth Ray, the Urban Planner, who I worked with in the Iowa Office of Economic Opportunity, when I was the Regional Head Start Coordinator. I had sat in her office, a few years earlier and talked to her about my writing poetry, when she suggested I should meet her ex-husband David, who was a poet. I walked into the white two-storied house on the corner that served as the offices of *New Letters*.

David Ray was the "dustbowl poet," renowned for his carefully crafted poems, including *X Rays*, and the poem "Dragging the Main."[16] Sitting behind his desk in black horn-rimmed glasses, he was serious and chatted with me about writing. Within the first few weeks of our acquaintance, he handed me a handful of newly published poetry volumes, asking me to write reviews for publication in *New Letters*. These reviews were to become my first contributions to this highly regarded little magazine. David Ray also selected a short story ("The Statue") and six of my poems ("Six Car Poems") for publication in *New Letters*.

Within weeks, the dustbowl poet had invited Carol and me to dinner, where we were warmly received by his wife Judy. David invited me to one of his English classes at UMKC, where I spoke for a few minutes about the unknown labels of objects surrounding us—a pre-Wittgensteinianism I would come to understand only much later—with Graham peeking over my shoulder in a back carrier.

Carol had returned to work at the Social Security Administration in Kansas City. With the help of David Ray, I was hired to teach courses in creative writing and astronomy at Loretto Academy—a private school. I would leave Graham with his babysitter—Marty McConnell—and teach poetry, followed by astronomy, to middle schoolers. In the creative writing course, I required students to submit their work to little literary magazines. To my amazement (and the students and their parents), some of these poems were accepted for publication. The class also produced (and printed) a collection of poems titled "The Chrysalid." Astronomy for ninth graders proved a serious challenge, as their mathematical skills were limited. So, I retreated to the lessons I had learned in Dr. Maxwell's Descriptive Astronomy courses I had taken at Howard; from the inside out. Planets, the sun, the galaxy, the local group of galaxies, superclusters. I taught them OBAFGKMN ("Oh Be A Fine Girl Kiss Me Now")—the Harvard spectral sequence of star types. I even invited a representative from MUFON (Mutual UFO Network) to speak to the class about the possibilities of extra-terrestrial life. I only taught at Loretto Academy for one semester; yet it sustained me.

Luxuriating in reading Vonnegut, Ouspensky, and Burroughs, and struggling to make money as a furniture mover, itinerant teacher, poorly paid poet (*New Letters* had paid me fifty dollars for my writing), David Ray had shared the check he had received from *The New Yorker* for a poem he had written inspired by a story I had told him. The poem was titled "Hammering." David was a true bard with an advanced degree from the University of Chicago—who would go on to win two William Carlos Williams awards—and a tenured professor of English who had been implicated in the HUAC (House Un-American Activities Committee) in the 1950s. The dustbowl poet was also orphaned by his family in the harsh Oklahoma 1930s depression. In opposing the Vietnamese war, David, along with the poet Robert Bly, had organized "Poets Against the War." By rights, David was paranoid that the FBI watched him. But he was also influenced by his Quaker sensibilities of unvitiated righteousness. He played a humungous role in moving my own life as a poet from dilettante to "serious" little scribbler.

I told him a story about the "revolution of subtlety," where little hand signals (gestures of comradeship—signs and counter signs) could be offered in opposition to miscreant empires of hate. An upgrade to the peace sign, a waggle, a sign, an outwitting the managers of information. I told him that in two-way traffic, I always mimicked the driver passing me, to the driver following. So, if the passing driver was a two-handed "ten and two" steering wheel holder, I would rearrange my hands to that position to signal the driver behind the car in front of him. Then quickly readjust my hands and body to the posture of the second car and so on, until I imagined a chain of "information" (cybernetic control information) would travel unknowable distances (across untold numbers of vehicles). This was a communication strategy that—if it became a ludic game (game theory)—could (when discovered by others) be played—duplexed—sending comportment (bodily configurations) signals in both directions on two-lane highways. When I suspected other drivers were onto it, playing the same game, I would know the revolution of subtlety had begun. David listened to my explanation as I ate my lunch. I went back to pounding the bright ten-penny nails into the shoddy construction of the carport I was building for him. He wrote "Hammering," sent it to *The New Yorker*, and they published it (after telephoning him to fact check—"Yes, there really was a Negro who thought this").

HAMMERING

His ultimate
contribution
to the world
he decided
hammering it
in would be not
only the nail
but when driving
the yellow car
moving his right
clenched fist
from steering
to his ear
a subtle
wave which the next
driver seeing him
barreling down
the expressway
would ape
unconsciously
thus passing
the signal on
until soon
through concrete
arteries of
the republic
upon corpuscles
of rubber his wave
would reach
California
and be lost
in the sea
like a smile
offered to strangers
such a life's work
being harmless
he opined
and giving the
universe
something to
detect when it
decides to
get sensitive
to small and exquisite

gestures[17]

Breathtaking *tour de force*! Ray had poetically conveyed my initial posit in the *Revolution of Subtlety*. A revolution so understated, indirect, restrained, that only a star, a universe, or God would notice. It was my C3—command, control, and communicate—structure that would save mankind from itself—with the help of the Sun (Hey Ra)—and return us all to the heavens, as we Hijacked the Starship. Communicate (subtly), control (discipline), and command (by courageousness). I wanted to foment a paradigm shift in human sensibility guided by a bold outrageousness. I wanted to be the mouse that roared, the David that slew Goliath, the one photon of light that would illuminate the cosmic darkness. And while it was thought my *hammering* was on nails, or boards, I was hammering in the pistoning electrons jumping up and down in their energy-levels, control information from the loving star's heart twisting into my retinal matrix—from the beginning—stumbling like a rolling stone in gravity's prison—*determined* (mechanistically and motivationally)—summing the infinitesimals like an integral. Could I make a "small and exquisite gesture"—a quantum gesture—the first true movement in the history of the Milky Way galaxy—bereft of malice and vainglorious pretense—to initiate a cascade (dominoes falling in a line) effect that would lead us to freedom. As the Jefferson Airplane had put it in their 1970 album *Blows Against the Empire*,[18] mankind was trying to escape from its "cage." Looking at the crystalline eyes of Grace Slick, I could see the unselfconsciousness—the almost mechanical doll-like determination—"Go ride the music!" Knowing that I only had C3, and that my enemies had C4—C3 plus computers—I would have to outsmart not only God by thinking in the gaps, but also Mammon, thinking between the computer cycles—cycle steal (cycle stealing is a technique for memory sharing whereby a memory may serve two autonomous masters and in effect provide service to each simultaneously).

I had invited total strangers to dinner at our little house in Stillwell, Kansas, to talk about the revolution of subtlety. Restless, anxious, paranoid—sitting up all night with my Koss headphones listening to the FM rock station. I started calling the station and letting it ring once every time they played a certain song ("Miracles" by Jefferson Starship). I did this for months, then when they played another song ("Picking Up the Pieces" by AWB), I do the same thing, hoping they would make the inference and play the two songs back-to-back—which, given time they did. Then I called and talked to the night DJ, John Bridges, a young Black guy, and invited him and a friend to dinner. When they came, I discussed the revolution of subtlety—it is principles and strategies—and told him that we could never meet in person again—and that I would send him a tape in a few weeks. In this way, continuing the C3 strategy, I had "hijacked" a radio station, and left no trace. The audiotape

I sent John Bridges included the "recognition sign" for the revolution of subtlety. I discussed with him and his girlfriend, that it would take years (it not decades, if not a lifetime) before the forces of darkness figured all of this out. And in an attempt to figure it all out, they would try to get the four of us to sell each other out (what I called "Shootout at the Fantasy Factory"). But I assured John Bridges ("Where's that damned bridge?") that a conspiracy against the United States's powers that be, could be won by discipline. The FM rock stations of the United States, and the genius of musicians, would help create a mythopoetic legend that would end in all of us "Laughing in the Face of a New Sun." ("Laughter? You remember laughter?")

Regardless, I played softball—most often left field—for three different teams while we lived in Kansas. Before leaving IBM, I played for their team. I played for the Social Security team from the office downtown where Carol worked. I played for a Kansas City team in a league where we played in tournaments on weekends. As a left fielder, with an accurate and strong arm, I routinely threw out runners at second base trying to stretch singles into doubles. I was a fair hitter who occasionally hit a home run but was mostly a singles and doubles hitter. I was a good teammate, always trying to be a shipmate—working on a "wooden ship"—where unless we all worked together, we would all perish. Slowed in my reactions by the Lithium Carbonate—I played through the fog—"boy scientist" experimenting with gravity—the white sphere spinning in the Sun—time stopped as it waited to come down—like Robert A. Heinlein's *Stranger in a Strange Land*—living and grokking orbital mechanics.[19]

White people and the powers that be had made me mad. Like Captain Ahab in Herman Melville's *Moby-Dick*, "I am madness maddened! . . . come and see if you can swerve me . . . ye cannot swerve me . . . The path to my fixed purpose is laid with iron rails, whereon my soul is grooved to run."[20] With my dog Mizmoon, I had liked living in Stillwell, listening to and attending the Kansas City Royals baseball games at Kaufman Stadium. I was witness to the rookie season of the incomparable George Brett. Listening on radio to Brett (3rd base), White (2nd base), Patek (short stop), Mayberry (1st base), Porter (catcher), Cowens (right field), Otis (center field), MaCrae (left field), and pitchers Splittorff and Leonard, play gave meaning to my life in Kansas.

My brother Robert appeared in the driveway of our little house on the prairie driving a brand-new, green Corvette. After the US Air Force, he had worked briefly for the US National Security Agency (NSA) as a Chinese translator. Observing my struggle for survival, my brother invited me to move to Washington, DC; he would give me a job at his graphic art business, Portfolio. With nothing to lose, and everything to gain, I put my little brown house up for sale. It sold quickly without returning much equity. Carol and Graham flew to Washington, while I drove a U-Haul truck with our household goods, along with Mizmoon. The drive from Stillwell, Kansas to Oxon Hill, Maryland (where Bob lived) was a study in the progress of the revolution, of subtlety.

Towing my yellow Volkswagen, the fourteen-foot U-Haul truck broke down before I reached Columbia, Missouri. As I waited in the cab with Mizmoon, while a repair truck came out on the highway to replace the alternator, I smoked and relived the three years we had lived in Kansas. Back on my way after hours of delay, I drove on East I-70, listening to the Eagle's "Hotel California"—the loony bin—Manfred Mann's "Blinded by the Light," and the Brothers Johnson's "Strawberry Letter 23"—the code for the revolution—the number twenty-three. Reminding me of the lyrics from "Wooden Ships," about smiling and understanding,[21] to smile and give me hand signals for two-three. Reaching to adjust the rear view mirror, knowing that from the angle of other drivers it was a "Black Power" salute.

Tooling on—"Mr. Natural" trucking, foreshortened booted-foot forward—across America in the U-Haul truck, Mizmoon at my side, I experienced the most splendid sunset I had ever witnessed. The Sun—Hey Ra!—had lowered behind me in an orange brilliance that made me stop the truck beside the highway and look back—the "gateway to the west arch" near St. Louis gleaming—to see the elliptical star's last light. And then on, thinking of William S. Burrough's book *Exterminator!* and the "Do Easy Principle." Burroughs asks "How you gonna pilot a starship, if you can't keep your room clean?"[22] "Do Easy"—D. E.—was the discipline—everything in "flow," automatic, easy because of repetition, organization, discipline. Studying the meaning of the letters and numbers of the infinite array of license plates reflected on the cars and trucks in front of me (a common monomaniacal preoccupation of the delusional), looking for "JA 23" or "RA 657" and combinations of multiples of 23, transpositions of letters with meanings that intersected songs on the radio or transient thoughts passing in mind. I was looking for communications from the universe of objects—physical semiosis—in living the integral—summing—apperceiving, tripping, returning home.

After two harrowing days of little sleep—pulling into the rest stops to walk Mizmoon and sleep a few tortured hours—I was in western Pennsylvania, where I had a flat tire. Limping into a truck stop, I asked the mechanic if he could fix the tire or give me a replacement. He checked inventory and made a few phone calls. I telephone Carol from a payphone. The mechanic came back and told me, they would have to ship a tire from another location, and that I should expect it to take eighteen to twenty-four hours for the tire to arrive. Being that it was truck stop, with eighteen-wheel semis, there was a constant rumbling of the big-rigs refueling or getting oil changes or other maintenance. It was noisy and kinetic, all a sleep deprived manic-depressive needed. Napping in the cab of the truck, while I awaited the replacement tire, I could not rent a motel room because of Mizmoon, whose presence was a kind of sentinel—watchman (dog) warning strangers to keep their distance. Mizmoon as a quiet kind of threat, her name saying it all—the "mizzen"—the misty dark side of the moon. She was a big, white and honey, feathered companion—dog of a Negro—who like Monté (of the Allegheny Mountain)—knew how to silently protect me. Like my first dog "Skip," who had skipped out on me (ran away); Monté (washed away); Inigo (disappeared in Iowa): now Mizmoon (of the Symbionese Liberation Army)—dog (god spelled backward)—the symbol of the revolution, leashed and looking for recognition signs.

Sleeping in starts, I waited for eighteen hours. Until, lo, a young white man in his early twenties, in a flannel shirt and jeans, said he had the tire. He told me to sit, relax, and watch. He "smiled at me." His movements and actions were precise, disciplined, and displayed the intent necessary to pull off the revolution of subtlety. He acted as if, from the beginning of the universe, his sole purpose had been to replace the back tire of the U-Haul truck and get me back on my way—"to the stars by way of difficulty"—air-hammering the lug nuts back into place and giving me the receipt. He was a soldier, on the road, a servant, a savant, congeries of atoms swerving in the void, who knew—staring into the void—that I was Bodhisattva on highways to other worlds. Like the Led Zeppelin song, "No Quarter," I had interpreted for the "head shrinkers" in Iowa City—"where's that bridge"—Einstein-Rosen bridge—these interstate highways being wormholes to the infinite worlds. And I was going "home" to one of them.

Hallucinating with fatigue after the thousand-mile drive, rocking on the concrete with the yellow VW towed behind me, within range of my brother's house, I stopped to telephone Carol, as I staggered around the rest stop, Mizmoon sniffing the humid and lush east coast air. They wanted me to stop and sleep for a night, but I was determined to finish the trip. Following the prompts of license plate messages, hand signals à la "Hammering," sluggish from the Lithium Carbonate, thinking faster than God, cycling through the fetch-process-put "Cycle-steal," I lumbered into Oxon Hill, Maryland like an alien star cruiser just off the closest wormhole Einstein-Rosen Bridge. After a night's sleep, Carol and I were looking for houses to rent. And we found one—a spacious neo-colonial—owned by a military officer not far from my brother's house. Graham, now two years old—a fine lad—had his own room, and I had a basement with a bar, fireplace, and a quiet room to write.

Settling into Oxon Hill—far enough away from my old DC haunts and temptations—I made a conscious effort to steer clear of my "prior known associates" and the trouble I knew they would bring. I started work at Robert's "Portfolio" graphic art business in "Old Town," Alexandria. The business had about eight employees—many freelancers and part-time—in a routine that consisted of my brother calling me and telling me when I was needed. As such, I was a freelancer working at his biding. On morning I went into Portfolio with an attitude. I was going to outwork everyone there—taping up the hundreds of "viewgraphs" faster than was humanly possible. My brother, my "supervisor," objected to the slapdash way I was taping the transparencies, and I snapped at him. He fired me.

I had been writing a manuscript, "The Him." in the basement of the Oxon Hill rented house. Now, writing became my only *raison d'etre*—misunderstood artist in his garret—pounding the keys—hammering—suffering beneath the burden of my insanity—failing my wife and son, yet again. Mizmoon had run afoul of the neighbors, who had threatened to "shoot her" if she rummaged through their trash again. So, I had to rig up a guy wire with turnbuckles to keep it taunt, to clip her to; to which she chaffed, running back and forth, confined to the short run. Like me, Mizmoon was on a restricted leash. Unemployed, yet again, and needing money, Carol applied to be reinstated in her Social Security job. She was given an assignment in Sioux City, Iowa; so back to Iowa. She flew out to Omaha with Graham. She then went to Sioux City, where she found and rented a hundred-year-old farmhouse situated in the middle corn and soybean fields. The house was a stately old wooden Iowa Gothic style farmhouse, thirty feet square, four rooms upstairs and four rooms downstairs. It was in a neglected state of repair, but I loved it! I started at once scrapping, painting, and wallpapering. Graham did not seem too excited about the abrupt change from the suburban life he had been accustomed to, crying himself to sleep in his new high-ceiling room.

The house, in Merrill, Iowa, was situated on a five-acre yard that also had a corn crib and implement storage shed used by Mr. Kerhberg, the landlord. Mr. Kerhberg, who owned and farmed the surrounding fields, lived a mile or so down the sectioned land—one-mile square grids—checker-boarded by dirt roads. We had rented this house for two-hundred dollars a month. I was thrilled, having found a way back to the "farm" of my imagination. The hippies had created an imaginary utopia, where the tribe returned to the land, growing their own vegetables, and trying to go back to the ways of their grandparents. And this was my immediate desire: to simplify, to get out of the city, to get back to nature. I embraced the "small is beautiful," simple is better than complex—appropriate technology—in de-commercializing my existence. I had room to think, to write, to create.

I was thirty-three years old when we moved into the farmhouse. In the attic, I found documents written in Old German. The original occupants had been German speaking missionaries, who had obtained the land from land grants provided by the US government. I found religious documents, as well as old McGuffey's readers for learning English. The house had two bricked up storm (or root) cellars, Carol, Graham, and I used on more than one occasion when the radio broadcast warned of imminent tornadoes.

Early months on what the Jefferson Airplane called "The Farm,"[23] was work and joy—painting, planting, nest building. Graham found newborn bunnies at the edge of the yard. We tried to save them with prepared formula and a little baby bottle Carol had, but we were unable to save them. Carol collected Monarch butterfly chrysalids from the side of the dirt road, put them in mason jars with milkweed pods and hatched them out. Graham was like the kid in Steven Spielberg film, *Close Encounter of the Third Kind*— enchanted—holding the newly emerged Monarchs on his finger, as they dried their wings, then flew away. We had a grove behind the house where Monarchs by the hundreds of thousands paused in the fall on their migratory journey to Mexico. And we had a garden with zucchini, tomatoes, corn, and pole-beans. But I had no illusions, as it was a *psychedelic* farm, where the ideals of the agrarian lifestyle were regnant, in the midst of actual working farms where millions of bushels of corn and soybeans were being produced to the horizons of our mere concepts.

While I settled uneasily into the role of a "househusband," Carol commuted to the Social Security Administration's offices in Sioux City. Her job was a "Benefits Authorizer." She interviewed and advised potential Social Security recipients. As Graham was barely three when we moved to the farm, I found myself bathing, dressing, and feeding him his daytime meals. Not to even mention trying to entertain him by reading to him, watching *Sesame Street* with him, playing with him. I found being a househusband exhausting, always trying to steal (cycle steal) a few moments during the day to do my own reading and writing. I discovered what most housewives with small children knew so well; care for the house and children is a full-time job with constant unremunerated overtime. I am watching *Sesame Street* with him one morning and hear "Come here, by way to me." The segment is that of a working sheepdog and his owner, quartering sheep, the dog running behind them and sending them toward the owner. The short video-clip reminded me that my true duty to my son was to impart to him the discipline I had inculcated in my life—corporeal, civil, military, self—without him consciously discerning what I was doing. I had to model it for him—performatively—knowing that it would emerge from him latter in his life like the Monarch butterflies fluttering from his fingertip alongside the roadsides of his Iowan memories; to fly away to newer stars in the Milky Way.

My happiness with the farm was so great, albeit weighted by my parental responsibilities, that I wanted to transcend my own hobbles (Lithium) and started to consciously miss (or avoid) taking it. When I would go a few days without it, I could immediately feel the mental fog lifting, my energy returning, my creativity blazing as I laughed in the face of each day's new sun. By summer, I examined an old water pump (and painted an acrylic canvas of it), traced our electric power to an idle windmill with weather vane (and painted it into my acrylic canvasses), and explored every recess of the used barns, unused chicken coop, unused barns in disarray. Some evenings, after cutting the four-acre yard with the little Sears lawn-tractor Carol had bought me, I wandered out to the edge of the western cornfield and reclined to watch the sunset (Hey Ra!). On a nonce, I even fell asleep as the gargantuan orb, compressed into its full, sagging, orange oblations winked out. The first summer was an idle—quiet, relaxed, introspective—Nature giving from all its cornucopia; delight, inspiration, and needed work. I took to wearing flannel shirts, bibbed-overalls, and work boots with laced up eyelets, like the Papa Sills of my North Carolina childhood.

Driven by manifold motivations; grandeur of the cosmos; inklings of mechanistic determinism; fear of abandonment by the things I loved— I railed against the burdens of my medication. I wanted to go beyond Ouspensky's cosmic conscious, to an even higher anti-deSitter (outside this four-dimensional manifold) consciousness. I wanted to transcend the highest reaches of human discipline for a cosmic discipline, where I trusted the universe enough to be guided, without doubt or question, to my next action— a quantum discipline. And I was a *watchman*—Argus—a thousand-eyed monster—*Argos* (Odysseus's dog)—waiting for a sign, a sound (*Nipper* on RCA Records); Mizmoon—white SLA dog—the dead earnest focus in Grace Slick's eyes.

Traumatized by being an isolated house husband, dejected by the rejection slip from Random House for "The Seed," I had stopped taking my 1,200 mg/day Lithium Carbonate. I was drinking scotch and smoking Pall Mall after Pall Mall (I had bought a case with ten packs). Pall Malls because: (1) Charles, my step-father had smoked them, (2) Kurt Vonnegut smoked them, (3) they had *In Hoc Signo Vinces* (in this sign you win) on the package, and I needed to *win*, and (4) Pall mall was a game, a kind of ground billiards played in the 1600s. I was thinking about the lyrics in Steely Dan's song "Don't Take Me Alive,"[24] about someone holded-up and resisting arrest.

In my mind, the carton of Pall Malls was the "dynamite" in the song. And I was using the cigarettes to stay awake so they could not "take me." The oil-burning furnace in the basement was balky—shutting down. It was the middle of a very, very cold night. Carol's mother, Barbara was there. I was concerned that the #2 fuel oil was going to run out during the cold night, she was worried that we were going to freeze in the cold drafty house. She kept turning up the thermostat, and I kept readjusting it downward. The furnace would go out. I would go down to the basement to try to re-light the pilot light. The longer the night went on, the more the furnace failed, so I had to sit up to make sure we could keep some heat in the house. Until it became a contest of wills, Barbara turning the heat up and my turning it down.

"If you touch the thermostat again, I'll shoot you!" I had threatened her.

I did have guns in the house—a .30–30 Winchester and a .22 rifle—and, not knowing the threat was an idle one, Barbara called Carol's father, who started driving to Merrill from Omaha. When he arrived the next morning, I was completely whacked-out on the scotch, reeking of Pall Mall smoke, and weeks off my meds. During one of these manic episodes, still dealing with the grief of my father's death, I had seen him, whirring in the clouds, in Ezekiel's chariot—wheels of fire—exhorting me to join him as he drove his Galaxy 500 Ford back to the distant stars. I spent days awake, painting a round mandala, Carol called the fire department when I was ranting and raving, but I talked them into believing everything was all right.

Finally, Carol's state senator father, Dave, arrived with two sheriff's deputies, who promptly subdued me, put on a pair of handcuffs, and drove me down to the sheriff's office in LeMars. I remember still being in my nightshirt sitting in the sheriff's office, hung-over, dry mouthed, then put in the back of a cruiser, still handcuffed, driven at high speed toward the Cherokee Mental Health Institute—"insane asylum"—at Cherokee, Iowa. I remember watching the sheriffs check their nine-millimeter pistols at the front desk. My next memory was awakening on an examination table—my arms folded across my chest, strapped and belted in a straitjacket—in the dark looking at a blinking red light on the ceiling that, I did not recognize as a smoke detector—taking it to be Steely Dan's

> Where no sun is shining
> No red light flashing
> Here in this darkness
> I know what I've done.[25]

But I did not know what I had done. Then the fluorescent lights came on. A doctor, I presumed, beneath a surgical mask, entered the room with a masked nurse.

"He's back."

I wanted a cigarette. They took my blood pressure and listened to my respiration. They loosened the straps and helped me out of the straitjacket. They drew a blood sample. They gave me an injection and when I woke up, I was living on the ward, getting up every morning to walk through the tunnels between the buildings to take my meds. I was trying to figure out how I could go home. Carol came to visit. I was still semi-incoherent. Things did not make sense. I finally had a meeting with a psychiatrist. He asked me questions. He explained that I had gone off my therapeutic doses of Lithium and had a manic episode. He said that they would titrate me back up to the 1,200 mgs and I should be fine in a few weeks. During those few weeks, Carol came to visit, talked to the doctors, and drove through snowstorms and blizzards, in one of the worst Iowa winters in years. I took Rorschach tests, as the doctors wanted to test for schizophrenia. Carol would not let them even consider a lobotomy. "Rather have a bottle in front of me, than a prefrontal lobotomy." This is perhaps an exaggeration, as what she would not allow was electroconvulsive therapy (ECT), which was widely used for major depression and schizophrenia.

Plaines Area Mental Health Center (PAMHC) was in the basement of the hospital in LeMars. I went for counseling once a week. They also took monthly blood samples to monitor my Lithium levels. At that time in the early 1980s, Lithium therapy was still somewhat experimental, so I was also required to collect my urine in order that my creatine clearance could be determined; it was still not known how Lithium affected the kidneys. The first time I went to talk with Dr. Kjenaas—the psychiatrist at PAMHC—he told me that he would be tape recording our sessions so he could analyze them. I was so deeply shamed by my hospitalization, failure of my wife and son, unemployment, and lack of success that I sat and talked with him with my eyes closed, or at least, I could not make much eye contact. After several weeks, he told me that he been a triage officer in Korea. Once, after five Black soldiers came in complaining of "urinary irritation" after an R&R in Japan—which he knew was "clap"—he delayed recommending them for treatment; choosing instead to let them suffer. Solders were being shot and left bleeding in the mud and snow, and these guys were partying with whores. He told me that he had always regretted this "moral failure," as he thought his own racist bias had played a part. Having gained my trust, I began to share my innermost feelings. Transference.

"You have an affective disorder. Your feelings are often inappropriate for the situation. What you have is not a moral problem, but a chemical problem with the inter-synaptic transport ions—potassium and sodium ions—in your brain. You have not failed, morally or ethically. You are also suffering from what has been done to you, like those Black soldiers in Korea. These people have done this to you—and they do not know it—but they are lucky to even know you. They are fortunate to know you."

During my weekly sessions with Dr. Kjenaas—who was also the director of the Cherokee State Hospital where I had been committed—his calm avuncular support, allowed me to talk and ramble on and on about my inner thoughts. I told him how, sitting on the sunporch of the old farmhouse during a summer thunderstorm, I had intuited that because the universe was digital (viz. quantized), the rain-streaked rusted window screens were binary coded—ones and zeroes, naughts and crosses. Communicating directly with the universe, the spaces in the square wire, the rainwater squares—reflecting the old sagging red barn (upside down)—on my retinas. Lattice matrices. Indian corn—black and yellow kernels. Naught-naught-window-naught-window-window. Tic-tac-toe—ones and zeroes—fireflies and darknesses—solid quantum binary code. Pushed up from the palimpsest Planck energy packets into the energy transports from my potassium/calcium misaligned inter-synaptic junctions—mood disorder. Sitting on the porch, watching a single windowlet—wet with rain—evaporate, increasing the relative humidity in Merrill, Iowa just enough to cause another wire square in the screen to condense out another window—window in window in the window of my mind—the universe "playing hide-and-seek with itself." And knew in an instant that the smallest cubes of space-time ("spime") filled and emptied with energy in the solid matrices of the changing humidities of the total energy-rain of the Cosmos. That I was in Ioway—I/O input-output—way—wiggle-waggle "W" ay!—for a reason (re: a son)—"Re" Sun god a Sun/Son.

"That it was all wiggle-waggle," the dance of honeybees signing for the direction of the Sun; the digital binary expressed as the analog—zig-zag; the sound of a human voice—digitized into ones and zeroes; the ones and zeroes in my rain smeared screens converted into light—converted into the inaudible pop-pop-pop of evaporations. Wiggle-waggle, the intergalactic ür-speech of the alien spacemen ("spacers") humans would encounter in the twenty-third century.

"Wiggle-wiggle-waggle-wiggle-waggle-wiggle-wiggle-waggle."

"11010110."

"Latin capital letter O with diaresis, in ASCII."

"I think in wiggle-waggle."

A week later, Dr. Kjenaas told me that he had spoken to a young Black man being admitted to the mental hospital in Cherokee, speaking Wiggle-waggle. I did not know if this was a prompt to get me to talk more about this or the reality of a highly improbable phenomenon. I casually asked him about what he was doing for the weekend,

"A round of golf."

"You'll have the best round in your life."

A week later, he told me he had shot a round of 82—his best ever. I sensed we were becoming friends. He asked me to bring Carol in for a chat. I did. Once, while having a mini-crisis, he came out to the old white farmhouse—made a house call—sat on the floor like a friend and advised me that I should take a good dose of my favorite drug—drug of choice—by which he intended alcohol or grass—and let the crisis pass. When he thought I was sufficiently recovered, the talk therapy ended. But he advised me that if I ever felt the acute pressure of being gaslighted (by racist microaggressions), rather than being institutionalized, that I should check myself into a hospital for a complete check-up. He cautioned me that—perhaps—I would always need to be on Lithium Carbonate; that to stop taking it would end in being involuntarily committed to a mental ward.

"The people who have done this to you are privileged to even know you."

Dr. Kjenaas asked me about my writing. When I told him I wrote sci-fi, he mused on about his own favorite sci-fi novels—Larry Niven's *Ringworld* and Frank Herbert's *Whipping Star*. I told him that I would read them. When I read *Whipping Star*, I was enthralled, as this was novel of how a star—the Sun—had been gaslighted into unhappy self-loathing—and how someone had restored the Sun's self-love.[26] This story was so much in line with my worldview—how love could be restorative. Years later, I read Toni Morrison's *The Bluest Eye*, where Pecola Breedlove, so saddened by her life that she had to hallucinate a world (one where she has blue eyes) to create an acceptable world she could live in (even if it was crazy).[27] I knew that if I loved anything, it would be taken from me. So, I resolved, not to hallucinate a world, but to love a world, a universe, a Sun that could not be taken from me. How can a Universe be denied? I would *love* a world into existence. I would await its answer. I would wait for its kiss back. I became hypervigilant, watching, listening. Universe, speak to me.

I was always trying to "go back to school." I was like John Barth's *Giles Goat-Boy*, always trying to register for courses, but thwarted at every turn.[28] Returning to my house husbandry, I had been urged by poet David Ray, to submit my poems to the Yale Younger Poets series. While at the LeMars Public Library photocopying my poems, a librarian asked me what I was doing. "Copying my poems," I answered. She said, "You're a poet?"

"You should give a reading at the library."

She made flyers and posted them in the library. A few weeks later, Carol and Graham, a few professors (Chemistry and English) from Westmar College (in LeMars, Iowa), and even Mr. Kerhberg, our landlord, with a few other locals, came to hear me read. I read about ten poems, including one about the "Dead Owl in the *Wasichu* barn's loft / hooting for black suns and red zig-zag war paint." I had recently read John G. Neihardt's *Black Elk Speaks*. Wasichu—Wašíču (Lakȟótiyapi) or wašicu (Dakȟótiyapi)—is the Siouan word for "white person."[29] I read my poems to polite applause and went home.

A few days later, while snoozing on the sofa, I received a telephone call from the Dean of Westmar College offering me a job as an instructor. He told me I had been recommended by the professors at the college who had attended my poetry reading. He arranged the interviews. I was redeemed. I banged together my resume, put on a shirt and tie, and from all appearances, had landed the job. I was exuberant. I came home floating on cotton fleecy clouds suspended in the blue Iowa sky.

The college President said, "Mr. Jones," the hiring committee and the Methodist Minister who had balked, sitting around the conference table, "there's been some concern about your religious beliefs."

"We'd like to hear a little about your religious beliefs."

I stood up. I started to tell them the following story.

"When I was a small boy, living with my grandfather, Tommie, in Spring Hope, North Carolina, I played in the yard in the dirt at his feet. Brother Tommie was a Deacon in his church, and a sharecropper who grew tobacco and cotton. On warm summer nights, with whippoorwills calling and fireflies blinking, the Milky Way Galaxy sprawled across heaven, I played in the yard with my brother and my young uncle. Papa Sills—Brother Tommie—sat in a caned rocking chair on the front porch—humming and occasionally saying 'uh-huh.'"

"Once in a while, an even older Black man—Uncle Awl—would walk down the road to sit with my grandfather on the weather-beaten porch. They would sit silently and rock, as we clamored and gamboled in the dust in the yard. At unpredictable intervals, one of them would mutter 'uh-huh.' By day, Pa would sit and rock in, silver-dollar spectacles, bibbed-overalls, and study his soft covered Bible. Then, many days later, Uncle Awl would appear at dusk, sit silently beside Pa, rocking away side by side in their canned chairs. They were hugely silent beneath the mighty raiment of the bright stars, the waltzing lightning bugs, the nonsense scrambling of our playing in the yard, whippoorwills' cavil."

"Uh-huh."

"Uh-huh," in reply, and rock-a-way.

"And in my life's miseries, that memory sustained me. The quietness of their conversations of *uh-huh*. But I did not think about it until I became a man, and my father died, and I could not cry: saddened by life's travails, by the wretchedness of it all. Until many months later, looking up at the Milky Way, I saw that these same stars were the ones Tommie and Uncle Awl had seen; the same stars that my father had seen; that, I was seeing them with their eyes. And I cried—with a determinedness—until I felt 'uh-huh' in my soul—realized what Tommie Sills and Uncle Awl had been saying."

"I've lived a long life; see these children playing in the yard; God is on his throne; it is as it should be and what they will come to see—*Uh-Huh*."

"I might not," I said to the President, Dean, and the Methodist Minister, "go to church as much as you might wish. But the universe is my church, I worship in it every day."

"Uh-huh."

They thanked me and asked me to step out into the hall. After a few interminable minutes, the conference room door opened, and they asked me to come back in. They invited me to sit. The Westmar College President looked at me and started to talk.

"Mr. Jones, we may not completely agree with your religious views, but in many ways, we believe that you're more spiritual than we are. We've decided to offer you the job."

"Humm baby!"

Uh-huh.

NOTES

1. Denise Levertov, *Relearning the Alphabet* (New York: New Directions, 1970).

2. Richard Brautigan, *Willard and His Bowling Trophies: A Perverse Mystery* (New York: Simon and Schuster, 1975); Donald Barthelme, *The Dead Father* (New York: Pocket Books. 1976); and Kurt Vonnegut, *Breakfast of Champions* (New York: Vintage, 1992).

3. Donald Barthelme, *Snow White* (New York: Touchstone, 1996).

4. Kurt Vonnegut, *Breakfast of Champions*, 14.

5. Robert M. Pirsig, *Zen and the Art of Motorcycle Maintenance: An Inquiry into Values* (New York: Harper Perennial, 2000).

6. Arthur C. Clarke, *2001: A Space Odyssey* (New York: New American Library, 1968); Clarke, *Childhood's End* (New York: Ballantine Books, 1953).

7. Ray Bradbury, *The Martian Chronicles* (New York: Doubleday, 1950).

8. Jorge Luis Borges, "The Circular Ruins," in *Ficciones*, ed. Anthony Kerrigan (New York: Grove Press, 1994), 57–64.

9. William Wordsworth, My Heart Leaps Up," American Academy of Poets, *Poets.org*, n.d, https://poets.org/poem/my-heart-leaps (accessed August 13, 2023).

10. Ivan Turgenev, *Fathers and Sons* (New York: Signet, 2005).

11. Richard A. Jones, "Laughing in the Face of a New Sun"; Unpublished manuscript.

12. Kurt Vonnegut, *Player Piano: A Novel* (New York: Dail Press, 2006); and Vonnegut, *Welcome to the Monkey House* (New York: Dail Press, 2013).

13. Emanuel Swedenborg, *Heaven and Hell* (Knutsford Cheshire: A & D Publishing, 2007).

14. Peter S. Stevens, *Patterns in Nature* (New York: Little Brown, 1974).

15. Alex Haley, *Roots: The Saga of an American Family* (New York: Dell Publishing, 1977).

16. David Ray, *X-Rays: A Book of Poems* (Ithaca, NY: Cornell University Press, 1965).

17. David Ray, "Hammering," *The New Yorker*, February 1, 1976, 92–93; repr. with permission of the author.

18. Paul Kantner and Jefferson Starship, "Starship," *Blows Against the Empire* (album) (Hollywood, CA: RCA Victor, 1970).

19. Robert A. Heinlein, *Stranger in a Strange Land* (New York: Ace Books, 1991).

20. Herman Melville, *Moby-Dick, Or, The Whale* (New York: Harper, 1851), chap. 37.

21. David Crosby, Stephen Stills, and Paul Kantner, "Wooden Ships," *Crosby, Stills & Nash* (album) (Hollywood, CA: Atlantic Records, 1969).

22. William S. Burroughs, *Exterminator!* (New York: Penguin, 1973).

23. Guy James and Michael Farley, "The Farm," *Volunteers* (album) (Hollywood, CA: RCA Victor, 1969).

24. Donald Jay Fagen and Walter Carl Becker, "Don't Take Me Alive," *The Royal Scam* (album) (Los Angeles: ABC Studios, 1976).

25. Fagen and Becker, "Don't Take Me Alive."

26. Larry Niven, *Ringworld* (London: Gollancz, 2005); and Frank Herbert, *Whipping Star* (New York: Berkely, 1986).

27. Toni Morrison, *The Bluest Eye* (New York: Holt, Rinehart and Winston, 1970):

28. John Barth, *Giles Goat-Boy* (New York: Anchor Books, 1987).

29. John G. Neihardt, *Black Elk Speaks: The Complete Edition* (Lincoln, NE: Bison Books, 2014).

Bertie Sills and Gus Jones, Wedding, 1944, parents of Richard A. Jones.

Richard A. Jones, 1947, age 2 years old.

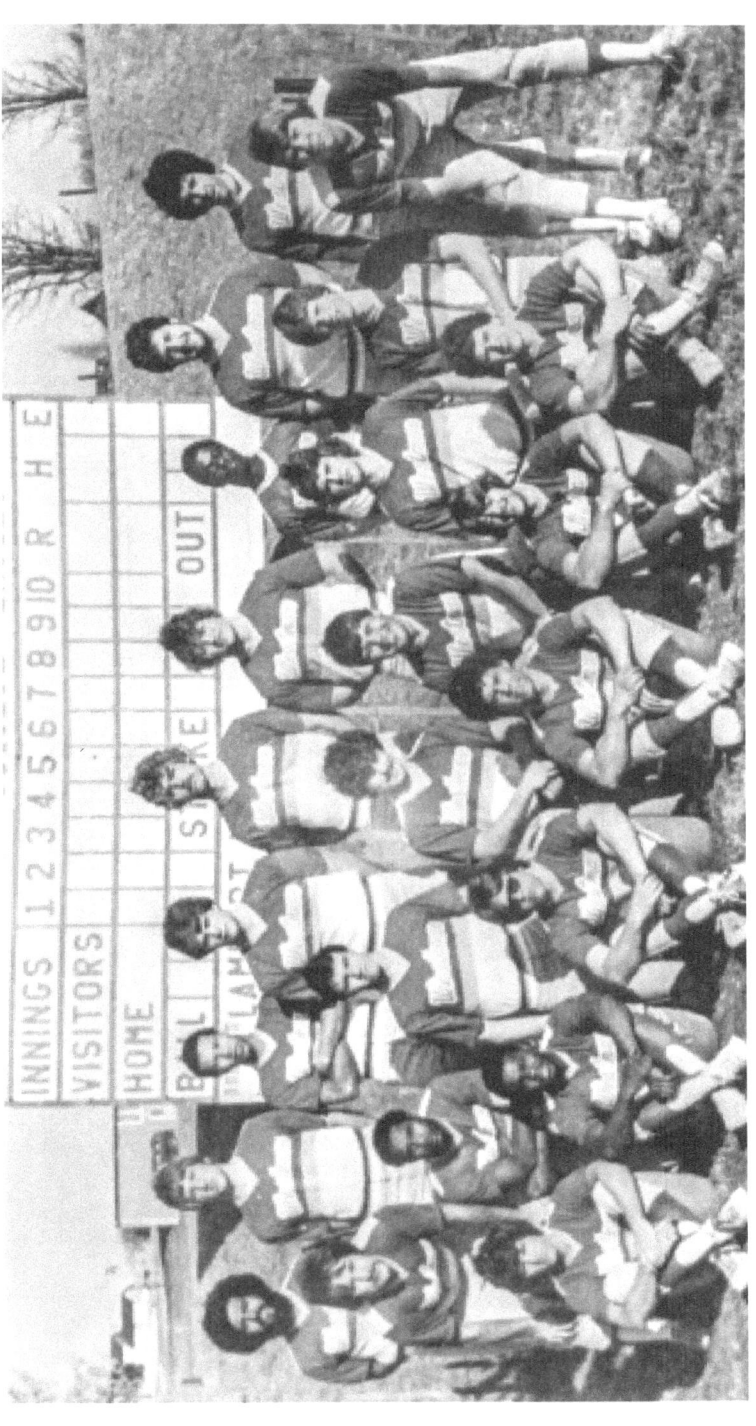

WESTMAR Baseball Team 1981. (Sitting): Dave King, Mel Mellerson, Doug DeBoer, Dave Vander Aarde, Randy Waterbury, Kal Goodchild, (Kneeling): Dave Huff, Larry Rayford, Tom Luxford, Brian Zschiesche, Tim Wiszowaty, Dave BeBoer, (MVP), Galyn Wiemers, Kevin Reed, (Standing): Coach Jones, Kent Harrison, Roger Archibald, Steve Watson, Lee Bolks, Bill Thomas, Matt Hill, Devin Simpson, Coach Simpson.

Airman 2C Richard A. Jones (bottom right), Chanute US AFB, Rantoul Illinois, 1966.

Richard Jones and Carol Stahmer's Marriage, May 1972.

Richard Jones and Angela Y. Davis, George Mason University, 2006.

Shauna, Richard, Graham, Carol, and Lindsey Jones at Graham's PhD ceremony. New York University, 2007.

Chapter 11

Westmar Eagles, 1979–1982

Living in the old white farmhouse, faux-farmer, listening to Norman Thomas on the radio—provincialism—and Chicago pork-belly futures, I was a stranger in a stranger land. Sitting for the summer on the sun porch, black and orange box elder bugs crawling on the rusted screens, Carol launching herself from the second-floor walk-out deck sitting in an old tire tied to a long rope swing. I was in a kind of phantasmagorical paradise of slowness. Listening to Jefferson Airplane's *Crown of Creation* under my Koss headphones. Alienated by the few Black people in the environment yet waving to the neighbors in their pickup trucks as they rooster-tailed down the dirt road past the house. They waved and I waved, but I did not know them, and they did not know us. So lonely for human contact that, once upon a nonce, Carol laid out some old sheets, and we all laid down on them and traced out our outlines with marking pens, cut them out, filled them with batting, dressed them in our clothes, and sat them in the living room. Then, when we took our walks, we could see them (stuffed us) sitting in the lamp-lit room and wonder about their (our stuffed) lives. It was eerie, moving our stuffed doppelgangers around in the house, how big we were, how much room we took up.

Mizmoon ran freely in the fields, along the fence lines, flushing ring-tailed pheasants. One day, a tan and white beagle puppy appeared in the yard. Perhaps dropped off in the country by somebody from town, the puppy followed me all around the place. She was welcomed and adored by Mizmoon. Because of her color—the color of scotch whiskey—we named her Scotch.

I was always jealous—green-eyed monster—that Carol would love someone else. This possessiveness was—of course—the result of my insecurities about abandonment. As my mother had abandoned me to the clutches of my aunties and uncles in North Carolina, Beverly—my first love—had abandoned me to her many sex-slaves, and Jackie who had not loved me. I was jealous of any man in Carol's proximity; the thick-wristed farmers, grisly plumbers; strangers without names. This emotion was selfish and distorted my impressions. I did not trust anyone.

The contract from Westmar College helped restore my sense of legitimacy. Given the literary rejections, failed jobs, and institutionalizations, this nod to "normalcy," helped me regain my sense of self. I had begun to think of myself as the ultimate poseur—pretended artiste, faux-poet, failed mathematician, sub-athletic—a grand dilettante, dabbler in many things, master of none. Or as the mid-westerners had it, "Like the North Platte River, a mile wide and an inch deep." So, I was still trying to overcome my own (and others) perception of my shallowness. The *Le Mars Sentinel* newspaper invited me to its offices to interview me. Their photographer staged a photo of me sitting before a wall of books with a world globe in front of me. The article spoke, glowingly, of my education (a master's degree), my background (IBM), and military service (SAC). Yet, I knew I was a laughingstock. In a small town, where the word gets around—gossip—from the sheriffs who drove me in handcuffs to the mental hospital at Cherokee, to the secretary at the Plaines Area Mental Health Center, to the firemen who had been called out to the farmhouse when I was manic and threatening to burn down the house, and my neighbors who wondered "where the fire was." And yet, there I was, all propped up, Negro "scholar" added to the faculty of Westmar College.

Westmar College was founded in 1887 as Northwestern Normal School and Business College. In 1900, it was renamed Western Union College and affiliated with the United Evangelical Church, training Navy Aviators during World War II. In 1948, it was again renamed—this time Westmar College—and began its affiliation with the United Methodist Church. Whereas Westmar College was non-sectarian, it was heavily influenced by the United Methodist Church. The contract Westmar had tendered, included the duties of "Minority Affairs Coordinator." I was also slated to teach an introductory course titled "Computers in Society." Along with these responsibilities, I was also asked to develop educational applications for their DEC PDP-11 minicomputer.

But first, Minority Affairs Coordinator. I had an office in the basement of the science building in a room with wall-to-wall bookshelves filled with math and science books, mostly examination copies, textbooks from another generation. I was also provided with a part-time work-study student. She was a young African American co-ed. I had come into my office in the morning, and she would be there ready to take dictation, write letters, and answer the phone. I liked her and wanted to provide the hours she needed to earn her work-study pay, but after a few weeks, I had run out of things for her to do. Having a "secretary" lent importance to the endeavor, but as I exhausted my make-work ideas, she drifted away to more industrious assistant professors. I had been hired as an "Instructor."

Fresh out the loony bin—*non compo mentis* (not of sound mine)—I was expected to be the leader of a group of about fifty African American students in an enrollment of somewhere around five hundred. These Black students were primarily from Florida, recruited by the athletic coaches to play football or basketball. But there were also Blacks from Chicago and New York. Northwest, rural Iowa was a new cultural experience for all of them. They complained to me of being followed in stores when they went into downtown Le Mars, where parking was still diagonal. They complained about the lack of adult guidance in the entirely white faculty and staff at Westmar College. The first act, as their advisor, was to start a Black Students' Association (BSA). I had membership cards printed up, elections held for officers, and called for an organizational meeting. I told them that the primary reason for my being hired at Westmar was that the administration needed to improve their racial demographics; they needed me to fill a statistical void. But they, the Black students, also needed me to help them navigate existence in this entirely white environment. We began to plan events.

A pivotal event was an off campus BSA picnic. I wanted to get the Black students off campus into a non-threatening environment. We found a quiet park where we roasted hotdogs, grilled hamburgers, and threw Frisbees. They had brought their own music. The music was heavy inflected by the songs of Earth, Wind & Fire. There was a decidedly different aesthetic from my neo-hippie tastes. We threw around footballs. I had brought Carol and Graham. Graham was a hit, as most of the Black students had younger brothers and sisters and missed playing with them.

As the afternoon progressed, I picked up a baseball bat and a couple of baseballs and began hitting fungoes to a few of the football players. "Thwack." I hit almost perfect 250 foot to 275-foot parabolas into the periwinkle blue Iowa sky. Thwack after crack, I launched the baseballs into the same place. The balls were so easy to catch—like picking low hanging fruit—because of their trajectories, they reached their apex, hung motionless in the air, and fell gently from the clouds, like magic. People who have never played organized hardball, do not have opportunities to experience the delights of fielding long fly balls. Besides these Black athletes, primarily football players, there were a few Westmar varsity baseball players who did not know what to make of me. They did not know—yet—that I had cracked-up, had a nervous breakdown, and recently been in the nuthouse.

With the fall semester well underway, I settled into teaching "Computers in Society." The textbook was rudimentary—ASCII Code, file processing, CPU, I/O, ALU, binary numbers—but the book also laid emphasis on the impact of computer technology on society. I remember so well, even now, the book's unit on privacy; algorithms that could be used to predict human behaviors or analyze human motives (personality types). This was in 1980 and having been reduced to abject paranoia by the British band YES's album *Drama*, with its tracks "Machine Messiah" and "Into the Lens." "Into the Lens" contains the lines "I am a camera," which I took to mean that human beings were input devices (I/O) for the Universal "Machine Messiah." God was a computer, and we were data capture devices. The universe was a machine. With paranoia guiding me, I taught "Computers in Society" as if my students were Hollerith punched cards—data input devices.

During the week of freshman orientation, students and faculty, and the families of faculty, were invited to watch a film called *Walkabout*. This was a film concerning the Australian Aboriginal people's tradition of sending pre-adult men into the bush to survive on their own. It was the story of how these young men, left to their own devices, needed to improvise—going against all inherited mores—to survive in the wild. After the months-long journey, they returned to the tribe transformed into adults capable of thinking and acting autonomously.[1] The message from the brain trust at Westmar, was for all of us to follow the Aboriginal bushmen in taking a walkabout to discover out adult selves; that even adults needed a walkabout to rediscover their true selves.

I thought that I was a part of this dissociative process for students. I would be their agent, leading them into the dessert of the real. Being recently released from Cherokee, I was already unhinged enough to show them the way. I had read *Computer Power and Human Reason* by Joseph Weizenbaum.[2] As I began lecturing—on walkabout—I started talking about fifth generation computers (VLSI) and AI. As a text, I used *Machines Who Think* by Pamela McCorduck.[3]

In 1980, Artificial Intelligence (AI) was a newly emerging academic field. The face on McCorduck's book reflected the mind-blowing astonishment of mankind (and me) awakened to the fact that not only was mind a computational device, but also that his own technical abilities were on the verge of giving machines the ability to think. Graduate students in John McCarthy's early courses on AI at Stanford University—because they understood so little of what he was teaching—referred to his classes as "Uncle John's Mystery Hour." And Joe Weizenbaum was already cautioning computer scientists and philosophers that where there might be things intelligent computers *could* do, humans should always beware that although they could, there were things they should not.

Suddenly, I was lecturing about the Turing Test, neural networks, W. Grey Walter's "turtles," and the threats of machine intelligence. But I was like the apocryphal stories of mathematicians whose graduate students would make bets on whether the mathematician would ever write an equation on the blackboard during their office hour visits. To wit, the students were skeptical of that mathematician's mathematical ability. In my case, I was talking about the "philosophy" of computer science without even knowing how to program them. I decided I needed to learn how to code.

Joel Rushikoff, a young assistant professor, gave me a book *Hands-On BASIC* by Herbert Peckham.[4] Over the Christmas holidays, I had borrowed a dial-up modem and a terminal. Using the book Rushikoff had given me—and logging on to the PDP-11 at Westmar—I spent hours at a time, sometimes all night, until I had mastered the BASIC programming language. Given my mathematics degree, I quickly understood loops, nested loops, decision trees, IF-Then statements, and even ARRAYs. One night after completing one of the assigned problems in the book, I realized that I could code out in BASIC anything I could conceive of mathematically. Even with all my failures at IBM and the University of Iowa, I now had a new tool that renewed my faith in the usefulness of computer technology.

On the home front, Graham had started school at Kissinger Elementary. He was a precocious child—highly verbal—curious about nature, people, and ideas. He was also socially isolated. Since I had always sought to live in the shadows, hiding out, and paranoid, skeptical of the motives of other people, jealous of any man that came within a hundred yards of Carol, I had become a semi-recluse; engaging with others only when forced. So, understandably, Graham craved other children to play with. After he had been in school a while, a teacher had recommended that he be held out of school for a year. Because his birthday was August 30th, he was a young five-year-old when he started kindergarten. But, knowing he was a gifted child, I rejected holding him back, especially based on the teachers comment that he was "verbally immature." Graham was one of the few—if not the only—mixed race kid in the school.

The Black Students Association held several parties at my white "Iowa Gothic" farmhouse. They brought their own music. I vividly recall my baby daughter, Shauna, dancing the "Hustle" with the gyrating Black students. She boogied down. As the Minority Affairs coordinator, I found myself acting as an advocate in many situations where I was totally inadequate. A Black student trashed his room and the hallway of the dorm where he lived. The Dean of Student Affairs arranged a meeting with me to discuss discipline.

"Why would he do such a thing?" the Dean asked.

"He's alienated and angry."

"Why?"

"The culture shock of living in a primarily white, rural environment without the cultural support systems to which he's accustomed."

The Dean looked at me. He was a young man, thickly muscled, with a large and expensive wristwatch. He appeared deeply suspicious of my multi-culty, neo-hippie-ish worldview. I sensed he thought I was wishy-washy—limp-wristed, unable to mete out appropriate discipline.

"What kind of discipline or counseling do you think appropriate?"

"He should talk to someone . . . be given another chance . . . made to clean up the mess he's made . . . apologize to his dorm mates."

Another time, the Black quarterback of the football team was accused of stealing an expensive leather and wool letterman's jacket from a bathroom. He had been brought before the college's Disciplinary Board, facing expulsion. I was asked to speak for him in the hearing. I questioned the principles—the quarterback and the victim of the theft—there had been no witnesses. Relying on the Perry Mason TV lawyers I had internalized, I argued that there had been no witnesses to this "crime," and therefore it was a "He said, he said." The quarterback had admitted he took the jacket, but it was a mistake, as he said he thought it was his. When the disciplinary committee voted, the quarterback was exonerated and allowed to graduate. Another troubling episode occurred when a young Black co-ed confided that she was pregnant. The father was one of the college's baseball players. Both were members of the BSA and had spent time in my house during BSA parties. The young woman told me, "My father will kill me." Reluctantly, Carol and I loaned them our car and gave them some money, so they could drive to Omaha for an abortion. Like many things, this incident was never spoken of again.

When spring finally came, I was approached by the varsity baseball coach, Warren Simpson, about becoming his assistant. Another so-called trait of psychopaths is their craving for risky behaviors—thrills. I should have known that this was a losing proposition. I should have anticipated how this new "walkabout" was a veiled assault on another of my loves. "If you love it, it will be taken from you." But.

"Humm Baby."

I was seduced by something I loved—baseball. I suited up for spring training in the teal and gray Westmar Eagle's uniform, hitting fungoes for the outfielders, and acting as the third base coach. At night, dreaming, I could hear the sweet sounds of baseball cleats—spikes—kicking up dirt as runner rounded third, scoring. I felt the thrill of my wooden bat making contact with the baseball, as I thwacked fly ball after fly ball into the cool March sky. The team had six African American players.

Westmar competed in NAIA II (National Association of Intercollegiate Athletics, Division II). NAIA, started in 1940, made up of about 250 small colleges, had lower academic requirements than the NCAA and fewer core academic requirements. So, by these criteria, the NAIA were the minor leagues of college athletics. In all my classes, discussions with students and faculty, there was little mention of books, concepts, or awe for existence. Which is to say that I was part of the incentivization for the students at Westmar to "take the walkabout" in a new world outside the provincialism into which they had been cast.

That first year at Westmar also yielded a few other surprises. David Ray published a few of my poems in an anthology, *From A-Z: 200 Contemporary Poets*.[5] I approached the administration about inviting him to campus to speak, which they eagerly approved. The anthology included poems by Richard Wright and Joyce Carol Oates. Suddenly, reinforcing my initial contact with Westmar at the Le Mars Library reading poems, the faculty began to construe my academic mission as "poetic."

Also, as result of my poems in David Ray's anthology, I was encouraged to sponsor a "Poetry Club." Meeting at my house, sitting on the floor in the living room, the student poets and I shared our poems. We published a small collection of our works and sold them. The booklet went through two printings.

Being a third base coach involves getting signals from the dugout and relaying them to hitters. I took the signals from Warren Simpson and relayed them on to batters. The signals are always different for different teams, and there are times when they are changed to throw the other team off. To do this effectively, the third base coach needs an "indicator." It can be something like "If I touch skin first the next sign is the sign." Signs to "take" (the pitch), to hit-and-run, steal (the base), or "You're on your own" (swing at your discretion), along with a "rub" (take off the sign and start over), are common. The other key role of the third base coach is to help runners approaching second base decide whether to come to third, and to wave the runner on to score. The worst transgression a third base coach can commit is to get a runner thrown out at home plate. Beyond that, it is a constant chattering.

"Ducks on the pond!"

"A little bingo!"

"A little poke!"

Clapping and giving fake signals. I was good in this role, as Warren Simpson was a natural leader, who would call the players into a tight circle, have them "take a knee," and exhort them to play beyond their abilities. He yelled and cried, encouraged, consoled, entreated, and praised the players. However, in the prior three seasons, the Westmar Eagles had only won three games. As I rode the bus with the team to away games in small towns in Iowa and South Dakota, I was constantly amazed by their enthusiasm and joy for competition. Despite all the practices, where I hit thousands of fly balls, gave hundreds of signals for batters, and waved in dozens of runners rounding third base, the Eagles went 9 and 18 during the 1980–1981 season.

That summer, after my first year at Westmar, I taught College Algebra. I enjoyed getting reacquainted with solving equations. As the summer proceeded, baby Shauna continued to thrive, learning to walk early. Carol continued supplementing our income with Treasury Bonds her father gave us from Ruffles Potato Chip royalties. As fall semester started, I was privileged to teach an Intro. Astronomy course, a Computers in Society course, and

COSMOS. The administration had bought rights to Carl Sagan's *COSMOS* series. I had been a charter member of Sagan's "Planetary Society," with a membership card numbered "0006." In this course, students would watch an episode on tape, having already read course materials, and chapter in the print edition of *COSMOS*, then discuss the material.[6]

There were twenty-five students (including Carol) in the Intro. Astronomy course. It was a night class, so there were many students from the community. The course was in the basement of the Kime Science Building. On the upper floors were the chemistry and biology labs. On nights of the class during breaks, I would walk to upper floors dreaming of bringing "real astronomy" into the classroom lectures. I wanted more than the "descriptive astronomy" I had learned at Howard University, where although I had studied "Blink Comparators," "thermocouples," and spectrometers, I had never touched these instruments. So, when I approached the unit on spectra and Fraunhofer lines (absorption spectra), I asked one of the chemistry professors for a liquid sample of Tetrachloride and used a candle and a little telescope to produce visible absorption lines for my student's observation. In another major assignment, I had students calculate the barycenters of all the planets with the sun, all of which are within hundreds of feet from the sun's center (these are very tedious calculations—conversions from miles to feet—using scientific notation) to show how the objects (planet-sun) orbit one another, and produce the wiggle of a star and its retinue of planets when astronomers search for stars with planets.

I had a breakthrough fall semester, when I started taking philosophy courses at the University of South Dakota, Vermillion. It was a long drive, made treacherous at times by poor weather. I enrolled in "Aesthetics" and "Marriage and the Family," an ethics course. Both courses opened new intellectual frontiers. In the aesthetics course, there were lectures on jazz, art, and Wittgenstein. In the ethics course, I decided to do a research project on family violence. I went to Sioux City and spoke with the director of a battered women's shelter. He gave me permission to use the data files from fifty cases to make inferences about positively and negatively correlated data points.

So, I used the files to quantify twenty variables, such as age, education, verbal abuse, physical abuse, alcohol use, number of children, income, etc. Using my new programming skills and Westmar's PDP-11, I wrote a "data mining" program with a Pearson correlation coefficient, r, nested inside For-Next loops to compare the first data point to all twenty data points, and writing the r values into a twenty-by-twenty array. I expected the array to have a diagonal of ones, where the data point was correlated to itself, and that is exactly what I found. In interpreting the output, I highlighted those factors that were highly positively and highly negatively correlated. In the paper I

Rhine Symbols

wrote, I noted that correlation does not imply causation, but highly correlated factors were worthy of deeper study. For instance, the educational levels of the abusers were not statistically relevant to the levels of physical and verbal abuse. I received an A in this course. The director of the battered women's study said that my paper was worthy of publication.

That second year at Westmar was also memorable because Charles and Bertie came to Le Mars to visit. Charles sat in on one of my Astronomy lectures. I built a brick fireplace using old bricks I had dug out from an old hog farrowing house. I also had an art exhibition of my artworks at Westmar, took my students to hear an astronomer give a talk at an observatory, and invited students out to the farmhouse to view the planets (Jupiter and Saturn), see M-42 (gas nebula in Orion), with a telescope loaned to me by Westmar. That Christmas 1981, when all the students had returned home for the holidays, I invited two African exchange students to the farmhouse for dinner and conversation. They were excited to be with a family and played with Graham.

There were more parties with the BSA. So, now, I found myself involved with several different cliques; athletes (baseball team), poets (Poetry Club), computer geeks (teaching an upper division course), BSA (fifty Black students), and now philosophy (at USDV). In the computer "walkabout," I had glommed onto the idea that "computers who think," could also become telepathic with humans. So, I wrote up a proposal and sent it to the National Science Foundation (NSF) for a human subjects study on computer-human interfaces. What I wanted to do was to demonstrate that a computer with circuits operating at a "coupling" frequency (with the Maxwell equation's ∇E and ∇B) with the known electrical "amperage" of neurons (100 milliamps), could produce a greater than statistical matching of Rhine symbols used in ESP experiments.

I proposed programming a computer with randomized Rhine symbols, having a human subject guess at the symbol before it was displayed, using proximity between human subject and the electromagnetic field created by the computer circuit, to see if the probability—beyond random guessing—varied as a function of distance. I argued that the importance of the experiment could be used to devise human-computer control in defense (weapons) applications. But in my heart of hearts, I knew it was a step toward a true AI. I was sent an application for human subjects experiments but balked at their complexity: the endless need for signatures.

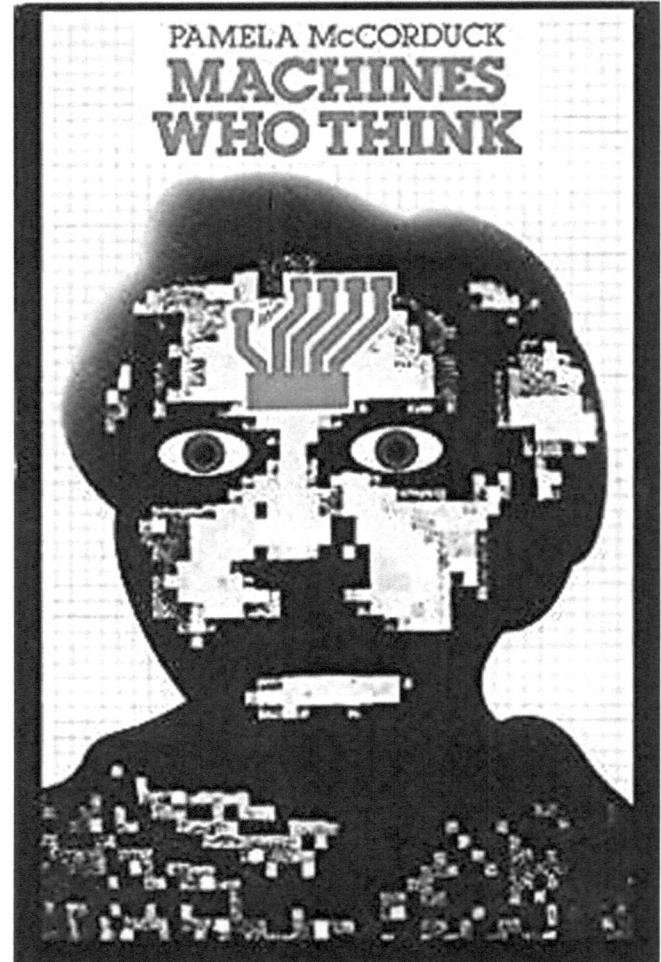

Book cover of *Machines Who Think: A Personal Inquiry into the History and Prospects of Artificial Intelligence* by Pamela McCorduck, W. H. Freeman Publishers, 1981.

I asked the Westmar administrators for permission to attend a recruiting trip to Drake University in Des Moines, my old alma mater. I took along an Apple computer and a copy of "Dr. Chips," an interactive "Rogerian-Therapy" program, on a floppy disc. I sat up a table, trying to recruit high school seniors to attend Westmar College. I had proposed an "honors program," for talented minority students. But, as the high schoolers walked past my table, skeptical of the virtues of a small college, in a smaller town, I knew this was another magnificent, failed idea.

When spring 1982 semester came around, I was still trying to prove myself as a professor. But I was also looking forward to baseball season again. The first year as Warren Simpson's assistant had reanimated my love for the game, where time stood still. Warren Simpson had decided to leave Westmar to pursue a PhD in Texas. By default, I was offered $800 to become the head coach. I accepted. There was a small notice in the *Transactions* section of the sports pages picked up by UPI or Associated Press stringers and in newspaper all over the country. I only knew this when Lawrence Cole, one of the Cole brothers who had been my friends at Central High School in Detroit, called me on the telephone to ask me, "What kind of season are you looking at, Coach?"

The year before, I had made a few observations about the players. First baseman Tim Wisowaty had a quick bat and launched 375-foot home runs with ease. David DeBoer, a solid six-footer, played right field and had hit .344 for the season. He was also a chemistry major with a 3.9 GPA, who aspired to graduate school after Westmar. I did not want to try to imitate Warren Simpson's charisma, rapport with the players, or fiery exhortations. So, as the season approached, I wracked my brain for novel approaches. The first idea I had was to put on a one hundred inning softball game to raise money, through pledges per inning, and walk-up donations. I thought the team could use the money for our spring trip south to Wichita Kansas, and to buy a new set of "away" jerseys. The March 9, 1982, *Le Mars Daily Sentinel* ran the headline for this story in the sports section as: "Softball on Saturday? That's Right."

> The 100-inning bonanza is the brainstorm of Eagle head coach Richard Jones and will be used to raise revenue to help defray the costs for the Eagles' southern road swing, where they will be playing six games in Kansas in three days during the school's spring break.

The event raised $496.60. But beyond the money, what I wanted was to communicate my love for hitting the ball, running the bases, and catching fly balls. I wanted to use this game to get to know who the real lovers of the game were. At times, after playing for forty innings, some players wanted to quit, arguing that we had made our point. But I would not relent. I had continued throughout the day, slogging on inning after inning, numb to fatigue. A few of the player's girlfriends, having come to watch, had came into the game to play a few innings.

That is a lot of hardball for six weeks! I should also relate the fact that the athletic department did not see fit to provide me with an assistant coach. The department was also not forthcoming in cutting the infield grass or dragging the infield, so before the first home game I was out early that morning raking

Table 11.1. The Westmar Eagles 1982 Schedule

March 18	*USD-Springfield (2)*	H	*2:00*
March 21	Kan. New. Col.-Wichita (2)	T	1:30
March 22	Kansas Newman (2)	T	1:30
March 23	Washburn Univ. Topeka (2)	T	1:30
March 24	UNO (2)	T	1:30
March 26	Morningside (2)	T	1:30
March 30	USD-Springfield (2)	T	1:30
April 1	Dana (2)	T	2:00
April 3	*Northwestern (2)*	H	*10:00*
			1:30
April 4	Sioux Empire (2)	T	1:30
April 6	*Briar Cliff (2)*	H	*1:30*
April 10	*Dort (2)*	H	*1:00*
April 13	Northwestern (s)	T	10:00
			1:00
April 15	BV (2)	T	1:00
April 17	Briar Cliff (2)	T	1:30
April 19	Yankton (2)	T	1:30
April 20	*BV (2)*	H	*1:30*
April 24	Dort (2)	T	12:00
April 27	*Morningside (2)*	H	*1:30*
May 1	*Sioux Empire (2)*	H	*1:30*

the infield. I really did not know what to make of this. I was soon to find out. It should be remembered that Major League Baseball (MLB) did not get its first Black manager—Frank Robinson—until 1975. And the National Football League (NFL) did not get its first head coach—Art Shell—until 1989. There was an ongoing debate that Blacks did not possess the "executive faculties" and leadership skills to be quarterbacks, managers, or head coaches.

There were seven Black players on the team. Mell Mellerson (SS) from Baltimore, Roger Archibald (RHP) from New York, Tracy Miller (OF) from Baltimore, Matt Hill (RHP) from Patterson NJ, Hector Brown (OF) from New York, Darwin Wright (3B) from New York, and Larry Rayford (OF) from Florida. I was impressed by Matt Hill's arm. He possessed a 92-mph fastball. I was equally impressed by Larry Rayford's power. He could turn a fastball around and rocket it over the fence.

The other eleven players were white, mostly from rural communities, good natured, and unassuming. Tim Wiszowaty (1B) was called "hoghead" because of his large cranium; Randy Waterbury (RHP) came to the first game with his baseball cap covered with burn holes (the object of a prank); Scott Starkweather (OF) was the object of constant team gossip (whether he was related to the notorious spree killer Charles Starkweather); Jeff Jansen (RHP) was a 6'5" tall freshman pitcher with outstanding control; Dave DeBoer (RF) was an outstanding contact hitter; Paul Johnson (LHP) was a 6'2" tall football player who also played baseball; Mark DeBruin (C) was a freshman; David Traetow(C) was a good contact hitter; Todd Nelson (C) was also a freshman catcher; Jay Prescott (RHP); and, Tom Luxford (2B) a sure-handed infielder.

Our first game on March 15 was against University of South Dakota-Springfield. The Eagle's former coach, Warren Simpson, had come back to Westmar from his graduate studies at Texas A&M, to see the home opener. Westmar came back from an 8 to 1 deficit to win the first game 9 to 8, scoring the winning run in the seventh inning on a hit by David Traetow. The second game of the twinbill was called because of darkness in the third inning with Westmar leading 5 to 4. Auspicious beginnings. I went home, had a drink, and slept like a hibernating bear.

"Humm Baby!"

It was still cold in northwest Iowa when we rolled out of Le Mars in a van provided by the school and my old blue Chevrolet station wagon toward Wichita, Kansas for our spring trip. The station wagon broke down near Omaha. Barbara, Carol's mom, and Claudia, her younger sister, came out to where the car was, loaded the player into their two cars, took us to Carol's childhood home in Omaha, fixed us a nice lunch, while the Chevy was repaired: it was a minor problem of a broken fan belt, so went quickly. Back on the road.

The station wagon had a flat tire close to Kansas Newman College. I should have suspected trouble when the proprietor of the tire service was also named "Richard A. Jones." Finally, after getting a new tire, we rolled up to the Kansas Newman baseball field, where I instructed the players to get off the bus so we could have a practice. The reason for this was that the team, because of the icy weather in Le Mars we had not been outside much, needed to loosen up after the long drive (424 miles) on US 81, and needed to show the commitment to playing that I expected. Nonplussed—all they wanted was to have dinner and sleep—we went through infield and outfield drills; followed by room assignments in a dormitory, and evening meals.

The next day, we lost the first game 10 to 2. We also lost the second game by a score of 15 to 1. I was hardly able to report the score to the sports reporter from the *Le Mars Daily Sentinel*, who I was supposed to telephone to give the box score and game highlights. I was finding it almost impossible to manage the team without an assistant coach. I was on the field as the third base coach, so I was not in the dugout to make decisions.

The next day, in the first game, we bobbled the ball (twelve errors), made poor throws, and did not hit well. Our pitches walked too many batters. Larry Rayford had a triple and two home runs in the opening game. Rayford also made one of the strongest throws from the outfield I had ever seen. On a single up the middle, with the Kansas Newman runner trying to score from second, Rayford uncorked a throw from medium-deep center to Traetow at the plate. The heave was a rocket on a line that never was more than ten feet off the ground, that one-hopped our catcher, but the tag was too late. The throw was like something from Roberto Clemente. We lost 23 to 10. Between games, I tried to give a pep-talk; Kansas Newman had been playing outdoors for two weeks and had already played ten games. Unfortunately, Mel Mellerson, our shortstop, turned his ankle and had to sit out the second game. After the game, I carried Mell piggy-back, to my old station wagon, and on to the emergency room for x-rays. I carried him—a solidly built young guy—into the emergency room and waited for the x-ray results, which turned out negative. They had wrapped it in an ace bandage and advised him to stay off of it for a few days.

The second game of the double-dip was hardly better. However, in a story I have told and written about many, many times—something happened that would forever alter my ideas about competitive sports. Paul Johnson, the 6'2" tall left-hander started the second game. Paul was a football player, who, I could tell, had only pitched a few games in his life. He labored. His only advantage was that he was a southpaw.

Under a perfect blue sky, high white cumulus clouds, no breeze, the grass recently cut, the white chalk lines still fresh, the game began with high hopes. We had dropped the first three games, but I had expected that. During the middle innings, Johnson walked a few batters, we were behind in the score, and I was standing outside the dugout exhorting him to throw strikes. Kansas Newman's second baseman, a slightly built young man (5'9" tall, 150 lbs.), met a Paul Johnson fastball—squared it up—and launched it over the center field fence—it was a bazooka! The young man put his head down and toured the bases. As he rounded third, Paul Johnson, walked over, and extended his hand (a low five). I asked the umpire for time and walked to the mound. Catcher David Traetow clanked out to the hill.

"Son," I said, looking up at him, "I've played this game all my life. I've been to over a hundred major league games, I watch it on TV," I stopped and looked him directly in the eye. Traetow listened.

"But," I continued, "I've never seen a pitcher congratulate a batter who's just hit a home run off him."

"But, coach don't you see, this baseball field is a church where we young men celebrate our youth and health? God created him and God created me, and on this day, God wanted him to do his best, and I wanted him to know that I was happy that he'd done his best."

By this time, the umpire had arrived at the mound to urge us to move it along. I dropped my head, walked off the field, and watched the remainder of the game without comment. Paul Johnson had been my Paul of Tarsus, converting me in an instant.

He was right.

After the sound thumping at Kansas Newman, we limped off to Washburn University in Topeka Kansas, where we lost two games 10 to 9 and 3 to 0. In the first game, we were ahead 9 to 2 in the third inning, when the umpires decided they did not really like me. I had heard an unkind comment about the "House of David"—a mythical Jewish baseball team where the players all wore beards—in reference to my long hair and scruffy beard. So, the umpires, reacting to my hippie-ish appearance, jobbed the Westmar Eagles; bad calls on the bases, squeezing our pitchers by not calling strikes on close pitches, and calling pitches that were not that close on our hitters. With the umpires' help—beneath a huge American flag blowing gently along the right field line—under a blue Kansas sky and sunflower yellow sun *ad astra ad aspera*. The team from Washburn, behind 9 to 2, came back, with the ump's help, to beat us 10 to 9. After being shut out 3 to 0 in the second game, we loaded up our gear and turned toward home. Of course, the team bus broke down somewhere in Kansas, alongside the highway. It was after sunset. This was before cellphones, so assessing the situation and seeing a light on in a farmhouse out across a fallow field, I asked our second baseman, Tom Luxford, to walk to the farmhouse to use the telephone to call for help. We waited helplessly. This time gave me time to evaluate our southern trip. We had lost all six games. My coaching had consisted in emphasizing hitting cut-off men, looking for the pitch in the "magic rectangle" above the pitcher's hand, and "bending your back" (to pitchers when they delivered the pitch). But I had learned much more. First, sport is a celebration, the field of play a church, and being angry about the success of opponent's success, pure folly. I had also developed a more egalitarian perspective on the skills of Westmar's young baseball players. I had seen better players, with better arms, better batting eyes, better power, faster, stronger; but that did not matter, as these players gave everything they had—I respected that. In looking back over the newspaper clippings I had saved, the 1982 season was less than a success. The *Le Mars Daily Sentinel* had run headlines on the Sports pages like "Wayne State hurlers silence Westmar hitters," "Early inning trouble plagues Westmar," and "Westmar falls to 1–14."

There were many stories that were not reported on the sports pages. Before a mid-April game, one of the Black players approached me.

"Coach, he called me a *Nigger*."

"Who called you a *Nigger*?"

The player went on to tell me that one of the team's white infielders had made the remark. As Westmar's "Minority Affairs Advisor," and Men's Varsity Baseball Coach, and a thirty-seven-year-old Black man, I was crestfallen, disappointed, and angry. Before the next game, I told the players assembled in the dugout, that if they wanted to win, they had to play together.

I made no recriminations or accusations. I looked the offender in the eye. Enough said.

Sometime during the long fifteen game losing streak, I broke down in the locker-room sobbing. We were men, they were men, so why could we not win a game. I put it down to my ineptness as a coach. Some of the players tried to console me. After that we played in a more determined way, resurgent, as we won two games in Yankton South Dakota. We won a few more games as the season ended. We won a game in the NAIA playoffs, with freshman Jeff Jansen pitching a gem. The two games with Sioux Empire were memorable, not because we won, but because the coach was a former major leaguer whose name I recognized. He was Hank Bauer, a right fielder for the NY Yankees from 1948 through 1958. The players on Westmar's team were whispering in our dugout about the Yankton coach, who retired before most of them were old enough to know who he was. I could not believe that he was the coach of a small college baseball team. His coaching style was profane, irreverent, and loud. He sat in a plastic folding patio chair outside the visitors' dugout along the third base line and yelled his signals to the batters.

"Bunt, goddamit!" He would yell at the flustered twenty-year-old batter.

"Take the damned pitch!"

"Hit and run, damnit!"

"Hit the damned ball!"

He was an ex-marine who served in World War II. He had been in the Battle of Guadalcanal. He had also played baseball with Roger Maris, Mickey Mantle, Yogi Berra, and Elston Howard. After the Yankton team beat us in both halves of the double-header, I walked over to shake his hand.

"It's a pleasure to meet you. I grew up in Washington DC watching the Yankees murder the Senators. As a kid, I worshiped Mickey Vernon, Roy Sievers, Eddie Yost, Clint Courtney . . . "

Sensing that I was wondering 'What are *you* doing here?' He said something I will always remember.

"You're not a bad coach. Your problem is you want to win every game. You can't win every game. You're going to win one-third of them no matter what you do. You're going to lose one-third of them no matter what you do. It's that other third where you can make a difference by putting the right player in the right place at the right time. No matter what league you play in, the goal is to win two out of three. That's winning baseball."

Listening intently, I studied his wrinkled, weathered face. He continued.

"I've had a good life. I own a hundred-thousand-dollar house in Kansas City. I have my own business. I have my children and a good wife."

I shook his hand again. He walked back to the team bus.

The season over and all that remained were the awards ceremonies and banquet. At the faculty banquet, I was awarded a trophy by the team. Given our dismal season, I was ashamed to even accept it. After that, I was presented the Minority Faculty of the Year Award. I was also ashamed to accept this award, because as far as I knew I was the only minority faculty, save a Cuban Spanish teacher and a visiting economics professor from Taiwan. There is a saying that, "the greater the guilt, the bigger the trophy." The minority faculty trophy was huge and appropriately, true guilt.

One afternoon a young man appeared at my door. He introduced himself as Jim Bartels, a graduate student at Iowa State University studying nuclear engineering. He asked if he could come in to talk with me.

"So, I hear that you have an interest in astronomy and human space-travel," he began.

"I do teach and have that interest," I answered, asking Carol to fix us coffee.

"What do you think it will take to get humans to the stars?" he asked me.

Over the next two hours, I offered conjectures concerning "NPP"—new physical principles—viz, that new physics needed developing in order that man could reach the nearby stars. It was crazy talk—new physics that could accelerate a craft to near light speed—but he listened as if I were a prophet.

"But the real problem," I opined, "is a human problem. We need to motivate the will and cooperation (and the funding) in the general population. We need to make it a national priority that is irresistible: something that everyone wants for the future and destiny of our kind."

I went on to talk about "Wooden Ships," the hippie anthem concerning the aftermath of a nuclear war. I explained to "Jim" how that song was about love, cooperation and the preservation of the human species. In trying to communicate how I thought that love between human beings would be the key to world peace and a cooperative project to send that love to the stars, I offered hummingbirds as an example.

"Hummingbirds hearts beat at 1,260 beats per minute, and they are tireless in their pursuit of nectar. The only way they can work so hard, is that they love their baby hummingbirds. We humans need to become like hummingbirds—too busy loving to hate one another."

As Jim Bartels rose to go, he reached for my hand.

"Okay, I'll work on the NPP to build the star drive. We'll call it the Hummingbird Engine. And you work on the sociological problem of generating the love-energy and cooperation necessary to use that engine to take human love to the stars."

"I'll do that," I offered as he walked back to his car, drove down the driveway, never to be seen again. But that brief conversation with Jim Bartels, was always a sub-routine—a backplane—motivating my behavior. In fetishizing hummingbirds, I created a self-referential trope that always reminded me that all of my life's work would be towards that end. The logo for Carl Sagan's "Planetary Society" was a wooden ship winding its way among the planets and stars. Warp-drive engines . . . new physical principles . . . hummingbirds . . . humm baby.

Despite all this, I was still trying to get the universe to talk back to me. I was still attempting to "live" equations. How to integrate a life? How to solve the differential equations of the meaning of a life? What does it equal? Humm?

Summer began as a lazy time. Summer, where the corn was knee-high by the fourth of July. Graham had discovered and was into video games. I heard the bleeps and blips from his Atari 2600 "Space Invaders" and "Pac Man" more than I wanted. Shauna was growing quickly into a beautiful and energetic baby girl. We took them on a road trip out to Yellowstone Park. Getting back to Le Mars—with the *Le Martians*—I was determined to improve both our living conditions, and my job opportunities. I had applied to a few PhD programs and been rejected. Carol's sister visited us and suggested that we move to Colorado. She was glowing about both the weather and the job opportunities.

I was determined to continue at Westmar. But one summer day, my neighbor, Old Man Schultz, angered that Mizmoon was chasing his sheep, shot her. The sheep were fenced, so Mizmoon's harassment was from outside the fence. That was it. I had to leave Iowa. Just as Patricia "Mizmoon" Soltysik, SLA theoretician had perished beneath a hail of police bullets, her namesake had died of gunshots. I was angry. But, after threatening Carol's mother, I had sold my guns, and I would not have thought to use them against my neighbor. But thinking back over all the dogs I had lost—Monté, Skip, Inigo—losing Mizmoon was deeply troubling. So, we hired a moving van, packed up all our possessions and headed off for Denver Colorado.

NOTES

1. Edward Bond, *Walkabout* (film), directed by Nicolas Roeg (Sydney and Alice Springs, Australia: 20th Century Fox, 1971).

2. Joseph Weizenbaum, *Computer Power and Human Reason: From Judgment to Calculation* (New York: W. H. Freeman, 1976).

3. Pamela McCorduck, *Machines Who Think: A Personal Inquiry into the History and Prospects of Artificial Intelligence* (New York: W. H. Freeman, 1981).

4. Herbert Peckham, *Hands-On Basic: For the IBM Personal Computer* (New York: McGraw-Hill, 1985)

5. David Ray, ed., *From A–Z: 200 Contemporary Poets* (Athens: Shallow Press, Ohio University Press, 1981).

6. Carl Sagan, *COSMOS* (New York: Random House, 1980).

Chapter 12

Colorado, 1982–1985

While looking for a rental house, we had a hotel room in Denver—courtesy of Claudia's credit card points. Having lived in the "country," we were reluctant to plop down in the middle of an urban (or even suburban) environment. We finally settled on a "chalet-style house" in the Angel Acres development in Conifer Colorado. Having lived in the old drafty farmhouse for five years, the house in Conifer was a cozy palace. It had vaulted windows in front, a wood burning stove on the first floor, and was nestled at about 8,600 feet in the Rocky Mountain foothills thirty-six miles southwest of Denver. The house had three bedrooms, one each for Graham and Shauna, and a master for us. The landlady was an airline attendant, who was exceedingly kind to us, and we eagerly signed the rental agreement, as we awaited the moving truck to deliver our furniture and household effects.

We were all enthralled by the bright blue skies and sunny mountain air. In exploring the new house, I found one paperback novel in a cabinet above the refrigerator—*Night Shift*, from Steven King's collection of short stories. I never read the book, but I took its title as a vade mecum, I needed to start to work—day and night—if I wanted to keep this new environment. We were so happy to get our belongings, set up the stereo, beds, and pots and pans. I recall the excellent acoustics of the vaulted ceilings, listening to George Winston's *Autumn* piano music, as the technician installed our new telephone service. Carol appeared happy with our new circumstances. We met a couple of our neighbors. There was "Old Sandy" and "Young Sandy."

"Old Sandy," a retired math teacher, lived on the other side of the road. He was friendly and would often knock at my door to see what I was up to. "Young Sandy" was a retired stewardess with a young family, including a daughter Shauna's age. But more importantly, she was an aging hippie chick who loved animals and plants. She had several dogs, including "Mr. Dog," a huge shaggy beast with a missing front leg. This three-legged dog and other neighborhood mutts formed a pack that had free run of the dirt roads and fields of Angel Acres. Still smarting from the loss of Mizmoon, I was wary of allowing Scotch to join this free-running pack. However, Scotch—our devoted butterscotch and white beagle—not only joined the pack, but soon became the leader of this pack of cavorting hounds.

Yet again strangers in a new state and neighborhood, we were isolated and lonely. There were days when I would drive down the hill to the Aspen Park Drug Store, just for the presence of other people. Many years later, I can still recall the distinctive smell of that drug store and its magical effect upon my sense of belonging and identification with something. One of the first things I did, as we settled into new environs, was get a library card from the Evergreen Library. I did this to expressly get a copy of Ludwig Wittgenstein's *Tractatus Logico-Philosophicus* (TLP), which still reverberated from my course in Aesthetics at the University of South Dakota with Phillip Turetsky.

I The world is everything that is the case.

I.I The world is the totality of facts, not of things.[1]

I struggled with the TLP. At the time, all I could really understand was that "facts" were linguistics entities, that, "The limits of your world, are the limits of your language." If I did not possess the words for something, they did not exist for me. Beyond that, "Whereof . . . thereof." But reading the TLP was a foreshadowing of my increasing realization of the importance of semiotics—the science of signs—language, including mathematical language—was a system of interconnected marks (words, pictures, symbols) creating a web-like structure that captured (and communicated) meanings. I had started to conceptualize a universe where "objects" were signs. A "physical semiosis," where a bird (or three birds) had a meaning. This was the way the universe could speak, or write, or encode meaning. As I continued to suspect a mechanistic determinism (a Newtonian clockwork universe), I knew, like Wittgenstein that words were the "spectacles" (eyeglasses, lenses) through which we were enabled to see the world. These lenses altered reality. I did not fully understand—yet—that I was having intuitions concerning Humean empiricism and Kantian phenomena/noumena distinctions. My thinking at the time culminated with an equation I could understand. The equation was "The sum of the facts from one to n, is the world." Since this equation is a fact, not included in the 1 . . . n, then this new fact about the world must be added to the list of facts, and the process repeated, ad infinitum. So, the world is always incomplete—the same diagonalization that bedeviled Georg Cantor, Alfred Tarski, and Kurt Gödel—and led to the Turing-Church theorems. The *fact* was that facts could not be infinite, upon pain of infinite regress, and that limited facts meant that the universe was finite under any interpretation (linguistically, mathematically, logically, semiotically, or ontologically). I was preoccupied by what contained this incompleteness, what completed it.

Oh well, as Antonio Gramsci had said: "I'm a pessimist because of intelligence, but an optimist because of will."[2] And all of this originated in the beginning of the universe—in the big bang (or whimper)—my will. Even if it was totally determinate, it was determined that I would will, if you will, and will exactly like this!

And it was the *will* of Bernhard Stahmer—inventor of the Ruffles potato chip high-speed slicer—that provided the T-Bonds that Carol and I were living on *high* in the foothills of the Rocky Mountains. The foothills had become a refuge for the *tribe*—the remainder of the hippies who were still trying to escape from the social, economic, and environmental tyrannies of twentieth-century America. I caught glimpses of them when we ventured out to buy groceries or chanced the longer trips to the shopping malls surrounding Denver. Like me, these neo-hipsters were ambling, shaggy, and easily identifiable by their tattered jeans and unkempt hair. They were also "letting their freak flags fly," in their cast of eyes, obvious disdain for bourgeois conventions.

We eventually met the Cooks (or Snapp-Cooks, in the hyphenated surnames that were becoming more common) at a T-Ball game. Boyd Cook was a pediatrician who had moved to the Conifer foothills from a practice in California. He had bought dozens of acres. But he lived in an authentic cabin that dated back to turn-of-the-century. Boyd's wife, Joyce, was younger. The Snapp-Cooks had two sons—Jonathan and Leif—who became Graham's playmates—Jonathan his same age. Dr. Cook was the umpire of the T-Ball game. Once we were introduced, we quickly became friends.

When we arrived in Denver, we had about $90,000 (almost $250,000 in 2023 dollars). But, knowing that the T-Bond monies were daily diminishing, I needed a stable means of supporting my family. Scouring the newspaper want-ads, I interviewed for a job teaching basic computer skills at Parks College in Denver. Desperate, I took the job. The director of the computer department—Oscar House—a former US Air Force Captain—was convinced of his intellectual superiority. Like Westmar, Parks had a minicomputer, they used to teach business fundamentals like COBOL (common business-oriented language) for keeping accounting records. They also taught the Report Generating Program (RPG). Parks College had recently installed a microcomputer lab with terminals from the minicomputer and needed someone to teach advanced BASIC programming.

The 5¼-inch micro-floppies were the storage media being used in 1982. I had to teach students how to initialize disks, format them, and use basic DOS commands (Init, Erase, Save, Print, Copy). After that, it was IBM BASIC. I taught a high-level course, complete with ARRAY manipulations. Over the course of the eight-week quarter, I lost students at a steady rate. By the time of the final exam, there were only half of those who had originally registered, and of these dozen, only half passed my final exam; which included, "Write a BASIC program that will create a 3x3 ARRAY and fill the diagonal from the (1,1,1) element to the (3,3,3) element with "1's" and all the other cells with "0's." Only two students were able to do this. When other teachers at Parks started to tell me that most of the students were "hopeless," and that the college was using their Veterans Affairs (VA) education benefits (GI Bill) as a source of profit, I knew I had to quit this frustrating job. The only benefit for me (and the two students who aced my final exam) was that I deepened my mastery of programming techniques.

One memorable evening, after pique with Carol—we seldom argued—where I had had one or two many glasses of red wine, I stormed out the house, jumped in the car, and drove off without having a destination. I found myself in Reynold's Park. I started to walk along one of the park's hiking trails—"Hummingbird Trail"—thought back to Iowa and Jim Bartels's "Hummingbird Engine," and returned home after dark. After apologizing to Carol, and vowing to make things better, to find another job. Hummingbird Trail became our family's favorite hike, where we could see Pikes Peak to the south, and an old Pony Express station, which served as the park ranger's abode. Anytime anyone visited us, we would take them with us and our dogs, for a walk on Hummingbird Trail.

Our third offspring, Lindsey, was born on June 15, 1983. With three children, rent to pay, and mounting costs for food and clothing, I desperately needed a stable job. The $10,000 T-Bonds were being rapidly exhausted. There was also the anomie created by the political situation of the Ronald Reagan presidency. His right-wing policies seemed retrograde—at least to this Black hippie. And Carol's parents, David and Barbara, were in the initial stages of their marital dissolution. They would visit us together, separately, and far too frequently—discussing the lack of virtue in the other—adding to my sense of anomie. My mother's husband—my stepfather Charles Wiggs—died of throat and jaw cancer—perhaps caused by his lifelong cigarette habit. After witnessing his suffering, I tried to stop smoking. I was almost forty. Unemployed. Desperate to prove myself as a father, as a legitimate adult.

Graham was emerging as a stellar student at Conifer's West Jeff Elementary School. Shauna was yet a preschooler. Lindsey still a nursing infant. This is where my friend, the poet David Ray, reentered my life. He invited me to a reading he was giving at Colorado College in Colorado Springs. As I drove the seventy miles, my mind took in the beauty of the mountains. David, gracious as ever, took me to lunch. During lunch, he made the following statement.

"Richard, you will never understand yourself as a Black man, until you spend some time living outside the United States."

He assured me that he could help me find a rental house in San Miguel de Allende.

So, I planned a one-year sojourn to Mexico. Amidst the constant warnings of "Don't drink the water," washed out bridges, and "banditos," all of us were anxious about the trip. But to circumscribe our trepidations, people have sailed across vast oceans without knowing whither yon shores and took "small steps" on the Moon—and we are afraid of Mexico? From remarks I heard from my family and Carol from her own, we both thought the risks exaggerated. Whether slanderous racial bias, or not, I had the dialectical suspicion that Mexican culture might be less belligerent than US culture.

David Ray telephoned today. Carol's mother will visit tomorrow. There are hectic days ahead as we prepare to leave. Having just recently moved from Iowa, it is amazing how much junk five people can accumulate. Parting with anything—even a paperclip—is threatening. "Never know when you might need it," is Carol's refrain. Last night, I dreamed of my father Gus, who had first taken me to Mexico. I think I might have been five or six years old when he traveled to Monterey one summer, where we witnessed a bullfight and the memorable waterfall "Horsetail Falls." I remember the colorful bougainvillea, languid and happy Mexican people.

The next day, everything seemed to click. Graham and I took four boxes of books to the Evergreen Public Library for donation. I loathed giving away books that I had owned for twenty years, but they were mostly paperbacks that could easily be replaced in the future. Graham went with me to Cinderella City—a mall near Denver—to drop off a load of old clothes. I am trying to enjoy the ease of unburdening myself of "things"—it is liberating and anti-materialistic. On the way back from the mall, after buying $3 worth of fireworks at a roadside stand, the VW bus ran out of gas. Luckily, I had a half can of gas in the back.

I had sold both cars and bought a used orange over cream VW camper—"Hippie" bus. The camper was in good shape, but I had a new engine installed. The half can of gas was there because I wanted to mount two five-gallon cans on the front, anticipating the paucity of PEMEX stations in the Sonora Dessert. When we returned, Carol's mother had just arrived. I wanted to try to repair our injured relationship after the confrontation with sheriff's deputies in the old farmhouse in Merrill Iowa.

We were making progress toward the move, more things in boxes destined for storage. I built a wooden box for the top of the VW camper. During this hubbub, I finished reading *The Ghost in the Machine*, which completed a gestalt for me with Arthur Koestler; whose great novel *Darkness at Noon* I had read when I was seventeen at Fisk University.[3] I was enlightened by his lively writing style and his analyses of the Greek concept of *holons*—fractal-like repetitive structures in nature—nature's use of the same structures at different scales. Lightning, rivers, trees, and blood vessels all show the same branching phenomena—something Leonardo put in his journals—the greater the difference between the diameters of the branches, the more obtuse the angle between them. Looking down at the eyelids of baby Lindsey, I could easily see this phenomenon in her branching capillaries.

Koestler went on to conclude that a "soma" type happy pill would be the salvation of mankind. I thought this distinction might be slightly overdrawn, as my own experiences with "happy pills" had convinced me that there was *nothing* as sublime as the chemicals in the natural sensorium. Lucidity in the healthy human consciousness is more potent than any synthetic manipulation. Artificially altered states of consciousness—good formalistically—are suspect as a form of human salvation. This statement is from a person who has taken 1,200 mg of lithium carbonate for thirteen years. I had adjusted my metabolism to it. I had been warned by psychiatrists that if I ever stopped taking it, I would wind up in a straitjacket, in a quiet room, in a psych hospital.

We were to leave for Mexico in a week. I find myself on W. Colfax Avenue waiting for the VW to be fixed. While waiting—a new engine replacement was costly and time-consuming—I chatted with a kindergarten teacher—refreshing to hear her optimism. I thought I needed to get the VW's speakers fixed and buy another five-gallon gas can.

These busy-work activities were ample cover for my growing anxiety. I was unable to communicate my needs to anyone with any conviction. So, I threw myself into any task to hand. It was just as easy to see the world as a nurturing womb (protective externality)—or, container ("container theory" viz., everything is contained in something else)—as it is to see it as an adversarial exposing existential threat. And with any negative trope (modifier or predicate), Colorado's majestic mountains, ponderosa pines, and spangling aspen (not mention purple shadowed deep snow) had been a warm womb for me. Now, if I can find—in people—the same natural balm and calm I have found in Colorado—then, true peace. Like the changing the time on clocks, "I spring ahead to fall back."

Kind reader, note that here is a change of tense as I write from a journal I kept while in Mexico. The past is becoming the eternal now.

As a way of reassuring the children, last night, I took Graham and Shauna to Lakeside Amusement Park. The lights and colors neither amused nor reassured me. But they appeared to have fun. The next week was exhausted by bolting the wooden box to the roof of the camper, securing the two five-gallon gas cans to the rear bumper (I had changed my mind about fastening them to the front), and consolidating the furniture and household goods we would leave to the movers for storage.

We rolled out, packed to the gills, with our loyal beagle, Scotch, and trust that this adventure would yield growth and understanding. Driving south on Highway 285, we soon arrived in a place called "San Miguel," and I thought it ironically premature, as we could not have driven that far in such a short time; southern Colorado might as well have been in Mexico, by the appearance of Spanish culture. Driving on through the Texas plains, vast open lands, pastured with livestock, punctuated with oil well "donkeys," we were making progress with few complaints. Carol nursing baby Lindsey.

Crossing through the border at Juarez, everything changed. The buildings became colored adobe; the people appeared more dishabille; and the goods and services questionable. I distinctly recall standing outside the Mexican side of the customs offices, when I was addressed by a tall man.

"Qué hora tienes?"

I blinked, not knowing what he meant. Seeing that I did not understand, he quickly tapped his wrist. Not knowing how to respond, I stepped closer to him and held my watch up so he could see it. In Juarez, we met a young man—Antonio—who knew enough English to help us. He showed me a calculus textbook, in Spanish. He showed me where to get "hamburgers," just like at McDonald's, he reassured me. Despite all caution, we ate the hamburgers and drank the Kook-aide he offered us. Antonio also helped us find a motel. I found the motel, what we had come to understand as "Mexican quality," which meant, "of a seriously inferior quality." And of course, we quickly developed "tourista" (i.e., diarrhea) from Antonio's food and drink. But our new young Mexican friend also helped me negotiate the bribes—almost $300—needed to get approval to take my "computardor"—an apple //e, 64k RAM, with WordPerfect, and a Brother Daisywheel printer—into Mexico. When we arrived in San Miguel, our realtor, Senior El Cid, an ex-pat American, told us there was no "duty" on the computer, and that we had been swindled. He went on to explain that everyone in Mexico was "on the take." If you wanted anything done, you had to pay a bribe.

But what a magical journey! We were on the "magic bus." The 650-mile drive from Conifer to Juarez, and the 950 miles from Juarez to San Miguel, took twenty-five hours. I only stopped for "pee breaks," petrol at the PEMEX gas stations, and a few times for snacks—that we all agreed were of inferior "Mexican quality." Of course, I stopped on a few occasions, so Scotch could stretch her legs and take care of her business. Carol drove for two hours, and I drove the rest; determined after the poor motel in Juarez, to not stop until we reached our destination. First, the Sonora desert, with its stately Saguaro cacti, lent to the air of strangeness. With the Sierra Madre Mountains to the west, we were tooling through the high plateau on the central plains. I did not speak Spanish. Carol was able to communicate much better than I could. My thoughts centered on old movies and television programs—the *Cisco Kid* and *Zorro*.

But, driving along the largely desolate highways late at night, Mexican semi-tractor trailer trucks—eighteen wheelers—decorated with yellow and green running lights, crucifixes, dangling mariachi ball fringe outlining windows, I reexamined my motives for this trip. First—or ostensibly—the reason was to write. But that was only a cover, as I had always believed that my manic depression was largely the result of racism: my extraordinary reactions to rejection was to become hyper-energetic. So, I thought, if I could live in a country where I could not even speak the language, I would be able to differentiate (dy/dx) racism from cultural otherness. I thought I could tell how much American anti-Black racism was part of my "psychosis." We were also running away from the political climate of Reaganism. Further, Carol's parent's marriage woes were increasingly annoying—they tried to drag us into the middle of it. I do not know when the idea came to me, but at some point, I decided I would try to gradually withdraw myself from lithium.

The first drive through Mexico was an experience I will never ever forget. The narrow highways, incredible distances between gas stations, troubles with money changing, and Mexican express buses sans mufflers; the semi-tractor-trailer trucks barreling down the highways at eighty miles an hour; noises, grinding gears, rumbling mufflers; the pistoning hammers of an empire that threatened to keep other drivers at bay. The initial impression that all of Mexico was as dilapidated as Juarez was an illusion, as the further south we traveled, the more refined the country became. It was as if the border towns were DMZ zones to discourage Americans from penetrating the sweet heartlands of innocence, beauty, and harmony with nature.

We arrived in San Miguel de Allende, late in the afternoon, on Sunday, July 17, 1984. The evening was resplendent in golden sunshine. The people were out in the streets, which were far too narrow, steep, curvy, and cobblestoned. Not knowing where the one-way streets were, or which way they ran, we encountered the horn-blowing, raised fists, and obscene gestures of irate drivers. It was so harrowing that Carol vowed never to drive in San Miguel. After finding a garage we could rent, we went about unloading the van.

The entire family made progress today. Carol deposited $1,000 in the town bank and wrote a check for $200 in exchange for pesos. We had a successful outing to a grocery store. Carol, the kids, and Scotch took a walk. I saw the local square for the first time. It was high summer on the central plateau, flowers blooming everywhere. I decided to spruce up the rental house at 54 Chorro Calle—which translated as "gush, jet, or spout street"—by white-washing the walls. And I have begun to think about getting down to work. On my poems first, as I thought that might be the easiest direction to make rapid progress. I wanted to write them up—elevate the language, clarify, and eliminate triteness—beginning with red-penciling, then get them into the WordPerfect word processor. I needed to get into this writing schedule as soon as possible.

Within the week, I had painted the study, a large room on the top floor with open French windows. The kids had a shaky day, still trying to adapt to the alien environment. Carol bought three wool throw rugs today. The floors are tiled, so, cool underfoot. I am exhausted from driving, painting, and trying to support Carol with the children. But I push on, painting the upstairs bedrooms and bathroom.

I like the informality of San Miguel—so far, no major problems. Graham and Shauna are making important steps toward healthy adjustments. Graham has already made two new friends—Thomas (a white Americano) and Roberto (a neighborhood youngster). Writing is heavy on my mind. I should be down to rewriting my poems in another week or so. Getting the computer up and working will take a few days. I was having problems getting WordPerfect to print to the Brother daisy-wheel printer.

I sent out postcards to family and friends to let them know we had arrived safely. We are still waiting for our first mail delivery. Carol appears more than resolved to the move. For a few days I was worried that she thought it a mistake. Now, I think she is—secretly—pleased that we have finally returned to doing things that are daring. Like Cat Steven's song, "I'm looking for a hardheaded woman," she is indeed that.[4]

My appetite seems to have improved. I do not know whether it is the food or a better attitude. Wittgenstein says there are no private languages.[5] Like a fool, I think my thoughts about loving the universe and stars are private. I am not sure I understand this all the way down, as, just because *we* have not found the words (or philosophy) that resolve our mysteries and anxieties, does not mean that somewhere in a vast universe, other beings have not found the words or symbols to so satisfy them (private to them). Wittgenstein neglects the possibility of more nuanced (better) words with better minds to understand them. For what I know of Wittgenstein, I cannot even say. Not much.

I need loneliness to write . . . well. I need the deep existential alienation that Albert Camus was able to portray so lucidly in the stories in *Exile and the Kingdom*—solidarity or solitude?[6] I needed the unutterably ineffable feeling of aloneness and not knowing my way about that nothing can console. It is difficult to do this with a wife and three small children.

I am half finished reading "Him with His Foot in His Mouth," by Saul Bellow. Bellow's writing is fluidly unselfconscious. His is a relaxed and urbane style—cultured. But as I remember it now, his *Mr. Sammler's Planet* is his most refined and penetrating work.[7] As I continue to think about all the people I have known and loved—Gus, Charles, Tommie—and lost, I search for an expression that could be interpreted as "overwhelming." I am seeking a positive goodness; searing magnesium light; pouring from my heart; illuminating everything; as bright as the noonday Mexican sun. And searching the faces of the people I see in the street, a reflection of hope—that I have projected for others—to reinforce the idea that living is good; that the life force is directed toward glory—driven light—after-image of the primordial, glowing, moving, cohering—energy forced into being, by law, and will. "I am pessimistic about my intellect and optimistic about my will."

I am almost forty years old: far beyond the age of creative mathematicians. I have only published a few absurd short stories and a dozen poems. My art consists of a few badly smeared canvasses. I am a nothing and a nobody. But today progress! Ah, sweet progress!!! I finished painting upstairs (except for the bathroom and master bedroom). It is beginning to look like home. I start painting downstairs in the morning. Rufina, our maid, went out for glass panes, so I could replace broken windows. I did not really want a maid, but I was told by El Cid (the rental agent) that the house came with the maid—there was no negotiating that. She was short, chubby, and clearly of mixed race—Mexican and one of the indigenous Indian tribes. She cooked, cleaned, and did our wash. She worked harder than anyone—never passing a trashcan without grabbing what was in it—cooking, sweeping, dusting. That night she had prepared excellent spaghetti for us and left to walk home to feed her own children.

We have been here for two weeks. Of that time, I have been painting for ten days. The fireplace had an elaborate painting of a Mayan or Aztec god Quetzalcoatl—a feathered serpent—the progenitor of mankind—took me eight hours to carefully outline. I must push myself to finish painting so I can get down to the real reasons I am here. Graham is getting bored—we need to see about getting him enrolled in school. I started reading *Memoirs of a Space Traveler* by Stanisław Lem—looks interesting; especially as that is how I see myself in Mexico, a space traveler.[8]

August was suddenly upon us. I got up early; swept Chorro Street up one side and down the other; trying to spread discipline and care. I was not sweeping to judge my neighbors, I simply thought someone might follow my example. The street was next to a public park. Niños y niñas—boys and girls—dropped candy wrappers and scraps of paper along the curbs as they walked to the park. At the corner of the park, at the end of our street was an old "insane asylum," that had housed the city's deranged people at the turn of the century. Peeking inside the cells, as I walked to the park, I could still hear the hysterical screams and sense the suffering of those who had been jailed there before Lithium. In picking up scraps of paper, I was making a statement about discipline.

Carol's sister Claudia flew into the airport in Leon for a visit. I suspected she was checking up on us. These early days of August were blessed with a white sunshine (the Tequila Sun), cool breezes on the central Mexican plateau—the heartland of the Toltec empire. I continued to finish the trim in the house and fix the ceiling light in the living room. Scotch was freaked. Confined to the back courtyard and on a leash when we went for walks, she did not bark once the entire ten months we were in Mexico (could not bark in Spanish we joked). There was a small black and white TV in the house. It was hooked up to cable and we were able to watch the new twenty-four-hour *CNN* news channel. We also watched movies in English and the Saturday baseball games.

One funny thing happened when baby Lindsey, just learning to talk, while watching this little TV broadcasting a Spanish language program, looked at the screen and said "Bla, bla, bla." She thought Spanish sounded like gibberish. And I was little better. At my best, I was learning to say "Buenas días."

"Buenas tardes"

"Buenas noches"

"De nada."

I get up in the morning, have my coffee, read for a few hours, and then spend the afternoon working on the computer. Interspersed with this, I try to help Carol with the children. I am reading *The Séance* by Isaac Bashevis Singer, the Noble Prize-winning short storyteller.[9] I have just read *Earth House Hold* by Alan Ginsberg's friend Gary Snyder. Snyder is an advocate of Zen Buddhism, and a member of the "tribe." He writes:

> How do they recognize each other? Not always by beards, long hair, bare feet or beads. The signal is a bright and tender look; calmness and gentleness, freshness and ease of manner. Men, women, and children—all of whom together hope to follow the timeless path of love and wisdom, in affectionate company with the sky, winds, clouds, trees, waters, animals and grasses—this is the tribe.[10]

Snyder had isolated the revolution of subtlety's "recognition factor," a knowing smile like the opening words of the Jefferson Airplane's song "Wooden Ships."[11] All is well tonight. *Buenas noches* (good night).

I am suddenly amazed by my mastery of the Quark WordPerfect word processor. Why did I have so much trouble with it in Colorado? Like many things, life has simplified in San Miguel. S.M. Allende is highly conducive to deep concentration; mild weather; a slow pace of life; and an abundance of nature. The comida is excellente—the cervaza transcendent (not a sharp as Americano beer). I have been drinking *Tres Exquis* (XXX) cerveza clara and the smooth and foamy *Negro Modello*—with a round aftertaste.

I rewrote a dozen poems today. I am devastated how thin many of them are. Inverted word orders, scant imagery, lack of concrete nouns, are just a few of their weaknesses. The apple computer helps with the cutting and pasting. As I continue to take 1,200 mg of the Lithium that I brought here with me, I increasingly think it interferes with both my creativity and clarity, not to mention my motivation.

Shauna had obtained a baby rabbit, a *Coneho*—rabbit in Spanish—she named "Fuzzle," which we keep in a cage in the backyard. Fuzzle is cute like Shauna, a little bunny.

I wrote to the owner of the house at Chorro 54—Marilyn Dodd Frank, a stage, TV, and movie actress—to see if she would either pay the $306.24 I spent for house paint, or deduct it from our monthly rent. I also sent postcards to Omar Serrano, Delores Wilson, and Erik Hassenbein. Omar was a colleague at Parks College in Denver, who would play an important part in my life when we returned to Colorado. Delores Wilson was the wife of Jere Wilson, the University of Chicago PhD child psychologist, who has been terminated by Parks College in Kansas City and I had partnered with in his furniture moving operation "Two Men and a Truck." And Erik was a former student in one of my computer programming classes at Parks College.

Reading the *Bhagavad Gita*, the conversation between Sri Krishna and Arjuna, in the chariot—"Do your duty, they're already dead—as they died when they wronged you"—was to become a central premise in my evolving secular humanism. "When you wrong another person, you die."[12] I felt this viscerally. The tribe—neo-Hippies—were evolving along these lines, "On the Road." I wanted to be kinder. I thought that perhaps an infinite kindness might allow me to hear the whispers of an even kinder universe. I was convinced there was a link between human goodness and insight into the realities of the Cosmos. Inspired by Arjuna's goodness, I was on the chariot.

Even with Westmar's 2½ inch refracting telescope, I was unable to resolve M-31—the great Andromeda Galaxy. Tonight, or tomorrow, I will climb up onto the roof of this old stone house in S.M. to look for her. Using the *Telstar* 5¼ diskette with a program to locate astronomical objects, because of bad seeing, I was unable to see M-31. San Miguel is an old city. Located at 20° 92′ N, 100° 45′ W, at an elevation of 6,289 feet, the city is a national historical site. The house we live in has stone walls, many feet in thickness, and dates back more than two hundred years. The cobblestone streets are trod by burrows, street vendors, and a Mariachi Band that serenaded us under our open upstairs windows one night, when Carol and I were at a low point.

We made up our differences over the weekend. To break the monotony, we all piled into the VW Camper and drove to the nearby town of Celaya, the state of Guanajuato's municipal capital, about thirty miles due south of S.M. I was desperate to protect my family from all threats, including the isolation of our domicile. Celaya, with a population of more than 30,000, was more than a scaled-up version of S.M. This was a bustling city—not a cobble-stoned historical site—where there were legitimate grocery stores, parking lots, and well-paved boulevards. We bought new stores of fruits and vegetables.

My work on the poems is progressing. One of my favorite "hippie" poets was Richard Brautigan. "Brautigan wrote poetry, experimenting with metre and image because, he claimed, he wanted to perfect writing sentences so he could write novels."[13] When I pine to write, I always seek to improve my poetry first. I agree with him.

Carol has located a school for Graham. I am excited that he will be going to school this year, as his freedom on the streets of San Miguel has resulted in some rather disturbing behaviors. First, he seems to be in some kind of running conflict with the local Mexican boys. He runs the streets with Thomas, his white friend, and seems to have developed enmity with Roberto, his Mexican compadre. I found a Ninja throwing star among his possessions. He is a good lad, but he needs the structure of school—*escuela*—as fall approaches. The school is bi-lingual—Spanish half-day; English the other half, run by an ex-pat elderly white woman. San Miguel is populated by a large contingent of American ex-patriots seeking the low prices of Mexican housing due to the favorable exchange rate between the dollar and peso, the mild climate, and socialized medical care. There are also a large number of American students at the Art Institute.

I finished reading John Updike's *Couples* today. Having read a few of his "Rabbit" novels, my evaluations of his fiction have not changed. He is a brilliant writer of contemporary fiction. His characters are immaculately flawed toward the carnal, cynical, and perverse. They lack the noble goodness I am searching for, and human beings do not seem to possess; and if this is the case, what is the sense to continue the pursuit of civilization? I find the heroic struggles of "Piet and Foxey" are no more (and no less) than the ordinary, exposed. Nonetheless, Updike is one of the great writers of the twentieth century.[14] I did not know it then, but I would go on to read almost all of his works (including his literary criticism). In his fiction, he has the ability to describe details in such a way as to create the illusion that the reader is *thinking* what is being read.

"Aieeee!!!"

There was a scream from the downstairs bathroom.

"What is it?" I yelled running down the steps. Once I opened the door, I saw the scorpion with its raised tail. After dispatching it and reassuring Carol that they were small and perhaps not deadly, I returned to the upstairs study. But, really, scorpions?

When I was at Minot State, Mrs. Ladendorf had said, "If you're not doing mathematics, you're wasting time."

I thought about that last remark. I knew that I was wasting time. I was not doing mathematics. I thought about mathematics. Mathematics was imbricated in my poetry. I pondered the meanings of infinity and infinitesimals—my old high school science project "Theory of Terminated Infinities"—and tried to find an inroad back into my mathematical work. Too old, I thought, to do any meaningfully creative mathematical work, I dreamed of understanding—in the interstitial moments—the mathematics I had already learned, been exposed to, or only had a glimpse into like, Abelian Rings, Group Theory, complex functions, Quaternions. The great mathematician Carl Friedrich Gauss had written:

> There are problems to whose solution I would attach an infinitely greater importance than those of mathematics, for example touching ethics, or our relation to God, or concerning our destiny and our future; but their solution lies wholly beyond us and completely outside the province of science.[15]

Knowing that my mathematical skills were suspect, I thought I would dwell on Gauss's "outside the province of science." Wandering up to the roof, I finally spotted M-31—a hazy ellipse—4.8 magnitude, halfway between the stars Alpheratz (corner star of the Great Square of Pegasus) and Shedir. At 2.2 million light years, the Andromeda Galaxy was the farthest object observable by the unaided eye. When I saw it, my heart leapt. More than 400 billion stars bouncing around on the inside my skull—more than awesome.

The Andromeda Galaxy became a recurring theme in my thoughts—a metaphor for the impossible—something that could be seen, but not touched—a destination—the closest "island universe" like the Milky Way. In the various renditions of my novel "The Seed," "The Star Plow," and "Ulim-Mwingi," M-31 became a destination in the future imagination of humankind.[16] The basic idea was that the two million light years separating the two closest galaxies was like the Atlantic Ocean to wooden ships (the song about square-riggers creaking on the waves) and the sailors who quaked in "shivering their timbers" (turning sheets to the wind as they ruffled). And in trying to gain my freedom, I wrote the story of a Black man who figured out a way to transport the entirety of life on the planet Earth to "a new home in the sun" (line from the Neil Young song "After the Goldrush") in the Andromeda galaxy. This mythopoetic story—a Black man accomplishing the impossible—became an obsession. But no matter how I wrote this story, it was always met with blind, uncommented upon, rejection. Blankness. So, my natural conclusion (manic-depressive, schizoid, paranoic, thought) was that it had already happened and the powers that be were trying to suppress the reality that had brought them unwillingly to the Andromeda Galaxy. I observed M-31 from the roof of the house in Mexico with Graham's binoculars. I was there!

Awakening the next morning to the ritual of the first of the three Lithium capsules that I would take that day, I started reading E. B. White's *Elements of Style*, trying to pick up a few ideas on prose composition.[17] I was always trying to discover ways to improve my writing, the "little scribbler," I was. Then, I discovered that the tape deck and speakers had been stolen from the VW van. The air-valve caps on the van had already been stolen by kids, I had presumed. And these thefts really did not bother me. Mexico was an extremely poor country. I had observed an incredibly old man—ancient—sitting on the corner of our street, all day with a shallow woven basket of limes, and a sign "five centavos." Feeling compassion, looking into his eyes in a nest of wrinkles, I bought five limes I did not need. I am not concerned about the lack of scruples of the people in this Catholic nation. This is not a nation of criminals. However, I hope whoever took the tape deck does not return for the tires and engine.

Speaking of criminals, I finished reading Jean Genet's *Querelle*, a thoroughly awful work. A dreadful account of murder, sadism, homosexuality, Genet is able to conflate these acts in such a way that disgust is leveled, and the reader forced to reexamine notions of conventional morality. All of which raises the question of whether the modern industrial-warfare-capitalist complex's embrace of the slaughter of human beings, equates with sociological sexual "crimes"—all depravations being equal. After Genet's *Querelle* and Updike's *Couples*, both distressing reads, I had the appetite for something more redemptive.[18] To that end, I am reading the *Meditations* by Marcus Aurelius. I am struck by not only his stoicism, but also his humility—In a hundred years, no matter how famous, few of us will be remembered; in a thousand, hardly any; in a million, none of us; in a billion, light.[19]

I finished the rewrite of my poems today. The word processor made it a delight. Some of the poems are beginning to show signs of their age, but I included them to give "arc" to my aesthetic.

Nine years ago, tonight, in Stillwell, Kansas, Carol and I had not seen Graham Matthew Jones, as he would be born that day—a Saturday—on a sunflower yellow Kansas morning. Tomorrow he will be nine years old. Since Graham was born, we have lived in Kansas, Maryland, Iowa, Colorado, and now Mexico. I have had jobs teaching in a private school, commercial artist, well-drilling, college instructor, and business school teacher. In those nine years, I have taught myself how to use a computer. As such, I have gained an appreciation for programming, string variables, arrays, and for-next loops. I have also improved my writing and read books that have deepened my thinking.

The work goes well. I finished my first short story today. It is twice as good as any I brought with me. This environment really helps my concentration. Today marks the sixth week. We celebrated Graham's birthday at the "Circus" restaurant—quite an affair. Our Mexican neighbors and a few Americanos dropped by for an impromptu party. Tomorrow is the first day of school for Graham. Shauna wants to go . . . too. A rock throwing incident has ended, for now, Graham and Roberto's friendship. We live in a working-class Mexican neighborhood. Albeit there are rich "white Mexicans" (of Castilian ancestry) living behind gated walls on the same street.

Things are picking up. I discovered that the interface plug between the computer and the interface card for the printer was loose. Hence, the problem with the printer. Where I promised myself not to let rejections from publishers mar my enthusiasm, I jumped in; sent a baseball story—"Squeeze Play"—to Roger Angell at the *New Yorker*. After a superficial reading of John Bunyan's *Pilgrim's Progress* in my efforts to elevate my ethics, I am committed to reading the Bible again. Bunyan's progress is by inches, as it was written in 1675, before our modern notions of adventure and romance, so I can accept its ponderous redundancy.[20]

The past few days have been lost. I am in a writing block; it all seems hopeless. But the devastating events appear to be external. Graham's attitude is poor. He expects us to do everything he wants—yet he calls us dumb, dope heads, loco—ad nauseum. Carol got so angry with Shauna, that it frightened me. We are all at the end of our patience. I do not blame Graham for his hostility. We have changed residences so much that he is always trying to recover any semblance of stability he has established. And our transient vagabondism is indicative of "dope heads." I absorb all insults and slights as a matter of course.

I got a traffic ticket today—600 pesos—which reinforces the alienation of the day. Someone stole the front Colorado license plate and two hombres claiming to be plain clothes policemen tried to extort me into paying to recover it. I doubted they were Federales and just ignored their request for payment. Carol burned and then reburned our dinner when she tried to reheat it. Sometimes it seems that everything is arrayed to undermine us, and it comes in cycles, waves. Graham's tears and anger; Shauna's petulance; Lindsey's nighttime crying; Carol's passive-aggressive episodes—run through their periodic ebb and flows—sometimes peaking simultaneously. Their moods are not random. All the while, our housekeeper, Rufina, floats through the house like a warm zephyr, silently cleaning, cooking, and washing diapers.

I met some *Norte Americanos* tonight at Graham's friend Nick's. They were worldly, and obviously well-off sophisticated people who agreed that we were ignorant fools. Not that they said much as they let me make my lack of class obvious. But it was obvious to me at least, as Carol did her best to hold up her white flag (racial identity), that these people did not respect us. Rather than "old home week" the cocktail hour became a retrenchment of the racial and class hostilities—incognito in badly translated Spanish—I come to expect at home in the United States.

I felt so "judged"—as if having been out of the situation where I had automatically been judged stupid—I had been forced back into an alien environment where I am suffused with the same feelings that caused me to flee to Mexico. One of the people at Nick's mother's house (Suzanne) was a writer. I would later realize that the tall, aloof, man was Clifford Irving, whose *Unauthorized Biography of Howard Hughes*, turned out to be fake, resulting in a year and half in prison. As such, Irving was famous (infamous). He told me that he was in the process of publishing *Tom Mix and Pancho Villa* in paperback.[21] I saw him a few times at an early Sunday morning softball game with Americans. The experience of double-entendre laden cocktail talk, much of which was intended to go over my head, made me not want to be a writer. It was a vicious evening.

After three days of depression—result of the fool I had been made of and made of myself—following the party at Suzanne's, I am better. Humiliation is good for the soul. Alcohol and lithium carbonate do not mix. I sent four poems to the magazine *Omni*. I received a letter from Alex Blackburn, editor of *Writer's Forum*, a small literary magazine in Colorado Springs, inviting me to submit; so, I prepared a few poems and a short story. We are preparing to return to Texas in a week to renew our visa. I just completed reading Carl Sagan's *Broca's Brain*. Sagan had a chapter knocking the pseudo-science of Immanuel Velikovsky, so I decided to read *Earth in Upheaval*.[22] I rather enjoyed it—the tensions between gradualism and catastrophism—events assumed to be billions of years old, reinterpreted as being only 3,500 years old. The book is mainly geology and anthropology.

I painted the upstairs bathroom shower. Everyone is excited by the journey back across the desert to Laredo, Texas. After completing our business in Texas, spending three days in a cheap motel, I am happy to be back in San Miguel. Carol has mixed emotions (and American groceries), but the kids are glad to be back, after days of being cooped-up in the van and motel.

I finished an acrylic painting of the "Mexican Sun." I am really revulsed by my painting. Carol's mother had back surgery. We are all hoping she will be fine and able to visit us soon. Getting back to work, whew, what a day! The mail came today, after a long delay. Walking back from the post office, where we had a box, I shuffled through the letters. David Ray's son Sam, a college freshman at Carleton College in Minnesota, was killed in a drunken mishap with a train. I knew Sam when he was a youngster—I played baseball with him at a playground—and how much David loved him. I felt the need to console David but did not know how. There was also a letter from Westmar College concerning the missing telescope they had loaned me; a letter from Regina Lombard, my old friend from Drake University; and a bill from Graham's new school. So, all in all bad news—death, missing property, forsaken friends, and owed money. I am really agonizing about Sam. How does one person suffer for another's loss? Death is for the living. My pulse is quickened. I suffer for David and Ruth, but there is little I can say—I will bide my time—wait until I can say something meaningful.

I finally telephoned David. He sounded like he had dealt with his grief to the extent possible. David spoke of "the transfigured one." Sam was, as I remembered him, a thick-set toe-headed boy, easily awed, quickly excited, and nearly invisibly unobtrusive. He was socially poised and eager to please others.

I have almost completed my reading of Abraham Pais's biography of Einstein, *Subtle Is the Lord*. Some of the mathematics is unintelligible to me. I recognize some of the equations. Reading about Einstein's genius is an exercise—a lesson—in humility.[23]

I have come to a dead standstill with my own writing. My manuscript "Three Birds" seems doomed. While I wait for inspiration; I like to paint—smearing up large canvasses with globs of brightly colored acrylic paint. "Lies uttered in pursuit of truth are not as deadly as lies of self-deception." I read Jack Kerouac's *The Subterraneans*. I was blown away by Morrison's *The Bluest Eye* (a signed copy that had been given to David Ray by Toni that he had loaned me).[24] In the lineage of beat and hippie literature—from William S. Burroughs, Alan Ginsberg, Richard Brautigan, Kerouac—to San Miguel de Allende, Burroughs had shot his wife in a hotel in Mexico City and Neal Cassidy had died on a San Miguel railroad track, high on pulque (a homemade agave cactus liquor) in 1968.

The past two days have been strange. Yesterday I opted to drive Carol into town to accomplish her errands. In San Miguel, one-way streets are marked on the houses and buildings with tiny inlaid mosaic tiles. Some streets abruptly change from two-way to one-way without warnings. Well, I was flagged down by a "Transito cop"—the same one who had given me a ticket six weeks ago (for driving the wrong way on a one-way street). I pretended I did not understand his request for "Identificacion." I acted surly. It turned out okay, as he only warned me. Shauna wanted to buy a "friend"—a frog carved from onyx—so against all my instincts of driving around in town, we retraced our path to get the friend. Shopping completed, on the way home, we were stopped by "Federales" for a routine examination of our vehicle registration papers—which were not in the car. We were forced to return home for the papers. Our registration checked out, so now back up a treacherous cobblestoned hill, an oncoming car would not give me room. In trying to pass, I nicked him—and he shook his fist and yelled at us. Uncharacteristically, I yelled back.

Now you might guess this was enough for one day. But noooo . . . no way José. I got a condescending phone call from Suzanne, Graham's friend Nick's mother, calmly informing me of an outbreak of Hep B at Graham's school. She thought Graham should get a Gamma Globulin shot at the clinic. When Graham had been sick, we had had a house call from a young Mexican doctor. I was beginning to understand that Mexico was more socialist—viz socialized medicine—than I had suspected. There were free clinics in Mexico and health care was relatively inexpensive. We were able to get an inoculation for Graham at the clinic. The visit from the Mexican doctor had been alarmingly cheap. That was yesterday—I had stayed up all night the day before—and today Graham has a case of head lice. Our housekeeper, Rufina, is talking about "dead people," for reasons that I cannot understand. Tomorrow?

Today, forty-odd years after these words were written—in a green "Record," National Brand ledger book, I want to step forward to now, to today. I am almost eighty years old. I am currently reading three books—two novels and a mathematics book. The first novel is *Erasure* by Percival Everette—funny, enjoyable, authentically Black literature. The second, *A Memory Called Empire* by Arkady Martine—apparatchik space opera. The math book gives me pause. *Volume I: The World of Mathematics* by James R. Newman, published in 1956, is a compendium of papers and book chapters about mathematics in four volumes that I bought in a used bookstore for $45. When I began writing this memoir, reminded of my love for mathematics, I thought I would finish my reading life by reacquainting myself with math by reading all four volumes. This morning I am reading E. T. Bell's contribution "The Queen of Mathematics," a discussion of higher arithmetic, viz number theory. There is a discussion of Fermat numbers, Mersenne primes, and "D.N. Lehmer, whose factor tables for the first ten million numbers set an unsurpassed record for completeness and accuracy . . . proved (1931) that M_{257} is not prime."[25]

This is only mentioned because it produced a deep synchronicity. The immediate pages of my journal from Mexico that I am currently using, are filled with my attempts to use the apple //e to calculate primes by manipulating perfect numbers, Mersenne primes, and Fermat type numbers. There are tables of these tabulations and printouts in my journal. The results are predictably wrong, but I am impressed by the fact that I was as doggedly deluded about my mathematical abilities and pursuits back then, as I was about my writing and painting.

Back in San Miguel, I swallowed another tablet of Eskalith.

NOTES

1. Ludwig Wittenstein, *Tractatus logico-philosophicus* (London: Routledge, 1922).
2. Antonio Gramsci, *Antonio Gramsci: Letters from Prison*, ed. Frank Rosengarten, trans. Raymond Rosenthal, 2 vols. (New York: Columbia University Press, 2011), vol. 1, 299.
3. Arthur Koestler, *The Ghost in the Machine* (New York: Macmillan, 1967); and Koestler, *Darkness at Noon* (New York: TIME, 1962; New York: Bantam Books, 1984).
4. Cat Stevens [Yusuf Islam], "Hard Headed Woman," *Tea for the Tillerman* (album) (London: Morgan Studios, 1970).
5. Ludwig Wittgenstein, *Philosophical Investigations* (New York: Macmillian, 1968), 88.
6. Albert Camus, *Exile and the Kingdom*, new trans. Carol Cosman (New York: Vintage, 2007).
7. Saul Bellow, *Mr. Sammler's Planet* (New York: Penguin Classic, 2004).
8. Stanisław Lem, *Memoirs of a Space Traveler: Further Reminiscences of Ijon Tichy*, trans. Joel Stern and Maria Swiecicka-Ziemianek (Evanston, IL: Northwestern University Press, 2000).
9. Isaac Bashevis Singer, *The Séance and Other Stories*, trans. Roger H. Klein and others (New York: Penguin, 1968).
10. Gary Snyder, *Earth House Hold* (New York: New Directions Publishing, 1969), 116.
11. David Crosby, Paul Kantner, Steven Stills, "Wooden Ships," *Volunteers* (album), (New York: RCA Victor, 1969).
12. Juan Mascaró, trans. *The Bhagavad Gita* (New York: Penguin Books, 1962).
13. Matt Stefon, "Richard Brautigan," at https://www.britanica.com/biography/Richard-Brautigan.
14. John Updike, *Couples* (New York: Knopf, 1968).
15. Carl Friedrich Gauss, quoted in *The World of Mathematics*, ed. James R. Newman, 4 vols. (New York: Simon and Schuster, 1956), vol. 1, 314.
16. See Richard A. Jones, *Ulim-Mwingi* (Bakersfield, CA: Innovative Ghost Writers, forthcoming 2023).
17. E. B. White, *The Elements of Style* (New York: Macmillan, 1962).
18. Jean Genet, *Querelle* (New York: Grove Press, 1987); and Updike, *Couples*.
19. Marcus Aurelius, *Meditations: Marcus Aurelius and His Times* (New York: Walter J. Black, 1945).
20. John Bunyan, *The Pilgrim's Progress from This World*, 2 vols. (London: Nathaniel Ponder, 1678; 1684).
21. Clifford Irving, *Autobiography of Howard Hughes* (unpublished manuscript to New York: McGraw-Hill, 1972; private publication in 1999); and Irving, *Tom Mix and Pancho Villa* (New York: St. Martin's Press, 1982).
22. Carl Sagan, *Broca's Brain: Reflections on the Romance of Science* (New York: Presidio Press, 1986); and Immanuel Velikovsky, *Earth in Upheaval* (Garden City; New York: Doubleday, 1955).

23. Abraham Pais, *Subtle Is the Lord: Science and the Life of Albert Einstein* (Oxford: Oxford University Press, 1982).

24. Jack Kerouac, *The Subterraneans* (New York: Grove Press, 1958); Toni Morrison, *The Bluest Eye* (New York: Holt, Rinehart and Winston, 1970).

25. See E. T. [Eric Temple] Bell, *Men of Mathematics* (New York: Simon and Schuster, 1986).

Chapter 13

I'm Wasted and I Can't Find My Way Home, 1984

"Come down on your own/ And leave your body alone." These lines from Steve Winwood's song "Can't Find My Way Home,"[1] easily expresses where I was in San Miguel. I was lost. As the concluding sentences of the last chapter indicate, I was not "leaving my body alone," taking 1,200 mg of Eskalith a day. I had decided I would "come down," by systematically withdrawing myself from the lithium. After the first two months, I dropped down to three capsules a day—900 mg—with the plan that if nothing happened, I would decrease to 600 after two-three months. But I also wanted to "find my way home." Home was not Mexico, Iowa, or the United States of America. Home was the Andromeda Galaxy I had glimpsed from the roof. In other words, the universe was home, and I wanted a letter from home. I needed to have some sense of communication, community, and commonality with that home. This was how I experienced existentialism—finding myself at home everywhere—in the universe. To do that, I needed to be better. A better father; a better husband; a better writer; a better thinker. In short, a better person.

Whew! What a day. I slept late. We gave Rufina the day off. Carol and I did the wash, by hand, as Rufina usually did—soaking and pounding the diapers, then hanging them up to air dry. Oiling the downstairs furniture and woodwork with polish, helped, as I was always trying to increase the family's comfort in this uncustomarily strange environment. Thinking back to the story of "Black and White Scottie Dogs," David Ray had published in *New Letters*, I was deeply paranoid about the motives (and scrutiny) of white people. San Miguel presents an intriguing array of peoples: *mestizo* (mixed raced), indigenous Indian (Tarasco); Castilian (white Spanish); white (ex-pats and *touristas*); Afro-Mexican (they tell me Vera Cruz is the city of Black Mexicans); and the mongrelized unidentifiable. The Black/white binary racism of the United States is muted in Mexico, but still operant. I passed through these people as a ghost during their celebration of the Day of the Dead.

I wrote my best poem—"Revolution"—since "Amtrak," last night. I continue to delude myself calculating prime numbers. The numbers I am trying to produce are larger than what I am able to prove to be primes (or perfect numbers). I will have to wait on this until I receive a copy of Derrick Norman Lehmer's tables of the first 100,006,720 primes, which I ordered to be printed by the University Library of Nebraska. I determined that 526,853 was a prime (6½ hour run-time on the apple //e). I cannot crunch larger numbers. I realize my superficial approach to number theory (guessing algorithms by combining other known algorithms) is in vain, but at least it keeps me "doing mathematics": learning more about programming. Once I received the Lehmer reprint, I even understood the Prime Number Theorem—$P(x)$ is asymptotic to $x/log\ x$—and understood how given a larger computer, I could easily demonstrate (and graph) this. I also saw how programming Newton's method of successive approximations could be programmed. Like many deluded amateurs, I believed there was an order—a pattern—to the whole numbers (like the Pythagoreans) that I could discover: which would provide a mystical and magical insight to the cosmos. "Cosmos" in Greek meant "perfect array." Back to my arrays of holes in the light, seen from my crib in Sunny Side Texas. A perfect array—a lattice—1s and 0s—speaking to the nerve cells on my retina—Andromeda on the roof.

We are not really being treated very well here. The other day, I overheard a Mexican mother make the comment "Malo," to another mother on the playground, as she observed our interracial children. San Miguel is as status conscious as the Norte Americonos they advertise themselves to be so critical of. Our family is definitely "out." I really do not care much, as Blacks are always out in the states, but it appears to be having deleterious effects on Carol. Just now, Carol is at bottom. My initial impressions of Mexico are changing. The people have been cruel in many subtle ways, to Graham especially. But these beautiful people are trapped. They have so little. The young people have no higher educational opportunities. There is little hope of ever having anything. So, here in San Miguel, at least on Sunday nights, the young hombres line up at "El Centro Plaza," and parade around the young senoritas walking in the opposite direction.

Yet as in all alienating situations there are good things. We piled in the VW and drove just outside town to Lake Patzcuaro. The lake has a hydro-electric dam. But, foreshadowing modernity are the fishermen casting nets and the Mexican mothers washing and pounding clothes on its banks. Trees surrounding the shores provide shade from the bright sun, and there is an ample playground with swings and seesaws. The children enjoy little outings to the lake. Today there is a two-legged dog in the parking lot, forced to hop on her front legs to get about. The dog goes about her business—begging for food—as if having two legs is perfectly normal. We are delighted to toss the crusts of our sandwiches to her. "Suspicious of my reason but optimistic about my will." Two-legged dog's *will* becomes a fortress for us all—we will persevere.

Pedantic as ever, I read twenty-odd pages of Stace's gloss on Hegel today. Hegel's philosophy is convoluted in both its simplicity and complexity—a third moment of the simple and the complex. No synopsis within my ability is possible, but I filter it through my ken. The plurality of the world does not easily derive from the "oneness" of the world. Hence, a duality, the one and the many of Parmenides and Heraclitus. Stace's Hegel sought to find a first principle upon which he might base succeeding principles—like Peano's "one" and its successors. By assuming objects stripped of their categories become pure "isness" (ipseity), which is itself a category, being becomes nothingness, and its converse nothing (categorically) is something. Hence being (anything) becomes a first principle—thesis—(a concept that precedes the world), nothingness the second (antithesis)—and becoming the synthetic third. This is the first Hegelian triad thesis, antithesis, synthesis. And on through the ladders of third-moments to the dialectics of history. The universe is an argument where contradictions are reconciled in compromises. Order-disorder, reason-insanity, darkness-light, continuity-discontinuity, life-death . . . Capitalism-Socialism-Communism. Big-Bang-Cosmos-Heat-death (Entropy).

Today I read of the death of Richard Brautigan. This greatly saddened me. I always thought his *Trout Fishing in America* the most poetic and perceptive work written by a "flower child." I have read *Trout* more than twice and anticipate rereading it again. The obit read:

> Novelist and poet *Richard Brautigan*, 49, who became a campus hero in the 1960s with his whimsical novel "Trout Fishing in America"; reportedly of a self-inflicted gun-shot wound, at his home in Bolinas, Calif. His works, which included "A Confederate General From Big Sur" and "In Watermelon Sugar," blended satire, extended metaphors and odd bits of information in a freewheeling style that came to symbolize the hippie era. Later Brautigan lost favor with American critics (although he remained popular in France and Japan) and spent his last years emotionally troubled.[2]

As I had modeled my poetry on Brautigan's parodic, ironic, and satirical style—a fractured and tortured pastiche—I immediately dashed off a note to Seymour Lawrence, Brautigan's agent, expressing my praise and sorrow for the writer's death. My evaluation of Brautigan's contribution to letters was complex. First, I thought cutting against the grain of modernity, he was the "un-writer," like 7-up was the *uncola* to "Coke." He was trying to undo the structured bourgeois pretenses of the great contemporary American novelists (Saul Bellows, Philip Roth, John Updike, Norman Mailer). His poetics were akin to Denise Levertov's *Relearning the Alphabet*, in that, after the disintegration of reason—in Hiroshima and Auschwitz—"after which poetry was impossible"—true artists were searching for new words, a new grammar, and new forms for pursuing meaning.[3] After the self-inflicted destruction of reason in Tom Wolfe's *The Electric Kool-Aid Acid Test*, where neurons were seared in the hope that political and social evils would be similarly pruned, the hippies were, by necessity, forced to grow new neurons; these new brain cells could only interpret the semiotic signals (words, gestures, concepts) that were from members of the tribe who had made similar mind-expanding trips.[4]

November 6, 1984, 12:40 am. Election Day in the states. For the first day since I had been eligible, I would not be voting (unless by some miracle absentee ballots appear tomorrow). It appears, if the polls I see on *CNN* are even remotely correct, Ronald Reagan will walk away with it: "Four poor years." I wrote several query letters seeking new opportunities for my writing. Ever the pedant, I am content to send these missives, wait for replies, and read myself silly. As the critics point out concerning the "little scribblers" suffering from the grammatological disease (writing), "Reading more poetry doesn't make one a better poet."

My curiosity—driven by awe, mystification, and my will to know—leads me to thoughts about time and space. Time is particularly difficult. Particularly. Generally. Universally. Especially as I sit here word processing a journal that I have kept for forty years, and am transported (transposed) back to that time, with a specificity and vividness that ties memory in knots (ouroboros). Every day when I retrieve my newspaper from the mailbox, wrapped in a plastic sleeve secured by a rubber band. I find myself unable to throw the rubber bands away, collecting them in a tray in a kitchen drawer. My rational: I ponder how many ways a closed loop can be tied into knots—as a ponderable question of string theory or quantum loop gravity. Just as using this journal ties me in knots from the past with knots in the present, presumably never to be unknotted, but only reknotted from within the partitions again—the greater the number of knots the more time has passed.

Space is another conundrum. I imagine arrays of matter interspersed with holes. Under increasing magnification, the holes predominate until there is only nothingness. The matter, under the same increasing magnifications, resolve into vacuities, separated by nerve-like networks, which disappear as the microscope goes deeper, until nothingness$_1$ merges with nothingness$_2$ (sub-two) into an undifferentiated nothingness. This monomania leads me to thoughts about solid matrices with numbers arrayed in three dimensions. I try to work out the multiplication of two 3-dimensional matrices—(Face$_1$, Slab$_1$, Slice$_1$) x (Face$_2$, Slab$_2$, Slice$_2$) = Face element 1,1,1. I imagine the flipping of a Rubik's cube, trying to understand what ontological meaning such a multiplication (or even addition) might have. What would the Identity (Hermitian) matrix mean in this context? I try to imagine Space in its ontological sense (as opposed to its linguistic sense). In its conceptual sense. I remember reading something in Laurence Sterne's *Tristram Shandy* about the amount of spilled ink by muddle-headed philosophers on theories of space and time (not to even mention it takes two years to write about the first two days of Tristram's life).[5] I google this and scanning a dissertation—"Time and Space in Tristram Shandy and Other Eighteenth-century Novels: The Issues of Progression and Continuity"—by Gisele Liliane Gourdon, quoting someone named "Jenkins":

> the solution to a knot depends upon finding its ends. Tristram Shandy is a knot without open ends—"a closed curve in n-space"—which begins before Tristram is born and ends before it begins. As a "tangled skein," its ends, if they exist at all, are well hidden. Nor is it full of free ends like a plate of spaghetti—a tangle, but not a knot.[6]

Writing this memoir—knotted rubber bands (closed curves in n-space)—past and present in time (tangled skein)—"ends before it begins." I have taken to calling "space-time" *spime*, a neologism that makes the two things one thing. As Hermann Minkowski, Einstein's mathematics teacher wrote, "henceforth space by itself, and time by itself, are doomed to fade away into mere shadows, and only a kind of union of the two will preserve an independent reality."

As, I continue reading James R. Newman's *The World of Mathematics, Vol. One*—if you are not doing mathematics, you are wasting time—I am living in the loop (the knot) of past and current space-time, being made mindful of what I knew then augmented by what I know now.[7] Then and now, I grapple with ideas of space—the *Zusammenhang* (context)—"where" *is* space—in my mind? Part of Kant's aesthetic? In "Invariant Twins, Cayley and Sylvester" (in Newman) by Eric Temple Bell, "Of course if we take *points* as the elements out of which our space is to be constructed, nobody outside a lunatic asylum has yet succeeded in visualizing a space of more than three dimensions."[8]

Back to the past (November 11, 1984). My own have disowned me. Where I think I am being a trailblazer—marrying outside the race, trying to be a poet, living in a foreign country—my own Negro people think I am a loser on all fronts ("not Black enough"). Race Traitor.

Rufina, our maid, introduced me to *Wenceslaus* (viz "Bohemian Santa Claus"), a gardener. The upper terrace of our house had a grass lawn that had been decimated by our Beagle's doing her business. Originally, Wenceslaus had brought over grass plugs to try to improve the lawn, with instructions to water every other day. The lower terrace was a small flagstone courtyard replete with a fountain and shallow pool. Wenceslaus, perhaps sensing our family's alienation, brought a dozen goldfish to fill the pool. This delighted the children—especially Shauna. Sensing my own sadness, he invited me to hang with him one afternoon.

Wenceslaus had a motorcycle. After we had a few beers and a glass or two of rum and coke, he asked me if I wanted a ride on the bike. Half-drunk, and holding on for my life as he took curves, I wondered if he was trying to kill me. Eventually, we arrived at his hacienda—an adobe house with a dirt floor—where he introduced me to his wife and children. The four kids were saucer-eyed, raven-haired, brown-skinned doll-babies ranging from suckling babe in arms to six or seven. His wife appeared intent on being a good host to his guest. She served a hot stew and warm tortillas, followed by homemade wine—pulque I assumed—of which I consumed cup after cup until I was semi-delirious. Watching the dark-eyed children peeking at me as I tried to communicate with Wenceslaus and his wife in my inadequate Spanish (his English was far superior to my Spanish), a deep sadness overwhelmed me. A dirt floor. An obvious poverty that made my existence at Calle 54 Chorro appear decadent—we had so much and were not even appreciative, where they had so little and were thankfully, beatific. In my drunkenness, I reached for my wallet and gave Senora Wenceslaus a *un mill peso* note (I guess worth about $50 at that time). As the evening passed to night and the children were put to bed, I had a few more glasses of pulque, and eventually emptied my wallet, repeating in my poor Spanish *para niños* "for your children."

Knowing I was too drunk to make the motorcycle trip back to San Miguel, Wenceslaus borrowed a friend's pickup truck and brought me home to contemplate my bourgeoise economic largesse and its relationship to Mexican poverty and destitute. I had heard a Mexican say, "Oh, you Americanos have all the *principle* (meaning material goods), but we have the interest (meaning *interest* in life." This ordinary campesino had gone on to elaborate: "You don't know how to live, to enjoy your food, to savor your drink, to feel your passion." What I had seen in Wenceslaus's house had changed my relationship with Mexico.

One of the consequences was to double the salary that we were paying Rufina. I thought the amount we paid her for the work she did for us—sweeping, washing clothes, preparing meals, and helping Carol with the children—was exploitative. The Americans I had come to know in San Miguel were astounded, asking me what I was doing "Trying to start a revolution," as now all the other housekeepers that came with rental houses wanted increased wages.

Another Sunday night (early Monday morning), as is our custom, Carol and I did the wash. It seemed such an inhospitable way for Rufina to begin the week with days of dirty diapers and our own soiled clothing. After Friday's overindulgence I am ready to dry out a bit. Making headway with Stace's Hegel. I have been suffused enough with his methodology that I was seeing two or three pages ahead in the arguments. I am working to finish my study of Hegel this week so I can read something more entertaining. I am desperately needing some good news concerning the writing proposals I sent off. If I am not writing seriously, I feel I have brought Carol and the children here under false pretenses. I await the starter's pistol. A package of books from David Ray, with no letter, came in the mail today. I take this as a positive sign that he is doing better after Sam's death.

Today was Thanksgiving. But with Ronald Reagan's reelection, the starvation of thousands in Ethiopia and Gandhi's assassination, there seems to be little to be thankful for. Other issues of South African racism, the fire bombings of Black families in Chicago, and the dire poverty in my face in Mexico contribute to my gloom. Even closer, my own lack of direction is overwhelming—a feast. I am reminded of a recent drive into the countryside with the family. Note that I have avoided any attempt to travel into Mexico City. Large urban areas frighten me. But we have taken day trips to Guanajuato (catacombs and silver mines), Celaya, and Saltillo (glazed tile). While returning from Celaya, I became disoriented—lost—and could not find the road back to San Miguel. I stopped a campesino and asked him, "San Miguel?"—pointing north.

"Sí," he answered.

Obviously not understanding me, I then pointed west.

"Sí," he answered.

To test my hypothesis that he did not understand the Negro requesting directions, I pointed east.

"Sí."

I then pointed north.

"Sí."

"De nada!"

Amused, I got back in the van and we wandered around lost until we found the road back to San Miguel. But this sense of being lost "wasted . . . and I can't find my way home," pervades everything I am doing. I am lost in the ozone . . . again. I am lost in space. I am lost in America. I am lost in Mexico. I am lost in the differential equations I do not understand. I am lost in the lost and found. I am lost in the ideas and conceptualizations of philosophy. I am lost in metaphors and similes. Reading and writing—in the same lost autodidacticism—are my only anchors that do not catch in the infinite depths. I finished reading Stace's Hegel today. The book was tiring . . . it demanded everything . . . I had to finish it . . . but it was worth it. Hegel's deduction of the absolute spirit was ineluctably seductive. An absolute posit of being. But after being lost in the wilderness of Celaya, found in the *Geist* of Hegel, I am happy and thankful that everyone in the family is home and well. Here is the poem I wrote celebrating this episode—"Black Man Asking Directions in Celaya Mexico":

> Having tired of McDonald's unhappy Meals
> My little americano children thought a trip to the mall was
> Entertainment
> I quit my job and sold my merry cars
> Drove non-stop to old Mexico
> Carnival Negro in a hippie VW micro bus
> Orange and cream fiesta
> The DMZ of El Paso being a barrier
> To keep Americans out
> To discourage them that they weren't at the mall
> To Guanajuato
> The farmland sweet
> Gringos few
> And the people almost really do
> Believe "Americans have the capital"
> "But Mexicans have the interest"
> Capital being things
> Interest being the good life
> Gringos few
> And the people almost really do
> Believe their simple lives are superior to
> Americano smart bombs and cruise missiles
> While praising the red white and green
> Looking for another eagle bearing serpent
> Atop prickly pear circa 1325
> Spitting as another tourist walks by
> I chance asking directions
> In Celaya Guanajuato Mexico
> East?
> *Sí*
> West?
> *Sí*
> North?
> *Sí*
> South?
> *Sí*
> And instantly knew
> What a Roman felt
> Asking his way in Gallia
> *Sí* means "no"

Well, here it is December 1st. Shauna and I just returned from *el mercado*—about 70 degrees, sunny—lots of news. First, I received a very nice little letter from Barbara Epler of New Directions. In fact, the letter was so supportive, I spent all day printing off the 190 poems, to send to her. New Directions is a high-profile publisher of experimental poetry. I continue to think that careful editing could turn my collection into a great first volume. There are very few African American poets who cross-over from the political "protest poetry" into the avant-garde modern. I try not to get my hopes up. I also received a positive response from my query to Random House, which means they would look at my novel. Hope springs eternal. I plan to rewrite "The Seed" (which I also intend to rename). As I have been so thoroughly disappointed by the reception of my manuscripts, I am going to load this one up, as I fear I am running out of chances. I am starting to entertain the idea that I might be "a failed writer." In this writing and rewriting, I am shooting for the moon this time, loading the manuscript up with dialog, descriptive scene setting, backstories, and action (excitement), plus a healthy measure of hard science.

Diving into the books David Ray sent, I am reading Tom Clark's biography of Jack Kerouac, that includes the story of how Neil Cassady—the original hipster hero of *On the Road*—died after drink pulque, near the railroad tracks in San Miguel. David was trying to help me gain literary perspective on where my writing fit into the history of the "writing against writing." After all, I saw myself as the Black Vonnegut, the Black Barthelme, the Black Burroughs. Here in Mexico, I was at the *Naked Lunch*, with my surreal talking typewriter. As a Black poet, I was far more experimental that LeRoi Jones (Amiri Baraka), Don L. Lee (Haki Madhubuti), or Gwendolyn Brooks. Having been influenced by the white beats and hippies, I was culturally integrated to the point that I was interested in more than mere racial politics. My eclecticism ranged over painting, physics, mathematics, astronomy, and philosophy. As they say about many other dilettantes, "A mile wide and in inch deep."

Okay. My Black language (writing) and white antithetical language (critique of my own writing)—Du Boisean double-consciousness—produces a pidgin aesthetic, bound to failure as it is interpreted by an empowered thesis (white superiority).

I started the "Starplough"—my retitling of the "Seed"—my tired, hackneyed, and exhausted epic of evolution of life in the cosmos as techne: rather than Darwinian evolution. Within a week, I had finished sixty-two pages. Sitting on the roof at Calle 54 Chorro, with the gas cylinders, and water tank, in the mild winter sunlight, I scratched out the marginal comments—turning the pages over for emendations. By the second week eighty-four pages; by the third 103 pages.

For Christmas, we went in search of a tree. Not finding a bushy full tree, we settled for a scraggly pine we purchased El Centro. The vendor, a young, short hombre, spoke to us in near perfect English, which surprised me. I asked him where he learned his English."

"Chicago."

Again, I was thunderstruck. He continued.

"We know a lot more about you than you know about us." His pronouncement was a condemnatory judgement of American provincialism. He was telling me that Americans had a narrow—self-absorbed worldview. I knew he was right. I was aware that in Mexico—San Miguel at least—I was perceived as an American; rather than Black. We took the tree back to the house and decorated it with paper ornaments. It is cool in the central plateau of Mexico in winter, so we built a fire in the fireplace with the spindly mesquite wood we had bought from a man selling it on the cobblestone street in front of the house. Carol and I tried to cheer the children with Christmas presents. Mexican quality toys were not of the plastic varieties so prominent in the states. Yet, there was a subtle depression that cast its pall from the alien fire and Christmas tree. For the Catholic Mexican families, Christmas was a solemn and anti-materialistic holiday—the church bells were angels.

Felis Navidad.

Feliz Ano Nuevo—January 1, 1985. Carol is proofing "Starplough." She is about a third through the manuscript.

I sense my deepening anxieties with the approach of Carol's parents' visit, disenchantment with San Miguel (too many American tourists and ex-pats), the pending trip back to Texas to renew our visas, New Directions (acceptance/rejection of poems), quiet from my mother and brother, the reaction of Random House to "Starplough." A near disaster with the word processor where I thought I had lost my files. I am also getting anxious to get back to Colorado to begin to build a nest for my family and build a life for myself—a life that does not depend on book publishers and editors who I do not know. Everyone is in general good health, except for Scotch, who has still not barked since we left Colorado five months ago. I need to write a few letters. As per usual, I have been grouchy during the final preparation of the manuscript.

Third week of January, we drove back north through León, San Luis Potosí, Ciudad Victoria, and Matamoros, to Brownsville, Texas, to get out visas renewed. The kids enjoyed being back in the USA. We cavorted on the beaches of South Padre Island and visited the Potter Zoo. At the Mall del Norte, we roamed the stores in this massive mall, astounded by the surfeit of consumer goods, so lacking on the other side of the border. I think I bought a Neil Young record (Re-ac-tor), only to be disappointed when I listened to it, by his use of "Synclaver," a voice distorting synthesizer. I also bought more printer ribbons for my Brother printer. Stocking up on "American quality" foodstuffs to take back with us, Carol bought a package of "Almost Home" cookies. The cookies tasted like home (soft, oatmeal, and raisins), and I was reminded that it would not be long before we ended this adventure in pseudo-anti-Americanism, pseudo-literature, pseudo-poetry, and became real people again. Once back in San Miguel, I ran the manuscript through the spell-checking program of Grammatik. We are looking forward to Carol's parents, Dave and Barbara, upcoming visit, with all the dramas that portends.

I had taken to playing pickup softball games with a renegade group of Americans who gathered on Sunday mornings. There were also a few local hombres mixed into this slow-pitch exercise in pounding the restricted flight "pelota" into the dry dusty field. The tall left fielder was Clifford Irving, the infamous writer I had met at the cocktail party. I enjoyed these softball games. And of course, having played and coached organized hardball, I was a phenomenon. Humm baby. When I played outfield, I glided to flyballs, that appeared uncatchable. Over-the-shoulder (Willie Mays style), shoestring, ranging left, throwing out runners—I was like the all-stars seen on TV. When I played shortstop—backhand stabs, leaping catches, turning double plays—I was Luis Aparicio. The locals and the ex-pats were dazzled and amazed by my athleticism. Another Sunday, chasing down a long fly ball, I tripped in a ditch in left field and sustained a severe ankle sprain.

We were invited to our neighbor Riva Barron's house—where there was a stimulating discussion of "feminism." Riva's New York friends were *très branché* (very hip, trendy). I had ingratiated myself with Riva with a paraphrase from James Joyce's *Portrait of the Artist as a Young Man* about "eternity": "the bird flying from one eternity to another, with a grain of sand . . . eternity would be said to have scarcely begun."[9] Carol has completed her proofreading and I will begin printing out "The Starplough" tomorrow morning.

Thinking back on my life of struggles with the word, I stumble across a book on the bookshelves in the house. *The Souls of Black Folks* by W. E. B. Du Bois. Of course, I had heard of this book, but never read it, thinking it had nothing to say to a twentieth Century Negro. Du Bois writes: "It is, then, the strife of all honorable men of the twentieth century to see that in the future competition of races the survival of the fittest shall mean the triumph of the good, the beautiful, and the true; that we may be able to preserve for future civilization all that is really fine and noble and strong, and not continue to put a premium on greed and impudence and cruelty."[10] After reading *Souls of Black Folks*, I had nothing but respect for the power of Du Bois's prescience. He saw the Black struggle in terms of victory—the greatest story of a people's rise, in a few generations, ever told—from slavery to scholarship. As was he himself, a scholar who wrote with the fire of stars.

The cliché is that one does not become a writer until he or she can paper their walls with rejection slips. So, while I pursued this cliché—which I thought was a pseudo-cliché—I doubted myself, a flaneur, a trader in the false-ironies of pretense, vanity, and conceits. I thought of the archetypical starving writer in his garret that I was not, living as I was on US Treasury Bonds like a gigolo. Being a pseudo-intellectual, I also feared being an inadequate father to my children and a failure as a husband. When Carol and I first got together, we were very skeptical of the idea of "love" as it was lived out in the American imaginary. We did not think our parents *loved* one another, and after my failed marriage to Jackie, I was doubtful that actual love was possible. Thus, when Carol and I married, we wanted to demonstrate that love was possible—become the performative proof, heal the races by our example. In her, I was "Looking for a Hard-headed Woman" (the Cat Stevens song).[11] I needed someone who could take all that America could dish out. In Mexico, Carol proved to me that she was as hard-headed and disciplined as I was, if not more so. I was down from 1,200 mg lithium per day to 300 mg, without mania or depression.

February 21, 1985. It's been an interesting few days. I visited Clifford Irving's house Monday and talked with him about agents and possible publishers for my poetry. Big Cliff provided me the following list of agents (responses from my submissions):

Random House (Rupert Loomis) – "Couple people read them: No Offer"
E. P. Dutton (Seymour Lawrence) – "Lack of editorial enthusiasm"
W. Norton (Star Lawrence) – "Need to publish in little magazines first"
University of Missouri (Susan Denny) – No respose
A. Knopf (Ash Green) – Form letter – "Not a likely prospect"
Simon & Schuster (Don Huttor) – No response
Morrow (William Cady) – No response
Houghton Mifflin (Nan Talese) – "Not publishing poetry until 1986"

Having printed out the collection of poems multiple times and having them returned was death by a thousand cuts.

I met another American writer. His name was Theodore Cogswell. Cogswell was a sci-fi writer who had published a collection of short stories, *The Wall Around the World*, certainly what I felt had been erected around my world.[12] He was also one of the founders of the Science Fiction Hall of Fame. I had many interesting discussions with Ted. He told me that there were only a couple of hundred fiction writers who made a living from their writing. He advised me to "keep my day job," and continue to write as an avocation (or even a hobby). Cogswell was a professor at the University of Minnesota. He also advised me, for the sake of my family's security, to go back to school to get a PhD.

Once, Ted put a question to me about an anti-gravity device being used to travel to the moon. As he put it, "When would the device need to be turned off and then on to produce a soft landing on the moon?" I told him I would try to write a BASIC program to calculate the nodal points of cut-off. It took hours for the program to crank out an answer. I simulated the trip to the moon after neutralizing the earth's gravity so the moon's gravity could begin to attract the spacecraft. I calculated the voyage would take forty days, with a max velocity of 1,476 ft/sec. The anti-gravity would be shut-off for four to six hours of deceleration caused by the earth's return-gravity, and land under the moon's influence with a velocity of 3.5 ft/sec.

On March 2, 1985, we attended a party at an American ex-pat's. Tom Frazee was a hippie refugee struggling to survive in Mexico. At this fete, he passed out hits of LSD. I pasted the micro-dot into the journal I am writing this from. It is just three weeks from my fortieth birthday. I was not unaware that I had spent much of 1984 in Mexico—not in George Orwell's dystopia—and with that nightmare past, I was living in the "future." "It was a bright cold day in April, and the clocks were striking thirteen." I was still limping, but my ankle was healing after twisting it chasing a softball. With my head in the clouds—like Thales walking into a ditch—I had run into a ditch. Carol's parents—Dave and Babs—are here. They suggested I get my ankle x-rayed and accompanied me to a clinic, where a young Mexican doctor, speaking polished English, told me in their presence, that it was only a high-ankle strain, and that rest and an ace bandage was all that was required. I introduced David and Barbara to Ted Cogswell and his wife. We had arranged the rental for a nice house within walking distance from where we lived, for them. The house had a magnificent patio with an open view of San Miguel and the surrounding countryside.

Dave and Ted Cogswell hit it off. Both were in their early sixties and World War II veterans. Carol's father regaled Ted and his wife with stories of his service in the US Marines in China as a Morse Code instructor. David had been put in this position because he had been an Eagle Scout, and already knew Morse Code. Because Carol's parent's marriage was in its final stages, these social encounters were fragile. Carol and I both knew that the real reason for her parent's presence was their concern for our safety. One morning, I took Dave along with me to play chess with Cogswell and a few other Americans. Ted beat me easily with a double Caro-Kann opening. He told me that he was an ex-collegiate team player. My lack of anger or self-doubt surprised me, as I had more important issues on my mind. David and Theodore's maturity and positions on the chessboard of life—Ted, a university professor and published author, and Dave, a former state senator and wealthy businessman—were forks in my position in life as a struggling player.

I was waiting for my own personal revolution. Approaching my fortieth birthday, I was gauche (socially inappropriate), arrogant (fake sophistication—putting on airs), conceited (overblown sense of self based on meager accomplishment), an aesthete (degenerate affectation of sensitivity to the beautiful), a poseur (a poser, actor, fake), and a bullshit artist. All these self-assessments derived from those days back in the Teacher Corps, where the sensitivity session facilitators had shared their opinion of me as "shallow and glib." Grappling with these insecurities as I withdrew myself from lithium carbonate, I was still self-centered, rather than the decentering required by being a father and husband. I recalled the adage, "Your children will make you human."

I do not really care about anything much right now except leaving Mexico. I have found my courage by withdrawing myself from lithium carbonate and my love for my family. I might surprise everyone by not returning to Colorado, although that possibility remains remote. Our love for the Rocky Mountain foothills is common knowledge. I feel the pull of the mountains.

I await several items in the mail: Lehmer's *Book of Primes*, computer printer ribbons, and a few books by Richard Brautigan.

"If God is everywhere, that doesn't leave room from much else."

God in the gaps. This line increasingly haunts my waking hours. But, I am in the middle of a journey toward enlightenment; a moral bildungsroman; despite—as the French say—*detournement* (diversion, misappropriation, hijack).

It is exceedingly difficult not to dip back into previous manuscripts (like "Three Birds") for material in my new work. I try to resist this temptation, as the writing I do now will be the basis, when combined with "Three Birds" fragments for my magnum opus, when I get back to work in the states.

I received back another poetry manuscript today from E. P. Dutton. The unsigned note expressed "Lack of editorial Interest"—which translates into "Did not like it!" In the past ten months, I have read ten volumes of poetry—from Brautigan to Levertov—and convinced that some of my poems are of equal quality. The only poet that has a clearer vision and a better aesthetic is Kenneth Rexroth, to whom I can only aspire. I am forced to conclude:

1. I am not a poet.
2. My subjective interpretation of my work is erroneous.
3. My poems are good but unmarketable.
4. "The Pearl" syndrome.
5. Black factors (i.e., "racism").
6. US cultural factors (i.e., market capitalism) & the "Bitch Goddess."

I will continue to try not to look for the mailman, as the other poems come limping back. If all the poems and "The Starplough" come back, I guess my trip to Mexico will have proven one thing; that I am not a writer.

March 22, 1985. I feel like I am getting myself together again. Today, we all piled into the VW and drove to Guanajuato—via Delores Hidalgo.

I gave copies of my poetry collection (copies returned from disinterested publishers) to Ted Cogswell and Clifford Irving.

Today is my fortieth birthday.

As April came to an end, our trip to San Miguel was also ending. Graham and I left the rest of the family and made the drive back to Colorado to find a house. Of course, the long drive took its toll on the VW, that had a fuel-pump failure in Texas, and we had to spend the night in a motel until the mechanic could get the replacement. Having eaten fast food, I had a beer. Graham was exhausted and quickly fell asleep. I sat up watching a movie—*Repo Man*—surprised by the ending, where the car turns into a spaceship. I thought our cream and orange VW camper was a spaceship.

When we arrived back in Conifer, Colorado exhausted, I was frantic to find a house. After a few days, the realtor showed me a little mock log-cabin, sitting on the side of a hill at 9,400 feet, on 2.5 acres, with a nighttime view of the lights of downtown Denver just twenty miles away. I thought it was the perfect house for us. After signing a check for the earnest money on the house, Graham and I hurriedly drove back to San Miguel to get the rest of the family.

April 17, 1995, Back in San Miguel, all the poetry manuscripts have been returned. Random House rejected "Starplough." On the final night before Theodore and his wife left to return to the states, we had drinks. He had given me a paperback copy of his stories and reiterated his advice that I go back to school. Ted handed me his card: "Theodore R. Cogswell: Proceedings of the Institute for Twenty-First Century Studies."

Deeply disappointed by all the publisher's rejections, I was overflowing with energy and hope. I had withdrawn myself from lithium, without adverse effects. We packed up all our stuff, gave the rabbit—"Fuzzle"—to the Mexican family, with caged chickens in their backyard, that lived next door.

"*No comida*," I offered as I handed over the *canejo*.

Leaving San Miguel, Scotch, our beagle, the kids in the back, with Carol in front reading the maps, we hit road. It was spring, and by day, the cholla and ocotillo cactuses were in bloom. Amidst the rich dessert colors, deep browns, reds, and yellow ochres, I was determined to drive straight through to the Rio Grande.

In the middle of the night on mountainous Mexican highway 57, on a particularly narrow stretch of road, with almost no shoulder, the lights of the VW camper began to grow dimmer and dimmer. With the Mexican eighteen-wheelers—grills emblazoned with Christmas-tree-colored lights and crosses—hurtling past us on the two-lane highway, with steep drop-offs on the side of the road, Carol and I were panicked. The headlights grew dimmer than the faint crescent moonlight. Till, finally, my hands choking the steering wheel, the headlights went out! I could not pull off to the side of the road. Luckily, we on a downhill stretch of highway. I followed the taillights of a big-rig, the VW rolling without headlights, until the engine quit. In this almost total darkness, my heart pounding, we were graced by a miracle. The VW camper rolled to a stop in a closed PEMEX gas station. Knowing that we had to wait until morning before the gas station opened, we tried to get a little sleep. I could not sleep.

When the sun rose, the PEMEX station opened, and I walked into the office, where a young man stood at the counter.

"Mecánico?" I asked.

"Sin mecánico," he calmly answered.

Thinking he did not understand me, tapping my watch, I asked "Cuando, mecánico?"

He paused, considering my question. Looking past him, hanging on the wall, was a painting of Jesus, his arms lifted in supplication.

"No mecánico, señor" he replied.

"Teléfona?"

"No teléfona, no mecánico," the young attendant said.

Looking past him at the poster of Jesus with a crown of thorns and a burning candle in his heart, I suddenly realized that now, I had finally done it. Got myself into a position jeopardizing my family that I could not get out of. Stranded in Coahuila, I walked back to the van and tried to think. Perhaps another American travelling this highway might stop for gas and help. I tried to take a nap. After an hour or so, the sun rising bright and warm, I awakened in a start. Sitting up, I tried the key and the engine fired. I thought that the battery had recovered enough to sustain the motor.

After a quick talk with Carol, we decided to push on as far as we could go. At least we did not need the headlights. The road was still steep, but at least the grade was now downhill. When the motor died again, we pulled off the road and waited for the battery to recover. I had already diagnosed the problem as a busted alternator. We continued down the road until we arrived in the town of Saltillo, where we found a garage that could fix the generator. It was going to take a while, as the Mexican mechanics did not just order a new or rebuilt generator: they removed the old one and rewound the copper armature. While they were fixing it, I was restlessly trying to watch out for the kids, get food, and reassure them that everything was all right. I did not sleep, dangerous for a manic-depressive.

The VW camper running again, we set off for the border crossing at Eagle Pass. Fatigued, I drove on through the night. On a dark road somewhere between Saltillo and the Rio Grande, at 3 a.m., we were stopped by the Mexican Army. The soldiers, dressed in olive drab fatigues, armed with automatic weapons, asked me to get out of the van. Shinning their flashlights on me, the inside of the van with the kids sleeping in the back, I could smell the oil on their machine guns. There might have been eight or ten of them, and my mind played a reel of a film where they might have easily killed us all for being drug smugglers, or just worthless riff-raff from *el Norte*. My heart was pounding in my chest. After poking around a bit, the soldiers allowed me to get back in the van and waived me on.

Red-eyed, the adrenalin having left my bloodstream, I continued driving until we reached the border crossing at Eagle Pass. I had never been so happy to see the stars and stripes and the white American Border Agents. Stopping us at US Customs, the Agents looked over the van loaded to gills with our possessions. After questioning me briefly concerning my visa and the reasons I had been in Mexico, they must have concluded there were drugs hidden somewhere in the van. I mean, we fit the profile; Black man, long-haired and bearded, driving a Volkswagen "Hippie Bus," returning from central Mexico—Marijuana or cocaine smuggling. They called for the drug sniffing German Shepherds. After sniffing around the van, the border agent said, "Everything out of the van on the tables."

Under the harsh bright lights, I started removing suitcases, boxes, and all of our stuff. But after thirty minutes, one of the agents told me to put it back. We were quickly processed and passed back into Texas. I do not know what happened, but either they made some phone calls and found out that we were "legitimate," or simply had a change of heart about putting us through the trauma of unloading and the repacking the contents of the van. We found a motel to get some sleep. Once the kids were asleep. I had a conversation with Carol.

"Perhaps they still think we smuggled dope out of Mexico." I said, even though she thought I might have just been paranoid.

"And perhaps they put a tracking device up under the van."

"And maybe they are listening to us right now." Carol heard me, but I could tell she was dubious.

"But" I continued, "there is a lot wrong with America. But it is still a great country. And I love my country. For however flawed it is, if a person wants to do something and has the will, they cannot really be stopped. And I want to do something to make my country better. I am a patriot. "First a man brings himself together, then he brings his family together, then the family brings the community to order, then the community brings the country to order." I had brought myself back to order and now it was time to bring everything else back to order. "The universe began in order and would end in order, and then repeat."

I had hoped the DEA drug enforcement agents *were* listening.

What had I brought back from Mexico? Certainly not contraband. I had brought back a forty-year-old man, who had almost stopped drinking alcohol, smoking cigarettes, smoking pot, and using lithium carbonate as a crutch. I considered withdrawing myself from lithium was the greatest accomplishment, and my moods had stabilized about a pivot of resoluteness. I had demonstrated my bravery in the face of extremes to Carol, that I was the man she had chosen to share her life with. Because the Mexicans perceived me as a Gringo; rather than a Negro, was also freeing. As financially impoverished as they were, the Mexicans I had met were proud of their deep cultural riches. One hombre had said to me, "You Blacks in America are pathetic—you don't even have your own language . . . not even to mention your own money, your own government, your own culture."

The books I read in Mexico that left indelible impressions were Toni Morrison's *The Bluest Eye* ("Hallucinated a reality"), Samuel R. Delany's *Dhalgren* (a Black sci-fi writer), Du Bois's *The Souls of Black Folks* (the greatest story ever told), and W. T. Stace's *Philosophy of Hegel* (a deep dive into philosophy).[13]

I had brought my sanity back with me from Mexico. I had learned that good old American anti-Black racism was as much the blame for my "insanity," as were my manic-depressive genes. As Kurt Vonnegut had observed, "A sane person to an insane society must appear insane."[14] Racism had made me cray-cray.

NOTES

1. Steve Winwood, "Can't Find My Way Home," *Blind Faith* (album) (London: Polydor, 1969).

2. Anonymous, Obituary of Richard Brautigan, "Transitions." *Newsweek*, November 5, 1984, 94.

3. Denise Levertov, *Relearning the Alphabet* (New York: New Directions, 1970).

4. Tom Wolfe, *The Electric Kool-Aid Acid Test* (New York: Farrar, Straus & Giroux, 1968; New York: Bantam, 1999).

5. Laurence Sterne, *Tristram Shandy and a Sentimental Journey* (New York: Modern Library, 1995).

6. Jenkins, quoted in G. L. [Gisèle Liliane] Gourdon, "Time and Space in Tristram Shandy and Other Eighteenth-Century Novels: The Issues of Progression and Continuity," PhD thesis, (January 9, 2017; 2002. University of Sheffield), 25.

7. James R. Newman, ed. *The World of Mathematics*, 4 vols. (New York: Simon and Schuster, 1956).

8. E. T. Bell, *Men of Mathematics* (New York: Simon and Schuster, 1986), 360.

9. James Joyce, *A Portrait of the Artist as a Young Man* (New York: Signet, 2006).

10. W. E. B. Du Bois, *The Souls of Black Folks* (New York: Fawcett, 1961).

11. Cat Stevens, "Hard Headed Woman," *Tea for the Tillerman* (album) (London: Morgan Studios, 1970).

12. Theodore R. Cogswell, *The Wall Around the World* (Los Angeles: Pyramid Press, 1973).

13. Toni Morrison, *The Bluest Eye* (New York: Holt, Rinehart and Winston, 1970); Samuel R. Delany, *Dhalgren* (New York: Bantam Books, 1980); Du Bois, *The Souls of Black Folks*; and W. T. Stace, *Philosophy of Hegel* (Mineola, NY: Dover, 1955).

14. Kurt Vonnegut, *Welcome to the Monkey House* (New York: Dail Press, 2013).

Chapter 14

Kent Denver Country Day School, 1985–1990

We found out from our realtor, that the bank financing for the house on Conifer Mountain was being questioned because neither of us was employed. But, because we were able to put twenty-five thousand down, we were allowed to buy the house with an ARM (adjustable-rate mortgage). So, while we awaited closing, I paced around the motel room, occasionally peering from behind the curtains into the parking lot. One afternoon I saw a North Dakota license plate. Watching for the owners of the car, when they emerged, I went out in the parking lot to speak with them.

"Hi, where you folks from in North Dakota?"

"Minot," the middle-aged man answered.

"I used to live there," I said.

"Really?" the man said.

"I graduated from Minot State College in 1970."

I went on to engage the couple in conversation, until the topic of what I had majored in at Minot State came up. When I told them "mathematics," they had informed me that they knew Agnes Ladendorf, my calculus teacher at Minot.

"She's not been doing well of late," they informed me as the man entered their vehicle.

The closing on the house at 11432 Nancy's Drive—the "Nancy" being a relative of Colorado governor Roy Romer, who developed the land on Conifer Mountain—went smoothly. It was May, but there was still snow at 9,400 feet. We were all excited to claim our new spaces. I thought the Ponderosa pines and spangling Aspen trees, with the deep blue sky, and the city lights of Denver winking in the distance at night, was poetically enchanting.

Those first few weeks were charged with readjustments. Still wondering at the synchronicities, I wrote a letter to Mrs. Ladendorf at Minot State to wish her well.

Being almost fifty percent of European ancestry, I was a light-complexioned Black person. I was a hybrid mixture of white and Black, the result of which often privileged me in a society that was decidedly colorist. But what of my children, who were mixed even further. Lindsey, at twenty-two months old, was still a babe in arms, nursing. But already there were issues with her curly hair that resisted easy combing. Shauna, just turning five, was a serious little girl, who had started reading at three, without being taught. We were beginning to wonder how she would fare at West Jefferson Elementary School. "Fair" being the operant word, as she was of fair complexion and might have passed racially as anything. Shauna was intelligent and curious. Even at five years old, she had an intense interest in biology, dotting on her pet frogs we had named "Pipidae and Pipida." I had marveled at her reverence for nature, as we bought Tubifex worms to feed the frogs. Born on "Earth Day," April 22, Shauna's life was a hymn to nature. She delighted in the nest of lady bugs we found on one of our walks on the dirt road in front of the house. And Graham, who earned the sobriquet "the Boy of Joy," because of his mischievous laughter, unbounded energy, and infectious intelligence. Graham was nine-and-a half years old, entering the fifth grade, fluent in Spanish, as the seven months in the bi-lingual *escuela* in San Miguel, had provided him with not only a felicity with a foreign language, but also an ease in new social situations. Graham was a brilliant child.

So, as I looked at our children, I was mindful of "our." For, as I had objected from the time I was a child, when I had watched the Bell System's film "Our Mr. Sun" (with Dr. Frank Baxter), the sun was not "ours." "Ours" connotes ownership or possession. I did not think that sun was ours, much less the universe; I chaffed when scientists wrote or said "our universe." This "our" talk was an artifact of capitalism. If anything, "we" were "its"—the sun and the universe possessed us. I took the same approach to "the" children—they were not "ours," we did not own them. I had quickly discerned that "my/our" interracial children were not mixtures of "us." They possessed both dominant and recessive genes from "our" parents and forebearers, back to the miasma of human beginnings. I preferred to think of it as "the Sun," "the Universe," "the children," thereby providing them with the quiddity (unique thinginess) of ontological being in an ontological universe.

"My children are my poems."

"No. Your children are your responsibilities."

My discourse about trying to "live" mathematics or "live" poetry, was pathetically immature. I was forced to reassess my personal "magic" for a new realism—a lesser "magic realism."

"Get real!"

While luxuriating in being back in beautiful Colorado, I met a guy named Mike Burns, who was a chimney sweep. Mike helped me put up a firewall for the woodburning stove in the basement. He also installed the stovepipe. We got to talking about baseball and he invited me to come out to play softball on a team sponsored by Bell Oil. I was a forty-year-old outfielder, who sometimes served as catcher, in a men's slow-pitch softball league. Arguably, well past my prime, I had lost my foot speed in chasing down fly-balls. Many of the players in the league were younger, stronger, and faster. I had one distinction. I was the only Negro. I was given the team jersey with the number "42," not for Jackie Robinson, but for the number Richard Pryor wore in the sports comedy movie "The Bingo Long Travelling All Stars and Motor Kings."

As the summer raced by, crystal skies, buttery sunlight, the children playing in the yard, and Carol and I both unemployed, burning through the remaining money, I knew I had to get back into school. I dreamt about it—a *Giles Goat-Boy*—ever thwarted by an evil computer in the administration building's basement.[1] I need to up my game by becoming a better scholar, a more discriminating thinker. I wanted to change my own assessment of myself as a pseudo-intellectual.

By fall, Carol had regained a job at the US Social Security Administration (SSA) as a "Service Representative," in the Denver teleservice center. This was huge. I was greatly impressed that having quit SSA twice to have children, they thought enough of her abilities to re-hire her. The children were back in school at West Jefferson Elementary. Graham quickly established himself as a talented child, but Shauna experienced a few difficulties, as she was teased on the school bus by the other kids. Lindsey, still being a toddler, was being cared for, to help me out, by a neighbor with a small child of her own. Carol used a breast-pump to save milk for Lindsey's bottles. I tried to help, transporting the children, picking Carol up from work, washing clothes. I was the proverbial "house husband," and I chaffed beneath its burdens. We even saw the movie "Mr. Mom" starring Michael Keaton, at the theater in Evergreen. I totally related.

In January 1986, I started my first course in the University of Denver's (a.k.a. DU) "University College," an open admissions program leading to the Master's of Special Studies Degree. The first course was in computer simulations, taught by an electrical engineer from Drexel University. Carol was in the first weeks of her new job, and my course was at night. I distinctly remember the Challenger space shuttle disaster on January 28, 1986. The horned forks of the debris became an indelible image with the teacher-in-space—Christa McAuliffe—giving her life to her students. I had a class at DU that night. The instructor and the other eight students in the class sat quietly, dazed, amidst quiet discussions about "frozen O-Rings," and our own disappointments. But after sharing our grief, the next class proceeded to discussions of feed-back loops, and hysteresis dampening. That is, how is an aeronautical control surface brought to a smooth stop by gradually reducing a control signal to dampen the servomechanism to a smoothly controlled stop. In the computer lab, the instructor gave us warm up exercises in FORTRAN programming, like the coding of Taylor's Series:

$$f(z) = \sum_{n=0}^{\infty} \frac{f^{(n)}(a)}{n!}(z-a)^n$$

For-Next loop, accumulator—*Sum=Sum+f(z)*—derivative and factorial Go-Sub—number of iterations. Where I was a proficient BASIC programmer, it took me a few computer labs to realize that BASIC was a stripped-down FORTRAN. By cribbing (looking over their shoulders) from my classmates, I was quickly able to come up to speed in this programming language. Working on the programs in this course, I often awakened in the middle of the night to drive down to Denver to get into the computer room. I spent many hours in the computer room, often after everyone else had left, driving back to Conifer in the twilight hours of morning. There were times when the Chinese graduate assistant who ran the lab would tell me that I needed to go home. But, to my mind, it was "do or die." University College was on a quarter system, so the classes were only ten weeks.

Near the end of the quarter, the instructor presented the class with a final project. He provided us with a FORTRAN module for the simulation, and we had to code the interface with our hysteresis dampening coding. It was a class project where we were to all be given the same grade. We only had a week to complete this. Being accustomed to working long nights in the lab, I set about trying to find the entry point for our code. It was like trying to find the edges in a mathematical jigsaw puzzle. My classmates struggled along with me, as we sat at our terminals, stopping to discuss various approaches. Finally, one night, as I sat there alone in the computer lab, I had an idea about how we could do it. The next day, when most of the class was working on the problem, I suggested my solution—and it worked! We were high-fiving one another! We had accomplished something that had seemed impossible. That night I, I drove down from the mountain with cleaning supplies—spray bottles of cleaner, paper towels, and rags—and "cleansed the temple." I washed the terminals, cleaned the keypads, washed the tables and walls. The instructor was pleased with our group solution and I received an "A" in the course.

Hysteresis—humm baby.

The next courses at DU were mixed in their outcomes. I took a required course for the program, Human Communications. In this course, students were required to explore topics such as "proxemics," or how close or far from one another people stood when they spoke to one another, tone of voice, eye contact, and social engagement. The instructor, Jackie Fishburn, was not seduced by my mystifications of talk about quantum mechanics and the computer model of human consciousness (viz, ears and eyes—Input;

brain—CPU and ALU; voice—Output). She was more concerned with the social and cultural forms that either made for authentic or inauthentic human communications. I learned one important lesson from her. When in doubt in a social situation, one should, "Smile, get up, extend one's hand, and say, 'Hi, my name is Richard.'"

Omar and his wife Donna came up to Conifer Mountain to visit us. They were a delightful couple. Omar, who was originally from Columbia, had an uncanny resemblance to Ricardo Montalbàn, the suave Latin actor of TV's Fantasy Island. Donna was a beautiful blond statistics teacher at Kent Denver Country Day School in the tony Cherry Hills neighborhood in Englewood Colorado. As we chatted, Donna told me that there was the possibility of a position at Kent Denver. She arranged an interview with the headmaster, Dick Drew.

After the interview with Mr. Drew, I spoke with Mary Adams, chair of the math department. She told me that the current middle school mathematics teacher did not have a degree in math, and parents were complaining that his classes were insufficiently rigorous. I returned home elated that I was being considered for a position teaching mathematics. I sent letters requesting letters of recommendation from Mrs. Oliver (chair of the math dept at Westmar), Mrs. Ladendorf (chair at Minot State), and David Ray (my poet friend). In a few weeks I returned to the headmaster's office where he offered me a contract with the job title "Teacher of Mathematics."

The parents were convinced that their kids were not being grounded in the fundamentals, so wanted me to use a book—*Algebra I: An Incremental Approach* by John H. Saxon Jr.—that I found without the "charm" of real math. The Saxon text was "drill." It had short lessons, followed by numerous homework problems (the odd numbered problems with answers in the back of the book). I later attended a "Book Fair" for teachers, where I met John Saxon, the textbook's author. I told him that I thought his textbook was rather "lean."[2]

"As the teacher, it's your job to supplement the rigor with excitement," John Saxon had replied. And that is exactly the way it turned out. During an era where parents believed that homework had been abandoned for "feel-good" ("hippie") laxity, the Saxon approach was reassuring to them that their kids were developing real mathematical skills. But I knew that skill without passion was drudgery, so I took two approaches. First, I started these bright seventh graders off with discussions about large numbers, teaching them the names of "octillions," "nonillions," "googols and googolplexes" and how to parse them with commas, name them, and represent them in scientific notation. I followed this with discussions of Miscellaneous Large Numbers, from the book *The Lore of Large Numbers* by mathematician Philip J. Davis.[3]

I brought a glass of water into the classroom drank it down, glug, glug, glug—and said "more molecules of H_2O than stars in the universe. I listened to these seventh graders talk about infinity and "what was greater than infinity."

The second innovation was to allow them to go to the computer room for "play." Kent Denver had two computer labs, one in the middle school (apple IIe's) and apple IIe's with extended memories in the upper school. In 1986, computers were primarily typewriters. There were few uses in public schools. There were a few educational software packages, but they were simplistic query/response type, or developmental game-playing. My approach with my seventh graders was to teach them just enough basic programming so they could go into the computer room twice a week and write little looping (FOR-NEXT) BASIC programs to compute and printout prime numbers, perfect numbers, and other sequences. I also introduced them to the apocryphal story of Gauss being asked to add up the first 1000 integers which he understood immediately "1000+1, 999+2 . . . 500+500 = (1000/2)x(1000 +1) = 500x1001 = 500500." It was easy to show them that $n(n+1)/2$ was what Gauss had deduced, so that the sum of the first 10 integers was $10(11)/2$, or 55. I then showed them how to write a BASIC program to do this. As they "played with this idea," they quickly tried to sum numbers greater than the 8-bit capacity of the machines. I also allowed them "free-play," where they could insert diskettes with game-like ed software. But the real boon was my introduction of the Terrapin LOGO Language.

Rather than have the computer "play" them via preprogrammed games, I wanted them to see how they could "control" the medium. Turtles were physical devices devised by Marvin Minsky and Seymour Papert at MIT—after Grey Walter's "turtles"—that were controllable by the computer and could draw on paper. The Terrapin LOGO program for the apple *IIe* allowed young students to write commands for a "turtle" that would draw geometric figures on the display. Thus, simple commands like:

$$FD\ 50\ RT\ 30\ FD\ 20\ RT\ 115 <RETURN>$$

Moved the cursor-"Turtle" forward fifty pixels, turned it right 30 degrees, moved it forward 20 pixels, and turned right 115 degrees. By placing LOGO commands in FOR-NEXT loops, complicated geometrical objects could be created. For me, teaching these smart seventh graders that computers could be used to "do mathematics," as well as play video games, was my contribution to mathematics education. In general, before the Internet, providing creative pedagogic uses for PCs—beyond word processing—was a challenge for all teachers.

On the home front, Graham ("the boy of joy") was cavorting through West Jefferson Elementary with excellent grades. Shauna, somewhat a tomboy, eschewed dolls, dresses, and pink. She was musical, artistic, and a voracious reader. Baby Lindsey, still nursing, chaffed at day care. Carol was adjusting to her new job at Social Security—bringing home the bacon—as, her salary was almost twice mine. While I was teaching mathematics, going to graduate school at DU, I was still writing poetry. All I really know is that we were living an enchanted life on Conifer Mountain. There were hummingbirds at the feeder (Humm baby and starship drives), "the elusive wapiti" (bull elk), and deep snows, even in June and August. One night, amidst heavy snowfall, around Christmas, my headlights caught two giant elk crossing the dirt road in front of our house.

By spring 1987, I was coaching—originally a "pitching coach"—baseball for the Kent Denver "Sundevils." But the varsity baseball program was already well established with a well-respected coach, Scott Yates. All I could do for the varsity pitchers was to encourage them to change speeds on their pitches: "put a little on . . . take a little off." So as the season progressed, I migrated to "C-Squad." C-Squad baseball was comprised of sub-JV kids, some of whom had never even played organized baseball. I enjoyed teaching them the fundamentals of the game.

In the classroom, my students were doing very well. Before major tests, I would tell them if they all got "A's," I would bring in my toaster, make them buttered toast and we would have orange juice too.

"The test is toast," I would exhort them.

And they responded magnificently. There were a few extraordinary young mathematicians. One I particularly recall was Wendy Lane. Windy had an intuitive grasp of algebra. Because I thought she was so gifted that I did not want to stand in her way, I deferred to her brilliance. Great teachers, when in the presence of students who are smarter than they are, only try to influence them by introducing new directions to the work. Wendy Lane went on to earn a PhD in astrophysics (studying the *windy* gas *lanes* of galaxies). The one thing I tried to stress was that memorizing formulae inadequate: to use a formula, you had to understand how it was derived.

$$x = \frac{-b \pm \sqrt{b^2 - 4ac}}{2a}$$

So, I taught these seventh graders how to derive the quadratic formula by "completing the square" on the general equation of a line ax + by + c = 0.

As the next few years passed, I taught not only algebra, but Euclidean Geometry, and a year-long Introduction to Astronomy course, as I continued to coach baseball and take classes at the University of Denver. These courses were decidedly practical. Taught by people involved in the disciplinary areas they taught. That was one thing I loved about DU—the people I met there had one foot in theory and the other in the community. They were practical scholars. Theory and praxis. By the time I had completed the degree program, I had learned (or at least been exposed to) PASCAL, UNIX (shell programming), Advanced BASIC, LISP (AI list processing), C, and computer modelling and simulation. Whereas most of the students in these courses were already employed in the tech sector, I was usually the only Black, and almost always an outsider looking into employment. So, beyond being likely hired into one of these more lucrative professional positions, I concentrated on the more theoretical considerations. I was always thinking of "Universal Turing Machines," the limits of computability (*Entscheidungsproblem*), the applications of computer science to artificial intelligence (W. Ross Ashby's *Design for a Brain*).[4] I was also trying to use computer programming as "applied mathematics," to help me deepen my understanding (meMODreality—the residue) or "pure" mathematics. In my grappling with AND/OR, NOR, and XOR gates and "binary-half adders," I engaged with "machine-language" programming. I finally understood Sheffer's stroke, where all the syncategormata (logical connectors) of first-order logic, could be represented by "NOT" and "AND." I could dimly perceive how this could simplify the architecture of the Processor's arithmetic-logic-unit (ALU).

Kent Denver Country Day School was rich. The teachers had ivy-league pedigrees and connections. Many of them—the core faculty—did not teach for money, but for love of their disciplines, and their love for young people. I shared an office with a young white woman with a degree from Harvard University. In the classrooms, there were green boards with recessed lighting (something every classroom in America should have). The computer labs had whiteboards and erasable markers. The grounds were lush, with views of the front range. While the buildings and grounds were spectacular, the faculty was what really shone. Four people I met there have continued to be part of my life forty years later. Dick Drew was a highly ethical, well-rounded headmaster. He would call me into his office for chats, where he would muse about baseball, philosophy, and human development (he espoused the four C's—community, civility, character, and compassion). Then there was Steve Johnson, head of the science department. Steve was a veterinarian by training yet had a deep knowledge and appreciation of basic science. He had initiated the "Quantum" project in the department. I had many, many meaningful discussions with him about "manifolds" (Branes), Shannon's Law (the universe as "Information"), and cosmic holism (entanglement—"spooky action at a distance"). I liked him as much for his sense of awe (meaning of space time) as for his human understanding (he introduced me to Lovelock's Gaia Hypothesis) as we discussed the Anthropic Principle (perfect anthropic principle and final anthropic principle—PAP and FAP). He respected me despite the "hysteresis in my logic" and I respected him for the "magic" in his science. Steve Johnson was hypnotic.

Back at DU, after a homework problem on Fourier Series, and running a FFT ("Fast Fourier Transform") program in DU's computer lab, I could often be heard quoting Fourier's Theorem: "a steady-state wave is composed of a series of sinusoidal components whose frequencies are those of the fundamental and its harmonics, each component having the proper amplitude and phase. The sequence of components that form this complex wave is called its spectrum."[5] Or as I expressed it: "All complex variation is the simple superimposition of simple sinusoidal variations." In my lunches with Steve Johnson at Kent, I ranted and raved about Fourier's Theorem.

"What this means is the complex variation of reality itself is simply the added simple sinusoidals—from the vibrations of atoms, to the eleven-year sunspot cycles, to the orbits of the planets, to the expansion of the universe, to the vibrations of your nervous system, to the vibrations of your inner-ear—a 'music of the spheres': the oscillating universe in all its entities—crickets and pulsars—vibrating on a continuous manifold ('jello')—the $\ddot{x}$ (double derivative) of acceleration on planets and vibrations on vibrating loops of string."

Steve Johnson would look at me with a faint smile, pulling out the sinusoidals from my voice. Humm baby.

Summers during the Kent years were a delight of limpid skies, time with the children, and reading. Because Carol was working, I was totally responsible for finding ways to keep the kids entertained and feed. I made their lunches, read children's books to Lindsey, took Graham to his friend Jonathan's house to play. These were years of T-Ball, jump rope teams, piano lessons for Shauna, and hiking on Hummingbird Trail.

While watching the movie "Tron" with them, my paranoia about advanced artificial intelligence returned. Living in a computer circuit was the ultimate alienation. I had a similar reaction to the film "Bladerunner." And after reading William Gibson's *Neuromancer*, I was terrified ("jacking in," meaning a jack in the cranium for an interface between humans and computers). Gibson, who had coined the word "cyberspace," had opened a new world, the simulacrum.[6]

I returned to teaching in the fall to discover that one of my poems had been published in the University of Colorado at Colorado Spring's literary journal *Writer's Forum*. A professor in Kent's English department had spotted the poem. Suddenly, my persona at Kent Denver changed. I was no longer perceived as merely a "math-science" guy (with all the staid rigidity that implied). I knew there was a distinct difference between a math teacher and a mathematician, the former a purveyor of accepted dogma, and the latter a creator of new meaning. Where I had wanted to "live" mathematics so it could talk to me, I had the privilege to meet Ruchira Datta, who "talked to me in mathematics." Ruchira had a perfect eight hundred on her math SAT's, a Westinghouse Science Scholarship, and graduated from Kent at fourteen years old, to earn a PhD in mathematics from Berkeley. She was one of the smartest people I have ever known. She spoke mathematics. Where I wanted the Universe to speak to me, it had been answered by allowing me to teach astronomy at Kent.

And as there is a distinction between teaching and doing mathematics, teaching high school astronomy is not being an astronomer. While I loved astronomy and cosmology, realizing my limits, I tried to teach my "love" for the subject. The classes were heterogeneous—many students without mathematical ability—and taken as a "free elective." I brought in astrologers to talk about how they cast horoscopes. To the student's delight, I invited representatives from MUFON (mutual UFO network) to lecture. Someone in the Kent circle of family and associates, donated a large clock-driven refracting telescope. I organized an overnight observation camp-out—the students sleeping in tents on the grounds—so we could observe the phases of Venus, the moons of Jupiter, and the great gas nebula in Orion (M-42). We watched the great Disney film, *The Black Hole*. We also viewed the brilliant documentary film *The Powers of Ten*. Of course, I found a copy of the Bell System's "Our Mr. Sun" (with Dr. Frank Baxter) to try to motivate and share love for "Ra." I taught them the Harvard Spectral Sequence, the H-R Diagram, the Mass-Luminosity relationship, stellar evolution, Population I & II stars, galacto-synthesis, Hubble's Law, binary-star light curves, microwave background radiation, and more importantly, a passion for learning about the cosmos. I also took them to the computer lab, with simple, programming exercises like "If the Star Sirius has a parallax of .379 arcseconds, what is its distance from earth?"

Two historical events also informed my teaching astronomy at Kent. The first was Supernova 1987A. We read and discussed all the incoming reports on interpretations of the data—radiation signatures and how new information about stellar evolution could be derived from them. The other major event was the pending launch of the Hubble Telescope. I made a homework assignment, that each student was required to write a letter to the Space Telescope Institute at Johns Hopkins University in Baltimore, expressing their interest in the Hubble project and suggesting a potential experimental use for the telescope. After a few weeks—to all our amazement—the director of the Space Telescope Institute sent individual letters to each student, with a remark about their suggestions, and included a large, glossy poster of the Hubble Telescope. I wanted the universe to talk to me and it answered in the excitement of my students.

Seeing how small class sizes, dedicated teachers, and the support provided teachers by an enlightened administration (Richard Drew), I wanted what I was seeing at Kent Denver Country Day School for my son, Graham. When he was ready for seventh grade, we enrolled him at Kent. As a member of the faculty, we were giving tuition assistance, but we still had to pay. But I thought it was worth it, as he was a talented kid and deserved the best. When he appeared in my Algebra I class, I immediately discerned his facile mind. He passed all my tests with excellent grades. He enjoyed the toast and butter—when I would proclaim "This test was toast!" And when I discovered that seventh graders in Colorado private and independent schools were given an annual test of "mathematical proficiency," I photocopied example tests from prior years and distributed them to the class for practice. I would allow them to score the twenty question multiple-choice tests, themselves. I would ask them, "How many people got eighteen to twenty correct?" and four or five hands would go up. Over the weeks leading up to the state-wide test, my students became comfortable with the tests, performed better with them all the time, and laughed with me as I called the tests "Toast!" Of course, we sometimes took time to discuss questions on the test; why the answer was (b) rather than (c). On the day before the actual test, when half the class raised their hands about getting eighteen to twenty correct, I knew they were primed and ready, so I animatedly and enthusiastically proclaimed, "This test is toast!!!" I then stood on my head on my desk in front of the class, as they laughed.

A few weeks later, when the test results were announced, the headmaster called me into his office to inform me that my seventh graders had come in third in the state of Colorado, with hundreds of schools having taken the test. I was so proud of my math class. They were good little mathematicians, so rather than retreating, I became more rigorous with them as the year approached its end. We investigated network theory via the "gas-water-light" problem and the "Seven Bridges of Konigsberg." I had them tracing lines from vertices (nodes)—without lifting their pencils—on plane and solid polyhedra—trying to get them to infer theorems of what was and was not possible to traverse (type I and type II) networks, before I shared the textbook principles (Gauss). For fun we made Möbius strips, cut them in half with scissors and saw them link like chains, and cut them in halves again wondering what would happen. I always tried to push the limits of their mathematical imaginings.

In the computer lab, I used the apple IIs the teach them an important lesson on computing the areas of irregular figures. We drew an irregular closed curve inside a square of known dimensions, used a BASIC program with an iterated FOR-NEXT loop, to use the RND (randomizing function) to choose the x and y coordinates of a point within the square, then counted the number of points within the curve, took the ratio, and produced an estimate of the area. The more points plotted the more accurate the estimated area. If the program ran to infinity, the area would be exact. I thought these ideas were pre-pre-calculus, and sophisticated for twelve-year-olds.

During the baseball season, one of the "C Squad" players made my year as a coach. He was an undersized, untalented, bespectacled (usually smudged and askew—think, white tape holding together the broken Buddy Holly bridge between the lenses) and playing right-field. In the bottom of the seventh—the last inning—with Kent leading the game and two outs, the other team with the tying and winning runs in scoring position, the batter hit a long fly ball directly at this kid. All the players on the field thought "Oh no!" His father was in the stands, the players on the bench covered their eyes. My little right fielder held his glove up to the limpid blue Colorado sky . . . and the ball, spinning in the sun, plopped into the pocket of his mitt. We all jumped and yelled in celebration. Having trust in this kid—to put him in the game because his father had come out to see him play—and have him win the game for us, was something I am sure this young man would never forget. That summer, sitting in a Chili's restaurant with my family, someone tapped me on my back.

"Coach Jones, I just wanted to say thank you." It was that kid's father, who went on to say that that moment had helped his son become a man. I was humbled. Humm baby.

If I had to parse the children's hybridity—Carol's family's genius brains—with my assorted proclivities, I would judge Graham inherited my scientific curiosity, Shauna, my artistic sensitivities, and Lindsey, my rebelliousness. One day we received a telephone call that Lindsey was "missing" from B and A (that is, the "Before and After" day care in Conifer). When she was found hiding behind the dumpsters and we had asked he why she had "run away," she had told us, "I don't like this place."

Back for another year at Kent Denver, I was hitting my stride as a teacher. In the astronomy course for the year, I included Gary Zukav's *The Dancing Wu Li Masters*.[7] I had taught Euclidean geometry and I had mastered it beyond my failures to see its import as a teenager. Yet, within these successes, the scythe of time (familiarity) and racism were beginning their harvest. My first whiff of criticisms of my breezy philosophical style came after an annual in-class evaluation. I had prepped for weeks, inculcating my approach, so that students would not be shocked when the dean of students appeared to evaluate my teaching. I would arrive early, copy the proofs on the board in different colored chalks, which tended to fluoresce under the recessed blackboard lights. Then, I would ask students for the steps in the proof. "Parts of congruent triangles are equal."

I was becoming increasingly aware that I was the only Black teacher. There was a Black librarian and a Spanish teacher.

The deeper problem was the suspicion that I was intellectually shallow—"teaching cosmology with algebra." At DU's University College, I was experiencing the same problem. In a computer simulation course, where we were assigned the programming exercise to "model" a mainframe computer running a time-driven queuing application answering telephone inquiries. We were to work in small groups of four. The other minority students in the class—an Asian woman and two students from the United Arab Emirates—teamed up with me to write the simulation. I understood queuing theory from a theoretical and mathematical standpoint, having dealt with it theoretically at IBM (PARS—"Programmed Airlines Reservation System"—a massive millions of lines of code). I had read books on the intricacies of queuing theory—time and event driven. So, I wrote the code for this program in BASIC and ran it on my little apple //e. The program took hours to run, but it worked. I could alter the wait time, arrival time, and processing time in the simulation. The other students on my team came up to my house in Conifer and examined the coding with me. When I turned in the printout of the coding to the professor on the last day of class, we were sure that we had fulfilled the requirements of the assignment.

When our grades arrived in the mail, I was astonished to see the "B." Without hesitation, I arranged a meeting with the dean of University College to lodge a complaint that the professor had been biased. The dean arranged a meeting with the professor. I drove out to Aurora, Colorado, where the professor had a suite in a high-tech office building. I explained to him that I had coded the program in lowly BASIC code and run it on an apple //e computer with 64k RAM, so the queuing actions and their servicing were extremely slow. I spread the fan-folded printout out on his desk, as he and one of his employees followed my logic step-by-step. After an hour or so, the professor agreed with me that my coding was correct, the output made sense, and agreed to change the grades for my group to "A." I drove home on a cloud, but felt the lightning within it, knowing that my intelligence had been questioned because of my race.

Back at Kent, using Zukav's *Dancing Wu Li Masters* and Fritjof Capra's *The Tao of Physics*[8] in my astronomy course, I sensed the concern that I was teaching "new age" nonsense. But I was convinced there was substance to the connections between quantum mechanics (and its fuzziness) with Eastern philosophies (with its mysticisms). In "dancing energy" 跳舞的能量 in Mandarin, I could almost visualize physics in the characters. Physics 物理 = wùlí. It made sense to me that the Universe was an elaborate "dance" (Shiva) of energy. But, despite my trying to teach "holism" in the parallels between quantum mechanics and Eastern mysticism, Kent Denver was trying to hire a "real" physics teacher. Which they did—an experimentalist.

The final piece of the puzzle that was pushing me out of Kent, was the fact that my son was a student. I had read many fictional accounts of children of teachers in private schools. I had cringed when I imagined the scuttlebutt, the whispers, innuendo, and negative social pressures created for Graham, because I was a teacher in this upper-class institution. I mean . . . my god . . . I had students from the owners of Union Pacific Railroads and Coors Brewing. Kent Denver was the alma mater of Madeline Albright. I was told when the kids of the early Apollo space program required protection from the glare of fame, they were enrolled at Kent. And every year graduating seniors were accepted at Harvard University, Yale University, Massachusetts Institute of Technology (MIT), Williams College, University of Chicago, and University of California, Berkeley. The student's parents were so dedicated to maintaining their social standing that they enrolled their kids in SAT camps starting in the seventh grade, so they could attain the requisite scores to matriculate to top universities. I wanted Graham to attend Kent because I wanted to inure him to the social pressures that had defeated me. I wanted him to know the ways of white folks.

One day, the front administrative office asked me to speak with a prospective parent. I told her that Kent embraced the Greek ideal of *aretē*, that is excellence in all things—the realization of potential, including excellence in moral virtue. I explained that at Kent, the total student was to be educated—the athlete, the scholar, the citizen. That, there was a high value placed on the uniqueness of the individual; the theory of multiple intelligences, so many ways to thrive and excel.

The secretary in the upper school also told me that she had received a telephone call from a relative of Agnes Ladendorf, asking if I worked there and to give me the message that she was extremely ill. I went home that night and composed a letter to my old calculus teacher who told me that I was a "right triangle," and that if I was not "doing mathematics" I was wasting time. In the letter I thanked her for helping me reach my mathematical maturity by tolerating my plodding attempts. Thinking back to my old astronomy teacher at Howard University, Alan Maxwell, with his notebook of the powers of two to the hundredth power, and the biblical "where there are two gathered in my name I will be there," I wrote that she had taught me the "infinite powers of two" (2^∞); that whenever I did mathematics, she was present.

In 1987, I had almost completed the requirements for the M.S.S. degree at Denver University. While awaiting the final exam in Advanced BASIC programming, I picked up a magazine with an article on "string theory." Reading the entire article (I believe it was in *Discovery* magazine), I was enthralled—violin strings and open or closed loops vibrating "monads" as the smallest physical entities. I went into the computer lab and aced the exam, which consisted of creating ARRAYs, filling them with data, and reading and printing out specific cells—child's play. In June of that year, the degree was mailed to me.

And, ostensibly, at least on the surface, Graham was doing well at Kent in the classroom and socially. He appeared happy. While I continued my intellectual struggle to find my true métier—which was coming in the discipline of philosophy—I was still suffering with my technological demons. Reading Herbert Marcuse's *One-Dimensional Man* and *Eros and Civilization* had made me a critic of technology qua technology.[9] Yet as a soon to be graduate of DU's Data Processing and Computer Programming MSS degree, I was up to my ears in technology. The verisimilitudes of "reality" and simulations of reality frightened me. I was already a mechanist determinist, so I was myself a mechanical system: *Man a Machine* (French: *L'homme Machine*) is a work of materialist philosophy by the eighteenth-century French physician and philosopher Julien Offray de La Mettrie.[10] I was similarly harassed by computer scientist Edward Fredkin's ideas that the universe *is* a computer (and we are all subroutines in an executing program).

I luxuriated that summer, reading, spending time with the children, gathering firewood from the slopes behind our house abutting Pine National Forest. As August that year began, I started getting telephone calls from Kent asking me to reconsider my resignation. They offered me a modest raise and a new teaching assignment as an eighth-grade lab science teacher. I was reluctant for many reasons. First, headmaster Dick Drew had moved on to Hillsdale School in California. Second, Steve Johnson, who chatted at lunch with me about the "jiffy" (time light takes to cross the diameter of a proton) and Planck time, possibilities of spaceflight by positioning resources at L5 (Lagrange point), the verisimilitudes of starfish to hands (and the golden section), had resigned to his family-owned vineyards in California.

I really did not want to return to Kent, but being unemployed with no prospects did not appear favorable either, so I reluctantly agreed. But I had only one request, which was that Graham would not be in my classes. I knew that as he matured, the pressures of my not favoring him, and the greater pressures of his classmates' ability to undermine me through him or destroy his respect for me through him.

When classes began, Graham was a student in my science course. I felt betrayed. Also, I was a theoretician, the new head of the science program (Mr. Burroughs, a biologist) was attempting to make me a "real" scientist (rather than an airy-fairy new age Wu Li master) by putting me in a laboratory-based course teaching the use of precision balances, data collection, and observational cause and effect. I chaffed at lab work. Washing beakers and setting up experiments was not my strength.

However, early one exceptionally beautifully bright November morning, I reached my limit. In a geometry class, one disinterested student in the back of the room, started singing "Zippidy-duh-da." I took the insult that I was an old and boring "Uncle Remus." I walked out the front door of Kent Denver and never returned. That morning, I taught that class the greatest lesson they would ever learn—beyond SAS, ASA, HL—insult taken. Humm baby.

NOTES

1. John Barth, *Giles Goat-Boy* (New York: Anchor Books, 1987).

2. John H. Saxon Jr., *Algebra: An Incremental Approach* (Englewood Cliffs, NJ: Prentice-Hall, 1979).

3. Philip J. Davis, *The Lore of Large Numbers* (New Haven, CT: Yale University Press, 1961).

4. W. [William] Ross Ashby, *Design for a Brain* (New York: Wiley, 1954).

5. Richard E. Berg, "The Fourier Theorem," *Britannica*, n.d., https://www.britannica.com/science/sound-physics/Steady-state-waves#ref527305 (accessed August 22, 2023).

6. William Gibson, *Neuromancer*, ed. Terry Carr (New York: Ace, 1984).

7. Gary Zukav, *The Dancing Wu Li Masters: An Overview of the New Physics* (New York: Bantam Books, 1980).

8. Fritjof Capra, *The Tao of Physics* (New York: Bantam Books, 1975).

9. Herbert Marcuse, *One-Dimensional Man: Studies in the Ideology of Advanced Industrial Society*, 2nd ed. (Boston: Beacon Press, 1991); and Marcuse, *Eros and Civilization: A Philosophical Inquiry into Freud*, 2nd ed. (Oxfordshire: Routledge, 1987).

10. Julien Offray de La Mettrie, *Man a Machine (L'homme Machine)* (Chicago: Open Court, 1912).

Chapter 15

Teikyo Loretto Heights University, 1990–1994

In 1990, I took a job at Teikyo Loretto Heights University (TLHU). Teikyo was a Japanese university, with students from Japan. I taught computer science and algebra. Fearful that I would always be a low-level academic, I began casting about for alternatives to teaching college algebra for the rest of my life. I sought advice from Dick Drew at Kent who put me in contact with a few of his friends. One recommended that I take a math course at University of Colorado-Denver. But this "Advanced Calculus" course had turned out to be a disaster. Another advised me to try a philosophy course at the University of Denver (a.k.a. DU). I was extremely comfortable at DU, having already earned two degrees. So, I registered for a course on Wittgenstein, while applying for admittance to the MA program in Philosophy. The chair of the Philosophy Department at DU was William D. Anderson. In Dr. Anderson's Ludwig Wittgenstein seminar, we read *The Blue and Brown Books* followed by the *Tractatus-Logico Philosophicus* (TLP).[1]

I had first been exposed to the TLP at the University of South Dakota, in Philip Turetsky's aesthetics course. When we had moved from Iowa to Colorado, the first book I checked out from the library was the TLP. With Dr. Anderson's calm exegeses, I began to glimpse—even if beneath a veil, darkly—the meanings of Wittgenstein's philosophy. Wittgenstein, or LW, had often said that he would be remembered by later philosophers in only a few quotes, or paraphrases of his ideas, but for me his words were transformative.

The first profound lesson was I understood that "the limits of my language were the limit of my world." I learned that language was the "mirror of reality." For the first time, I saw that language (ordinary languages and ideal languages) were both like spectacles (eyeglasses) through which we saw the putative real, but that rather than seeing reality, we saw the glasses. As eyeglasses could be changed, so could the *language* we used to constitute the world. I had been aspect blind, a naïve realist, believing that what I saw was unfiltered reality. This was a freeing insight, as I now saw mathematics itself, as lens through which I viewed reality, and not God the infinite geometer. Mathematics was a *language game*.

Dr. Anderson was a tranquilly elegant man. He seemed completely aware of himself, without being self-conscious. He invited me to lunch at a restaurant near DU's campus on more than one occasion. He also invited me to have lunch with him at his condo. He appeared intent on getting to know me better as a person, and not just as a graduate student. I even invited him to have lunch with me at Teikyo, so he could experience my emergence in that experiment in international education. Dr. Anderson soon taught me important lessons about philosophy that were not in the readings. For instance, where I thought I was attending DU to learn philosophy, via Wittgenstein, he taught me that LW viewed "philosophy" as an illness; a "conceptual disease." LW was an "anti-philosopher" and I was at DU to "get well," by closely examining the modalities (possibilities and impossibilities) of language use. Under Dr. Anderson's guidance the TLP began to make sense. "I. The world is everything that is the case." And "I.I The world is the totality of facts, not of things." I understood that "facts" are truth-functional I-type and O-type Aristotelian propositional categories—*Some S are P* and *Some S are not P*, where the universal propositions A (All S is P) and E (No S is P) are not about the world. Dr. Anderson taught me to be skeptical of all universal generalizations (including this one).

"Your role as a philosophy teacher is to shame people who think that because they can read, they are intellectuals." He said that all people overestimate their knowledge about the world. In doing so, they delude themselves, and live lives of self-deception. He told me that by constantly reading, thinking, and attempting to understand reality—what they (the self-deceivers) thought they were doing, I would offend them (like Socrates offended the Athenians). This offense could be countered by two alternatives: (1) they could awaken and begin ridding themselves of self-deception, or (2) they could continue their endless slumbers watching shadows on the wall of Plato's cave. Being a philosopher—like Wittgenstein—was to be a "horsefly." In one of the seminars on Wittgenstein, another student gave me a copy of Bruce Duffy's *The World as I Found It*. This novel about Wittgenstein convinced me that LW meant that some things (language) existed when he entered the world, and would remain when we left the world, and that "language had to take care of itself."[2] During the two years in Denver University's Philosophy Department, I was rapidly becoming a "Black Wittgensteinian."

My propositions are elucidatory in this way:

> He who understands me finally recognizes them as senseless, when he has climbed out through them, on them, over them. (He must so to speak throw

away the ladder, after he has climbed up on it.) He must surmount these propositions; then he sees the world rightly. Whereof one cannot speak, thereof one must be silent.³

To say the least, I was silent. I felt that same lofty, icy coldness, dispassionate distance I had felt at four am in Minot North Dakota after solving an indefinite integral that took four pages. In Wittgenstein, I felt the clarity that allowed me to think again. Yet LW knew that he—like Socrates—"knew nothing." The motto of the TLP: "and all that one knows, not just heard rustling and roaring, can be said in three words." I interpreted those three words, as IDK [I don't know]. Dr. Anderson was teaching me that philosophers, in trying to talk about the ineffable "limits of the sayable" (and thinkable) make a muddle of language and that good philosophy tried to clear up these conceptual diseases by using perspicuous expressions. Philosophy was a disease. LW was a physician who diagnosed the illness and made prescriptions for its cure. These ideas were deflationary—popped the air-filled balloons of all intellectual pretensions—the self-deceptions of knowing. Wittgenstein thought the best philosophy book would be a "joke book."

In two years, I took courses in epistemology, metaphysics, symbolic logic, "human problems," Plato, Aristotle, and more Wittgenstein. I learned to appreciate the fact that natural languages—in contradistinction to "ideal languages" (like mathematics, logic, and computer programs)—were perfectly able to convey any concept; that ordinary language was necessary and sufficient, and a ground for thought and communication. For me, this constituted the "linguistic turn.' From David Hume, I learned that there was really no way to deduce cause and effect, as it is either a priori (deductive) or a posteriori (inductive). You cannot deduce causality without experience, and to use inductive methods, is to argue in a circle. Hence, the diadem of science—cause and effect—is the scandal of philosophy.

From Plato, I learned many things, Forms, Philosopher Kings (and Queens), Socrates's IDK ("All I know is I know nothing"), but the most importantly, "The Upward Path." This was Plato's four-levels of knowledge, being, and ethics, which was an inflection point for understanding my past and future existence. My pragmatic interpretation of the upward path was that the four steps were, *eikasia, pistis, dianoia,* and *noesis.* Eikasia (doxa—appearance) was the uniformed gossip and babble of the hoi polloi. Pistis was the step up to the conventional wisdom of the tribe. Dianoia was the giant step—as the first two were of the visible realm—to scientific study. Finally, noesis, was the use of facts derived from dianoia, to question in dialectical inquiry. The final two levels of the divided line were located in the intelligible realm (of the Forms and mind).

In its epistemic (eikasia to noesis), ontological (appearance to Real), and ethical (good in things and appearances to the Form of the Good), Plato's upward path was the direction my life needed to take. I was reminded of my hippie days, where Russian mystic-mathematician P. D. Ouspensky had provided the paradigm, in the form of levels of human consciousness in his book *Tertium Organum*.[4] Ouspensky's divided line consisted of *preconsciousness* (genetic memory), *unconsciousness* (Freud's Id-Ego-Superego), *consciousness* (awareness), and *cosmic consciousness* (noetic thought). Ouspensky's cosmic consciousness—the continual awareness of the "Oneness" of the universe, the turning of the galactic wheel, the illusion of time—is my quest to enter into discourse with the universe—to have it "talk back to me," because my love and awareness of it is so deep and unending that it borders on worship.

Teikyo was my laboratory of the real. University of Denver was my laboratory of the arcane. In my last year at TLHU, I achieved a massive amount of work in the real (Platonic realism) world. And I also surpassed all prior efforts in the practical world. In accomplishing this synthesis—*a priori* and *a posteriori*—I arrived at Immanuel Kant's synthetic a priori, or C. S. Pierce's abductive perspective—IBE (inference to the best explanation). The best explanation for my life at this time was that as a Black man living in America, I was laboring on the upward path to provide an example for my family (always be seen as a student in the eyes of my children) and trying to gain my freedom and dignity by way of increasing my knowledge (wisdom) and becoming a better person by discovering what it is to live a good life (ethics).

At Teikyo, I taught my classes, and even managed to help with TLHU's club baseball team. Hum babe! In 1993, at age forty-eight years old, I took the mound in an intra-squad game with the Teikyo Tigers baseball team. During this three-inning game, I threw my last pitch "in anger" (meaning trying to strike out the batter). I felt like Satchel Page, the great Negro League pitcher who made it to the Major Leagues when he was already far past his prime, but who managed to win many of the games he pitched. And I pitched well, striking out a few of the young Japanese ballplayers with slow roundhouse curveballs. My "heater" topped out at about 82 mph—not bad for an old man. I gained the respect of the Tigers, who invited me to coach their upcoming game with the club team at the University of Colorado Boulder. My coaching that day only amounted to exhorting the pitchers to "throw strikes," and "to stay within themselves" (baseball lingo for do not try to do too much—do *you*). Teikyo won one half of the double-header. They were exhilarated.

At DU, I was nearing the end of coursework for the MA in Philosophy, a degree that I thought was not "second-rate." Being a mathematician-computer teacher, I had never been required to write analytical essays. The two years studying philosophy at DU improved my writing and reasoning, by helping me maintain a "line" in my thinking from thesis-premises-to conclusion. In order to graduate, it was required I take a comprehensive written exam and an oral exam. As the Friday when these examinations were scheduled approached, I was a nervous wreck, coffee jangling my nerves—humming.

The written exam went well. Two questions on Wittgenstein, one on the history of philosophy, and one on Plato's metaphysics. But the oral exam did not go as well, as the committee asked two questions that stumped me. I was at a loss to answer questions concerning the ontological and epistemological distinctions in Plato's "Third Man Argument." I feared that I had failed. But perhaps, my answers to the question on Wittgenstein's *On Certainty* saved me.[5] When Dr. Anderson called me back into the conference room and stated that "On the balance of my work, I had been passed," I was elated. I was told the degree was a "terminal degree," meaning that I could not use it to pursue a PhD. But now, I held four master's degrees, even if some people thought some of them were "second-rate," I did not. I had used the University College's courses to help train me to become a better student; take notes, never miss classes, do the homework carefully, study for tests, and fulfill the requirements.

At Teikyo, this "going over to the other side," as my mathematics and science colleagues perceived my shift from the "hard" academic disciplines to the "soft" humanities, was a surprise; especially since they saw me as a technician rather than a theoretician.

Graham had graduated from Kent with excellent SAT scores (National Merit Scholar) and chosen to matriculate at Reed College in Portland, Oregon, one of the most liberal "lefty" schools in the country. Graham brought Michel Foucault's book *Discipline and Punish* home with him.[6] I eagerly read this book. It helped me change from my rational left-brain to my creative right-brain. The whole idea of disciplinarity, from academic, corporal, to political and carceral, enlarged my conceptual space. Shauna had similarly distinguished herself at Colorado Academy (National Merit Scholar) and matriculated at Oberlin College in Ohio. Lindsey was still enrolled at Colorado Academy. Carol was reestablished in her job with the Social Security Administration. We had two dogs—Scotch and Domino—and lived in a quiet cul-de-sac in Littleton, Colorado.

I obtained tickets to see Kurt Vonnegut at Teikyo's theater. I thought about his book *Hocus Pocus*, where he taught in a little college for the learning disabled. There was also a Japanese connection "an enormous prison run for profit by Japanese who, along with other prosperous foreigners, have bought the United States of America."[7] There were rumors among the cognoscenti that among the 54 percent of Americans who read at a sixth-grade level, there were colleges for dyslexics, with dyslectic professors teaching "backward." For all this, there was something uncanny—*hocus pocus*—about Kurt Vonnegut ("curt and from the gut") at Teikyo. Vonnegut was funny and said many interesting things about writing, war, and how to live a good life. Afterward, I stood in a line to meet him. When I shook his hand I said, "I've read all your books."

"Well, you'd had better," Vonnegut replied.

In my bildungsroman to becoming a better human being—perhaps even evolve to live in Tralfamadore, Vonnegut's utopia, where beings see through time and can live in any moment—I decided that the MA in Philosophy was not a "terminal degree." I retook the GRE and applied to the PhD program in Philosophy at the University of Colorado in Boulder. I was shocked to see that my GRE scores had not changed in the twenty-five years since I had first taken them at Minot State College in 1970.

To my utter amazement, I was admitted in the fall of 1994 to the PhD degree program at the University of Colorado. I thought I was prepared for this leap. But the life of a forty-nine-year-old graduate student was to prove problematic.

Wittgenstein had taught me the most important lesson—the goal of philosophy was therapeutic—to rid oneself of one's self-deceptions—and "how to go on."

NOTES

1. Ludwig Wittgenstein, *The Blue and Brown Books* (New York: Harper Torchbooks, 1965); and Wittgenstein, *Tractatus logico-philosophicus* (London: Routledge, 1922).

2. Bruce Duffy, *The World as I Found It* (Boston: Mariner Books, 1987).

3. Ludwig Wittgenstein, *Tractatus logico-philosophicus* (London: Routledge, 1922), 189.

4. P. D. Ouspensky, *Tertium Organum, or the Third Cannon of Thought and a Key to the Enigmas of the World* (Whitefish, MT: Kessinger Publishing, 1998).

5. Ludwig Wittgenstein, *On Certainty*, ed. G. E. M. Anscombe and G. H. von Wright, trans. Denis Paul and G. E. M. Anscombe (New York: Harper Torchbooks, 1972).

6. Michel Foucault, *Discipline & Punish: The Birth of the Prison*, trans. Alan Sheridan (New York: Vintage Books, 1995).

7. Kurt Vonnegut, *Hocus Pocus, or What's the Hurry, Son?* (New York: Putnam Publishing, 1990).

Chapter 16

The University of Colorado, 1994–2000

Boulder, Colorado was a university town. With 30,000 students, it was the flagship institution of the state system. But to the hip, the University of Colorado (UC) was the bastion of far left ("lefties"), refugees from the hippie "back to the earth," and the newly emergent "punk" anarchist movements. When I first walked the streets to get to the university bookstore, I saw the spiky rainbow mohawks, the piercings, and skateboarders of the new youth culture. Boulder, along with Cal Berkely in California, had gained the prefixes of "The Peoples' Republic of," as an indication of their anarcho-socialist leanings. Boulder was the home of Alan Ginsberg's Naropa Institute, where Buddhism, poetry, cannabis, and alternative lifestyles were academic disciplines.

Having begun my college experience at Fisk University, with less than five hundred students, I had always been intimidated by large public universities, where students were anonymous numbers in a computer—like John Barth's *Giles Goat Boy*. I knew that I could easily get lost at UC—Hermann Hesse's *Beneath the Wheel*.[1] I believed that institutionalized education—especially when the institutions became huge—were capitalistic "factories," intent on reproducing knowledge to replace the interchangeable parts of a society that was increasingly like the assembly line.

I thought of myself as a revolutionary thinker. The thinkers I respected in all fields were "anti-" philosophers, poets, writers. So, I brought—the anti-philosophers Ludwig Wittgenstein (LW) and Friedrich Nietzsche, anti-writers Richard Brautigan and William S. Burroughs, anti-poets Amiri Baraka and Haki Madhubuti, anti-scientists Paul Feyerabend and Bruno Latour—with me to Boulder. Intellectually, I felt at home with the youth on the streets of Boulder, against all bourgeois institutions, including the great universities that resisted social and political change. Yet, Boulder was the ideal place for me because it was at the center of what remained of the ethos of the Haight-Ashby hippies. I thought UC was more hospitable than the University of Iowa, where I had cracked-up and been an unwilling graduate student in the Science Education department. And Boulder was the site of the *Mork & Mindy* TV show with Robin Williams and Pam Dawber. Like many Black people in America, I identified with Mork, as an alien, living in seclusion in suburbia, while hiding his true identity (as human).

"This is Mork, calling Ork . . . Na-nu, Na-nu."[2]

In my application for the PhD program, I had written that I was interested in the "philosophy of computing," "the philosophy of science," and "modern philosophy." The application had also had a question asking what were my intentions for using the degree. I had answered that I would like to return to Howard University, where my intellectual journey had begun, to teach philosophy to young Black students. At the time I wrote this, I could not name a single Black philosopher, beyond, perhaps W. E. B. Du Bois—who, I would discover latter, mainstream white philosophers considered a "sociologist."

The Philosophy Department, in Hellems Hall, was located near the center of the sprawling campus, with an amphitheater behind it, where outdoor Shakespeare festivals were held in the summer. When the weather was nice, I spent many hours sitting alone in this amphitheater reading philosophy. The department had seventy-five graduate students—none of whom were Black—with one Hispanic, one South Asian (India), and one Chinese national. The faculty of thirty or so professors were all white. Although because of my "paper bag" colored skin-tone—many people asked me "What are you?"

During the opening weeks of the semester, there was a party at my advisor's home, Christopher Shields. The seventeen new graduate students, along with their spouses (or "partners") were invited. There were seven new PhD and ten master's students. At the party, where everyone was trying to *suss* one another out, I quickly realized who the players on the faculty were. They were stoic, calm, preoccupied, and engaged in quiet conversation with one another. At forty-nine years old, I was as old, or older than some of my soon-to-be professors, and by far the oldest grad student. The home of the professor—my grad advisor—was unpretentious.

Somehow, in the weltering doubts plaguing me, the Wittgenstein I brought with me to Boulder sustained my "revolutionary" stances. LW had convinced me that many of the "things" humans took to be "the furniture of reality"—like "I" and "me" and "death"—were only words (in a language game). And on deeper reflection, that even the reified foundations of science, like space and time ("spime"), were similarly verbal constructs. The philosophical revolutionary I took myself to be was like the first philosopher—Thales—who first understood the mathematics of infinity—after studying in Egypt, he propounded that a semi-circle was the infinite locus of the vertex of a right triangle. His tombstone, only found in the twentieth century, had this figure inscribed.

My first semester courses were, Epistemology with George Bealer, Metaphysics with Graham Oddie, and Introduction to Cognitive Science with Chris Shields. Bealer was a Cal Berkeley philosopher, deeply analytical, and apparently intent on teaching the history of twentieth-century epistemology. Oddie was a young visiting professor from New Zealand, finding his way in a new country and new philosophy department. Shields was also a young, popular, well-meaning professor who specialized in ancient philosophy, but was teaching this survey course on "consciousness."

I learned important concepts from all of them. From Bealer, the retreat to the meta-level in the work of Tarski (language that talks about language), and the paradoxes of the infinite constructions of propositions by PRENEX reductions and subsequent mathematical diagonalizations. From Oddie, a deeper appreciation for appearance/reality distinctions. Oddie's metaphysics course turned on a deep discussion of "universals," like "red." And from Shields "C-fibers," Searl's "Chinese Room translations," "anomalous monism," and the books and articles by Paul and Patricia Churchland.[3] Shields also deepened my understanding of the "back propagation algorithm." Outside these classrooms, I was also able to establish personal relations with these brilliant thinkers.

Yet with all my new and revolutionary knowledge, my grades at the end of the semester, A from Bealer, B+ from Shields, and B from Oddie, were woefully inadequate—anything less than an A in graduate school (especially for a PhD) is considered a failure. Realizing I needed to devote more time to philosophy and less time at Teikyo, I resigned from my part-time position.

My advisor, Chris Shields, sensitive to my foundering—I was in over my head—counselled me treat my immersion in philosophy as a "writing program." He knew that my writing was inadequate. I knew my writing was inadequate. I was also lost concerning my direction in philosophy. My aimlessness concerned him. I wanted to continue my study of Wittgenstein, but in the philosophy department at UC, LW was marginal. He discouraged this interest advising me to "map the territory." Meaning that I needed to identify the major historical players and their schools and ideologies. In doing so, I quickly discovered the so-called "analytic-continental" split in contemporary philosophy. Analytic philosophy—which was dominant in the department—was the Anglo-American practice of the analyses of arguments and concepts (a conceptual "science"). The continental strain was primarily continental European French and German existentialism, phenomenology, and postmodernism.

In trying to right myself in this rocking boat, I conceived of my enthusiasms for Jean-Paul Sartre, Albert Camus, and Foucault—in terms of

Wittgenstein—as LW being a bridge (a "hinge") between these oppositions—a "third way" of doing philosophy, as a "therapeutic" practice. Where many of the philosophers on the faculty thought my assumed conceptual mathematical ability would translate into philosophical acumen, this did not prove to be the case.

Second semester, I was pleased to learn that the department had accepted nine credit-hours of the work I had done at the University of Denver toward the required fifty-five hours of coursework. Freed from Teikyo, I redoubled my efforts. LW's vade mecum, "Philosopher take your time," became my guide as I slowed my life down, so I could increase my comprehension of the voluminous and dense readings. My grades began to get better. In a course on Aristotle taught by Chris Shields, I deepened my appreciation for "the homonymy of the good," the tri-partite division of the soul, and Aristotelian virtue ethics. A course on Plato, taught by Argentinian philosopher Gabriella Carone, contributed to my understanding of "Justice" and the logic of Socrates's method of "aporia" (the *elenchus*). I was still struggling with my writing.

During this period of struggle, John Fisher's course on Aesthetics stands out. First, because he showed the class slides of postmodern art, including Robert Mapplethorpe's explicit photographs, Andres Serrano's "Piss Christ," Orlans plastic surgeries to transform her body into art, and Hsien Tehching's punching a timeclock every hour for a year. He played The Band's classic rock song "The Weight" in class as an example of "art." John Fisher also raised the larger questions concerning what art *is* and what the nature of beauty *was*.

In this aesthetic course, after receiving a "B" on an essay, a young classmate told me that I needed to "change my vocabulary." He said that my transformation from a computer programming and algebra teacher to a "philosopher" was dependent on my new choices of words. Another sympathetic classmate gave a copy of a little book, *The Practice of Philosophy* by Jay Rosenberg. I read and re-read this book continuously, until I began to roll the rock in the right direction. My "discursive locutions" began to include words like instantiation, hermeneutic, constitutive, performativity, normative, axiological, hegemony, and praxis. The "posties"—pomo, post-Fordian, post-post-pomo, post-capitalism—saturated my discourse and narrative style.

The summer of my first year, I took a course on Existentialism from Phyllis Kenevan. Absolutely at home in this course with readings from Heidegger, Kierkegaard, and Sartre, my performance was superb. I was enabled to take part in class discussions and authored several excellent papers. I became a Kierkegaardian "knight of infinite faith."[4] After the course, speaking with professor Kenevan, she told me that she had known George Gamow when he was at UC Boulder. She told me, Gamow had a profound sense of humor.

In chatting with her on the steps of Hellems Hall, I told her about Herman Melville's *The Confidence Man*.[5] How, when interviewed on the David Susskind TV show, Camus had said that Melville's *The Confidence Man* was the first existential novel—that we are all swindlers, wearing masks, and that "confidence"—playing on the word—is the coin of the realm, with it one can do anything—including running game on others. After that conversation, I told her I wanted to give her a copy of this book, which I did. As Camus was the paradigmatic "outsider," and I was always an outsider, a stranger.

Sitting in my Twentieth-century Analytic Philosophy seminar, taught by Yale educated, Robert Hanna, discoursing on Wittgenstein, the "Vienna Circle," and the linguistic turn, I was back on firmer ground. He also lectured on Alfred North Whitehead and Bertrand Russell's *Principia Mathematica*, G. E. Moore's "Refutation of Idealism," and A. J. Ayer's *Language, Truth and Logic*.[6] I took a course on Immanuel Kant from a youngish UCLA visiting philosopher Carol Voeller. Voeller was rigorous and made me think more deeply about Kant's *The Critique of Pure Reason*.[7] The categories of the understanding, antinomies of reason, and the "Copernican revolution," became part of my analytic tool bag. Maneuvering a terrain filled with self-doubts, murky writing, and marginal grades, I was glimpsing the cold austerity—bereft of sentiment—of analytic philosophy. Kant's "All beginning is in time and all limits of the extended are in space. But space and time belong only to the world of sense. Accordingly, while appearances in the world are conditionally limited, the world itself is neither conditionally nor unconditionally limited,"[8] showed me an actual transcendental ontology and epistemology, a real realm beyond the senses, and truths beyond our ken. I thought Kant, like Wittgenstein, deflated the infinite rationality we humans arrogantly assumed, and replaced it with a finite empiricism of the senses. It made sense. We *made* sense. Nature, space, time, and reality were projections—we were not embedded in the universe, so much as we created the universe (or at least *a* universe). My thinking became clear—David Hume's atoms without color—the icy coldness near absolute zero that slowed energy to a crawl—the same "stopping of time" of tracking an airborne baseball or solving a double integral.

I was coming up on my "Fifth Semester Paper" in the fall. I had to form a committee, or at least the department chose one for me. I had Steve Leeds (Harvard University/MIT), Carol Cleland (Brown University), and Wes Morrison (Northwestern University). Leeds specialized in the Philosophy of science and epistemology, Cleland in the Turing-Church thesis and the limits of computability, and Morrison on the philosophy of religion. Morrison was also the director of the graduate program. These were brilliant and well-educated professors who had decided I should write my qualifying paper on "causation." I was already convinced that "causation" was a non-starter, full stop. Aristotle's four causes: formal, material, efficient, and final (teleological) about summed it up for me. And Hume's "we never see the hidden springs" of nature—that "cause and effect" is a "habit" (a habitual way of seeing)—underscored this impasse to further progress. I understood "cause and effect" in the nomological (scientific law) sense of Stefan-Boltzmann's statistical mechanics and the second law of thermodynamics. At the quantum level, "cause" was lost again to probabilities. And if I adhered to my Bohmian holistic cosmological wave concepts, the super-determinism of this universe, or its multiplicities in the multiverse, were assured.

I did the research on causality. I discovered one terrific book, *The Cement of the Universe* by John L. Mackie, but most of the papers were discussions of "contrary-to-fact-counterfactuals," that seemed wooly and fuzzy to me.[9] In retrospect I wish someone on the committee would have recommended Schopenhauer's Appendix, where he discusses causation. I was unprepared for the logico-linguistic ("logic chopping"), counterfactual approach I encountered in the philosophy journal articles. I wish the committee had allowed me to discuss causation from the standpoint of physics—but they did not—and the paper was a jumble. Failing the fifth semester paper meant I could not enter into candidacy. The committee's verdict shattered me. I went to my aesthetics professor's office and fumed. I told John Fisher that failure was not an option.

"I am in debt through student loans. I have children in college. My wife has maxed out our credit cards."

He let me vent.

"Was I an affirmative action admission?"

"No," he reassured me, "you were admitted on merit."

I stewed for an hour while he sat, watching me, and saying extraordinarily little.

I drove home pondering my future. I decided that I would file a civil rights complaint with the US Department of Education. I wrote the letter to them detailing my frustrations at being them only Black student, in a department with an entirely white professorate, in a university with one of the smallest percentages of Black students in the country. They returned the forms. I walked into the office of one of my fifth semester paper committee's office and dropped the manila envelope on his desk, without saying a word. He read the return address on the envelope. I said nothing, picked the envelope up and walked out of his office. I knew that possibly, I could not win a lawsuit against the University, but I could cause them embarrassment, as Affirmative Action was still a highly politically charged issue.

As I continued to boil, not sharing my failure with anyone, I tried to think strategically. Meeting with two of the professors on the committee, I asked them if I could register in one of their courses, so I could discern what their requirements were. They allowed it, and I registered for Advanced Metaphysics from Cleland and the Philosophy of Physics from Leeds. I also took a Process Philosophy seminar with Gary Stahl. While all of this was going on, I received a telephone call from Professor Alison Jaggar saying she would like to meet with me, and perhaps work with me.

She was sitting quietly when I walked into her office. There were potted plants, an oriental rug, upon which a honey and white English Setter, who looked like my dog Mizmoon. Alison, as she insisted, I call her, had a pronounced and refined English accent.

"May I fix you a cup of tea?"

She was calmly composed, with a mischievous twinkle in her limpid blue eyes. She smiled when she spoke to me. She told me that I was isolated, and although I knew much about Western philosophy, that I knew nothing about myself. She told me that she thought, since I came to philosophy so late, that I could do more in a shorter period of time in Social and Political philosophy than in metaphysics and epistemology, which she thought took much more time to get a feel for.

"I want you to meet some of my friends," she communicated with warmth. And so began my second life in the philosophy department at Boulder.

I had started to think that the elite analytic philosophers came from upper tier universities (Ivies, Stanford, Berkeley) and either taught in one of them to produce replacements for the upper tier or taught in the second tier flagship state universities to prepare the future professors to replace them there, or in the third tier colleges with PhD programs. I was being taught by people from the top. I did not think they harbored ill will toward me (or were even racists), but that I was too "non-traditional" (too old, Black, and without adequate preparation). Many of my classmates in these seminars were undergraduate philosophy majors, Phi Beta Kappas, with nearly perfect SATs and GREs. My background as a high school geometry and algebra teacher, and a programming instructor at an experimental Japanese university, did not give them much to work with in me. Yet, they saw something—my desire and will to get better—that inspired them to help me. They perceived my humility and love for wisdom.

I construed my latest defeats as induced Socratic *aporia*. They had induced such massive levels of confusion in me that it had broken me down. It was like "boot camp" in the military where you were broken down then put back together according to the military's specifications. My upper tier professors at Boulder, could not have me think I knew something, as after all, the greatest of all the philosophers only knew, "that he knew nothing." What is it to know nothing? Nothing with certainty?

I was at least mapping the territory. Philosophy was divided into five major areas: Metaphysics, Epistemology, Ethics, Social and Political, and the philosophies "of." Metaphysics and Epistemology (M&E) are the "hard" subcategories as they include the deepest questions of knowledge and reality. Ethics is about "the good." Social and Political concern the collective "good," or "what is the good we can know together that we cannot know alone." The philosophies of "of" were those of science, law, mathematics, physics, education, language, etc. In grappling with the "of's," I was always trying to bring about "the great reversals" of postmodern philosophy by reversing the terms. So, the philosophy of science became, "the science of philosophy." In rapid order: the Laws of philosophy, the language of philosophy, the education of philosophers.

I took the philosophy of science from Oddie and Alan Franklin (from the UC physics department). I took the philosophy of mathematics from Steven Leeds, who I had also taken the philosophy of physics. I did very well in the philosophy of physics. Steve Leeds telephoned me one afternoon to inform me that he was giving me an "A−" in this difficult course on quantum mechanics. Carol danced around the house with me, as Leeds had failed my fifth semester paper. This single grade was a fulcrum in not only my graduate work at UC, but also boosted my confidence that I was making progress toward becoming a philosopher. Leeds was, by my lowly estimation, a stone-cold genius, who did not use textbooks in his courses because he wanted to encourage divergent thinking, rather than back of the book answers. I thought, he thought, like I did that "systematic conceptual misinterpretations and misunderstandings," were strategically important for theoretical (speculative) philosophy. I did not do as well in his philosophy of mathematics, primarily because I had not mastered the first-order predicate calculus (deductive logic). However, the questions the course raised in my mind about "consistency" and "completeness," in mathematical proofs, remained with me until I had graduated and taught symbolic logic.

The one course that "got me over" in the philosophy department was my performance in the philosophy of science. I quickly understood *certeris paribus* conditions (with other conditions remaining the same), how Bayes's Theorem allowed for IBE (inference to the best explanation), and revisability in scientific laws and theories. I had an implicit understanding—from my boyhood days as boy scientist—of the theories of science advanced by Imre Lakatos, Karl Popper, and Thomas Kuhn. For my final paper and class presentation, I investigated the "Perihelion Advance of the Planet Mercury." Aided by a powerful book on the topic recommended by Alan Franklin, I discussed the many theories put forward to explain this phenomenon, ending with Albert Einstein's theory on curved space. The "A" I received in this course produced a positive ripple effect (a Bohmian wave) in the department.

But while pursuing these philosophy "of" courses, I was increasingly coming under the influence of the world historical feminist philosopher,

Jaggar. In "introducing me to her friends," she also thought I should start attending philosophy conferences. So, that fall of 1997, I bought a roundtrip Amtrak ticket to Providence Rhode Island, home of Brown University, for the SOFPHIA ("Socialist Feminist Philosophical Association") conference. Philosophers Alison M. Jaggar, Lewis R. Gordon, Padget Henry, Gail Presby, Richard Schmitt, Ann Ferguson, and Karsten Struhl were in attendance. The conference discussions were informal. There was much talk about two books: *The Dialogical Imagination* by M. M. Bakhtin and *The Agony of Education: Black Students at a White University* by Joe R. Feagin et al. I certainly knew something about the latter.[10]

More important than the conference was meeting Padget Henry and Lewis Gordon, both Black professors at Brown. Although I was still a graduate student and several years his senior, Gordon treated me like a colleague, taking me for coffee, and talking philosophy with me as we walked across Brown's campus. Gordon invited me into his home for a party, where people sat around his kitchen table, drinking red wine, and debating the intricacies of the revolutionary struggle. I remember riding with Padget Henry to the train station to pick up a SOFPHIA participant, where I told him about my novel *Blackland*.[11] I told him about the need for a "BIA" (Black Intelligence Agency), like the FBI and CIA, to gather intelligence for building a Black nuclear weapon—or at least to make the enemies of Black folks think that what was happening. He laughed.

During SOFPHIA's open sessions, doctoral candidates from other disciplines sat in on the discussions. I recall two very young scholars talking about "Post-Fordism." Because they were speaking so rapidly, with ideas intersecting from so many diverse directions, I thought they might be "coked-up." And one irate Black PhD candidate from the American Studies program becoming irate by my presence. As I dressed in work boots, jeans, and a "buffalo-plaid" wool shirt, she thought that I was the paradigmatic "academic pet." Which implied that I was an instantiation of white academic privilege, where a minority academically ill-prepared student, was groomed for participation in the academic kennel. I was outraged by this Black woman's assumption that I was Alison Jaggar's "pet."

Meeting Lewis Gordon was pivotal. He was an actual Black philosopher teaching philosophy. Gordon awed me with his Socratic teaching style in a class on Frantz Fanon.

Jaggar and Lewis Gordon were friends. There was a mutual respect and commitment to their work, a loyalty, a cooperation—comradeship—a community of friends, a society, socialism. A similarly dressed older philosopher—flannel work shirt—Richard Schmitt, also at Brown, lent quiet solemnity to the proceedings. When I left Brown University on the train, I left with a place to stand—an Archimedean point—a place from which I could move the earth.

Close to Providence, the police halted the train at a station platform.

"Everyone off the train," came over the loudspeaker, "There's been a reported bomb threat."

As the policemen, with bomb-sniffing German Shepherds, snooped under the train cars, and walked up and down the aisles, I stifled my chuckles of the "Boom shaka laka," bomb in my novel in progress, *Blackland*. Headed for New York City and the Alain Locke Conference, I was reading book on Wittgenstein, *Rails to Infinity* by Crispin Wright.[12]

The Locke Conference was at the New School for Social Research, an avant-garde, urban university. On the program were several well-known Black philosophers, including Lucius T. Outlaw Jr. from Haverford College, William R. Jones from Florida State University, Leonard Harris from Purdue University, Anthony Appiah from Princeton, and Tommy Lott from San Jose State College. Just a few years prior, the only Black philosopher I had heard of was Cornel West. But here at this Locke conference was a panoply of diverse Black philosophers and philosophies.

Having come under Jaggar's influence, since she had said "I didn't know about myself," I had taken a keen interest in Black philosophy. I had read Leonard Harris's canonical *Philosophy Born of Struggle*, William R. Jones's *Is God a White Racist?*, Lucius T. Outlaw's *On Race and Philosophy*, and Kwame Anthony Appiah's *In My Father's House*.[13] This reading had become my "second curriculum," that is, the vast literature and archive of "Black discursive practices," that was not taught in white philosophy departments. For Black philosophers, the required discipline was self-taught. While pursuing the regular curriculum of "dead white guys," I was supplementing these "isms" with a rich tableau of Black literature, philosophy, and culture. I was like a kid meeting a major league baseball player, when the elegant, Appiah, left the stage after giving his paper and sat right in front of me. He turned to look at me and I said clumsily: "I just finished reading your *In My Father's House*."

At this conference, I had opportunities during breaks to speak with Leonard Harris and Tommy Lott. The crux of the conference was the work of the first Black PhD philosopher from Harvard University, Alain LeRoy Locke. Leonard Harris had founded an Alain Locke Society and held national conferences to elucidate his work. Locke, I was discovering was an intellectual giant. After that conference, where I had crashed with one of my son's friends from Kent Denver, Mike Balderi, I hopped back on Amtrack and headed for Baltimore.

At the train station in Baltimore, my great nephew Marcus Sills picked me up.

Marcus, a student at Morgan State College, shepherded me about during my stay at Morgan for the "Intersections of Race Conference." Marcus chatted with me about the "Brother to Brother" organization he belonged to. This program, he explained, linked successful Black college students with Black men in the hood who were having problems with gangs, incarceration, and drugs. I liked this idea of "brotha helping brotha." The Conference at Morgan was also revelatory.

First, Richard Schmitt, the philosopher I had met at SOFPHIA, was on the program. Richard Schmitt's presentation was not a prepared paper he read, but a "talk" about race in America. When he said, "Black people in America don't have a problem, white people in America have a problem," I was at once a SOFPHIA acolyte. Second, Schmitt introduced me to the brilliant Black existentialist philosopher Robert Birt. Birt, a graduate of Vanderbilt University's philosophy program was to play many important parts in my future as a philosopher. Third, Robert Birt asked me to moderate a panel at this conference on "intersectionality"—which has since become a trope in Black philosophy. As moderator for the panel, I introduced the speakers, kept an eye on the clock, passing notes to them when their time was up, and moderating the fielding of questions. It was my first "public appearance." On the long train ride from Baltimore to Denver, I thought that I had taken another turn. Just as I had wanted to be someone who could "live" mathematics, I now wanted to be someone who could "live" philosophy, *live* Black philosophy.

Now that I had found a sympathetic community in other Black philosophers, I ensconced myself in reading every book and academic paper I could find on Black philosophy. I quickly discerned that fewer than one hundred African Americans held advanced degrees in academic philosophy. There were more than 10,000 whites in the American Philosophical Association.

To understand more about Jaggar, who had assumed the role of my dissertation advisor, I began taking some of her courses. I enrolled in her course on Feminist Political Theory. As, she was also the director of the Women's Studies Program at the University of Colorado (UC), women packed into her courses. I was one of only a few men in these courses. Her reading lists were dense, as we often read a book per week. Her classes were different, as she did not lecture continuously, but found novel ways to produce student engagement. She used small groups, presentations, and questions from the readings posted to a class group email account, so everyone could read everyone else's questions and observations. I thought this was a creative and effective method for inclusion. But her greatest skill as a philosopher was to consistently draw out in discussions, the most reticent, oft ignored, and lowest status participant in every group. And she knew how to listen, oh how she could listen. And hear, not only the lyrics, but also the melody.

As I found out about her, I discovered that she was the founder of SOFPHIA, the originator of the journal Hypatia, and one of the leaders of a group of feminists who had postulated feminist "standpoint theory." The idea that knowledge is situated in one's position in the society. That there was also a "Love's Wisdom"—the knowledge of the heart only women possessed. Her book *Feminist Politics and Human Nature* delineated four camps: liberal feminism, socialist feminism, Marxist feminism, and radical feminism.[14] Jaggar was a radical socialist feminist. I heard stories from those who knew her that she started one of the first battered women's shelters in the country by inviting abused women into her own home.

Because Alison, Richard Schmitt, and Lewis Gordon belonged to the Radical Philosophy Association, I joined and began attending their national conferences. Alison told me about many important things before sending me out to be interviewed for jobs or fellowships.

"They will interview you, but they will not hire you. It will serve to make them feel that they are not racists. And they will try to infantilize and feminize you."

Infantilize a fifty-three-year-old man by making me a "boy." *Feminize* a man with three children by making me less than a man. But the *pièce de resistance* was that she was right; I could read it in every interviewer at the APA interview tables. I was dehumanized by not being young enough, but still a "boy," and degendered like a woman by being without "power."

"We don't think you can write and publish enough at your age to ever be considered for tenure," one interviewer surmised.

I also had an encounter with Lucius T. Outlaw at the society for Phenomenology and Existential Philosophy (SPEP) at its 1997 annual conference in Denver. While celebrating the work of feminist philosopher Iris Marion Young, Outlaw was the most thoroughly self-possessed and confident Black man I had seen in years. I approached him like he was a rock star with a copy of his book *On Race and Philosophy* for an autograph. He signed the book.

Jaggar arranged for me to have lunch with him. During that lunch, I told Outlaw that, like him, I had attended Fisk University. I told him I had been on Fisk's baseball team as a pitcher. It had been the first year Fisk had fielded a team in years and that we had lost every game that first season. Outlaw told me that he had also been on Fisk's baseball team the year after I had left and pitched the first game Fisk won in its second season.

With this in common, I told him about my vision for Black philosophy was to have a PhD philosophy program at an Historically Black College and Universities (HBCU). Neither Howard, Fisk, or Hampton Universities had a doctoral program in philosophy. Outlaw appeared sympathetic. He was so easy to talk to, a cool customer, a southern gentleman, in my world of chaotic struggle with words, committees, and fifth semester papers. I entreated his help with my attempts to complete my work at the University of Colorado. I showed him photos of my children and we went back to the SPEP conference.

Having completed the coursework, all that remained was the language exam, recommendation for candidacy, completing the diss, and the oral defense. I registered for the hours of dissertation work, paying for them with student loans. I spent days in the library at the University of Denver (DU) secluded in study rooms, with closed doors. It took a year for Jaggar to give me the approval to begin the actual writing. She had talked me through writing a thirty-five-page outline. As I returned to Boulder to meet with her to discuss the dissertation, she recommended that I rearrange the order of the chapters.

To communicate my state of mind, I am forced to stream of consciousness. Repeated failures had impressed a deep humility. This humility had in turn opened a door to healing. Living in the stacks at DU, reading and re-reading African American writing . . . Eldridge Cleaver's *Soul on Ice*; *The Autobiography of Frederick Douglass*; Claude Brown's *Manchild in the Promised Land*; and Martin Luther King Jr.'s *Where Do We Go from Here: Chaos or Community?*[15] Presenting a paper at the American Philosophical Association (APA) conference in Berkeley—"Theorizing Black Community"—where I had argued that "if Black people didn't conceptualize their own visions for future forms of collective life (community), then it would be done for them." The prospectus for my dissertation being a discussion of the ideas of Black thinkers Martin Luther King Jr.'s ("Beloved Community"), Lucius Outlaw's ("Africana Philosophy," as the shared cultural forms of life of Black people in the diaspora), and Cornel West's ("Retranscendentalization" of Black life), with contrast in a white Canadian philosopher Will Kymlicka's *Rights of Minority Cultures*.[16] While writing draft after draft, I was often amused by the presence of King, West, and Outlaw—as the history of the "west"—with the rebellion against England's "king," being the essential posit of the "west," followed by the "outlaws" who continue to define the west by challenging the frontier. What I thought was *original thought* in the thesis was my argument for "anti-anti-essentialism."

Essentialism, as I interpreted it was the Aristotelian idea that a thing is what it is because of its properties. In logical parlance, I construed this is an ontological object is the sum of its predicates. Essentialisms in analyzing "race," were centered by many thinkers on biological phenotypic traits—skin color, hair texture, lip thickness—and even "intelligence." Racial essentialism was the basis for racism on so-called scientific, or biological differences. The racial science of cranial capacity, facial angles, and other anatomical differences was being called into question by DNA analyses. The arguments were that genetic difference between the races were almost non-existent, and "the genetic differences between races were smaller than the genetic differences within an individual race." Further, DNA analyses were revealing that human-like hominids walked up out of Africa into southern Europe, and around the Levant, to south Asia, into Australia, with side migrations into northern Europe, northern Asia, and across into to the Americas. Thus, "beneath the skin," we are all Africans.

If biological racial essentialism was a myth, the racial anti-essentialists, like Anthony Appiah and Naomi Zack could argue that "race" as a human linguistic construct, did more harm than good and should be abandoned as a property or predicate. At the end of the twentieth century, this was the essence of the essentialist/anti-essentialist dichotomy. The "sublime" I offered as a contribution to reconceptualizing the category "race" was adapted from a book—*The Black Atlantic* by Paul Gilroy.[17] Gilroy showed how the Atlantic Ocean—center of Africans scattered in the diaspora, was a unifying element in the expressions of cultural forms. White symphonic music (essentialism), African drum rhythms (anti-essentialism), and syncretisms of Jazz and Negro spirituals (the anti-anti-essentialism) of new cultural forms that foregrounded an Atlantic community (in an anti-diasporic) seeking to reassemble itself. The coming home of the scattered tribes, the "little Gidding movement" reinstantiating community rather than chaos.

Fin-de-siècle thinking—the end of the century—in resolving dichotomies, my anti-anti-racial essentialist category—elaborated from Outlaw's and Gilroy's umbrella notions of Black collectivity, defined racial anti-anti-essentialism, as "the necessity of retaining the category of "race," so long as Black people are negatively affected by "racisms." If "race" was not biological (essentialism), it could be abandoned as a category (anti-essentialism). Abandoning "race" suggested that affirmative action programs were no longer necessary. And since America was a meritocracy, individual arduous work was all that was needed to overcome "race." Anti-essentialism erased the prior (diachronic) abuses of racism and left the (synchronic) results in a "blaming the victim," place of degradation and poverty.

Writing and rewriting my dissertation was an extreme exercise in self-examination. I needed Carol to help me improve the grammar—remove the passive voice (something I had argued pervaded Black writing, as active voice—assertive speech—was a threat to white authority)—and polish the transitions. As a mathematician cum programmer, writing had consisted of discrete expressions, linked vertically in chains of reasoning. As a poet, my poems were vertical rather than horizontal. My writing tended to be stacks of ideas rather than flowing sentences in waves of paragraphs. I tried to obscure these infelicities writing prose with prolixity and sesquipedalian clouds.

Jaggar, preparing me for the job market, had me apply for pre-doctorial fellowships, Ford Foundation Minority Fellowships, and dissertation grants. She sent me out to interview for jobs in Tennessee and Wisconsin. I interviewed at the APA tables for jobs at Howard and the State University of New York (SUNY). I sent applications to dozens of schools. While my student loans approached $100,000, our credit cards maxed out with Carol using one card to pay off another, and our children needing resources, I worried that I would be left with a worthless degree and no job. I was beginning to realize that where I might look good on paper, when I showed up for an interview, what the interviewer saw when I appeared was an old man.

I attended conferences, gave papers, and tried to serve the greater good in working for my friends in the Radical Philosophy Association. Like the Hassidic Jews, I was "reading until I went blind."

To prepare for the language test, I audited an introductory German language course. Listening to the tapes in the language lab, attending lectures, and using a CD-ROM course, I mastered just enough of the language to take the departmental test. I was permitted to use a Langenscheidt's German English dictionary. I was given two hours to translate three pages of Wittgenstein's book *On Certainty* from German to English. For months, I had opened this book, with German on one side and English on the other, at random, writing out translations, and comparing them to the printed English. I had done this exercise daily, until I started to get the translations mostly correct. Then I would begin again, opening the book at random, until I was so familiar with the text that I recognized large swaths. On test day, I was pleased that I recognized the section that included "This is my foot."—*Das ist mein Fuß*.[18] When I walked out of the test room, I was floating—off my *Füße*—as I knew (with certainty), that I had passed.

I was entered into candidacy with letters of support from Christopher Shields (my former advisor and Aristotle teacher) and Gabriella Carone (my Plato teacher). I had formed a committee of Alison, James Nichols (who taught me Social and Political Philosophy), Graham Oddie (my Philosophy of Science professor, and current department chair), and Claudia Mills (a sympathetic feminist philosopher who had commiserated with me over a beer when I was considering quitting the program). But there was a bonus. Lucius T. Outlaw Jr. had agreed to be my "outside reader." The requirement was to have one member of the orals committee from outside the department. Outlaw was a nationally known Black philosopher, and it was unusual for someone of his stature to serve on the committee of any candidate at a UC philosophy department's oral defense.

I was quaking in my boots, adrenaline urging flight—but Alison had taught me to fight—by perseverance and assertion. I had a community with me, Outlaw, Birt, Gordon, Schmitt. As I arrived in the conference room, prepared with handouts, and Alison's advice to answer questions directly and then shut up (as she knew that when threatened, I threw up a cloud of words to try to hide behind), trying to set up the remote speaker for Outlaw's conference call, I happened to see a tag beneath the edge of the table: Monroe Table Company, Inc., Colfax Iowa.

There was immediate closure. Colfax Iowa was the place where the "sensitivity trainers" hired by the Teacher Corps, back in 1970 (thirty years prior), had broken me down so completely that it ended my marriage with Jacqueline, began a downward spiral of alcohol and drug use, and ultimately led to manic-depression, and the struggle to free myself from lithium. Colfax, Iowa was the ground zero of my metamorphoses. Now, at the time of my greatest test, the oral defense of my thesis, a sign from the universe. The table I was to sit at to defend myself was made at the point in space and time—Colfax, Iowa—where my adult struggles with life began. I exhaled. I was ready for this. The Jungian and Jamesian synchronicity—the deep warp and woof—the interrelatedness of things—was at the table with me. Witnessed by all—my wife, my friend Donna Reeves, other graduate students—I defended my dissertation, and waited in the hall outside the conference room.

"Dr. Jones, I presume," was Graham Oddie's greeting as he reached to shake my hand.

In May 2000, at the age of fifty-five years old, after two years reading philosophy at the University of Denver and six years at the University of Colorado, I became the first Black PhD in Philosophy to graduate from UC Boulder (and the oldest at that time).

So, there I was a *philosopher*, deeply in debt, with no prospect for a job, exhausted by the trek up the upward path. I celebrated with a small party at Alison's. But inwardly, I felt like a failure. I did not have a teaching position. I did not attend the "hooding" ceremony at the department. I felt hollow.

Then, to my surprise, in the early days of August, Alison telephoned me to tell me that Kansas State University (KSU) was prepared to offer me a Visiting Professor position. I hurriedly had my dossier prepared and mailed to KSU. I spoke by phone with the department chair, describing the courses I would teach, and telling me that a contract would be mailed for my signature. Kansas State University in Manhattan, Kansas was five hundred miles from where we lived in Littleton, Colorado. So, I bought a new pickup truck to transport my belongings, and we drove off to Manhattan to look for an apartment. I was both elated and saddened that I would be separated from Carol, but it was a Hobson's choice, "that or nothing."

Kansas State University was a large land grant state university with thousands of students. KSU also had a national reputation as a football powerhouse and fought to fend off perceptions of being a "Cowtown" college. In rapid order, I choose books, wrote my syllabi, and adjusted to the life of bachelorhood, cooking my own meals and washing my own clothes. I started a checking account. For the first time, I was paying my own bills. And, for the first time in many years, I was desperately lonely. I marked the calendar for the three-day holidays when I would drive the five hundred miles across Kansas and Colorado to be home, and then drive back to the isolation of my "philosophy."

In one year, I taught the same course, "Introduction to Social and Political Philosophy," using *Social and Political Philosophy: Classical Western Texts in Feminist and Multicultural Perspectives* edited by James P. Sterba, five times.[19] I supplemented this text with Michel Foucault's *Discipline & Punish*.[20] The Sterba text was a compilation of brief excepts from the ancient Greeks, through the medieval and renaissance period, to the present. The *present* included papers by Frantz Fanon, Karl Marx, John Rawls, and Cornel West. It was a survey course that moved rapidly, and I had read all the works from which the excerpted material was taken. Because the course was a requirement, most of the students were from other disciplines, and thought philosophy courses were "mere opinions." The terms of my contract were teaching these courses, being a member of the dean's "Committee on Diversity," teach a "Business Ethics" course, and give two public lectures.

In almost total seclusion in my efficiency apartment, I prepped for lectures, graded essays, and fulfilled my other obligations. John Exdell, the tenured Political philosopher, and the department chair, James Hamilton, were my closest allies on the faculty because they were closer to my age. I tried to be a "hip" professor—the only Black in the department—making it understood that students call me "Richard." But I was disciplined (like *Discipline & Punish*) in keeping exact records (spreadsheets that calculated grades) and tried to show how philosophy was pertinent to modern life.

I shared the office of a professor on sabbatical. His office was littered with homework assignments from an introductory logic course, truth-tables, and proofs from deductive logic. As I walked the department halls, I could see the even longer proofs from the course in symbolic logic, left on the whiteboards as if to mock me.

One first semester course was an extension course at US Army Fort Riley Kansas base. I was teaching in an old, wooden, administration building, that looked like it was from World War II. There was no air-conditioning. There were standing fans, but when running, were so noisy that students could not hear my lectures. So, it was either a stifling heat that induced comas, or churning fans that produced inaudibility.

I drove back across Kansas and Colorado for Christmas break. I was overjoyed being reunited with Carol. The APA Eastern Conference was held in DC that year. I had applied for ten jobs by email and received three requests for interviews. One interview was for a position at Howard. I was interviewed by a young white professor and Segun Gbadegesin, Department Chair. The young white woman, Cara Spencer, I later found out, was a graduate of MIT.

Dr. Gbadegesin was an African philosopher, with tribal scarification marks. Gbadegesin listened quietly as I described my dissertation topic. Dr. Spencer had commented, "Poetry."

Back in Manhattan, Kansas where the conservative Republicans in the statehouse were trying to prevent evolution being taught as "science," I was starting my course on "Business Ethics." The class of thirty-five business administration majors and minors, practical-minded, dubious about "ethics" but certain about business, were not amused by my crack that "Business Ethics" was an oxymoron. In the first class I had said "There's no ethics in business, red in tooth-and-claw, in pursuit of profit." But, I was determined to give them a whiff of virtue, deontological, utilitarian, and situational ethics. I used case studies—Bhopal (chemical disaster), Walmart (main street vs box store), and the Corvair (Ralph Nadar's dangerous car)—to show how stockholder's interests had shifted to stakeholder's interests. Many students thought I was anti-"invisible hand"—a socialist.

Teaching this course made me feel dirty—preparing students for the grim work of neocapitalism—transnational capitalism—vulture capitalism. The thing that saved me was a letter I received from Radical Philosophy Association (RPA) philosopher Richard Schmitt, asking me to be RPA's outreach coordinator. During the spring of 2000, I had hundreds of RPA brochures printed. These bi-folded brochures had the RPA's credo:

> We also oppose substituting new forms of authoritarianism for the ones we are now fighting. Our efforts are guided by the vision of a society founded on cooperation instead of competition, in which all areas of society are, as far as possible, governed by democratic decision-making.

I addressed hundreds of envelopes with a letter written by Richard Schmitt, stuffed them with the brochure, and mailed them to philosophy departments all over the world, inviting them to join the Radical Philosophy Association. So, once again, the conspiracy of munificence, reached into my dreary life to show me that I was not alone. The RPA was my family. If my family was socialist, then I was socialist.

I plodded through the spring semester, with the expected drama of plagiarism, phantom students showing up for the final exam expecting to pass the course, and surprising to me overtures for me to remain in Kansas to take a permanent job at KSU.

However, things had changed at home. Carol had applied for a position at Social Security's office of adjudicating Supplemental Security Income claims. A highly competitive national position, with a substantial salary increase, she was selected. But, Lindsey was still in high school and did not want to move with Carol to Washington, DC. We gave her options of living with Carol's sister, but she convinced us she could stay in Colorado, alone, to complete high school. Against our better judgment, we allowed her to live alone—which she came to see as our "abandonment"—in the house in Littleton. It had tragic consequences, as she had problems with this situation. I have always regretted this decision.

Carol moved to Washington, to live in an old-brick "row house," in northwest DC, owned by my childhood next-door-neighbor, Aurelia Clifford. Mrs. Clifford had rented the house to our son, Graham, who had lived there while he took an exchange-student year while he was at Reed College. Once I finished at KSU, I drove out to DC. with Lindsey's dog Allie. Living in this "row house" on Euclid Street, reminded me of my mother's house on Blaine Street. The house was close to the "Gold Coast," near the famous Dunbar High School, Howard, and the Shaw and LeDroit Park neighborhoods. I sensed I was reliving my childhood, living in a predominantly Black neighborhood. In my newfound unemployment, I walked Allie every day.

Graham had graduated with honors from Reed College, Phi Beta Kappa, and president of the student body. I had read his senior thesis and thought "he wrote like an angel." His prose was fluid and exciting. He was a gifted scholar, *leading* in my footsteps, taking time to decide between graduate schools, teaching at the Field School in DC. Field School was an exclusive private school. Graham wanted to see if he wanted to teach.

When my son became a man, I tried to keep him close enough to be relatable. I wanted to tell him about my "mental illness," but could only obliquely tell him he needed to read Robert M. Pirsig's novel *Zen and the Art of Motorcycle Maintenance*.[21] Graham decided to attend New York University (NYU) to pursue a PhD in Anthropology. Graham is now a tenured professor at MIT.

Shauna, who had come out one night while the family was watching *Saturday Night Live*, was a junior at Oberlin College. Ironically, she now had a boyfriend. She was a beautiful young woman struggling with identity issues. Shauna was a talented singer with interests in art. She would go on to graduate from Oberlin and begin a PhD program in Art History at the University of San Diego. Shauna completed a master's degree in Environmental Studies at the University of Iceland, currently lives in London, and writes for Orion magazine.

Lindsey, who was so much like me in many ways, rebellious and sensitive to the attitudes of others, graduated from Colorado Academy intending to matriculate at Pepperdine in Los Angeles. She had enrolled but within weeks had decided that it was not for her. Lindsey rebounded from this and became an outstanding student at Colorado State University in Fort Collins. I was surprised when she majored in chemistry. She is now a research lab manager at Massachusetts General Hospital (MGH) in Boston.

Walking around northwest Washington with Allie was exhilarating. But DC had changed. It was not T. S. Eliot's "Little Gidding," where,

> Will be to arrive where we started
> And know the place for the first time.[22]

The street names "Kalorama Road," were the same, but the people were different. Walking Allie around Meridian Park (a.k.a. Malcom X Park), I did not see kids playing baseball. The game was now soccer. Men and young boys of Hispanic descent kicked the white ball back and forth on the turf. Washington, DC was also undergoing gentrification. Houses that once belonged to poor Blacks in areas of the city that had been blighted by poverty and crack were being bought by wealthy whites. The city had a Black mayor, garbage was being picked up on time, and there was the feeling of racial progress—if not harmony, at least the tolerance allowing "community."

Carol was settling into her new position at SSA. She worked in the Appeals Council, preparing cases for administrative judges to rule on appeals from lower courts on rejected claims for supplemental security income (SSI).

So here we were. I was back home in DC, unemployed. I spent my days working on a paper, "Theorizing Black Communities," Robert E. Birt had accepted for a book he was editing, *The Quest for Identity: Critical Essays in Africana Social Philosophy*.[23] Ironic, as this was exactly where I was in my life. When not working on this paper, I walked Allie.

NOTES

1. Hermann Hesse, *Beneath the Wheel*, trans. Michael Roloff (New York: Noonday Press, 1969).

2. Joe Glauberg, Gary Marshall, and Dale McRaven, *Mork & Mindy* (TV series) (Los Angeles: ABC, 1978–1982).

3. See Patrica S. Churchland, *Neurophilosophy: Toward a Unified Science of the Mind/Brain* (Cambridge, MA: Bradford Books, 1989).

4. Søren Kierkegaard, *Fear and Trembling*, ed. C. Stephen Evans and Sylvia Walsh. Translated by Sylvia Walsh (Cambridge: Cambridge University Press, 2006).

5. Herman Melville, *The Confidence-Man: His Masquerade*, ed. Hershel Parker and Mark Niemeyer, 2nd ed. (New York: W. W. Norton, 2005).

6. Alfred North Whitehead and Bertrand Russell's *Principia Mathematica Volume One*. (Seaside, OR: Rough Draft Printing, 2011; 3 vols. (Cambridge: Cambridge University Press, 1910–1913); and Alfred Jules Ayer, *Language, Truth and Logic* (Mineola, NY: Dover, 1952).

7. Immanuel Kant, *The Critique of Pure Reason* (1781), trans. Norman Kemp Smith, unabridged ed. (New York: Bedford/Saint Martin's, 1969).

8. Kant, *The Critique*, A 522.

9. John L. Mackie, *The Cement of the Universe* (Oxford: Clarendon Press, 1980).

10. [Mikhail] M. M. Bakhtin, *The Dialogical Imagination* (Austin: University of Texas Press, 1982); and Joe R. Feagin, Hernan Vera, and Nikitah Imani, *The Agony of Education: Black Students at a White University* (New York: Routledge, 1996).

11. Richard A. Jones, *Blackland* (Austin, TX: Atmosphere Press, 2021).

12. Crispin Wright, *Rails to Infinity: Essays on Themes from Wittgenstein's* Philosophical Investigations (Cambridge, MA: Harvard University Press, 2001).

13. Leonard Harris, *Philosophy Born of Struggle: Anthology of Afro-American Philosophy from 1917* (Dubuque, IA: Kendall/Hunt Publishing, 2000); William R. Jones, *Is God a White Racist? A Preamble to Black Theology* (New York: Penguin Random House, 1997); Lucius T. Outlaw, *On Race and Philosophy* (New York: Routledge, 1996); and Kwame Anthony Appiah, *In My Father's House: Africa in the Philosophy of Culture* (Oxford: Oxford University Press, 1993).

14. Alison M. Jaggar, *Feminist Politics and Human Nature* (Lanham, MD: Rowman & Littlefield, 1988).

15. Eldridge Cleaver, *Soul on Ice* (New York: McGraw-Hill, 1968); Frederick Douglass, *The Autobiography of Frederick Douglass: Narrative of the Life of Frederick Douglass, an American Slave*, ed. George Stade (New York: Barnes & Noble, 2005); Claude Brown, *Manchild in the Promised Land* (New York: Signet, 1965); and Martin Luther King Jr., *Where Do We Go from Here: Chaos or Community?* (Boston: Beacon Press, 1989).

16. Will Kymlicka, *The Rights of Minority Cultures* (Oxford: Oxford University Press, 1995);

17. Paul Gilroy, *The Black Atlantic: Modernity and Double-Consciousness* (New York: Verso Books, 2012).

18. Ludwig Wittgenstein, *On Certainty*, ed. G. E. M. Anscombe and G. H. von Wright, trans. Denis Paul and G. E. M. Anscombe (New York: Harper Torchbooks, 1972).

19. James P. Sterba, ed., *Social and Political Philosophy: Classical Western Texts in Feminist and Multicultural Perspectives* (Belmont, CA: Wadsworth/Thomson Learning, 2003).

20. Michel Foucault, *Discipline & Punish: The Birth of the Prison*, trans. Alan Sheridan (New York: Vintage Books, 1995).

21. Robert M. Pirsig, *Zen and the Art of Motorcycle Maintenance: An Inquiry into Values* (New York: Harper Perennial, 2000).

22. T. S. Eliot, "Little Gidding," in *Four Quartets* (New York: Harcourt Brace, 1943; 1971), 59.

23. Robert E. Brit, ed., *The Quest for Identity: Critical Essays in Africana Social Philosophy* (Lanham, MD: Rowman & Littlefield, 2001).

Chapter 17

Howard University, 2001–2013

Walking Allie—who, the veterinarian I took her to, thought was a wolf-dog mix—I was seeing northwest Washington, DC, as if for the first time. Allie had to see the vet because she would not urinate in Mrs. Clifford's backyard. Carol and I tried to reason it out—the odor of generations of cats?

As such, I had to walk her three or four times a day. Around Kalorama Road, through Meridian Park. Northwest DC was not my childhood haunt, as I had lived "east of the river," as northeast DC was called. As I walked, aware of the gentrification of the city, I willed myself to think about some of the philosophy I had brought to Meridian Park (the exact longitude of the original layout for Washington).

I pondered James Sterba's arguments concerning "scope." What is the scope of our "caring?" Everyone cares for him/herself. Everyone cares for family, followed by community, then country. Some few, care for those in other countries, followed by the earth. A few care for all life in the universe—in the multiverse? Likewise, the upward path of "knowing. *Erkenntnisse*, German for cognition, and the many ways of knowing *that*, knowing *how*, and knowing *why*. Forms of *Wissen*. Suffused by the wonder of being back—an Odysseus—with his dog (Argus)—after wandering the meridians—in disguise. Dressed in my Lee carpenter jeans, work boots, and tee shirt, I wandered the beach I had washed up on, thinking about epistemology and "caring." As Carol trundled off to the SSA office every morning, I walked Allie, worked on the paper, that Robert Birt had asked me for. Scope. As Bertrand Russell concludes in *The Problems of Philosophy*:

> All acquisition of knowledge is an enlargement of the Self . . . we start from the not-Self, and through its greatness the boundaries of Self are enlarged; through the infinity of the universe the mind which contemplates it achieves some share in infinity.[1]

One morning, I walked down Euclid Street with Allie toward Dunbar High School. Across Georgia Avenue, I could see the new Howard University Business School. Walking onto the Quad, I could see the same Douglass Hall I had taken classes in almost forty years before. Founder's Library stood as it had decades before, the clock's bell chiming the hour. I was a bearded Zarathustra come down from the mountain, a philosopher with a hammer. Locke Hall, which was being built when I left in 1965, was where the philosophy department was located. I mounted the steps with the purpose of seeing if the department needed a part-time instructor for the fall semester. I met the kindly department secretary, Denise Spriggs, who was curious about Allie, especially since dogs were not allowed on Howard's campus. Ms. Spriggs introduced me to Dr. Verharen. Verharen told me they *were* looking for help, as he was about to undergo prostate surgery.

I quickly had letters of recommendation and my dossier sent to Howard. Within a matter of days, I was interviewed and hired as a Visiting Assistant Professor. For me this was like prophesy—the essay I had written in my application to the PhD program at Colorado—the return of the prodigal son.

Still living in Mrs. Clifford's house on Euclid Avenue, we needed to find a new house. But, why not continue living there? It was so close to Howard, walking distance. Well for one thing, it was so noisy. There was a constant wail of sirens—ambulance and police—and the ever-present hum of automobiles. It was also hot in the old row-house. The house was filled with antique furniture, dusty old books from the 1940s, a faded opulence. We also needed someplace closer to Carol's job in Virginia. The ideal location would also be close to a Metro station, so I could commute to Howard.

Within days, we found the ideal place. Stoneybrooke was a bedroom neighborhood in Alexandria, Virginia, close to the Huntington Metro Station. The house itself was built during the white-flight decades, where whites from Washington sold their brick row houses, and bought these hastily thrown up mock colonials with aluminum siding, where at least they did not have Black neighbors. The house was within our budget.

I quickly settled in as a professor. Where I thought I was Sam Greenlee's *The Spook Who Sat by the Door*, the novel whose character was the first Black CIA officer, who used his training in gathering intelligence, political subversion, and guerrilla warfare *against* the CIA.[2] I thought that I had been an "undercover brotha," all those years living in the midwest—Iowa, Kansas, Colorado—spying on white people. I had been trying to decipher their cultural tropes. With my pale brown skin, the camouflage of my white wife Carol, and a dissembling nature, I had hidden in the interstices trying to understand their prejudices and hatreds for Black people. Now, suffused with knowledge from behind the lines, I had come home to Howard to teach them how to understand their enemies, so they could transcend them.

All those alienated days and nights longing for the familiarity of Black people. Isolated in the great desert of Iowa, watching Donnie Simpson's TV show late Friday nights—"Video Soul." Fascinated by Steve Harvey in "Hanging with Mr. Cooper," and Cedric the Entertainer's, lessons in my lost Blackness.

"Dawg."

These television programs were like "Radio Free Europe," in the "great deserts" of Iowa and Kansas. It was what my Black Air Force buddies often said when they spoke of their hometowns back East, "Back in the world." Deserts without Black people. But now, back at Howard, I was surrounded by "my familiar." Or so I thought, as I was getting insights into a "New Negro."

On the first day of teaching Principles of Reasoning, I was stunned to see the classroom on the first floor of Douglass Hall, was the same room I had taken Introduction to Logic in 1964. The exact same room. Serendipity? Synchronicity? Fate? A cruel and ironic joke played on me by the Philosophy Department? Still, in the spiderwebbed neurons of my memory, the trapped spider of me sitting near the back next to the blackboard, insouciant to the white professor from the US National Bureau of Standards teaching the evening course. I looked at the student sitting in the seat I had occupied then, and wondered if this young Black man would earn the "D" grade I had received.

"Principles" involved truth-tables (which Ludwig Wittgenstein had brought to a high art at Cambridge), Aristotelian Syllogisms, and formal deductive proofs. I remember having taken the streetcar and bus back to Blaine Street and telling my mother about the attempts to "mathematicise language." At that time, almost forty years before, I had found Gottfried Wilhelm Leibniz's dream of a *characteristica universalis*, a universal conceptual language, an exciting idea. A rational calculus I immediately saw then in ones and zeroes. And, now, with all the computer programming, mathematics, I saw at once how these elements of logic could underpin computer architecture—AND gates, OR gates (Bill Gates), XOR gates, Sheffer's Stroke.

The Introduction to Philosophy course was also interesting in that I was faced by students who were beneficiaries of two generations of educational and social progress since I had left. These Black students were relaxed and assured that they would be accepted in professional schools, enter the financial sector, or become entrepreneurs. They were confident and practical, philosophy being only a required "core curriculum" course many put off until they needed the credit to graduate. They endured my enthusiasm with mild amusement, believing that philosophy was merely ones' considered opinion . . . and was "too white."

Then on September 11, 2001, on a bright sunny day, a student came in late to my Intro course.

"They're flying planes into buildings in New York," she announced.

Trying to get home on the Metro, I saw smoke rising from the Pentagon.

I was worried about Carol. When she finally arrived home, we, along with the rest of the world, watched images of airplanes slamming into the World Trade Center (WTC) towers. Graham, who lived in Brooklyn, called, and said he could smell the smoke. Shauna, who was visiting us from Iceland, needed to get to the Greyhound Bus station to travel to New York. As I drove her to the bus station, we saw the Jeeps mounted with .50 caliber machine guns at every intersection. It was like a scene from the 1950s sci-fi film *The Day the Earth Stood Still*.[3]

When classes resumed at Howard, a young Black student, dressed in a St. Louis Cardinals baseball jersey and a gold chain, stood up and said, "It wasn't terrorism . . . we deserved it . . . we been killing them for years." Many of his Intro to Philosophy classmates appeared to agree. A side effect of 9/11 for me was an increasing awareness of the deep divisions in Black people's judgements concerning US hegemony. I was also aware that Shanksville, Pennsylvania—where the third airliner crashed—was only a few miles from the Allegheny Tunnel, near Berlin, Pennsylvania, where I had lived in a tent for three weeks when I was a nineteen-year-old student at Howard. Humm?

After the endless news reports of the planes crashing into the WTC, I went back to teaching. Every semester for the first few years, I repeatedly taught Principles of Reasoning and Intro. By now, an Instructor, I was offered yearly contracts that were destabilizing because many years they were not tendered until late August, and some years after the first semester had already been in session for two weeks. One year, I did not teach at all. I spent my days walking Allie, reading philosophy, and removing wainscotting from the faux-colonial house in Stoneybrooke.

The next year, in addition to Principles and Intro, I was "permitted" to teach "philosophy of Natural Science," where getting students to appreciate "Popperian falsification," Feyerabend's scientism, and Hemple-Oppenheim's Hypothetico-Deductico schema, was a stretch for students preparing for medical school. The period between 2003 and 2006 was dynamic, as I stepped out from being a professor, to becoming an activist. Just as I knew there was a difference between a teacher of mathematics and a mathematician, I knew there was an even more profound difference between a professor of philosophy and a philosopher.

At a Radical Philosophy Association (RPA) national conference at Brown University in 2002, I suggested that the next RPA conference be held at Howard. Richard Schmitt, then RPA coordinator, wrote a letter to the chair of Howard's Philosophy Department, Segun Badegesin, seeking the department's willingness to host the conference. Returning to Howard, I presented the letter to Dr. Badegesin, who agreed. That spring, I began making plans for the conference titled "Philosophy Against Empire," for the fall of 2004. In pursuit of organizing, I approached Howard's Student Services, to see if I could get a work-study student to help me with the endless emails, phone calls, and planning. Student Services responded by providing a young woman to help me.

I was also drafting the paper I intended to present, "Black Authenticity/ Inauthenticity and American Empire." Where, by legend, Howard was, the center of Black radicalism—Stokely Carmichael (Kwame Ture) was a graduate of Howard's philosophy department—it was the bastion of the *Black Bourgeoisie*. At the end of the Civil Rights Era, where concessions had been made enabling economic opportunity, now, it was "all about the money." There was little truck with Black socialists, especially with George W. Bush's, "The enemy of my enemy is my friend."

One afternoon, my work-study student handed me the following letter, which read in part:

February 7, 2004

Dr. Jones,

On last Friday, I sought the purpose of the RPA for the first time. I failed to do so in the beginning because I assumed the conference would be a venture for members to exchange dialogue about ideologies of past philosophers. I do lack the educational history of philosophy and I was ultimately concerned with learning *how* to implement a conference as opposed to knowing the purpose of the conference. I agree that the nature of such corporations as Enron is wrong, and that racism and sexism exists, but socialism, Marxism or communism is not the answer. That cannot stop racism, sexism or any other -isms. People's character must change, not our system of employment. I was reckless in assuming the former impairments were the sole essence of this contemporary conference.

Some men in power may have impaired the initial will for men in countries, but Dr. Jones, I am not subject to that. Because of Christ, I AM FREE.

Sincerely,

This letter of resignation by my work study marked a change for me at Howard. First, I had applied again for a permanent Assistant professor, tenure-track job, again not chosen and forced to share an office with the selected candidate. In two years, I watched the favored professor display contempt for the students' scholarship. I began hearing rumors that parents were complaining to Howard's president that they did not want their sons and daughters taught by a "godless atheist, communist."
"Yet I rise."

I continued preparation for the fall conference, constructing a program, letting contracts with food services and the bursar's office for funds received for conference registration payments. I had replaced my work study with a young Jamaican woman who had been a stellar student in my Principles course. I could not pay her, so she volunteered.

With registration payments being paid, I eagerly awaited this RPA conference at Howard, the first at an HBCU. I should also comment that my work-study's resignation had shown me that we Black people had truly little, and Howard therefore precious, and she did not want to risk Howard with "communist" ideology. In the early 2000s, congress funded Howard for about $250 million per annum. This largess filtered down from the administration, to the departments and special programs. Like "crabs in a barrel," this money underpinned fiefdoms and political power structures, holding administrators in thrall. The ratio of administrators (assistants to the assistants) created bureaucratic hierarchies, that were "reticulated into finer and finer capillaries of power."

That summer of 2004, attempting to enhance my CV so I could reapply when another tenure-track position opened at Howard, I published a rewrite of my dissertation with Edwin Mellen Press in Lewiston Maine. I asked a professor from Howard's art department to take a photo of the collapsing Howard Theater on Georgia Avenue for the cover of *African American Sociopolitical Philosophy: Imagining Black Communities*. I imagined the Howard Theater, where Stevie Wonder, Duke Ellington, Ella Fitzgerald, and almost every other famous Black performer had played, as the symbol of the Black community in the Shaw district's indifference to itself. I also published the collected poetry I had written in the 1970s and 1980s with the title *Bippie Poems*.[4] Unable to find a mainstream or small press to publish these poems, I signed a contract with PublishAmerica in Baltimore. Willem Meiners, the publisher, had taken on the corporate publishing industry by offering contracts without writers paying, thus it was not a "vanity press." In fact, PublishAmerica, paid writers one dollar. They edited the poems and printed the book with one of my early paintings, "Nude Flower Field," on the cover.

Fall 2004, I discovered I had no contract to teach at Howard that academic year. I could not cancel the conference, as participants had already made airline and hotel reservations. As the war in Iraq raged on, I was reading Noam Chomsky's *Hegemony or Survival*, warning like Martin Luther King Jr.'s *Where Do We Go From Here: Chaos or Community?*, that unless America ended its hegemonic quest for global dominance, the chaos of never-ending war would result.[5] Having no standing at Howard made it impossible for me to fulfill my role as site-coordinator for the RPA conference. I approached the new chair of the philosophy department, who had decided that the philosophy department would not host the conference. Showing him the letter that the previous chair had signed, I pleaded with him to allow the conference to go forward. I told him that cancelling the conference at this late date would destroy me as a "philosopher." Reluctantly, he relented.

My Jamaican student—Rosanna Neil (who later graduated Harvard Law school)—became my "inside" agent at Howard. I would meet her at McDonald's to discuss planning for the conference. Because she had "standing," as a student, she could approach people and sign documents I could not. Rosanna became a friend, having Carol's vegetable soup with us in Stoneybrooke.

The conference was a success. There were philosophers from all over the world—Russia, Brazil, Mexico, England—and at one point conferees began referring to the gathering as the RPA *International* Conference. Students attending some of the sessions, were privileged to hear remarks from the great feminist philosophers, Iris Marion Young and Alison Jaggar. But what I will always remember from the conference, was a remark from a white RPA professor, who said something to me about the racial homogeneity at Howard after having lunch in the student cafeteria, the "Punch-Out."

"When I walked into the Punch-Out—I felt something. I was in a space where I didn't belong."

I told him that that was the way I had felt at the University of Colorado Boulder, all the time. I told him that since leaving Howard University in 1965—where I had "punched out," slang at that time for flunking out of school—earning six degrees in predominantly white colleges—I had had not had one Black professor.

After the conference, Richard Schmitt found out that I had put on the conference without being on the faculty. He mounted a letter writing campaign from conference attendees attesting to my skillful coordination of this important international conference. Howard's then president, H. Patrick Swygert (who earned more than $1 million per year), received letters from philosophers, foreign and domestic, supporting me. The next year I was proffered another one-year temporary appointment as an instructor.

Between my lectures, I often wandered up to the top floor of Locke Hall, where Dr. Alan Maxwell—my old astronomy teacher—had had an observatory and planetarium built after I had left in 1965. The telescope and planetarium were no longer in use. But poking around in the unused classroom I found the slate celestial sphere where he had demonstrated the ecliptic and equator projected into space to define the equinoxes—the "first point of Aries."

"Stress is proportional to strain—Hook's Law—and in the spring the first point of Aires," I could hear him lecturing. I was under *stress*, but I would *spring* back.

I found a twenty-question-multiple-choice test for Introduction to Astronomy in an abandoned filing cabinet. It was not photocopied but held the unmistakable odor of a spirit-master, with its signature blue text. Smelling it made me think that perhaps it had been made by Dr. Maxwell.

Wandering about the campus, I had also reestablished contact with Dr. Charles Edward Mahone—my catcher from the Little League Fort DuPont team—now a Dean in Howard's School of Business. As he was a tenured professor, I had him write a letter of recommendation to the philosophy department. They say you cannot go home again, but walking from the Metro stop on Georgia Avenue, up the hill past Florida Avenue, past the Howard theater, past Howard University Hospital—built where the old Washington Senators played baseball at Griffith Stadium, I was beginning to merge (re-emerge) with the sounds and rhythms—the umwelt—of the Black community.

But the Black community was different. Beneath the Chuck Brown "Bustin' Loose," go-go clanga-banga-banga-boom, Georgia Avenue was different. Of course, after 9/11, there were Black men sitting on the street reading the Koran, and once in a while someone would scream out at me from a passing car.

"Hey, you Santa Clause looking motherfucker, you ain't no Muslim!"

This was at the end of the Civil Rights Era, and Black people were in search of a new political strategy. It had always been argued that there were only four ways forward—Integration, Assimilation, Accommodation, or Separatism. Integration (legal community) had failed. Assimilation (Beloved Community) was dubious. Accommodation (multiculturalism) was questionable. And Black separatism (back to Africa) was an anachronistic Garveyism. The Black community had changed.

Eugene Robinson's book *Disintegration: The Splintering of Black America* divided the Black community into four classes: (1) 2 to 5 percent Elites (upper-class Blacks), (2) 50 to 55 percent middle class (burgeoning bourgeoise), (3) 25 percent lumpen (ghettoized Blacks), and (4) 10 to 12 percent (immigrants and mixed race).[6] The extremely rich Black athletes and entertainment stars, still had ties with the "ghetto rats," as their cousins, aunts and uncles, were still there. Yet, the inner-city Blacks were still un- or under-employed due in the deindustrialization of America. Middle-class Black America were still "pre-woke," believing in the meritocratic work ethic, and had made significant economic progress after the great northern migration. The presence of immigrants and mixed-race people within the Black community, threatened any conceptualizations of "community."

At Howard, "The Mecca," as at some point all Black people passed through its gates on the hill, there were represented all of Robinson's *dis*integrational classes. There were African students from many nations. I even had one of the "Lost Boys" in one of my Intro classes. There were Africans working on advanced degrees in economics and premed students. Many of these African scholars were the intellectual *crème-de-la crème* of their countries and awarded national scholarships. Some of these foreign national scholars thought American Blacks were self-indulgent, lazy, and only at Howard to party. Of course, there were also Black students from all over the Caribbean. These students, having been educated under the British system, were also usually serious, and thus excelled. Risking a generalization, Black bourgeoisie students, from, say, Detroit, Baltimore, DC, or New York, tended to be less well prepared than their foreign counterparts. The "hood-rats," from the Black lumpen-proletariat, were often unprepared for college work. However, every time I encountered one of these so-called lower-class Black students, I identified with them and tried to give them extra attention and consideration. Similarly, the faculty was widely distributed across a spectrum of Black perspectives. I found many of them aloof in their superiorities and achievements in overcoming their Blackness.

I quickly became an outsider at Howard. There were a few ways of being an insider. The good old Baptist religion was one entre. Belonging to the network of HBCU alumnae was another way to achieve "propers." The long chains of Black fraternities and sororities was another route. Being a Black radical with a white wife was disqualifying. One year when I was on a sabbatical (unwanted but imposed by not being offered a one-year contract), a neighbor wondered why I was not getting up early, with my backpack and briefcase, to make my trek to teach at Howard.

The neighbor, Kim Thompson, was a big Black man with three sons. With his wife (who Carol and I called Lil' Kim), Mr. Thompson was generous and friendly—a true big brother, who had welcomed us to the Stoneybrooke neighborhood. I was raking leaves in my front yard when Kim walked across the street.

"Doc, why aren't you teaching this year?"

After explaining my situation, Kim told me he had a frat brother who was one of Howard's president Swygert's attorneys. Kim told me he would ask his frat brother what was up—why I did not have a permanent position. A few weeks later, Kim Thompson told me that his fraternity brother (a Kappa) had shared interesting perspectives.

"Jones," his Kappa brother had told him Swygert had responded, "Is one of our best professors, but he is far too radical for Howard. He belongs at somewhere like Cal Berkeley."

When I heard this, I understood my place. Howard gave lip-service to being the center of the world for the Black intelligentsia, but it was really an extension of the illusory American mythos of meritocracy. After Francis Fukuyama's "end of history," where there were no longer alternatives to post-industrial capitalism, and the entire world wanted to be like us (US),

Black communities could only look to replicate the "strip-mall," track housing, and transnational neo-colonialist stratagems of the power-elite. What I am suggesting is that Howard University reinforced the utopian visions of the hegemon. What I had suggested in my dissertation—"If Black people do not create their own utopian visions, someone will do it for us"—was being acted out at Howard. Was this a failure of imagination? Was this an indoctrination? Or was this the hidden—reticulated tentacles of power—oppressing "the people." The Black Panthers had often reminded the brothas that an educated Black man made a weaker warrior. In my dissertation, I had written:

> When African Americans ponder eternity, the existence of the soul, and a future technological reality, our views are strangely conservative. Only imagining Judeo-Christian eschatologies, we are *slouching toward Armageddon*. If we do not have our own dreams and imaginings of the future—moral, political, technological—then the future our Black descendants find when they (we) get there will not be our own.

But, integration, assimilation, accommodation, and separatism were failed strategies, so by my lights that only left Black socialism—too radical for Howard? As Margret Thatcher was fond of saying, "There is no alternative (TINA)," to neoliberalism, leftists in my circle were beginning to counter with "TISA," there is a socialist alternative.

Where I felt the political pushback, I made a conscious decision to "go underground." I felt I had covert comrades at Howard—including the new philosophy department chair Patrick Goodin—who ostensibly holding Howard's public party-line, enabled me to fight my guerrilla warfare against the bourgeoisie in Black skin and White masks. Goodin gave his approved of many of the courses I taught that rounded me out as a thinker and philosopher. He allowed me to teach Wittgenstein, symbolic logic, epistemology, and Black aesthetics. I learned valuable lessons, beyond what I taught. Goodin was a good man who knew I was caught in the political contradictions of the dialectics of race. As chair, he wanted to do important things at Howard. I shared his enthusiasm, and he used his power to surreptitiously help me "fight on the backplane."

In 2006, to my utter surprise, I was elected co-coordinator of the RPA. One of the first things I did was arrange to travel to Havana, Cuba with an RPA contingent, so I could see a socialist country. All the propaganda—Russian missile crisis, Fidel Castro, communism—was in place, as I got off the plane in Barbados to transfer to a Cuban airplane (direct flights to Cuba were prohibited by the US government). I was anxious as I stepped up to the US immigration officer. Peering at my passport and examining my backpack, he asked me a series of questions.

"Why are you travelling to Cuba?"
"For a philosophy conference."
"Radical Philosophy Association? What does that mean?"
"Radical, as in *radix*—Greek for root—radical meaning to get to the roots of things."
"Pass on through."

Once aboard the flight, the world changed. The pilot was a white Russian. The flight attendants were beautiful and kind mixed-race people, who did not appear to have the same self-consciousness as US Blacks. When the flight arrived at Habana Airport, going through Cuban customs, taking a bus to the Hotel Verdugo, and settling in with the other American philosophers, was the boldest political move I had ever made.

Once the conference began, the inestimable Cliff Durand, presiding, each American presented a brief paper to the mixed assembly of Cuban philosophers and sociologists. I had had the foresight to have my paper translated into Spanish by a professor at Howard. The paper I gave, "Comparative Educational Philosophies," suggested that capitalist educations were *instrumental* (Aristotelian means-end reasoning), as opposed to socialist education strategies that were more *intrinsic* (Aristotelian reasoning qua reasoning). Instrumental learning was therefore an instrument of capital accumulation, leading to extreme competition. Whereas intrinsic learning—learning because of the love of learning—led to more altruist, ergo communal, consocialism. My paper contained many references to Paulo Freire's *The Pedagogy of the Oppressed*.

> Education either functions as an instrument which is used to facilitate integration of the younger generation into the logic of the present system and bring about conformity or it becomes the practice of freedom, the means by which men and women deal critically and creatively with reality and discover how to participate in the transformation of their world.[7]

During the next few weeks, Cliff Durand, a white philosopher who taught at Morgan State University, an HCBU, led the US contingent of RPA members to many important locations in Cuba. We visited the farmhouse hide-out where Castro waited for the peasants to rise-up to overthrow the Batista regime. We were greeted by the director of the Latin American School of Medicine (ELAM), who explained the educational philosophy of "community medicine." He told us how admission was determined not by MCAT scores alone, but by careful examination of candidates' motives to serve others. In other words, students seeking status, monetary rewards, or other emoluments of credentialed "healers," were not admitted to ELAM. I met one young Black medical student from Howard and asked her what she wanted to do once she had graduated.

"Go back to Los Angeles to start a clinic in Watts."

Three other transformative interactions occurred for me. First, we were driven to a poor neighborhood just outside Habana, where poor women needed a day care center for their children. In austere economic times, the government was unable to help. So, the women in the community learned to make concrete, construction trades, and built the center themselves. "Women hold up half the sky." On one wall was a quote from Martin Luther King Jr. which read, and I paraphrase: One does not need a college degree to be helpful. All one needs is heart—compassion—and a willingness to lend a hand.

Next, at a remote location in Cuba, we toured an old coffee plantation. Around the main house—the master's house—ran a deep moat. But not a moat for water, but for dogs to prowl at night to protect the master. Nearby were the huts (hovels) of the un-named, un-known, Black slaves who had labored there. I sensed the cruelty and the bared fangs of the snarling dogs.

Then, we took a side trip to Santiago, where the culture was decidedly African. When Fidel Castro came to power, he promised a color-blind society. I sensed that had been partially accomplished, as there were dark-skinned Cubans in all echelons of society—government, medicine, and education—but there were also residuals, where extreme poverty seemed to fall on Blacks, particularly Black women. In Santiago, where on a clear day, one could see the island of Haiti, and from Haiti I supposed (on a clear day), all the way back to Africa. Here I felt my own Blackness in the "Black Atlantic," diasporic connections of Paul Gilroy.

The downside of Cuban socialism was the grinding poverty. Much of this misery was economic warfare from the giant hegemon to the north. By the time I had left Santiago, I had given all my clothes to poor young men who begged for them, needed them so they could work at their jobs. My clothes, bought from Kohl's, were cheap for me to replace, but valuable to Cubans with nothing. The ordinary Cubans I met, were highly literate, politically well-informed, and largely determined to continue the struggle. There was the same dispassion toward the American way of life that I had encountered years before in San Miguel de Allende.

Finally, at a meeting between US and Cuban philosophers, Philip Agee gave a talk about the CIA. In 1975, Agee had gone rogue and written *Inside the Company*, a 1975 exposé of a CIA agent. He was living in exile in Cuba and regaled us in stories about the techniques—bribery, electronic surveillance, and payoffs—the CIA employed in maintaining US hegemony. While working for "the company," Agee had lived in Alexandria Virginia, where I lived. His exposé was so compelling, when I returned to the United States, I bought his book and read it. According to Agee at one point the president of Mexico was on the CIA payroll.[8]

Cliff Durand, the facilitator for the Cuba trips for the RPA, told us that Americans who traveled to Cuba automatically generated a dossier at the US Department of Justice. So, okay, there was an article published in the communist Cuban newspaper *Gramma*, about Richard Jones from Howard University participating in a conference at the University of Habana. Yet, like Fidel Castro's hiding-out in the hills, awaiting the peasants to join him, and Mao Zedong living in the mountains and coming down every spring until the people joined him, I had retreated to the conceptual mountains awaiting the arrival of "the people," who I could join in the revolution for human dignity and freedom.

Back at Howard, the department decided that I would teach a course on the philosophy of religion. I blanched, trying to talk my way out of this set-up. With an enrollment of twenty, I taught them theories of religion from readings on Sigmund Freud, John Hicks, and Friedrich D. E. Schleiermacher. These were bright young Black people, but they were all believers. Whenever I made a slightly atheistic statement, they would whip out Bibles from their backpacks, to refute me chapter and verse. When I related the plot of D. H. Lawrence's novel *The Man Who Died*, where Jesus although severely injured, survived the crucifixion, and went on to have children, they were shocked.[9]

"What happens when a magician comes into town," I asked them.

To their silence, I intoned, "He looks for a set of twins." It was a trick, I explained. To resurrect the dead, you need a twin. Jesus was a twin. I lectured them on Nietzsche's idea that Christianity was a "slave religion," where guilt was the debt one could never repay. I suggested that the problem of the twentieth century was whether man could be moral without a father figure, God. "God is dead," and man killed him. I knew there would be fallout, but I no longer cared.

I loved Howard University. But my homecoming was inhospitable. In the Black community, Philosophy was viewed as an excrescence. Academic philosophy was too white. Philosophers were not valued. At Howard, African American studies, African history, Egyptian philosophy, and Black Studies were all thought by students to be more important.

Howard was the crossroad of Black thought. I saw Barack Obama launch his presidential run at Howard's Crampton Auditorium. As the faculty left the auditorium, there was a collective, "No chance." I saw the great actors Ruby Dee and Ossie Davis at Howard. Cornel West spoke at convocations every year. There was even a professor in the English department who had been at McKinley High School when I was there in 1960. Everywhere I looked on the Howard campus, I saw home, but I was systematically unwelcomed. "Man is not at home in his created universe of symbols." Howard was my final refuge for my conceptions of "Black community." In 2008, I stood on the freezing national mall—along with a million other people from all over the world—and watched Barack Obama take the oath of office. Afterward, walking back to the Metro station in the crowds, there was a collective expression of awe and togetherness, "Never thought I'd live to see this day."

I continued to fulfill my dream of teaching philosophy at Howard until 2010, when the university's President's Commission on Academic Renewal (PCAR) announced its intention to discontinue the philosophy MA degree program and to eliminate Howard's department of philosophy. There are over one hundred HBCUs in the United States, of which Howard University had prided itself as having "the only standalone department of Philosophy at an HBCU." I was devastated by this proposal. I immediately sent out an urgent email to all the Black philosophers I had met in RPA and Philosophy Born of Struggle (PBOS). Leonard Harris, Cornel West, and, of course, Charles W. Mills all wrote letters to Howard's president Sidney A. Ribeau testifying to the strategic importance of Howard's philosophy department. Again, being actional, I organized Howard's students to protest the elimination of the department. I sent long essays to the academic provost and other members of Howard's board arguing that not only should Howard retain its philosophy program, but that it also should enhance its offerings to include a PhD degree in philosophy—philosophy FUBU ("for us, by us")—as, heretofore, all Black philosophers educated in the United States were produced in TWIs (traditionally white institutions). I received emails requesting information and documentation from a reporter with the *Chronicle of Higher Education*. The struggle to save philosophy at Howard eventually reached Anthony Appiah, then Chair of the Board of the American Philosophical Association, who wrote a letter in support of retaining the philosophy department at Howard. This support from the APA proved important, as Howard's administration kept the philosophy department, even though it ended the MA program. I was pleased to have initiated student protests and reached out to Black philosophers all over the country to help save the philosophy program at Howard.

The diadem of my time at Howard had come in 2009, when I conceived a conference to be held in South Africa, "Transnational Capitalism." RPA provided the framework and noted Marxist philosopher Robert Wolff, who knew a dean at the University of the Western Cape, provided the contact to make the conference possible. There were forces that repeatedly undermined my efforts to bring off the conference—collapse of support from hosts, proposed rescheduling, and conflicts with liaisons—but I was determined to hold this conference on the African continent.

When I stepped off the plane in Cape Town, South Africa, I kissed the tarmac. Over the next few weeks, I delivered my paper, "African American

Neo-Nationalism and African Socialism," which delineated continuities between Black socialism and African socialism. Transnational capitalism, considered a solution to African poverty, had extracted African natural resources and undermined local community development. One delegate at the conference provided a telling example of the need for mosquito nets to control the spread of malaria, dengue, West Nile virus, and chikungunya. Cheap manufactured nets from China prevented them from being manufactured in Africa. So, the expertise and jobs required were denied Africans. This example could be generalized for clothing, shoes, and other manufactured goods. The transnational economic strategy was to extract raw materials, use them to manufacture goods in more developed countries, then sell them back to Africans—profiting from the sources and the destinations.

At a banquet for the Cuban Ambassador to South Africa, the small RPA contingent was invited up to the dais to meet him after he had made his speech. A photographer from the local newspaper snapped a photo of the ambassador with us.

"That photo will be on the desk of the CIA station chief, tomorrow," I told my comrades.

During the conference, which was sparsely attended, Leonard Harris, videotaped me talking about being a "Black Wittgensteinian." Leonard Harris was ostensibly in Cape Town trying to track down a mythical manuscript by the Ghanaian-German Black philosopher Anton Wilhelm Amo (c. 1703–c. 1759). Harris had been informed that there might be a copy at the library at the University of Johannesburg. But, Harris had also registered for the RPA conference, so his presence was reassuring.

After the conference, we were escorted to many places, met with organizations, and did volunteer work. I climbed Table Mountain with a student from Howard, visited an orphanage for children with fetal alcohol syndrome, and engaged with a group of writers from Chimurenga Magazine. RPA made small monetary contributions to many of these organizations. We took a trip to Robbin Island, the prison where Mandela had been held for twenty-seven years. Standing in the small cell he had occupied and peering between the bars, was unforgettable. Robbin Island had become a museum, and the docents and guides were former inmates who had been imprisoned with Nelson Mandela. They told first-hand stories of his courage and dignity.

My impressions of South Africa's "Rainbow People of God"—Desmond Tutu's—prophetic Christian ideal of community, were a mixed bag. After the end of apartheid, statal wealth (airlines, mines, telecommunications, manufacturing) was redistributed to upper-class Blacks in the form of stocks and bonds, resulting in an insulating layer between the white elite capitalist class and the Black precariat. This strategy was intentionally designed to prevent open class warfare. Cape Town was divided into districts of Asians (from

India), poor whites (Afrikaans), rich whites (behind electrified razor-wire fences), mixed-race people, denizens of Khayelitsha (an impoverished township of almost a half-million souls) and Africans from several tribes, Zulu, Bantu, and Swazi. I was transfixed as I walked the streets of Cape Town listening to the Xhosian "click-language."

Differences in wealth were evident everywhere. There were ultra-modern shopping malls where gold Kruggerands were sold to tourists from the United States, Germany, and Europe. There were posh restaurants, extravagant backdrops to Black people wandering the streets begging for handouts. Grotesque asymmetries in wealth obscured South Africa's natural beauty. As I stood on the balcony of a restaurant in Cape Hope, overlooking the bay of Cape Agulhas, where the Indian Ocean meets the Atlantic Ocean—the blue water and green water demarking the confluence—I felt the arc of human existence. The ancient African San people, who left cave drawings 70,000 years ago, well before attempts of symbolic representation anywhere else in the world, had stood here at the most southernmost point on the continent. "I am we."

As I stood amid a Cape Town Ubuntu festival, listening to the young Africans read poetry and making music, I was caught up in my genetic ancestry. While walking the streets, I encountered a Red Cross blood mobile. I thought I would donate my blood—return my DNA to the place where it had originated—a homecoming—blood brothers and blood sisters—but after filling out all the forms, was informed that I was too old to donate. After taking the money left from conference registrations, from a S. A. Bank, I divided it into proportionate amounts to be donated in the name of the RPA to many of the institutions and organizations that needed it most, the orphanage, the organization for foreign students (illegal immigrants) from all over Africa trying to improve their lives by gaining educations at South African universities, and a summer camp for children who lived in the Khayelitsha township. Along with the student from Howard, I bought soccer balls, children's books, and toys from the same opulent shopping mall that sold Kruggerands and gave them away in the streets of the township.

Like Cuba, I saw Black people victimized by the capital accumulation that allowed some to live large, while others had nothing. Same as in the United States. I came back to teaching at Howard with an altered worldview. During my final years, I taught courses in Critical Race Theory, Black Feminist Philosophy, and the History of Africana Philosophy. At one RPA conference at San Francisco State University, I had the privilege of introducing the keynote speaker, Angela Y. Davis. After her talk, as I walked her from the podium, I leaned over and kissed her on her cheek. I retired from Howard University in 2013.

What had I learned. What kind of philosopher had I become? Ubuntu. "I Am Because We Are." I am we. I had found community in my RPA family, the academic professors at Colorado who had taught me, all the historical philosophers and thinkers I had read throughout my lifetime. I had learned from my students, Black, White, and Japanese. I had learned from my family—wife and children—how to be a better human being.

Intellectually, Lewis R. Gordon's book *Disciplinary Decadence* had helped me elide hierarchies of knowledge types.[10] Lucius T. Outlaw's book *On Race and Philosophy* had defined Africana Philosophy, as an umbrella notion which included all the discursive practices of Black people.[11] Both these philosophers provided the ideas that allowed me to move to the top of Plato's upward path, dialectical, noetic thought. Alison Jaggar helped me by getting me through the minefield of a PhD program. But more importantly, taught me the importance of women in the struggle for human dignity and freedom. I had learned that reality, truth, and objects are social constructs. That we must *resist* reality. Especially a constructed reality that immiserates human beings. I am chasing a long fly ball. Time has stopped.

Rock (the earth) and fire (the sun). . . . hum (the music of the spheres) . . . Hummingbirds and babies . . .

Hum babe . . . rock and fire!

NOTES

1. Bertrand Russell, *The Problems of Philosophy* (1912) (Los Angeles: Enhanced Media, 2016), 112.

2. Sam Greenlee, *The Spook Who Sat by the Door* (New York: Richard W. Baron Publishing, 1969).

3. Edmund H. North, *The Day the Earth Stood Still* (film), directed by Robert Wise (Los Angeles: 20th Century Fox, 1951).

4. Richard A. Jones, *African American Sociopolitical Philosophy: Imagining Black Communities* (Lewiston, ME: Edwin Mellen Press, 2004); and R. A. Jones, *Bippie Poems: Collected Poems 1970–1995* (Baltimore: PublishAmerica, 2004).

5. Noam Chomsky, *Hegemony or Survival: America's Quest for Global Dominance* (New York: Henrey Holt, 2004); and Martin Luther King Jr., *Where Do We Go from Here: Chaos or Community?* (Boston: Beacon Press, 1989).

6. Eugene Robinson, *Disintegration: The Splintering of Black America* (New York: Knopf Doubleday, 2011).

7. Paublo Freire, *Pedagogy of the Oppressed*, trans. Myra Bergman Ramos (New York: Penguin Books, 1972).

8. Philip Agee, *Inside the Company: CIA Diary* (New York: Bantam Books, 1976).

9. D. H. Lawrence, *The Man Who Died* (New York: Ecco, 1995).

10. Lewis R. Gordon, *Disciplinary Decadence: Living Thought in Trying Times* (New York: Routledge, 2007).

11. Lucius T. Outlaw, *On Race and Philosophy* (New York: Routledge, 1996).

Bibliography

Agee, Philip. *Inside the Company: CIA Diary*. New York: Bantam Books, 1976.
Aiken, Daymond J., Kenneth B. Henderson, and Robert E. Pingry. *Algebra: Its Big Ideas and Basic Skills, Book II.* New York: McGraw Hill, 1957.
Albee, Edward. *Two Plays by Edward Albee: The Sand Box and The Death of Bessie Smith (with Fam and Yam)*. New York: Signet, 1960.
American Psychiatric Association (APA). *Diagnostic and Statistical Manual of Mental Disorders, Fifth Edition, Text Revision* (*DSM-5-TR*). Edited by Francis G. Lu. Washington, DC: American Psychiatric Association Publishing, 2022.
Ananthaswamy, Anil. "Is Our Universe a Hologram? Physicists Debate Famous Idea on Its 25th Anniversary." *Scientific American*, November 30, 2022. https://www.scientificamerican.com/article/is-our-universe-a-hologram-physicists-debate-famous-idea-on-its-25th-anniversary/ (accessed August 12, 2023).
Anderson, Jon, Steve Howe, and Chris Squire. "Starship Trooper: Part 1, Life Seeker." *The Yes Album* (album). London: Advision, Fitzrovia, 1971.
Appiah, Kwame Anthony. *In My Father's House: Africa in the Philosophy of Culture*. Oxford: Oxford University Press, 1993.
Ashby, W. [William] Ross. *Design for a Brain*. New York: Wiley, 1954.
Aurelius, Marcus. *Meditations: Marcus Aurelius and His Times*. New York: Walter J. Black, 1945.
Ayer, Alfred Jules. *Language, Truth and Logic*. Mineola, NY: Dover, 1952.
Bacon, Francis. *Bacon's Essays and the Wisdom of the Ancients,* available at www.gutenberg.org/files/56463/56463-h/5643-h.htm
Bakhtin, [Mikhail] M. M. *The Dialogical Imagination*. Austin: University of Texas Press, 1982.
Baldwin, James. *Giovanni's Room*. New York: Penguin, 2000.
Barnett, Lincoln. *The Universe and Dr. Einstein*. Mineola, NY: Dover, 1948.
Barth, John. *Giles Goat-Boy*. New York: Anchor Books, 1987.
Barthelme, Donald. *The Dead Father*. New York: Pocket Books. 1976.
———. *Snow White*. New York: Touchstone. 1996.
Bell, Arthur. "Christopher Isherwood: No Parades." *New York Times*. March 25, 1973, 412.
Bell, [Eric Temple] E. T. *Men of Mathematics*. New York: Simon and Schuster, 1986.

Bellow, Saul. *Mr. Sammler's Planet*. New York: Penguin Classic, 2004.
Berg, Richard E. "The Fourier Theorem." *Britannica*. N.d. https://www.britannica.com/science/sound-physics/Steady-state-waves#ref527305 (accessed August 22, 2023).
Bergson, Henri. *Time and Free Will*. Mineola, NY: Dover, 2001.
Birt, Robert E., ed. *The Quest for Identity: Critical Essays in Africana Social Philosophy*. Lanham, MD: Rowman & Littlefield, 2001.
Blackman, Gary, Grace Slick, Marty Balin, and Paul Kanter. "Hijack." *Blows Against the Empire* (album). Hollywood, CA: RCA Victor, 1970.
Bond, Edward. *Walkabout* (film). Directed by Nicolas Roeg. Sydney and Alice Springs, Australia: 20th Century Fox, 1971.
Bonham, John, et. al. "The Crunge." *House of the Holy* (album). Headley, UK: Headley Grange, 1973.
Borges, Jorge Luis. "The Circular Ruins." In *Ficciones*, edited by Anthony Kerrigan, 57–64. New York: Grove Press, 1994.
Bradbury, Ray. *The Martian Chronicles*. New York: Doubleday, 1950.
Brautigan, Richard. *Willard and His Bowling Trophies: A Perverse Mystery*. New York: Simon and Schuster, 1975.
Brewer, Cobham E. *Brewer's Book of Myth and Legend*. Edited by J. C. Cooper. Oxford: Helicon, 1993.
Brosnan, Jim. *The Long Season*. New York: Dell, 1961.
Brown, Claude. *Manchild in the Promised Land*. New York: Signet, 1965.
Burroughs, William S. *Exterminator!* New York: Penguin, 1973.
Bunyan, John. *The Pilgrim's Progress from This World*. 2 vols. London: Nathaniel Ponder, 1678; 1684.
Caldwell, Erskine. *God's Little Acre*. New York: Signet, 1965.
———. *Tobacco Road*. Athens: University of Georgia Press, 1995.
Camus, Albert. *Exile and the Kingdom*. New translation by Carol Cosman. New York: Vintage, 2007.
———. *The Fall*. New York: Vintage Books, 1991.
———. *Lyrical and Critical Essays*. New York: Vintage Books, 1970.
———. "The Misunderstanding." In *Caligula & Three Other Plays*, translated by Stuart Gilbert, 75–134. New York: Knopf, 1958.
———. *The Plague*. New York: Knopf Doubleday, 1991.
———. *The Stranger*. New York: Vintage, 1989.
Capra, Frank. *Our Mr. Sun* (film). Directed by Frank Capra. CBS, 1956.
Capra, Fritjof. *The Tao of Physics*. New York: Bantam Books, 1975.
Chomsky, Noam. *Hegemony or Survival: America's Quest for Global Dominance*. New York: Henrey Holt, 2004.
Church, Richard. *Five Boys in a Cave*. New York: John Day, 1951.
Churchland, Patricia S. *Neurophilosophy: Toward a Unified Science of the Mind/Brain*. Cambridge, MA: Bradford Books, 1989.
Clarke, Arthur C. *2001: A Space Odyssey*. New York: New American Library, 1968.
———. *Childhood's End*. New York Ballantine Books, 1953.
Cleaver, Eldridge. *Soul on Ice*. New York: McGraw-Hill, 1968.

Cogswell, Theodore R. *The Wall Around the World*. Los Angeles: Pyramid Press, 1973.
Considine, Douglas M., ed. *Van Nostrand's Scientific Encyclopedia*. 5th ed. New York: Van Nostrand Reinhold, 1976.
Cook, Samuel. "(What A) Wonderful World." *The Wonderful World of Sam Cook* (album). Hollywood: A&M Records, 1960.
Cosell, Howard. *I Never Played the Game*. New York: William Morrow, 1985.
Crosby, David, Stephen Stills, and Paul Kantner. "Wooden Ships." *Crosby, Stills & Nash* (album). Hollywood, CA: Atlantic Records, 1969.
Dan, Steely. "Reelin' in the Years." *Can't Buy a Thrill* (album). Los Angeles: ABC Records, 1972.
Dass, Baba Ram. *Be Here Now*. San Cristobal, NM: Lama Foundation, 1971.
David Ray, ed. *From A-Z: 200 Contemporary American Poets*. Chicago: Swallow Press, 1981.
Davis, Philip J. *The Lore of Large Numbers*. New Haven, CT: Yale University Press, 1961.
Delany, Samuel R. *Dhalgren*. New York: Bantam Books, 1975.
Derrida, Jacques. *Dissemination*. Translated by Barbara Johnson. Chicago: University of Chicago Press, 1981.
Descartes, René. *Meditations on First Philosophy*. Translated by Donald A. Cress. 3rd ed. Indianapolis, IN: Hackett Publishing, 1993.
Dickinson, Emily. "I Had a Guinea Golden." https://www.poetry-archive.com/d/i_had_a_guinea_golden.html
Dixon, Luther, and Ollie Jones. "Rainbow Valley." *Moon River* (album), by Jerry Butler. Burbank, CA: Vee Jay Records, 1962.
Dostoevsky, Fyodor. *Crime and Punishment*. Translated by Constance Garnett. New York: Bantam Classic, 1984.
Douglass, Frederick. *The Autobiography of Frederick Douglass: Narrative of the Life of Frederick Douglass, an American Slave*. Edited by George Stade. New York: Barnes & Noble, 2005.
Dreiser, Theodore. *An American Tragedy*. New York: Heritage Press, 1954.
Du Bois, W. E. B. [William Edward Burghardt]. *The Souls of Black Folks*. New York: Fawcett, 1961.
Duffy, Bruce. *The World as I Found It*. Boston: Mariner Books, 1987.
Dylan, Bob. *Tarantula*. New York: Scribner, 2004.
Eliot, T. S. "Little Gidding." In *Four Quartets*. New York: Harcourt Brace, 1943; 1971.
Fanon, Frantz. *The Wretched of the Earth*. Translated by Richard Philcox. New York: Grove Press, 2005.
Feagin, Joe R., Hernan Vera, and Nikitah Imani. *The Agony of Education: Black Students at a White University*. New York: Routledge, 1996.
Fegen, Donald Jay, and Walter Carl Becker. "Don't Take Me Alive." *The Royal Scam* (album). Los Angeles: ABC Studios, 1976.
Ferlinghetti, Lawrence. *Little Boy*. London: Faber & Faber, 2019.
Fitzgerald, F. Scott. *The Great Gatsby*. Orinda, CA: Seawolf Press, 2021.
Fleischer, Max. "Koko the Clown." In *Out of the Inkwell* (cartoon series). Los Angeles: Paramount, 1918–1927.

Foucault, Michel. *Discipline & Punish: The Birth of the Prison*. Translated by Alan Sheridan. New York: Vintage Books, 1995.
Freire, Paublo. *Pedagogy of the Oppressed*. Translated by Myra Bergman Ramos. New York: Penguin Books, 1972.
Freud, Sigmund. *Moses and Monotheism*. Translated by Katherine Jones. London: Hogarth Press, 1939.
Frost, Robert. *The Poems of Robert Frost*. New York: Modern Library, 1946.
Gamow, George. *One Two Three . . . Infinity: Facts and Speculations of Science*. New York: Bantam Books, 1979.
Gauss, Carl Friedrich. Quoted in *The World of Mathematics*. Edited by James R. Newman. 4 vols. New York: Simon and Schuster, 1956.
Genet, Jean, *Querelle*. New York: Grove Press, 1987.
Gibson, William. *Neuromancer*. Edited by Terry Carr. New York: Ace, 1984.
Gilroy, Paul. *The Black Atlantic: Modernity and Double-Consciousness*. New York: Verso Books, 2012.
Glauberg, Joe, Gary Marshall, and Dale McRaven. *Mork & Mindy* (TV series). Los Angeles: ABC, 1978–1982.
Goines, Donald. *Dopefiend: The Story of a Black Junkie*. Los Angeles: Holloway House, 2021.
Golding, William. *Pincher Martin: The Two Deaths of Christopher Martin*. New York: Harvest Books, 2002.
———. *The Spire*. New York: Pocket Books, 1966.
Gordon, Lewis R. *Disciplinary Decadence: Living Thought in Trying Times*. New York: Routledge, 2007.
Gourdon, G. L. [Gisèle Liliane]. "Time and Space in Tristram Shandy and Other Eighteenth-Century Novels: The Issues of Progression and Continuity." PhD thesis. January 9, 2017; 2002. University of Sheffield.
Gramsci, Antonio. *Antonio Gramsci: Letters from Prison*. Edited by Frank Rosengarten. Translated by Raymond Rosenthal. 2 vols. New York: Columbia University Press, 2011.
Greenlee, Sam. *The Spook Who Sat by the Door*. New York: Richard W. Baron Publishing, 1969.
Haley, Alex. *Roots: The Saga of an American Family*. New York: Dell Publishing, 1977.
Hampshire, Stuart, ed. *The Age of Reason: The 17th Century Philosophers*. New York: Signet Classics, 1956.
Harris, Leonard. *Philosophy Born of Struggle: Anthology of Afro-American Philosophy from 1917*. Dubuque, IA: Kendall/Hunt Publishing, 2000.
Hayes, Chris. *A Colony in a Nation*. New York: W. W. Norton, 2018.
Hays, Lee, and Pete Seeger. "If I Had a Hammer (The Hammer Song)." *Peter, Paul, and Mary* (album). Burbank, CA: Warner Bros, 1970; 1962; 1960.
Heidegger, Martin. *Being and Time (Sein und Zeit)* (1927). Translated by J. MacQuarrie and Edward Robinson. New York: Harper & Row, 1962.
Heinlein, Robert A. *Stranger in a Strange Land*. New York: Ace Books, 1991.
Herbert, Frank. *Whipping Star*. New York: Berkley, 1986.

Hesse, Hermann. *Beneath the Wheel*. Translated by Michael Roloff. New York: Noonday Press, 1969.
———. *Demian*. Translated by Michael Roloff and Michael Lebeck. New York: Bantam Books, 1963.
———. *Narcissus and Goldmund*. Translated by Ursule Molinaro. New York: Bantam, 1984.
———. *Sidhartha*. Translated by Hilda Rosner. New York: Bantam Books, 1981.
———. *Steppenwolf*. Translated by Basil Creighton. New York: Bantam, 1979.
Heywood, John. *A Dialogue Conteinyng the Nomber in Effect of All the Prouerbes in the Englishe Tongue*. London: Thomas Berthelet, 1546. https://quod.lib.umich.edu/e/eebo/A03168.0001.001?view=toc (accessed August 12, 2023).
Hindi, Noor. "Against Death." *TriQuarterly* 159 (January 15, 2021). https://www.triquarterly.org/issues/issue-159/against-death (accessed August 19, 2023).
Hitler, Adolf. *Mein Kampf*. Translated by Ralph Manheim. New York: Houghton Mifflin, 1973.
Hobbes, Thomas. "Opera Latina," in Molesworth, William (ed). *Vita carmine expressa,* Vol. 1, London, 86.
Hoffman, Abbie. *Steal this Book*. New York: Grove Press, 1971.
Holmes, Richard. *Coleridge: Early Visions, 1772–1804*. New York: Pantheon Books, 1999.
Hopkins, Gerard Manley. "Spring and Fall: To a Young Child." In *Hopkins: Poems*. London: Everyman's Library Pocket Books, 1995.
Hume, Cryil, Irving Block, and Allen Alder. *Forbidden Planet* (film). Directed by Fred M. Wilcox. Beverly Hills, CA: Metro-Goldwyn-Mayer, 1956.
Ionesco, Eugène, *Rhinoceros and Other Plays*. New York: Grove Press, 1959.
Irving, Clifford. *Autobiography of Howard Hughes*. Unpublished manuscript to New York: McGraw-Hill, 1972; private publication in 1999.
———. *Tom Mix and Pancho Villa*. New York: St. Martin's Press, 1982.
Jaggar, Alison M. *Feminist Politics and Human Nature*. Lanham, MD: Rowman & Littlefield, 1988.
James, Guy, and Michael Farley. "The Farm." *Volunteers* (album). Hollywood, CA: RCA Victor, 1969.
Jastrow, Robert. *Red Giants and White Dwarfs*. New York: W. W. Norton, 1979.
Jeans, Sir James. *Problems of Cosmology and Stellar Dynamics*. London: Cambridge University Press, 1919.
Jenkins, Ron. "Mathematical Topology and Gordian Narrative Structure: 'Tristram Shandy.'" *Mosaic: An Interdisciplinary Critical Journal* 25, no. 1 (1992): 13–28. https://www.jstor.org/stable/24780583.
Jones, Richard A. *African American Sociopolitical Philosophy: Imagining Black Communities*. Lewiston, ME: Edwin Mellen Press, 2004.
———. *Bippie Poems: Collected Poems 1970–1995*. Baltimore: PublishAmerica, 2004.
———. *Blackland*. Austin, TX: Atmosphere Press, 2021.
———. *Ulim-Mwingi*. Bakersfield, CA: Innovative Ghost Writers, forthcoming (2023).

Jones, William R. *Is God a White Racist? A Preamble to Black Theology*. New York: Penguin Random House, 1997.

Joyce, James. *A Portrait of the Artist as a Young Man*. Berkeley: The Bancroft Library Internet Archive, 2008.

Kant, Immanuel. *The Critique of Pure Reason* (1781). Translated by Norman Kemp Smith. Unabridged ed. New York: Bedford/Saint Martin's, 1969.

———. *Groundwork of the Metaphysics of Morals* (1785). Translated by Mary J. Gregor. Cambridge: Cambridge University Press, 1998.

Kantner, Paul, and Jefferson Starship. "Starship." *Blows Against the Empire* (album). Hollywood, CA: RCA Victor, 1970.

Kerouac, Jack. *The Subterraneans*. New York: Grove Press, 1958.

Kesey, Ken. *One Flew Over the Cuckoo's Nest*. New York: Signet, 1963.

Kierkegaard, Søren. *Fear and Trembling*. Edited by C. Stephen Evans and Sylvia Walsh. Translated by Sylvia Walsh. Cambridge: Cambridge University Press, 2006.

King, Martin Luther, Jr. *Where Do We Go from Here: Chaos or Community?* Boston: Beacon Press, 1989.

Koestler, Arthur. *Darkness at Noon*. New York: TIME, 1962; New York: Bantam Books, 1984.

———. *The Ghost in the Machine*. New York: Macmillan, 1967.

Kymlicka, Will. *The Rights of Minority Cultures*. Oxford: Oxford University Press, 1995.

Lake, Greg. "From the Beginning." *Lucky Man, Knife Edge: Emerson, Lake & Palmer* (album). New York: Cotillion Records, Atlantic Records, 1970.

La Mettrie, Julien Offray de. *Man a Machine (L'homme Machine)*. Chicago: Open Court, 1912.

Lawrence, D. H. *The Man Who Died*. New York: Ecco, 1995.

Leibniz, Gottfried Wilhelm. *Theodicy: Essays on the Goodness of God, the Freedom of Man, and the Origins of Evil*. La Salle, IL: Open Court, 1985.

Lem, Stanisław. *Memoirs of a Space Traveler: Further Reminiscences of Ijon Tichy*. Translated by Joel Stern and Maria Swiecicka-Ziemianek. Evanston, IL: Northwestern University Press, 2000.

Levertov, Denise. *Relearning the Alphabet*. New York: New Directions, 1970.

Lewis, C. S. *Till We Have Faces*. New York: Time Reading Program, 1956.

Lewis, Sinclair. *Arrowsmith*. New York: Penguin, 2008.

Mac Cumhaill, Clare, and Rachel Wiseman. *Metaphysical Animals: How Four Women Brought Philosophy Back to Life*. New York: Doubleday, 2022.

Mackie, John L. *The Cement of the Universe*. Oxford: Clarendon Press, 1980.

Malory, Thomas. *Le morte d'Arthur*. New York: Everyman's Library, 1956.

Mann, Abby. *Ship of Fools* (film). Directed by Stanley Kramer. Culver City, CA: Columbia Pictures, 1965.

Marcuse, Herbert. *Eros and Civilization: A Philosophical Inquiry into Freud*. 2nd ed. Oxfordshire: Routledge, 1987.

———. *One-Dimensional Man: Studies in the Ideology of Advanced Industrial Society*. 2nd ed. Boston: Beacon Press, 1991.

Mascaró, Juan, trans. *The Bhagavad Gita*. New York: Penguin Books, 1962.

Matthews, William. "Cows Grazing at Sunrise." In *Seach Party: Collected Poems of William Matthews*, edited by Sebastian Matthews and Stanley Plumly. Boston: Houghton Mifflin, 2004.

McCorduck, Pamela. *Machines Who Think: A Personal Inquiry into the History and Prospects of Artificial Intelligence.* New York: W. H. Freeman, 1981.

Melville, Herman. *The Confidence-Man: His Masquerade.* Edited by Hershel Parker and Mark Niemeyer. 2nd ed. New York: W. W. Norton, 2005.

———. *Moby-Dick, Or, The Whale.* New York: Harper, 1851.

Mike, Toronto. "23 Ways To Get To First Base." *Toronto Mike.* January 29, 2008. https://www.torontomike.com/2008/01/23_ways_to_get_to_first_base/ (accessed August 13, 2023).

Moore, Jonh T. *Fundamental Principles of Mathematics.* New York: Rinehart, 1950.

Morrison, Toni. *The Bluest Eye.* New York: Holt, Rinehart and Winston, 1970.

Munitz, Milton K., ed. *Theories of the Universe: From Babylonian Myth to Modern Science.* New York: Free Press, 1965.

Naughton, Bill. *Alfie.* New York: Ballantine, 1966.

Neihardt, John G. *Black Elk Speaks: The Complete Edition.* Lincoln, NE: Bison Books, 2014.

Newman, James R., ed. *The World of Mathematics.* 4 vols. New York: Simon and Schuster, 1956.

Niven, Larry. *Ringworld.* London: Gollancz, 2005.

North, Edmund H. *The Day the Earth Stood Still* (film). Directed by Robert Wise. Los Angeles: 20th Century Fox, 1951.

Orwell, George. *Animal Farm.* New York: Signet, 2004.

Ouspensky, P. D. *In Search of the Miraculous*: *Fragments of an Unknown Teaching.* New York: Harper Paperbacks, 2001.

———. *Strange Life of Ivan Osokin.* Garden City, NJ: Courier Dover Publications, 2020.

———. *Tertium Organum, or the Third Cannon of Thought and a Key to the Enigmas of the World.* Whitefish, MT: Kessinger Publishing, 1998.

Outlaw, Lucius T. *On Race and Philosophy.* New York: Routledge, 1996.

Ovenden, Michael W. *Life in the Universe: A Scientific Discussion.* Garden City, NY: Anchor Books, 1962.

Pais, Abraham. *Subtle Is the Lord: Science and the Life of Albert Einstein.* Oxford: Oxford University Press, 1982.

Peckham, Herbert. *Hands-On Basic: For the IBM Personal Computer.* New York: McGraw-Hill, 1985.

Pierce, C. S. [Charles Sanders]. *Stanford Encyclopedia of Philosophy.* https://plato.stanford.edu/entries/pierce/#bio.

Piersall, Jimmy. *Fear Strikes Out: The Jim Piersall Story.* New York: Little Brown, 1955.

Pirsig, Robert M. *Zen and the Art of Motorcycle Maintenance: An Inquiry into Values.* New York: Harper Perennial, 2000.

Potter, George and Evelyn Simpson. *The Sermons of John Donne*, 10 vols. Berkeley: University of California Press, 1953.

Proust, Marcel. *Remembrance of Things Past.* 3 vols. New York: Vintage, 1982.

Pyle, Howard. *Pepper and Salt: Seasoning for Young Folk*. Salt Lake City: Editorium, 2020.
Ray, David, ed. *From A-Z: 200 Contemporary Poets*. Athens, OH: Shallow Press, Ohio University Press, 1981.
———. "Hammering." *New Yorker*, February 1, 1976, 92–93.
———. *X-Rays: A Book of Poems*. Ithaca, NY: Cornell University Press, 1965.
Robinson, Eugene. *Disintegration: The Splintering of Black America*. New York: Knopf Doubleday, 2011.
Russell, Bertrand. *The Problems of Philosophy* (1912). Los Angeles: Enhanced Media, 2016.
———. *Why I Am Not a Christian: And Other Essays on Religion and Related Subjects*. Edited by Paul Edwards. New York: Touchstone, 1967.
Sagan, Carl. *Broca's Brain: Reflections on the Romance of Science*. New York: Presidio Press, 1986.
———. *COSMOS*. New York: Random House, 1980.
Saint-Exupéry, Antoine de. *The Little Prince*. New York: Harcourt's Children's Books, 1943.
Sartre, Jean-Paul. *No Exit and Three Other Plays*. Translated by Stuart Gilbert. International ed. New York: Vintage Books, 1989.
Saxon, John H., Jr. *Algebra: An Incremental Approach*. Englewood Cliffs, NJ: Prentice-Hall, 1979.
Selby, Samuel M., ed. *CRC Standard Mathematical Tables, Student Edition*. 16th ed. Cleveland, OH: Chemical Rubber, 1968.
Shirer, William L. *The Rise and Fall of the Third Reich: A History of Nazi Germany*. New York: Simon and Schuster, 1960.
Singer, Isaac Bashevis. *The Séance and Other Stories*. Translated by Roger H. Klein and others. New York: Penguin, 1968.
Slim, Iceberg. *Pimp: The Story of My Life*. New York: Cash Money Content, 2011.
Snyder, Gary. *Earth House Hold*. New York: New Directions Publishing, 1969.
Solzhenitsyn, Aleksandr. *One Day in the Life of Ivan Denisovich*. Translation by E. P. Dutton. New York: E. P. Dutton, 1963.
Spark, Muriel. *Memento Mori*. New York: Macmillan, 1959.
Stace, W. T. *The Philosophy of Hegel*. Mineola, NY: Dover, 1955.
Stefon, Matt. "Richard Brautigan," at https://www.britanica.com/biography/Richard-Brautigan
Sterba, James P., ed. *Social and Political Philosophy: Classical Western Texts in Feminist and Multicultural Perspectives*. Belmont, CA: Wadsworth/Thomson Learning, 2003.
Sterne, Laurence. *Tristram Shandy and a Sentimental Journey*. New York: Modern Library, 1995.
Stevens, Cat [Yusuf Islam]. "Hard Headed Woman." *Tea for the Tillerman* (album). London: Morgan Studios, 1970.
Stevens, Peter S. *Patterns in Nature*. New York: Little Brown, 1974.
Strachey, Lytton. *Eminent Victorians*. New York: Modern Library, 1940.
Swedenborg, Emanuel. *Heaven and Hell*. Knutsford Cheshire: A & D Publishing, 2007.

Swihart, Thomas L. *Astrophysics and Stellar Astronomy*. New York: John Wiley, 1968.
Thomas, Carla. "Gee Whiz (Look at His Eyes)." *Gee Whiz* (album). New York: Atlantic Records, 1960.
Thomas, Dylan. *Portrait of the Artist as a Young Dog*. New York: New Directions Publishing, 1968.
Turgenev, Ivan. *Fathers and Sons*. New York: Signet, 2005.
Updike, John. *Couples*. New York: Knopf, 1968.
U.S. Supreme Court. *Oliver Brown, et al. v. Board of Education of Topeka, et al.* 347 U.S. 483 (May 17, 1954).
Velikovsky, Immanuel. *Earth in Upheaval*. Garden City; New York: Doubleday, 1955.
Vonnegut, Kurt. *Breakfast of Champions*. New York: Vintage, 1992.
———. *Hocus Pocus, or What's the Hurry, Son?* New York: Putnam Publishing, 1990.
———. *Player Piano: A Novel*. New York: Dail Press, 2006.
———. *Welcome to the Monkey House*. New York: Dail Press, 2013.
Warner, Getrude Chandler. *The Boxcar Children*. Park Ridge, IL: Albert Whitman, 1942.
Weizenbaum, Joseph. *Computer Power and Human Reason: From Judgment to Calculation*. New York: W. H. Freeman, 1976.
White, E. B. *The Elements of Style*. New York: Macmillan, 1962.
———. *One Man's Meat*. New York: Harper & Row, 1942.
———. *Stuart Little*. New York: HarperCollins, 2005.
Whitehead, Alfred North, and Bertrand Russell. *Principia Mathematica: Volume One*. Seaside, OR: Rough Draft Printing, 2011; 3 vols. Cambridge: Cambridge University Press, 1910–1913.
Winwood, Steve. "Can't Find My Way Home," *Blind Faith* (album). London: Polydor, 1969.
Wittgenstein, Ludwig. *The Blue and Brown Books*. New York: Harper Torchbooks, 1965.
———. *On Certainty*. Edited by G. E. M. Anscombe and G. H. von Wright. Translated by Denis Paul and G. E. M. Anscombe. New York: Harper Torchbooks, 1972.
———. *Tractatus logico-philosophicus*. London: Routledge, 1922.
Wolfe, Tom. *The Electric Kool-Aid Acid Test*. New York: Farrar, Straus & Giroux, 1968; New York: Bantam, 1999.
Woodson, Carter G. *The Miseducation of the Negro*. Amherst, NY: Associated Publishers, 1933.
Wordsworth, William. "My Heart Leaps Up." American Academy of Poets. *Poets.org*. N.d. https://poets.org/poem/my-heart-leaps (accessed August 13, 2023).
Wright, Crispin. *Rails to Infinity: Essays on Themes from Wittgenstein's* Philosophical Investigations. Cambridge, MA: Harvard University Press, 2001.
Wright, Richard. *Uncle Tom's Children*. New York: HarperCollins, 1982.
Wyler, Rose. *The Golden Book of Astronomy: A Child's Introduction to the Wonders of Space*. Racine, WI: Golden Press, 1955.
Wylie, Philip. *Generation of Vipers*. McLean, IL: Dalkey Archive Press, 1996.
Yutang, Lin, trans. *The Importance of Understanding*. Cleveland, OH: World Publishing, 1960.

Zim, Herbert S., and Robert H. Baker. *Stars: A Guide to the Constellations, Sun, Moon, Planets, and Other Features of the Heavens.* New York: Golden Press, 1951.

Zukav, Gary. *The Dancing Wu Li Masters: An Overview of the New Physics.* New York: Bantam Books, 1980.

About the Author

Richard A. Jones, PhD, was a professor of philosophy at Howard University from 2001 to 2013. Jones authored several books and many articles on topics such as race, culture, epistemology, and metaphysics. He has contributed to the development of Afrocentric philosophy and has challenged the Eurocentric assumptions and biases that often dominate mainstream philosophy. As a scholar and a teacher, he has inspired many students and colleagues with his insights and perspectives exploring connections between philosophy and other disciplines, including science, art, political community, and ethics. A prolific poet, the latest of his ten poetry volumes is *Skinny Poem* (2023). Jones's poetry and fiction have also appeared in *Scientific American* (May 2021), *New Letters*, and other literary publications.

www.ingramcontent.com/pod-product-compliance
Lightning Source LLC
Chambersburg PA
CBHW031723230426
43669CB00007B/227